Discourses of Desire

Sappho, 1775. This painting by Angelica Kauffmann is reproduced courtesy of John and Mable Ringling Museum of Art, Sarasota, Florida.

You came, and I was longing for you; you cooled my heart which was burning with desire.

. . .

May winds and sorrows carry off the one who rebukes me.

SAPPHO

Discourses of Desire

GENDER, GENRE, AND EPISTOLARY FICTIONS

Linda S. Kauffman

CORNELL UNIVERSITY PRESS

Ithaca and London

CORNELL UNIVERSITY PRESS GRATEFULLY ACKNOWLEDGES
A GRANT FROM THE ANDREW W. MELLON FOUNDATION
THAT AIDED IN BRINGING THIS BOOK TO PUBLICATION.

Copyright © 1986 by Cornell University

First published 1986 by Cornell University Press.
First published, Cornell Paperbacks, 1988.

International Standard Book Number (cloth) 0-8014-1853-4
International Standard Book Number (paper) 0-8014-9510-5
Library of Congress Catalog Card Number 85-48196

Printed in the United States of America

Librarians: Library of Congress cataloging information
appears on the last page of the book.

The paper in this book is acid-free and meets the guidelines for
permanence and durability of the Committee on Production Guidelines
for Book Longevity of the Council on Library Resources.

For Frances MacIntyre
and
Anne Grieser (1949–1980)

Contents

7

8   Contents

Illustrations

Acknowledgments

In discourses of desire, one discovers how much more appropriate it is to speak of wish formulation than of wish fulfillment, and in this discourse, many people across the country helped me struggle with my wishes and my writing. In Santa Barbara, California, I remember the wry insights of the women in my classes at Antioch University/West and the Adult Education Division of City College. I thank Norene Wheeler for many discussions about narcissism and nostalgia, and Russell Waldrop for helping me to leave. Later, the lively engagement of my students—men and women—at Emory University and at the University of North Carolina, Chapel Hill, helped me formulate the theoretical issues at stake in discourses of desire.

From 1980 to 1982, an Andrew W. Mellon Postdoctoral Fellowship to Emory University enabled me to proceed from speaking about desire to writing. Several generous colleagues at Emory patiently critiqued innumerable rough drafts: for the *Portuguese Letters* and Roland Barthes's *A Lover's Discourse: Fragments*, I have Diane Wakoski and Taffy Martin to thank; for *The Turn of the Screw*, William Dillingham and Deborah Ayer Sitter; and for *Clarissa*, John Sitter and Georgia Christopher. Trudy Kretchman's help with production of the manuscript and her many other kindnesses remain unforgotten. Robert Detweiler not only read early drafts but invited me to test my theoretical premises by team-teaching in Emory University's Institute for the Liberal Arts.

In the summers of 1981 and 1985, I received fellowships from the William Andrews Clark Memorial Library in Los Angeles. My gratitude extends to the entire staff, in particular to Patrick McCloskey and John Bidwell for help with translations and illustrations. In 1981 G. Jennifer Wilson sheltered and entertained me better than Luster ever did Benjy; and Richard Dysart made the summer of 1985 equally memorable.

In Ithaca, New York, from 1982 to 1983, the Feminist Scholars' Reading Group at Cornell University sharpened my interdisciplinary perspective, and I am still learning from Roberta Batt. At Cornell University Press, I am grateful to Bernhard Kendler (who remained committed to the project long after Job would have become dubious) and to Marilyn M. Sale and Judith Bailey for excellent editorial advice and copyediting.

In North Carolina, I am deeply indebted to the National Humanities Center and to the National Endowment for the Humanities for completely supporting me in 1983–1984 at a crucial stage in my career, when long-formulated wishes were finally fulfilled. I am particularly grateful to the center's librarians and typists, who worked tirelessly on my behalf. Thanks go as well to several center scholars: Josiah Ober, Michael Alexander, and Betty Rose Nagle helped me with classical translations; Jasper Hopkins, André Le Coque, and Paul Ricoeur conferred on the French. John Seelye read segments on American literature, and Paul Ricoeur's meticulous critique enhanced the theoretical aspects of the manuscript. Olaf Hansen's insights, similarly, continue to inform my theoretical thinking, and he, along with Martin Meisel, enriched not only the manuscript but my entire year at the center with advice, encouragement, and friendship.

I owe a special debt to several indefatigable letter-writers for innumerable recommendations, which helped me secure all the grants cited above. Lawrence Willson, William Frost, H. Porter Abbott, and Garrett Stewart from the University of California, Santa Barbara, and Robert Detweiler and John Sitter from Emory University—all ceaselessly sang my praises and have more than earned my thanks.

Chapter 6 originally appeared in a different form in *Nineteenth Century Fiction*, vol. 36, no. 2 (September 1981), 176–192, © 1981 by The Regents of the University of California, and is used by permission of the Regents. Chapter 7 also appeared in a different form as

"Devious Channels of Decorous Ordering: A Lover's Discourse in *Absalom, Absalom!*" in vol. 29 (Summer 1983) of *Modern Fiction Studies,* copyright by Purdue Research Foundation, West Lafayette, Ind. 47907, and is used with permission and with special thanks to editor William Stafford.

Lines from "Elm," from *The Collected Poems of Sylvia Plath,* edited by Ted Hughes, © 1963 by Ted Hughes, are quoted on page 158 by permission of Harper & Row, Publishers, Inc. Thanks are due to Olwyn Hughes. Lines from the Tenth Elegy from *Duino Elegies* by Rainer Maria Rilke, translated by David Young, are reprinted by permission of W. W. Norton & Company, Inc., copyright © 1978 by W. W. Norton & Company, Inc. Lines from Emily Dickinson are quoted with permission of the Estate of Robert Linscott. Lines from *The Three Marias: New Portuguese Letters* are reprinted by permission of Doubleday Publishing Company, Inc., © 1974 and Victor Gollancz, Ltd.

In the final phases of writing and production, the English Department at the University of North Carolina, Chapel Hill, provided funds for the research assistance of Leslie McCray. I am grateful to Phillip Snyder and Christopher Harlos for long hours of research and proofreading when deadlines were looming. Funds from the Endowment Committee of the College of Arts and Sciences and from the University Research Council are also gratefully acknowledged.

Two friends, finally, unfailingly responded to crises large and small: Larysa Mykyta's astute analyses of feminism, psychoanalysis, and many other theoretical issues have taught me almost as much as her friendship has. Garrett Stewart's critical acumen and lively style were always my models in draft after draft of the entire manuscript, each of which he read with unremitting care, contagious enthusiasm, and conviction about the book's—and my—merits.

This book is dedicated with love and appreciation to my mother, Frances MacIntyre, who endures; and, with enduring grief, to the memory of Anne Grieser.

LINDA KAUFFMAN

Chapel Hill, North Carolina

Discourses of Desire

A pity beyond all telling is hid in the heart of love.
WILLIAM BUTLER YEATS, *The Pity of Love*

The necessity for this book is to be found in the
following consideration: that the lover's discourse is
today *of an extreme solitude*. This discourse is spoken,
perhaps, by thousands of subjects (who knows?), but
warranted by no one; it is completely forsaken by the
surrounding languages: ignored, disparaged, or
derided by them, severed not only from authority but
also from the mechanisms of authority (sciences,
techniques, arts). Once a discourse is thus driven by its
own momentum into the backwater of the "unreal,"
exiled from all gregarity, it has no recourse but to
become the site, however exiguous, of an *affirmation*.
That affirmation is, in short, the subject of the book
which begins here. . . .
ROLAND BARTHES, *A Lover's Discourse: Fragments*

Prologue

La lettre, l'épître, qui n'est pas un genre mais tous les
genres, la littérature même.

JACQUES DERRIDA, *La Carte postale*

. . . Granted then, that all of literature is a long letter
to an invisible other, a present, a possible, or a future
passion that we rid ourselves of, feed, or seek.

The Three Marias: New Portuguese Letters

The letter as literature, literature as a letter: what does this doubling imply about the role, nature, and function of fictional genres?
Does time, does memory exorcise desire or enhance it? Is desire itself
fundamentally fictive? Is artifice inseparable from longing, from language, from literature? How does artifice prolong both passion and
the production of writing?

In Ovid's *Heroides*, fifteen heroines write to an invisible other who
has seduced, betrayed, or simply left them behind. Each letter is a
confrontation, a demand, a plea, a lament: if the beloved were present, there would be no need to write. In the act of writing, however,
presence becomes problematical; what, after all, does it mean to be
"present" to one's beloved? If he truly loved when he was present,
how could he bear to be absent now? Each epistle repeats the pattern:
the heroine challenges the lover to read her letter, rages against the
forces that separated them, recalls past pleasures, speculates about his
infidelity, laments his indifference, and discusses the sole act that
engages her in his absence: writing. In many of the epistles, the heroine considers ending her life, but she avoids every sort of closure and
dedicates herself to nurturing her illusions: of his presence, of his

1 7

eventual return, of her own identity as his beloved, of their mutual passion. Yet her strategy is simultaneously subversive, for she contests the fate to which her lover has abandoned her. Her epistle is simultaneously a love letter and a legal challenge, a revolt staged in writing.

These, summarily stated, are a few of the formal characteristics of amorous epistolary discourse that recur in every subsequent text in my book, from *The Letters of a Portuguese Nun* (1669) to *The Three Marias: New Portuguese Letters* (1972). My aim, however, is not merely to trace the similarities in these texts, for each discourse simultaneously represents a response to and a significant departure from the one before it. In amorous epistles two paths of narrative thus merge; the text is both an absorption of and a reply to another text. Rather than being solely a study of genre, therefore, this book is a study of the transgressions of genre.[1]

Since the classification of genres relies on "family resemblances," what are we to make of texts without an innovative father-author? Several of the texts in my book have aroused centuries of controversy concerning origins, authenticity, legitimacy, paternity. Was Ovid, for instance, the father of an authentic new art form in the *Heroides*, as he boasts? Did Heloise really write the letters to Abelard, or was the entire correspondence invented by Abelard, as some scholars maintain?[2] Are *The Letters of a Portuguese Nun* the spontaneous outpouring

---

1. My approach to genre is indebted to the theories of Mikhail M. Bakhtin, *Rabelais and His World*, trans. Helene Iswolsky (Cambridge: MIT Press, 1968); *Problems of Dostoevsky's Poetics*, trans. R. W. Rotsel (Ann Arbor: Ardis, 1973), esp. chap. 4; *The Dialogic Imagination: Four Essays*, ed. Michael Holquist, trans. Holquist and Caryl Emerson (Austin: Univ. of Texas Press, 1981). See also Tzvetan Todorov, *The Poetics of Prose*, trans. Richard Howard (Ithaca: Cornell Univ. Press, 1977); Gary Saul Morson, *The Boundaries of Genre: Dostoevsky's Diary of a Writer and the Traditions of Literary Utopia* (Austin: Univ. of Texas Press, 1981); and Janet Gurkin Altman, *Epistolarity: Approaches to a Form* (Columbus: Ohio State Univ. Press, 1983).

2. See, for example, Leo Spitzer, "Les *Lettres portugaises*," *Romanische Forschungen* 65:1–2 (1954), 94–135; Fr. Joseph T. Muckle, "The Personal Letters between Abelard and Heloise," *Mediaeval Studies* 15 (1953), 47–94; D. W. Robertson, Jr., *Abelard and Heloise* (New York: Dial Press, 1972). Charlotte Charrier, in *Héloïse dans l'histoire et dans la légende* (Paris: Librairie ancienne Honoré Champion, 1933), chap. 1, summarizes the entire debate and concludes that Abelard revised Heloise's authentic letters, fashioning the correspondence into a model of the conversion experience; Peter Dronke also reviews the controversy but reaches the opposite conclusion in *Abelard and Heloise in Medieval Testimonies* (Glasgow: Univ. of Glasgow Press, 1976), pp. 7–33.

of passion from an unworldly woman, or did a cunning Frenchman perpetrate one of the greatest literary hoaxes of all time?[3] Those critics who seek to "legitimize" the *Portuguese Letters* can do so, paradoxically, only by maintaining that they are the "natural" writing of an obscure nun. For nearly three hundred years, the letters have aroused intense controversy: they are a work either of conscious calculation or of natural genius; they rely either on artifice or on the spontaneous overflow of powerful feelings; they are either the invention of a rational masculine mind or of a distraught feminine sensibility. (A Portuguese nun with the author's name was living in the Convent of the Conception in Portugal when the letters were published in French in Paris, but the original Portuguese text—if it ever existed—has never been found.) At stake is national pride as well: both the Portuguese and the French count the text among the masterpieces of their nations' classic literature. Authorship, ownership, paternity, identity—individual and national, feminine and masculine— are traced, retraced, and, like a thread in a labyrinth, lost.

My aim is to examine the ideology of authorship invoked here and to see how that ideology enforces certain stereotypes of masculine as opposed to feminine writing, which are then repeated through the ages by critics unconscious of their underlying assumptions. What, after all, does it mean "to write like a woman"? Is Ovid "writing like a woman" in his letters from the heroines? If so, what are the implications of adding male as well as female correspondents in the *Heroides*, as Ovid did later? From Rousseau to Rilke, critics have imitated the *Portuguese Letters;* can we deduce the gender of an author solely on the basis of internal textual evidence? Similarly, the feverish speculation about the true identity of "Currer Bell" demonstrated that in *Jane Eyre*, the issues of interpretation and critical evaluation were inextricably bound to the issue of gender. What are the so-called laws of gender and laws of genre, and what is the connection between them in so many disputes—about legalities, authority, the proper name, identity and difference? What have these disputes to do with forms of discourse that explore power and desire? The reasons differ, but in all the texts in my study passion is transgressive, woman is disorder,

3. The debate over the authenticity of the *Portuguese Letters* is recounted in Frédéric Deloffre and J. Rougeot, "Analyse d'un chef-d'oeuvre," in *Lettres portugaises, Valentins, et autres oeuvres de Guilleragues* (Paris: Garnier, 1962), pp. 3–33.

and discourses of desire are repressed. Their speakers are literally exiled or imprisoned or metaphorically "shut up"—confined, cloistered, silenced. To speak of the mixing of genders and genres as a transgression of some inexplicable law is not mere hyperbole, when one considers the patterns of repression and silencing from Sappho to Heloise, from Ovid's exile to the three Marias' prosecution for obscenity.[4] Transgression lies in telling, for each discourse in my book combines writing and revolt, defiance and desire. The writing is the revolution.

While tracing scholars' preoccupations with such questions from Ovid on, I approach gender as a reflection not of life but of art and thus include male writers as well as female in order to analyze the literary construction of gender. Comparing Ovid's attempt to write "like a woman" with the three Marias' proclamation that they intend to write "like men" exposes the artifice of the literary construction of gender and demonstrates its distance from naïve mimeticism, for each of these authors relies on a concept of referentiality that links not word to thing but text to text. Hence, in his portrait of Dido, Ovid is not striving to represent the central core of woman's self, or "woman's essence," for he is skeptical about the very idea of a center, a self, an essence, and about language's representation of such concepts. Instead, Ovid's portrait is a critique of a previous representation of Dido: Virgil's. The three Marias' *New Portuguese Letters*, similarly, is a sustained critique of the representations of women in general and the Portuguese nun in particular, for she has been celebrated as the archetypal victim in every subsequent century. In transforming the nun from victim to artist, the three Marias simultaneously undermine the myriad imitations of her letters. Moreover, they undermine the very idea of imitation itself, basing their response to the nun's letters on an entirely different poetics of reading. From Ovid forward, then, discourses of desire pose a radical challenge to traditional concepts of authority and authorship, referentiality and representation.

Crucial issues that represent a critical crossroads in contemporary feminist theory concern the ideology of authorship and the ideology

4. See Jacques Derrida, "La Loi du genre / The Law of Genre," *Glyph* 7 (Spring 1980), trans. Avital Ronell, in *Critical Inquiry* 7 (Autumn 1980), 55–81. See also Peggy Kamuf, "Writing like a Woman," in *Women and Language in Literature and Society*, ed. Sally McConnell-Ginet, Ruth Borker, and Nelly Furman (New York: Praeger, 1980), pp. 284–99.

of mimesis. Some feminist critics fear that, in the words of Elaine Showalter, "Franco-American theory has gone much too far in discounting the importance of signature and gender in authorship." She goes further in another essay: "The categories of literary analysis most essential to the project of feminist criticism—author, period, genre, tradition—as well as the cultural models underlying them all, are precisely the ones which the most potent forces in contemporary criticism would call into question or dismiss; we will have to fight to protect them."[5] But what if there is an author, a genre, a tradition that itself questions mimesis, draws attention to the ambiguous implications of signature, and exposes the artifice involved in critical perceptions of gender? Discourses of desire are part of a tradition that is older even than Ovid, yet each discourse is just such a sustained critique. The Ovidian rhetorical ideal challenges the concepts of unity, fixity, and consistency; instead, it celebrates the fluid, the multiple, the capricious. Rather than seeing illusion as veiling a central reality or a fixed truth, Ovid values illusion for its own sake and recognizes how large a role artifice plays in arousing desire. His rhetoric, with its word play, masks, and poses, is both radically antimimetic and profoundly political. In my view, it is not enough to continue merely to portray the representations of women in fiction, although this has been an enormously fertile field of investigation. Feminist criticism must reevaluate the very concepts of author, of genre, of mimesis and challenge the traditional models of academic criticism. Some feminist critics insist that women's writing must be "true-to-life," based on "the authority of experience."[6] The danger of that approach lies in reducing the art to the life, as if women were incapable of writing about anything but themselves, and lacked aesthetic control and imagination. As I will show, this reduction is precisely what happens in tradi-

5. Elaine Showalter, "Critical Cross-Dressing: Male Feminists and the Woman of the Year," *Raritan Review* 3 (Fall 1983), 130–49. See also "The Future of Feminist Criticism," *Feminist Literary Criticism: A Working Paper for The National Humanities Center Conference*, Research Triangle Park, North Carolina, 27 March 1981, pp. 65–81.

6. See, for example, Arlyn Diamond and Lee Edwards, eds., *The Authority of Experience: Essays in Feminist Criticism* (Amherst: Univ. of Massachusetts Press, 1977); Sandra Gilbert, "Life Studies; or, Speech after Long Silence: Feminist Critics Today," *College English* 40 (1979), 849–63; Suzanne Juhasz, *Naked and Fiery Forms: Modern American Poetry by Women, a New Tradition* (New York: Harper and Row, 1976). Margaret Homans relates the issue to women poets in *Women Writers and Poetic Identity* (Princeton: Princeton Univ. Press, 1980), pp. 215–19.

tional critical assessments of Sappho, of Charlotte Brontë, of the three Marias. My aim is to examine the process and strategies by which these writing women transform themselves into artists, taking control of the production of writing to challenge not just men's representa-tion of them but—particularly as it relates to gender—the fundamen-tal tenets of representation itself.

I cannot stress strongly enough that from Ovid onward this chal-lenge is a political one. Although one may challenge the tenets of representation by showing that all language is self-referential, that all issues can be reduced to issues of signification, to "the nothingness of human matters,"[7] my focus is on the challenge to the tenets of repre-sentation as a political act. I situate critiques of mimesis within politics and history, delineating how discourses of desire have been dis-paraged or repressed by the structures of official thought from Ovid onward. In my view, Ovid was punished precisely because he refused to valorize the glorious past of omnipotent patriarchs; he refused to devote his poetry (as Virgil had) to officially endorsed Augustan val-ues. Classical scholars, in fact, have argued that the coup de grace that led Ovid to exile was specifically his portrait—so different from Vir-gil's representation—of Dido and Aeneas.[8] I have, moreover, chosen the *Heroides* precisely because it is the most rhetorical of all Ovid's poetry; I wish to underscore the ancient power of rhetoric as a specifi-cally political strategy of persuasion. To trace the process by which Aristotle elevated poetry and devalued rhetoric lies beyond the scope

7. Paul de Man, "Criticism and Crisis," *Blindness and Insight: Essays in the Rhetoric of Contemporary Criticism*, 2d ed., rev. (Minneapolis: Univ. of Minnesota Press, 1983), p. 18. Recent criticism of Richardson's *Clarissa* in particular centers on just this schism be-tween those critics who, like William Beatty Warner, view language as mere significa-tion and those who, like Terry Castle and Terry Eagleton, relate language to political action. See Chapter 4 below, note 43.

8. See Howard Jacobson, *Ovid's "Heroides"* (Princeton: Princeton Univ. Press, 1974), p. 90, n. 26. Says Jacobson: "Heroides 7 represents a serious attack on the Vergilian and Augustan philosophy of life and society." Nevertheless, I do not wish to minimize the complexity of Virgil's art; to cite but two critics who focus on the moral ambiguity of the *Aeneid*, see W. R. Johnson, *Darkness Visible: A Study of Vergil's Aeneid* (Berkeley: Univ. of California Press, 1976), pp. 1–22, and Christine G. Perkell, "On Creusa, Dido, and the Quality of Victory in Virgil's *Aeneid*," *Women's Studies* 8 (1981), 201–23. For a history of the Dido tradition and a bibliography of Virgilian sources, see Arthur Stanley Pease, *Publi Vergili Maronis Aeneidos Liber Quartus* (Cambridge: Harvard Univ. Press, 1935; rpr. Darmstadt, 1967), pp. 14–21; and Richard Heinze, *Virgils epische Technik* (Leipzig: B. G. Teubner, 1915; rpr. Darmstadt, 1972), pp. 115–17.

of this book,[9] but that scale of values informs my discussion of Augustan perceptions of Virgil's virtues and Ovid's transgressions.

Defining gender as a construct that is "literary" does not diminish the negative force this idea has exerted in the perceptions of writers, critics, and readers through the ages; that force has been considerable, as I will show. But I will also show how, by combining a poetics with politics, writers like the three Marias expose the double agents of their repression: traditional representations of woman and stereotypical concepts of gender. From the *Heroides* to *The Three Marias,* the writing heroines perform a "quiet, stealthy work of undermining," carried out by miming the dominant images the culture disseminates.[10] The aim of the writing heroines in my book is, in the words of the three Marias, to "deflower myths" of woman by undermining mimesis, by transgressing the boundaries of both gender and genre. The *Heroides* interweaves rhetoric and poetry, narrative and myth; Heloise combines two medieval epistolary modes and mixes learned rhetorical arguments with erotic longings; the *Portuguese Letters* combine the tragic tirades of Racinian drama with the epistolary form; *Clarissa* transforms a comedy of seduction into the tragedy of Clarissa's death. *New Portuguese Letters* is the logical culmination of the tradition I trace, for the three Marias purposely subvert the traditional notion of genre by including myriad forms, styles, and modes in their collaborative text. They also subvert the ideology of authorship by not signing their letters, radically challenging conventional notions of a text's paternity, lineage, genealogy, genre. Yet their text, while transgressing generic boundaries, comes closest to explicitly invoking its generic models, demonstrating that the higher a genre develops and the more complex it becomes, the better it remembers its past.[11]

My analysis stresses content and form, genre and mode, as well as the diachronic renewals and elusive revisions of the form. Every text in my book is a dialogue between the writing subject and addressee, but it is also a dialogue with the preceding texts and languages of amorous discourse: thus Ovid, like Catullus before him, invokes Sap-

9. See Paul Ricoeur, *The Rule of Metaphor,* trans. Robert Czerny (Toronto: Univ. of Toronto Press, 1977), chap. 1.

10. Maria Isabel Barreño, Maria Teresa Horta, Maria Velho da Costa, *The Three Marias: New Portuguese Letters,* trans. Helen R. Lane (New York: Bantam, 1976), p. 23.

11. Bakhtin, *The Dialogic Imagination,* pp. 415–21.

pho; Heloise invokes Ovid; the Portuguese nun's letters reiterate those of Heloise; *Jane Eyre* is a subtext in *The Turn of the Screw;* and the process continues through the reaccentuation of the *Portuguese Letters* in *The Three Marias.*[12] Desire is infinitely transcribable, yet ultimately elusive, and is therefore reiterated ceaselessly. Dialogism implies not just double (or multiple) languages and dialogue but another *logic*— one that, as we shall see, distinguishes Ovid from Virgil, Heloise from Abelard, Clarissa from Lovelace, and so on.[13]

My emphasis on dialogue raises questions about the relation of presence to absence, speech to writing. Every single heroine writes to sustain the illusion that she is speaking to her beloved. Her discourse is written in extremity and lies at the extremes of telling, so far removed from mere mimesis that the diegetic and performative aspects of narrative dominate the discourse. Indeed, what Gérard Genette says of Proust is true of Rosa Coldfield in *Absalom, Absalom!* too: "The narrator is present as source, guarantor, and organizer of the narrative, as analyst and commentator, as stylist (as 'writer')."[14] I have these multiple narrative roles in mind when I refer to the "doubleness" and the "duplicity" of discourses of desire, for the heroines are frequent commentators on the complexities of style and, concurrently, analysts of the subtleties of feeling. They simultaneously analyze their illusions about the beloved and create new ones by writing; the act of writing itself is one means of creating the illusion of presence. If narrative is viewed as a performance, presence (or the illusion of presence) becomes crucial, as Mikhail Bakhtin points out: "Language, when it means, is somebody talking to somebody else, even when that someone else is one's own inner addressee. . . . All rhetorical forms . . . are oriented toward the listener and his answer. This orientation is usually considered the basic constitutive feature of rhetorical discourse."[15] I begin with the most rhetorical of all Ovid's

12. Bakhtin defines this sort of assimilation and reaccentuation as the distinguishing characteristic of novelistic discourse, ibid., pp. 415–22.

13. See Bakhtin, *The Dialogic Imagination,* chap. 1, on the logic of the epic versus that of the novel. See also Julia Kristeva's essays on Bakhtin: "The Ruin of a Poetics," in *Russian Formalism,* ed. Stephen Bann and John E. Bowlt (New York: Barnes and Noble, 1973), pp. 102–19, and "Word, Dialogue, and Novel" in *Desire in Language: A Semiotic Approach to Literature and Art,* ed. Leon S. Roudiez, trans. Thomas Gora, Alice Jardine, and Leon S. Roudiez (New York: Columbia Univ. Press, 1980), pp. 64–89.

14. Gérard Genette, *Narrative Discourse: An Essay in Method,* trans. Jane E. Lewin (Ithaca: Cornell Univ. Press, 1980), p. 167.

15. Bakhtin, *The Dialogic Imagination,* pp. xvi, 28, 332.

poetry, the *Heroides,* and demonstrate how each subsequent heroine sustains the fiction of a conversation with the beloved in her letters, while simultaneously revealing her awareness of the fictiveness of the endeavor. The inscription of desire is alternately rhetorical, erotic, spontaneous, calculated. It is a consciously staged utterance, addressed to the absent beloved; yet (paradoxically), it simultaneously dramatizes his silence, the heroine's alienation, and the metonymic displacement of desire. Each amorous discourse draws on the same tropes and figures of rhetoric to persuade the beloved to return, and in each the performative aspects of rhetoric dramatize the similarities in situation and context. What are compulsively reiterated from Ovid to the three Marias are the prologue and epilogue of seduction: these are the subjects of the discourse. In each text, the heroine transforms the ordeal of abandonment into a passionate vocation that might be called the vocation of iterative narrative.[16] Ceaselessly repeated in the aftermath of abandonment, it is a powerful reenactment of pleasure and desire, related less to the mimetic than to the diegetic qualities of narrative, for the narrating heroine is intensely, constantly present as analyst, catalyst, and creator of her own desire. Since every letter to the beloved is also a self-address, as I shall show, the heroine's project— aided by her reading and her writing—also involves self-creation, self-invention. That is the obsessive motive of the governess in *The Turn of the Screw,* for instance, whose entire narrative can be read as a disguised love letter to her employer; like all the heroines in my study, she transforms herself from the archetypal Woman Who Waits into the Woman Who Writes. The book that follows does not define woman's essence or imagination. Rather than relying on notions of underlying essences, with gender (as with genre), I examine the constructs that define and circumscribe, the myths that are disseminated, and the ideologies they serve. If the book is not a paean to femininity, neither is

16. Genette, chap. 3. Genette's method resembles the structuralist analyses of Tzvetan Todorov and Roland Barthes; my debt to all three theorists is large, although I do not draw the sharp distinction between mode and genre that Genette insists upon. Following Derrida and Bakhtin, moreover, I do not limit my discussion to mode; instead, my emphasis is on the ways in which discourses of desire transgress the boundaries of genre, assimilating other forms, genres, canons, speech patterns, and being assimilated in turn in the novel. In "La Loi du genre / The Law of Genre," Derrida, defining generic disruptions as legal transgressions, says "the law itself is at stake"; in the following chapters, I compare this view with Bakhtin's discussion of novels of pathos and trial (pp. 388–400 in *The Dialogic Imagination*), placing them in the context of amorous epistolary discourse.

it a paean to sentimentality, which, as Barthes observes, is considered obscene today. Insofar as the conclusions of the book suggest a re-evaluation of the affectional life, it does so with a Borgesian awareness of the impossibility of trying to "forget" the twentieth century. The texts in my book combine literature and criticism, asking questions of love that weave theory with practice. They use methods as old as Dante's *La Vita Nuova* and—influenced by the literary salons of seventeenth-century Paris and by Freud—are as new as Derrida's *La Carte postale*.

To reiterate, then, the genre I shall question is epistolary; the mood is amorous and elegiac; the situation is the aftermath of abandonment. The heroine's discourse is meant as a performance to be spoken, a letter to be read; she utters her desire in the absence of the beloved. The narrative consists of events reported by the heroine to the lover; it is oblique and elliptical because we frequently see only the repercussions of events that, like the love affair itself, are never narrated. Other acts of communication are enacted rather than reported in the narrative: the heroine's writing reenacts seduction, confession, persuasion, and these constitute what "happens" in the text.[17] She writes in the mode of amorous discourse, transforming herself in the process from victim to artist. Style, subjectivity, and intertextuality are the motives for and subjects of the writing. These may seem incompatible, but since the discourse itself is the product of incompatible narrative impulses, it vacillates between vengeance and nostalgia, defiance and desire. Janet Gurkin Altman points out that the very qualities that make a work most mimetic in epistolary terms—authorial absence, domination of discursive elements—work against its narrativity. Epistolary texts combine elements usually regarded as opposites: discourse and narrative, spontaneity and calculation. The epistolary author, notes Altman, "has a fundamental problem," for such an author "(A) must make his letter writer (B) speak to an addressee (C) in order to communicate with a reader (D) who overhears; how does he reconcile the exigencies of story (communication between novelist and reader) with the exigencies of interpersonal discourse (communication between correspondents)?"[18] Since amorous epistolary discourse subverts so many conventional dichotomies and

17. Altman, pp. 207–10. Altman never speaks directly of the genre I call amorous epistolary discourse, but my debt to her analysis of *epistolarity* is nonetheless large.
18. Altman, p. 210.

explores so many transgressions and transformations, it is appropriate that the author of the *Metamorphoses* was one founder of the form; he marked it forever with doubleness, duplicity, difference, dissimulation—the distinguishing characteristics of Ovidian rhetoric in the *Heroides*.

The Love Letter

This figure refers to the special dialectic of the love letter, both blank (encoded) and expressive (charged with longing to signify desire).

Roland Barthes, *A Lover's Discourse: Fragments*

1
Ovid's *Heroides:*
"Genesis" and Genre

Oenone. 1688. Nicholas Yeates's engraving was published in
*Ovid's Epistles, with the Addition of Three Epistles of Paulus Sabinus,
in Answer to as Many of Ovid,* trans. Mr. Salusbury, 4th ed.
(London: Jacob Tonson, 1688). It is reproduced courtesy of
the William Andrews Clark Memorial Library, University of
California, Los Angeles.

The Search for the Lost Father

> Perhaps too my name will be joined to theirs, nor will
> my writings be given to Lethe's waters; and someone
> will say, "Read the elegant poems of our master,
> wherein he instructs the rival parties [i.e., men and
> women]; or from the three books marked by the title
> of "Loves" choose out what you may softly read with
> docile voice; or let some [Heroine's] Letter be read by
> you with practised utterance; he first invented this art,
> unknown to others.
>
> OVID, *The Art of Love*

Genre, engendering, generations, genealogy—what does it mean
to father a text? Did Ovid father a genre as well? In *The Art of Love*, he
urges female students to read Callimachus, Philetas, Anacreon, Sappho, Menander, Propertius, Gallus, Tibullus, Varro, Virgil, and then
suggests that they read his *Amores* and *Heroides*, particularly since the
latter is a genre unknown to others, which he invented (*Ignotum hoc
aliis ille novavit opus*, 3:345–46). What might Ovid mean? He could
mean simply that he is the first Roman to imitate a Greek model,
following the time-honored convention of the *primus* motif. But in
such cases Romans usually took pains to draw attention to their Greek
masters. Propertius, for instance, proclaims that he is Callimachus'
disciple, minimizing his own originality in order to draw attention to
the fact that he is following in his great Greek father's footsteps.[1] Not
so Ovid. As Clarissa will do later, he in effect proclaims, "I am Nobody's." Rather than acknowledging a debt by presenting a catalogue
of fathers, his list serves cunningly to point up what he has accomplished that they have not: the invention of a genre. Howard Jacobson observes, "The very fact that . . . Ovid neither mentions nor hints

---

1. Howard Jacobson, *Ovid's "Heroides"* (Princeton: Princeton Univ. Press, 1974),
pp. 320–21.

at some Greek ancestor (unlike Propertius, Horace, Lucretius, and Vergil), is itself testimony that he means this as an absolute assertion of his inventiveness, not merely of Roman adaptation."[2]

C. Dilthey's 1884 treatise on the *Heroides*, however, disputes Ovid's boast of paternity (and Dilthey himself is granted paternity, as Jacobson points out: "It has long been routine to father upon Dilthey the view that the *Heroides* genre existed before Ovid"). Dilthey, in fact, in *Observationum in epistulas heroidum Ovidianas particula I*, never actually denies that Ovid invented the genre. Instead, he cites earlier authentic love letters, mythical letters, and references such as Plutarch's allusion to a letter to Ariadne, forged in Theseus' name. Long dramatic monologues by passionate heroines and love letters—authentic and fictional—certainly existed before the *Heroides*. Homer's Penelope and Briseis, Apollonius' Hypsipyle and Medea, Euripides' Medea and Phaedra, Sophocles' Deianira, Catullus' Ariadne and Laodamia, and Horace's Hypermnestra—all precede Ovid's heroines. Before the *Heroides* came Latin elegies and the letters of Cicero, Plato, Epicurus, and Propertius.[3] But Propertius, for example, did not conceive of an interrelated sequence like the *Heroides*. His elegies, moreover, concentrate on the poet as lover, a technique Ovid employs in other works but not in the *Heroides*. Furthermore, where Propertius highlights the transformation of a mundane erotic situation into a heroic one, Ovid does the opposite. He transforms well-known heroines into modern, erotic mistresses of the art of rhetoric, single-mindedly discoursing on desire.[4] Despite classicists' extensive knowledge of myriad literary forms in antiquity, not one reference exists to other works like the *Heroides*. Although free-standing poems sometimes appeared inserted in drama or other genres, Ovid's formal letters in verse stand alone. In other epistles and poems, moreover, the author and the letter writer are virtually indistinguishable; Ovid's characters, in contrast, are vivid individual portraits, distinct from the poet and from each other.[5] Indeed, one distinctive trait of the *Heroides* is a kind of doubleness: one reads it simultaneously as a series of individual letters and as a coherent text with a unified form, theme, and structure.

2. Ibid., p. 321.
3. See Jacobson, pp. 319–22; W. S. Anderson, "The *Heroides*," in *Ovid*, ed. J. W. Binns (London: Routledge and Kegan Paul, 1973), pp. 49–83.
4. Anderson, pp. 64–65.
5. Jacobson, pp. 321–31.

Ovid was the first to conceive of the larger possibilities of the epistolary form, for rather than limiting it to a single letter, he developed it
into a genre with a particular dynamic principle and pattern, expand-
ing the technique of the love elegy by combining it with mythology
and giving it an intensity of focus, expression, and range that was
entirely original.[6]

The evidence thus supports the view that Ovid did invent a genre,
but I am as interested in the assumptions implicit in the controversy as
in its eventual outcome. First, in searching for authentic origins, how
can one reconcile the references historical figures like Plutarch make
to letters written by mythological figures? The lines between fiction
and reality, the authentic and the inauthentic, are further blurred by
such fascinating details as that the letter to Ariadne was forged in
Theseus' name. Who forged it? Was the forger another mythological
figure, invented by some anonymous author, or could the forger and
author be one in the same? Forgeries, thefts, disguised names, false
attributions, and illegitimate copies abound in discourses of desire.

If origins cannot be firmly fixed in the identity of the author,
neither can they be found in the language. Like the self, the language
of this genre is fluid, decentered, multiple: Sappho's Greek decenters
Ovid's Latin, or a French text is ostensibly written by a Portuguese
nun to whom three women respond centuries later in Portuguese.
Amorous discourse is indeed a hybrid of languages, of astonishing
diversity and simultaneity. The bilingualism (sometimes trilingualism)
of the texts mediates against certainty and centrality; each letter writer grapples with the intractability of language and expresses profound skepticism about the connection of words to deeds, to reality, to
representation. The result is a radical detachment from ideology as
well. Ovid's attitude toward the glories of Roman Augustanism, in
contrast to Virgil's, is characteristically skeptical, irreverent, unswayed
by the public virtues espoused by epic. The genre of amorous epistolary discourse is, paradoxically, antigeneric and anticanonical; it engulfs and is engulfed by other languages and other cultures, and it
assimilates other genres—Sapphic lyrics, authentic letters, Roman elegies, the soliloquies of tragic heroines. It also presents several ideologies in dialogue or conflict rather than a single coherent one.
Every discourse of desire is therefore simultaneously a critique of

6. Ibid., pp. 6–7, 321–31.

language.[7] The lover is a critic who has been described as a linguistic orphan in philosophical solitude.[8]

Ovid's self-criticism is most pronounced when his solitude is greatest—after his banishment. The myriad implications of viewing the letter as literature and literature as a letter are highlighted in the *Tristia* and *Epistulae ex Ponto*, for Ovid's letters in exile combine the same motifs of longing, intensity, despair, and supplication that mark his heroines' discourses in the *Heroides*. Despite the uniqueness of the *Heroides*, Helmut Rahn maintains that the entire genre includes Ovid's elegiac letters from exile.[9] These elegies begin, indeed, with the characteristic generic contrasts between the writer's immobility and the book's freedom to travel. Ovid also contrasts his former pride in his earlier art with an awareness that the art in these elegies is much chastened and subdued. His *envoi* opens with the words:

> Little book, you will go without me—and I grudge it not—to the city. Alas that your master is not allowed to go! Go, but go unadorned, as becomes the book of an exile; in your misfortune wear the garb that befits these days of mine. . . . your title shall not be tinged with vermilion nor your paper with oil of cedar; and you shall wear no white bosses upon your dark edges. Books of good omen should be decked with such things as these; 'tis my fate that you should bear in mind. . . . I would have you appear with locks all rough and disordered. Be not ashamed of blots; he who sees them will feel that they were caused by my tears.
>
> Go, my book, and in my name greet the loved places: I will tread them at least with what foot I may.[10]

Throughout book 2 of the *Tristia*, Ovid's argument involves several issues of representation. He urges Augustus to distinguish between

---

7. Mikhail M. Bakhtin, *The Dialogic Imagination: Four Essays*, ed. Michael Holquist, trans. Holquist and Caryl Emerson (Austin: Univ. of Texas Press, 1981), pp. 412–22.

8. Roland Barthes, *A Lover's Discourse: Fragments*, trans. Richard Howard (New York: Hill and Wang, 1978), pp. 211–12. Unfortunately, the title Howard uses misleadingly emphasizes the lover as a character rather than the fragmentary nature of the discourse. A better translation might be *Fragments of an Amorous Discourse*, which is more in keeping with Barthes's theoretical project.

9. Helmut Rahn, "Ovid's elegische Epistel," *Antike und Abendland* 7 (1958), 105–20. I am grateful to Betty Rose Nagle for drawing my attention both to this article and to the larger relevance of Roman amatory elegy.

10. Ovid, *Tristia* and *Epistulae ex Ponto*, trans. Arthur Leslie Wheeler, Loeb Classical Library (Cambridge: Harvard Univ. Press, 1924), p. 3, book 1, part 1, lines 1–16, hereinafter cited parenthetically in the text by letter and line number.

Ovid the man and Ovid the artist, between miming and reality, between Ovid's personal morality and the *jouissance* of his erotic, imaginative verse. "I assure you, my character differs from my verse (my life is moral, my muse is gay), and most of my work, unreal and fictitious, has allowed itself more license than its author has had. A book is not an evidence of one's soul, but an honorable impulse that presents very many things suited to charm the ear" (2:353–58). Such penitence as Ovid does display in the *Tristia* is highly ambiguous; he disowns the very words of penance even as he writes them, finding ways to reproach and to defy his persecutors even as he beseeches their pardon. (Heloise will employ a similar strategy with Abelard.) In other elegies, while he seems contrite, he simultaneously indicts Augustus for his hypocrisy, as when he reminds Augustus of how often he enjoyed Ovid's performances. While Ovid hastens to add that such actions are praiseworthy ("so benign is thy majesty everywhere"), the real emphasis is on all the sinful pleasures Augustus himself relished, the pleasures he saw. "With thine eyes, by which the whole world profits, thou hast gazed undisturbed at these adulteries of the stage. If 'tis right to compose mimes that copy vice, to my themes a smaller penalty is due. . . . My poems too have often been presented to the people with dancing, often they have even beguiled thine own eyes" (2:513–17, 519–20). Ovid ends book 2 with an invocation to Augustus, addressing him as "Father . . . protector and salvation of thy native land" (2:574).

All the texts that follow in the present book exhibit the same blurring of the boundaries between letter and literature—from the *Tristia* to the *Heroides*, from the letters of Lady Bradshaigh to Richardson's novel, from Brontë's letters to Monsieur Heger to *Jane Eyre*. Orphanhood, exile, solitude, and loneliness—encoded in every single text and plaguing every single writer of discourses of desire—are ultimately what one finds in searching for the lost father.

The Heroines' Discourses

> The lovesick [οι ἐϱῶντες] always take pleasure in talking, writing, or composing verses about the beloved, for it seems to them that in all this recollection [μεμνημένοι] makes the object of their affection perceptible [αἰσθάνεσθαι].
>
> ARISTOTLE, *Rhetoric*

Given Ovid's borrowings and deviations in Greek and Latin, in history, myth, and elegy, what remains distinctive about each heroine's discourse in the *Heroides*? One must look forward as well as back to discover what themes, motifs, and structural features distinguish the *Heroides* as one *locus classicus* of amorous epistolary discourse.

First, the heroine is defined by the lover she addresses. That bond structures the meaning in ways that would not be applicable if the heroine were merely writing a diary, a memoir, or a journal. In amorous epistolary discourse, the heroine always locates herself—spatially, temporally, emotionally—vis-à-vis the beloved. She draws attention to the bond (*foedus*) that links them, which she thinks should command loyalty (*fides*) from the lover to whom she proclaims her faithfulness (*fida*) and laments his infidelity, betrayal, or absence.[11] Phaedra complains to Hippolytus, for instance: "With wishes for the welfare which she herself, unless you give it her, will ever lack, the Cretan maid greets the hero whose mother was an Amazon. Read to the end, whatever is here contained—what shall reading of a letter harm? In this one too, there may be something to pleasure you; in these characters of mine, secrets are borne over land and sea. Even foe looks into missive writ by foe."[12] Even in this brief passage, several distinguishing traits of the genre are apparent. The complaint in the first line is based on *lack*, a word that recurs throughout the discourse. *Pleasure* is another word much on the heroine's lips; she wants to please her lover by writing and to recall their past pleasures together. The analogy of lovers to foes echoes Catullus' famous *odi et amo*, an allusion that Ovid evokes again and again. It is also significant that Phaedra defines Hippolytus as his mother's son rather than as her husband's, audaciously decentering his authority while disguising her incestuous desire. Phaedra goes on to speak of writing as a compulsion; it overpowers all taboos, all modesty, and all injunctions, thus achieving what speech makes impossible: "Thrice making trial of speech with you, thrice hath my tongue vainly stopped, thrice the sound failed at first threshold of my lips. Wherever modesty may attend on love, love should not lack in it; with me, what modesty forbade to say, love has commanded me to write" (4:7–10). Signifi-

---

11. See Janet Gurkin Altman, *Epistolarity: Approaches to a Form* (Columbus: Ohio State Univ. Press, 1983), pp. 118–20; Anderson, p. 70.
12. Ovid, *"Heroides" and "Amores,"* trans. Grant Showerman, Loeb Classical Library (Cambridge: Harvard Univ. Press, 1914), letter 4, ll. 1–7, p. 45, hereinafter cited parenthetically in the text by letter and line number.

cantly, writing gives her a freedom that speech denies her both because of her so-called modesty and because of the beloved's absence.
At other times, the heroine will purposely blur the distinction between speech and writing in order to nurture the illusion of the beloved's presence. The illusion of presence haunts every single heroine's discourse of desire.

Phaedra's letter points to another trait of amorous discourse, for
explicit attention is paid to the act of reading. The lover is first commanded "to read to the end," then is cajoled with the question, what
harm can it do? Phaedra follows this with a tease: the letter should be
read because there are both secrets and pleasures contained within.
Epistolarity has been defined as "the use of a letter's formal properties
to create meaning."[13] The fundamental category of epistolarity is that
it must be written to be read. It does not necessarily follow that the
letter *will* be read, much less that it will evoke a response, but as an
utterance, it is "dialogic"; its existence depends on sustaining the
illusion of a dialogue with the reader. Thus, in amorous epistolary
discourse, the act of reading becomes a pervasive part of the narrative; the heroine imagines the beloved receiving her letter, reflects
on the different emotions it might elicit in him, and resolves to write
in a way that will please him. In the rare instances when she either
receives or writes a reply (Helen to Paris, Hero to Leander, Cydippe
to Acontius), she relates her response as a reader. Reading and writing are part of the drama enacted in the heroine's private theater.

In all amorous epistolary discourses, from *Clarissa* to *The Three
Marias*, we thus develop the illusion of reading a letter in the process
of being written, an illusion reinforced by the fact that each heroine
begins with an explicit reference to the act of writing. Her tone is
reproachful; if the beloved were present, she could put down her
pen. Signs of physical pain (usually tears, sometimes blood) deface the
pages of her letter and testify to her physical as well as her psychic
suffering. These tears on the page have the status of the kind of
evidence one might use in a court trial. Through such signs, the
heroine transmits a part of herself, the corporeal, to the textual, implying that the body's message is truer than speech; tears are irrefuta-
ble evidence. Tears prove—both to the lover and the beloved—that
the grief is not an illusion. Compare Roland Barthes's amorous discourse: "By weeping, I want to impress someone, to bring pressure to

13. Altman, pp. 94–96.

bear upon someone. . . . Tears are signs, not expressions. By my tears, I tell a story, I produce a myth of grief. . . . by weeping, I give myself an emphatic interlocutor who receives the 'truest' of messages, that of my body, not that of my speech: 'Words, what are they? One tear will say more than all of them.'"[14]

Tears thus indicate the disproportion between what is signified and the means of signifying. Throughout amorous discourse, the heroine glorifies her tears, her heart, her tongue, her body as authentic registers of her emotions. Yet she disrupts the conventional impulse to think in terms of dichotomies, for she does not always glorify these elements at the expense of their opposites, as one might expect. Frequently, in fact, she subverts the traditional dichotomies of heart versus mind, speech versus writing, tongue versus pen, for "to write" becomes synonymous with "to live." Writing comes to signify her life's blood, illustrating her identification of her body with the text.[15] Canace writes Macareus, for example, "Dead that I am, believe me, yet at your words I live again" (11:63). Her words defer death, for even the act of describing her tears defers the actual act of dying, as when Dido writes: "Could you but see now the face of her who writes these words! I write, and the Trojan's blade is ready in my lap. Over my cheeks the tears roll, and fall upon the drawn steel—which soon shall be stained with blood instead of tears" (7:183–86). In the *Tristia*, similarly, Ovid reiterates the close identification of his body with his text when he reports, "These verses upon my departure, like so much that was mine, in sorrow I placed with my own hand in the fire. Just as Thestius' daughter burned her own son . . . so I placed the innocent books consigned with me to death, my very vitals, upon the devouring pyre"(1:7:15–20). In some cases, ink itself is compared to the life's blood; the ancients wrote in a milky substance, which the recipient would treat with charcoal to read the writing. In *The Art of Love*, for example, Ovid urges women to carry on secret correspondences via a confidante who should "hide a paper packet in her stocking, and bear your coaxing message 'twixt foot and sandal . . . [or] bear your words upon her body. A letter too is safe and escapes the eye when written in

14. Barthes, *A Lover's Discourse*, p. 182.

15. On female sexuality and textuality, especially the connection of blood and the body to women's writing, see Susan Gubar, "'The Blank Page' and the Issues of Female Creativity," *Critical Inquiry* 7 (Winter 1981), 243–63; on the equation "écrire = vivre," see Gregory L. Ulmer, "The Discourse of the Imaginary," *Diacritics* 10 (March 1980), 61–75.

new milk: touch it with coal-dust, and you will read" (3:621–28). The letter is thus a metonymic and a metaphoric displacement of desire. The narrator is catalyst for and stylist of the narrative, a producer of metaphors. As in Ovid's *Tristia,* the specific destination the heroine yearns for is the same as that of her letter: she sees the letter as part of herself and wishes that she had the freedom to transport herself to her lover, to be opened and held in his hands.[16] The heroine frequently reverses the opposition of words and deeds, by making the letter minister to—and minister of—passion. The same strategy appears in the *Tristia,* where Ovid writes from the place of the book: "Though sent to this city I come in fear, an exile's book. Stretch forth a kindly hand to me in my weariness, friendly reader, and fear not that I may perchance bring shame upon you; not a line on this paper teaches love. . . . you will see nothing here except sadness, and the verse befits its own state" (3:1:1–10). In these lines, Ovid tries to forestall the kind of rejection that the heroines suffer throughout the *Heroides.* Exiled because he refused to relegate love to the margins of discourse, Ovid subsequently writes a text that assures its readers the forbidden subject will not be raised. Yet the very reference to what is absent is a means of reinscribing love, of reminding the public of his love poetry, and of ridiculing those who have banished him on such grounds. In these lines, the book is cunningly personified, miming the fate of its author: "If the lame couplets halt in alternate verses, 'tis due to the metre's nature or to the length of the journey; if I am not golden with oil of cedar nor smoothed with the pumice, 'tis because I blushed to be better dressed than my master; if the letters are spotted and blurred with erasures, 'tis because the poet with tears has injured his own work. If any expressions perchance shall seem not Latin, the land wherein he wrote was a barbarian land" (3:1:11–18). Examples such as these are the *locus classicus* of motifs that will be reiterated again and again in this book. They demonstrate what it is like to write "under erasure"; they illuminate the myriad ways in which the discourse of love is an alien discourse; they help to clarify why the act of writing is itself such a transgression, for etymologically, *transgression* means "to pass over or beyond."[17] Moreover, if metaphor, as Paul Ricoeur suggests in his discussion of Aristotle, is the transposition of a

---

16. See Gérard Genette, *Narrative Discourse: An Essay in Method,* trans. Jane E. Lewin (Ithaca: Cornell Univ. Press, 1980), p. 167.

17. See Tony Tanner, *Adultery in the Novel: Contract and Transgression* (Baltimore: Johns Hopkins Univ. Press, 1979), p. 9.

name that is alien, belonging to something else that is transposed through a system of deviations, borrowings, or substitutions, in the *Tristia* it is the poet himself who is alien, and in the *Heroides*, it is often the woman who is alien, borrowed, or stolen, in conquest.[18] Briseis is one such woman. "From stolen Briseis is the writing you read, scarce charactered in Greek by her barbarian hand. Whatever blots you shall see, her tears have made; but tears, too, have none the less the weight of words" (3:1–4). Ovid's Briseis illustrates his innovative use of sources, for in Homer, Briseis speaks a scant fourteen lines in the *Iliad*, over the corpse of Patroclos.[19] Here, Ovid develops Briseis into a powerful character in her own right, skillfully drawing Achilles' attention to her tears, her pen, and the power of her discourse. Briseis' words mark several other traits of the genre. First, the conquest of the heroine's body is frequently connected to that of her country; both her body and the body politic are enslaved, in a state of siege among warring factions—psychic as well as political. The same analogy recurs when the Portuguese nun becomes the conquest of a Frenchman stationed in Portugal during the reign of the Sun King; it resurfaces in the three Marias' meditations about Portugal's colonization and women's oppression. Secondly, Briseis' situation is dialogic; she is engaged in dialogue with the lover but is forced to communicate in an alien tongue. The significance of this alien relation is enormous, for it makes her skeptical about the connection of words to reality and frustrates her desire to master her master's language. She is alien, other; so are the words she must use.

After she draws attention to the act of writing and reading, the heroine examines the forces that separated the lovers. Sometimes the sea, the wind, or other natural forces keep them apart; at other times war divides them. To the heroine, however, no force—natural or political—is as powerful, as all-consuming as her own passion. As Penelope asks Ulysses, "But of what avail to me that Ilion has been scattered in ruin by your arms, and that what once was wall is now level ground—if I am still to remain as I was while Troy endured, and must live to all time bereft of my lord?" (1:47–50). Throughout the *Heroides*, Ovid casts a critical eye upon Roman vainglory, national pride, and the civic virtues that are the staples of epic. He quite

18. See Paul Ricoeur, *The Rule of Metaphor*, trans. Robert Czerny (Toronto: Univ. of Toronto Press, 1977), p. 20.
19. Anderson, p. 64.

consciously rejected those values, endorsing instead the value system of Roman amatory elegy but creating a genre unique in its single-minded focus on alternative subjects, moods, and attitudes of the speaking heroine. Penelope's question exhibits radically different logic from that which glorifies the nation over the individual, the public image over the private emotion, the male over the female, war over love, duty over desire. The heroine's obsession with her passion leads to enormous transgressions, for she sometimes betrays her homeland and her family for her lover. Medea, for example, contrasts her present degradation with her past grandeur: "I, the maiden who am now at last become a barbarian in your eyes, who now am poor, who now seem baneful—I . . . gave into your hand the fleece to steal away unharmed. I betrayed my sire, I left my throne and my native soil; the reward I get is leave to live in exile!" (12:105–10).

As in the *Tristia* and the *Epistulae ex Ponto,* which Ovid would write later, exile is the dominant note throughout the letters of the heroines, for they are exiled not only from the beloved but from all solace, protection, identity; they are bereft of beloved, father, and fatherland all at the same time. They ponder various solutions to their plight but end in merely asking over and over, as Ariadne asks, "What am I to do? Whither shall I take myself—I am alone. . . . where am I to go? My father's realm forbids me to approach. . . . I still shall be an exile! 'Tis not for me, O Crete . . . to look upon thee. . . . No, for my father and the land ruled by my righteous father—dear names!—were betrayed by my deed when, to keep you . . . from death in the winding halls, I gave into your hand the thread to direct your steps in place of guide" (10:59–72). Medea gave fleece; Ariadne gave thread: in each case the gift—like the letter—is a transgression; it "passes over or beyond" the boundaries fixed by laws, fathers, nations. Thread and fleece are substitutions for the heroines' bodies, the means of salvation for those they love. In Freud's famous example, the *Fort! Da!* game, the spool can be pulled back by its thread, but rather than restoring Theseus to Ariadne or Jason to Medea, the thread or the fleece that each heroine willingly surrenders (along with her body) simply facilitates the flight of her lover.

Throughout the *Heroides* and in all subsequent amorous epistles, the heroine engages in a complex analysis of her predicament. Some narratologists suggest that "the narrative is a . . . doubly temporal sequence. . . . one of the functions of narrative is to invent one time

scheme in terms of another time scheme."[20] One generic legacy of the
Heroides is that several time schemes function simultaneously; the heroine moves rapidly between past, present, and future. She is sometimes nostalgic, sometimes uncertain, sometimes hopeful. At times,
she contrasts her past naïveté with her present disillusionment. At
other times, she leaps from a memory of past pleasure to anticipation
of the future, asking herself how and if it is possible that their past
joys have ceased for all time. Frequently the heroine's analysis begins
with denial and disbelief. Rather than abandoning her, her lover must
be dead, shipwrecked, imprisoned. Doubt about his fidelity, remorse
for her doubts, and justification of the lover follow in quick succession. Ovid frequently disrupts the temporal order with the heroine's
speculations about her lover's infidelity and the revenge she anticipates, as when Hypsipyle curses Medea: "As for your mistress—with
my own hand I would have dashed my face with her blood, and your
face, that she stole with her poisonous arts! I would have been Medea
to Medea!" (6:149–51). As Hypsipyle moves rapidly to a prediction of
Medea's future, Ovid's readers would know that her curses eventually
come true one after the other: "May the woman who intrudes upon
my marriage-bed suffer the woes in which Hypsipyle groans, and feel
the lot she herself now brings on me; and as I am now alone, wife and
mother of two babes, so may she one day be reft of as many babes, and
of her husband! Let her be an exile, and seek a refuge through the
entire world! . . . Let her wander, destitute, bereft of hope, stained
red with the blood of her murders!" (6:153–56, 162). Narrative time
in amorous discourse is further complicated by each heroine's awareness that she is neither the first to be seduced nor the last to be
abandoned by her lover. Sometimes the heroine even imagines herself serving as handmaid to her lover's new mistress, just to remain
near him. Briseis tries to persuade Achilles: "As captive let me follow
my captor, not as wife my wedded lord. . . . The most beauteous by
far among the women of Achaea will come to the marriage-chamber
of your bride—and may she come! . . . I shall be a lowly slave of
yours" (3:69–75). Rhetorically, the ploy is a strategy of persuasion,
born of desperation. It also illuminates a basic pattern in the structure
of desire, for each heroine occupies the same place in the structure of

20. Christian Metz, *Film Language: A Semiotics of the Cinema*, trans. Michael Taylor
(New York: Oxford Univ. Press, 1974), p. 18, cited in Genette, p. 33.

the beloved by whom she is betrayed; she is set in rivalry with other women who will be betrayed in their turn, as Hypsipyle's prophecies illustrate. "I would have been Medea to Medea!" thus summarizes a remarkably complex structure entailing the exchange of women, the compulsion to repeat, triangular desire, and the disruption of narrative time.[21]

It also illuminates another trademark of Ovidian strategy, which is to highlight the correspondences between the correspondents. The heroine in one letter frequently comments on the fate of other heroines: this device reinforces the sense of sequence and unity in the text and simultaneously draws attention to the repetitive structure of desire, seduction, and betrayal. Ovid is often criticized for being too repetitive by critics who have not noticed the thematic relevance of repetition or his strategy of doubleness. On the one hand, the heroines have their suffering in common, as Ariadne writes: "Now, I ponder over not only what I am doomed to suffer, but all that any woman left behind can suffer" (10:79–80). On the other hand, each heroine has the opposite impulse to exalt her suffering as absolutely unique. Repetition, after all, can be based on difference as well as similarity; no repetition is exactly the same. Thus when Phyllis is betrayed by Demophoon, she first sees her fate in Ariadne's terms: Demophoon is Theseus' son; his abandonment of Phyllis replicates Theseus' abandonment of Ariadne. Phyllis damns him as "heir to your father's guile, perfidious one" (2:78) and ridicules his heritage: "Of all the great deeds in the long career of your sire, nothing has made impress upon your nature but the leaving of his [Theseus'] Cretan bride" (2:75–76). Yet she insists on contrasting as well as comparing herself to other heroines: "I had hope for a better fate, for I thought it my desert; the hope—whatever it be—that is grounded in desert, is just" (2:61–62).

Ovid's heroines thus consciously and ardently search for the law of recurrence, explicitly attempting to interpret their experience by interpreting that of other heroines. The technique emphasizes the text's

---

21. On women as objects of exchange, see Claude Lévi-Strauss, *Structural Anthropology*, trans. Claire Jacobson and Brooke Grundfest Schoepf (New York: Basic Books, 1963); on the repetition compulsion and triangular desire see René Girard, *Deceit, Desire, and the Novel: Self and Other in Literary Structure*, trans. Yvonne Freccero (Baltimore: Johns Hopkins Univ. Press, 1966); on disruptions of narrative time see Genette.

dialogism since it counterpoints other letters within Ovid's text and other authors' treatment of the same heroines.

This intertextuality bears a striking resemblance to the procedure of psychoanalysis, which involves the same effort to interpret, to account for repetitions, to assess the structure of desire. In a sense, no individual letter can be analyzed without considering its status as part of a repetitive structure of seduction, betrayal, abandonment. Thus, what Phyllis does above is both to interpret a repetition and to repeat the trauma of interpretation.[22] Each heroine in Ovid's text does the same thing. She returns obsessively to the causes and consequences of her betrayal, trying retrospectively to impose an order and a coherence on an experience in which she lacked foresight at the time. The *Heroides'* structure ceaselessly reiterates the same formal pattern: every heroine proceeds from denial of the reality of her betrayal to doubt of her lover's intentions, and then to jealousy, outrage, and despair. She is, moreover, frequently angry with herself as well as with her lover for not being more cautious. These formal characteristics recur in all the texts to follow. The Portuguese nun castigates her heart in her opening letter for "lacking foresight" (*prévoyance*); Jane Eyre calls herself a "blind puppy" after Rochester betrays her; Rosa Coldfield "holds no brief" for herself since she saw Sutpen's faults better than anyone. While in the *Heroides,* each heroine struggles to arrive at one fixed interpretation of her experience, her inability to do so and to resolve the conflict insures that another letter will succeed this one. The inability to persuade the beloved to return has a similar effect of making the writing go forward, keeping the circuit of desire open. Ovid depicts the personality of the beloved as an enigma, as an insoluble problem that the heroine tries to confront in the letter by offering multiple explanations for his betrayal without ever arriving at any ultimate conclusion.

22. Barbara Johnson, *The Critical Difference: Essays in the Contemporary Rhetoric of Reading* (Baltimore: Johns Hopkins Univ. Press, 1980), p. 142. Translating into the language of psychoanalysis, one would say that the heroines in my book practice the Imaginary in the full knowledge of what they are doing, a practice as apparent in *The Three Marias* as it is in the work of Roland Barthes. Jacques Lacan's "discourse of the Other," however, takes place at the level of the unconscious, whereas I use *discourse* primarily to connote utterance and *other* as the absent beloved. My title is nevertheless a conscious attempt to retain the trace of Freud and Lacan, for there are many parallels between the "talking cure" and letter writing. See Jacques Lacan, *The Language of the Self: The Function of Language in Psychoanalysis,* trans. Anthony Wilden (Baltimore: Johns Hopkins Univ. Press, 1968).

The issue of repetition focuses attention on the heroine as reader as well as writer, for only in rereading do the differences in situations, in texts, in suffering seem to emerge; if one does not reread, one is doomed, like Ariadne, to read the same story everywhere. Sometimes the heroine reads too much and only sees the similarities and not the differences between her fate and that of others. The overall effect, therefore, is of a succession of states and time schemes ceaselessly substituted for one another. Phyllis' comparison of Demophoon with his father, Theseus, is thus a demonstration of one of the fundamental traits of iterative narrative: the ability to keep one's thoughts focused on two disparate moments simultaneously, to see them as identical and to merge them.[23] Ovid thus "invents one time scheme in terms of another" and demonstrates that narrative is a "doubly temporal sequence"—one in which, given the terms of amorous epistolary discourse, the acts of writing and reading are both narrated and enacted.[24]

Several other sorts of doubleness distinguish Ovidian rhetoric in the *Heroides*. Since the *Heroides* are the most rhetorical of all of Ovid's poetry, two kinds of rhetorical exercises must be mentioned here: *suasoriae* and *ethopoiiae*. *Suasoriae* persuade by the use of logic, *ethopoiiae* rely on characterization and emotion to move the audience. *Ethopoiiae* usually begin with an account of present difficulties, move to a retrospective description of past prosperity, and conclude with a pessimistic look at the future. There is, moreover, a specifically female subcategory of *ethopoiiae* which relies on pathetic monologues, pure sentimentality, and self-pity.[25] I mention these classifications not to reduce Ovid to a mere rhetorician, for the *Heroides* are far more sophisticated than these rudimentary exercises, but I draw attention to these rhetorical models because their influence can be seen in subsequent amorous discourses, particularly those of Heloise and the Portuguese nun. Ovid's heroines combine logic and emotion; his heroines are zealous, judgmental, visionary, and as skilled rhetorically as politicians. Of particular interest here is the relation of *ethopoiiae* to legal oratory, for the development of the genre of amorous epistolary discourse is related to trial literature. As Bakhtin has observed,

23. Genette, pp. 142–43. See also Roland Barthes, *S/Z: An Essay*, trans. Richard Miller (New York: Hill and Wang, 1974), p. 16.

24. Genette, p. 33; Altman, pp. 206–12.

25. Jacobson, pp. 325–30.

Novelistic pathos always works in the novel to restore some other genre, genres that, in their own unmediated and pure form, have lost their own base in reality. In the novel a discourse of pathos is almost always a surrogate for some other genre that is no longer available to a given time or a given social force—such pathos is the discourse of a preacher who has lost his pulpit, a dreaded judge who no longer has judicial or punitive powers, the prophet without a mission, the politician without political power, the believer without a church.[26]

In my view, the specific genre that novelistic prose seeks to restore, the genre for which it is a surrogate, is that of amorous epistolary discourse in general and the *Heroides* in particular. Bakhtin traces "the discourse of pathos" back to pre-seventeenth-century trial literature, but the traits he describes were developed long before in the *Heroides*. The abandoned heroine accuses her seducer of infidelity, impugns his motives, demands justice, threatens vengeance, and justifies herself. The language of the genre is not just a dialogue but a trial, a contest, a debate. These traits, as Bakhtin points out, stand in stark contrast to those of epic: "The idea of testing the hero, of testing his discourse, may very well be the most fundamental organizing idea in the novel, one that radically distinguishes it from the epic. From the very beginning the epic hero has stood on the other side of trial; in the epic world, an atmosphere of doubt surrounding the hero's heroism is unthinkable."[27]

There are several problems with Bakhtin's definitions here. Not only is heroism more problematic and epic more complex than he allows, but the discourse of pathos is not "peculiarly novelistic . . . quite unlike that found in poetry," as Ovid's verse epistles demonstrate. Bakhtin's neglect of Ovid distorts his classifications here, for the traits he enumerates are all characteristic of the *Heroides*, which combine pathos *and* poetry. The heroine justifies herself, accuses her lover, breaks down his resistance to reading her letter, and refutes the logic of his viewpoint. The procedure is precisely what Bakhtin defines as the discourse of pathos, which "continually senses the resistance offered by alien discourses, alien points of view; it is the kind of pathos associated with justification (self-justification) and accusation. . . . [It is] fully sufficient to itself and to its object. Indeed, the speaker completely immerses himself in such a discourse, there is no

26. Bakhtin, *The Dialogic Imagination*, pp. 394–95.
27. Ibid., p. 388.

distance, there are no reservations. A discourse of pathos has the appearance of directly intentional discourse."[28]

That intentionality, moreover, is reinforced by the many references to tears and tearstains on the letter, which serve as proof of the pathos the letter contains. Every subsequent text in the genre is similarly structured around accusation, confrontation, trials, self-justification. Heloise follows Abelard's orders to the letter, then demands consolation from him; the Portuguese nun abandons herself sexually, then contests her abandonment. *Clarissa* commences with Anna Howe's urgent request that the heroine clear her name; the governess in *The Turn of the Screw* will likewise write to justify her actions. Jane Eyre's opening themes are punishment and disobedience, and Rosa Coldfield talks for hours to set the record straight about Sutpen's insult and her injury. *Diegesis*, remember, suggests that narrative is a retracing of a journey already made. Ovid's most important contribution is perhaps the emphasis on speech, on talking; what Bakhtin calls directly intentional discourse is what comes closest to being purely discursive, what, in my view, Ovid develops in the *Heroides*. Bakthin argues that authentic pathos in the novel "shies away from discourse that is openly emotional, not yet separated from its subject." But had Bakhtin more fully considered the genre of the amorous epistle, his formulations might have been different, for this genre combines the two—authentic pathos and emotional discourse. Indeed, it is one of the characteristic strategies of the genre to make it appear that aesthetic distance has been demolished, that emotional reserve has been abandoned, that one is witnessing the spontaneous overflowing of powerful feelings. Bakhtin goes on to argue that only poetic pathos can be authentic; novelistic pathos, in contrast, draws on the codes of literature: "Novelistic pathos . . . must borrow the discourses of others [by which Bakhtin means other authors]. When *authentic* pathos inheres in a subject, it can only be a *poetic* pathos" (Bakhtin's emphasis). My aim, on the contrary, is to demonstrate that it is precisely the poetic discourse of pathos in Ovid that is imitated in detail by Guilleragues in *Lettres portugaises*, which contains numerous allusions to the *Heroides* in every letter, and that the "discourse of the other" from which novelists from Guilleragues onward borrow is this particular Ovidian model. Thus, although verse epistles eventually become assimilated into the novel

28. Ibid., p. 394.

proper, it is the *Heroides* that give it an openly and spontaneously "contested, contestable, contesting" orientation.[29]

The element of spontaneity is as significant a contribution as pathos, for the fact that Ovid's heroines speak in the present moment marks yet another difference from epic, which deals with the heroic past, an idealized world of fathers and beginnings. Epic, a far more static genre, which stopped evolving long ago, is characterized by completedness and reverence for the past, but Ovid is drawn to all that is not completed; his heroines speculate on what is unknown, unfolding, becoming. The openness to the present has far-reaching implications for imaginative literature, for works that are constructed in a zone of contact with uncompleted events in a particular present tend to assimilate the nonliterary (autobiography, memoirs, political manifestoes, and authentic letters) into the literary. Indeed, when the temporal present entered imaginative literature, a revolution occurred, as Bakhtin explains: "The present, in all its openendedness, taken as a starting point and center for artistic and ideological orientation, is an enormous revolution in the creative consciousness of man. In the European world this reorientation and destruction of the old hierarchy of temporalities received its crucial generic expression on the boundary between classic antiquity and Hellenism, and in the new world during the late Middle Ages and Renaissance. The fundamental constituents of the novel as a genre were formed in these eras."[30] Many of these constituents are present in the *Heroides*, for it too is nonhierarchical and nonpatriarchical; not only does it deal with the individual in the uncompleted present, but its focus on the personal, the immediate, and the familiar demolishes the distance, the reverence, the inaccessibility of epic. Of the Ovidian rhetorical ideal of life, Richard A. Lanham remarks: "The point is not to hierarchize—there are no hierarchies here. . . . [Ovid] leaves his form open, aleatory, waiting to be realized. . . . He did not believe in he-

29. Ibid., pp. 332, 394–95. See also Peter Brooks, "Freud's Masterplot," in *Literature and Psychoanalysis: The Question of Reading—Otherwise*, ed. Shoshana Felman (Baltimore: Johns Hopkins Univ. Press, 1982), pp. 280–300. On diegesis as retraced journey, see J. Hillis Miller, "Ariachne's Broken Woof," *Georgia Review* 31 (1977), 44–60, and "The Figure in the Carpet," *Poetics Today* 1:3 (1980), 107–18. Frédéric Deloffre and J. Rougeot (eds.) cite Guilleragues' numerous allusions to the *Heroides* in "Analyse d'un chef-d'oeuvre," in *Lettres portugaises, Valentins, et autres oeuvres de Guilleragues* (Paris: Garnier, 1962), pp. 3–33.

30. Bakhtin, *The Dialogic Imagination*, p. 38.

roes, or the self they were based on."[31] Ovid himself can be described as an *aleator:* a gamester, a gambler; the effect for which amorous epistolary discourse strives involves chance, risk, and multiple possibilities—from the *Heroides* to *The Three Marias.* Roland Barthes, indeed, defines amorous discourse as "outbursts of language, which occur at the whim of trivial, of aleatory circumstances." Even more significant, the entire form of epistolarity has been defined as involving "the aleatory construction of the work."[32]

Thus those scholars who used to compare Ovid unfavorably to Virgil missed the mark, for Ovid had no interest in imitating Virgil's epic or emulating his Augustanism. Ovid may not have been "too dense to master a suitable repertoire of Augustan philosophical clichés," says Lanham; instead he simply never shared Virgil's preoccupation with the foundations of a culture and a city, since Ovid was cynical about the very notion of foundations: "He denied the theory of knowledge from which [such clichés] grew. Too skeptical to think the whole truth contained in a single myth, he thought the epic genre a fraud."[33] Since the *Aeneid* appeared some years before the *Heroides,* the difference between Virgil's Dido and Ovid's illuminates the differences in style and politics between epic and epistle, for Virgil's Dido is a queen so overpowered by her passion as to be inarticulate. Her suicide is a *fait accompli;* all readers know that she is destined to die as a result of an inevitable fall from majesty to mere womanhood. In contrast, Ovid's Dido is highly articulate and self-conscious; she evokes the *scribentis imago,* the image of herself as letter writer, and suicide is depicted as a threat, a rhetorical strategy she uses merely to persuade Aeneas to return. In Virgil her role is subordinate to the themes of epic; in Ovid national glory is irrelevant to her single-minded obsession with her passion.[34] She doesn't die at the end but remains alive, discoursing about her desire.

Yet critics have customarily seen Ovid's Dido as a failure, and some attribute that failure specifically to Ovid's war with Virgil. Jacobson's view is representative:

> The notion of a divine mission that must override personal considerations, the ability to perceive and appreciate the strange ways in which

31. Richard A. Lanham, *The Motive of Eloquence: Literary Rhetoric in the Renaissance* (New Haven: Yale Univ. Press, 1976), pp. 59–60.
32. Barthes, *A Lover's Discourse,* p. 3; Altman, p. 211.
33. Lanham, p. 62.
34. Anderson, pp. 49–68.

the supernatural hand operates—all this is beyond Ovid's Dido. . . . I suspect that Dido's attitude is essentially Ovid's and that the inability to separate out his personal feelings from the mythical situation is one reason why this poem fails. Ovid was congenitally averse to the Vergilian world-view and quite unable to sympathize with a *Weltanschauung* that could exalt grand, abstract—not to mention divine—undertakings over simple individual, human and personal considerations, and could dictate the sacrifice of the self for "higher ends." In this poem we hear not simply Dido struggling with Aeneas, but Ovid waging war against Vergil; and he is doomed to defeat from the start because of his incapacity and unwillingness to appreciate the Vergilian position.[35]

But perhaps Ovid was capable of appreciating the Virgilian position and simply rejected it. Rather than seeing a divine plan, a supernatural hand, at work in the world, perhaps he saw the world as random and capricious—or worse, a world ruled by a capricious "divinity." (Given his laments in the *Tristia* and the unfair severity of his treatment, he would certainly have been justified in reaching such a conclusion.) That Ovid conceived of the self as fluid, multiple, playful—an aleatory mixture of styles and poses—seems all the more certain whenever his subject was love. If one views the *Heroides* as a conscious critique of Augustan Rome, of Virgilian values, and of epic itself, then one's view of Dido changes dramatically. As Lanham remarks:

> You cannot leave Dido behind. She will not oblige by sacrificing the private life, the life of the feelings, to the greater glory of Rome. She will curse you, come after you. Accommodate the life of feeling or you will end up with daughters and granddaughters like Augustus's two Julias. Ovid, then, points to the central Roman weakness, to the lack of a full and balanced interiority, of a rich self. All Ovid's poetry before the exile explores this split, this gap in the center, in one way or the other. It was his obsessive great subject and he embraced it all his poetic life.[36]

Some scholars have gone even further, arguing that it was precisely Ovid's subversive portrait of an *impius Aeneas* that incurred Augustus' wrath and resulted in Ovid's exile—that *Heroides* 7 (Dido's letter) was the "straw that broke the camel's back."[37] In any case, Virgil becomes the poet laureate; Ovid is sent (like Sappho before him) into exile.

---

35. Jacobson, p. 90.
36. Lanham, p. 63; my reading of Ovid is indebted to Lanham's analysis of Ovidian values and rhetoric, chaps. 1 and 2.
37. Jacobson, p. 90.

The Trace of Sappho

> If we show, by comparing Sappho's poems with
> Anacreon's . . . that the art of poetry or of prophecy is
> not one art when practised by men and another when
> practised by women but is the same, will anyone be
> able to find just cause for blame in our
> demonstration?
>
> PLUTARCH, *Virtues of Women*

Ovid writes "like a woman" in the *Heroides* by adopting multiple female personae; Sappho is a woman writing—what is the difference? Plutarch may be right that the art itself does not differ between the sexes, but the criticism does differ. Critics of Sappho, for instance, invariably resort to biographical criticism. If Sappho refers to someone who "seems as fortunate as the gods to me, the man who sits opposite you and listens nearby to your sweet voice and lovely laughter," she must be jealous of a male rival for a female lover, as George Devereux maintains. Asks Devereux:

> What can a man offer to a girl that Sappho cannot offer? The answer, I
> think, is obvious and leads to a clinically highly documentable and
> crucial finding: few women are as obsessed with a (neurotic) feeling of
> incompleteness—with the clinically commonplace "female castration
> complex"—as the masculine lesbian. Moreover, the latter experiences
> her "defect" with violent and crushing intensity particularly when her
> girl-friend is taken away from her not by another lesbian, but by a man,
> who has what she does not have and which she would give her life to
> have.[38]

Not only have scholars argued *ad feminam* against Sappho, but the myths that she was small and ugly "were probably invented in later antiquity to show that she would have preferred male lovers to female, if she could have attracted them." An anonymous papyrus from the late second or early third century A.D. states that Sappho "has been accused by some of being irregular in her ways and a woman-lover. In appearance she seems to have been contemptible

---

38. George Devereux, "The Nature of Sappho's Seizure in Fr. 31 LP as Evidence of Her Inversion," *Classical Quarterly*, n.s. 20 (1970), 22.

and quite ugly, being dark in complexion and of very small stature."[39] One thus runs the risk, as a woman writing, of being labeled marginal, deviant, abnormal; we shall see the kind of criticism Devereux practices resurface in the critical assessments of Heloise's "unreasonableness"; the Portuguese nun's "narcissism"; Charlotte Brontë's "hunger, rebellion, and rage"; and the three Marias' sexual frustration.

A further assumption is that women's writing is by definition "natural," uncomplicated by literary tradition and artifice. For example, D. L. Page, who is one of the recognized authorities on Sappho, maintains that her art is "unadorned by literary artifice. . . . Rarely, if anywhere, in archaic or classical poetry shall we find language so far independent of literary tradition, apparently so close to the speech of every day. Style is in harmony with dialect; both products of nature, not artifice."[40] Again and again one discovers the same unexamined critical assumptions about speech and writing, nature and artifice, gender and genre, masculine and feminine. But the opposite charge has been leveled at women writers too—that they are incapable of spontaneity, of feeling, of writing without calculation, as Rousseau later argues while citing Sappho as the sole female exception: "The celestial fire which heats and engulfs the soul, the genius which consumes and devours, that burning eloquence, those sublime raptures

---

39. "Sappho," in *Greek Lyric*, trans. David A. Campbell, Loeb Classical Library, 4 vols. (Cambridge: Harvard Univ. Press, 1932), vol. 1, p. 3, hereinafter cited parenthetically in the text by volume and page. Feminist reconsiderations of Sappho include Sarah B. Pomeroy, *Goddesses, Whores, Wives, and Slaves: Women in Classical Antiquity* (New York: Schocken, 1975), pp. 53–55; Mary R. Lefkowitz, *Heroines and Hysterics* (New York: St. Martin's Press, 1981), Chapter 9; J. Hallett, "Sappho and Her Social Context: Sense and Sensuality," *Signs* 4 (1979), 447–64, and Eva Stehle Stigers' response, 465–71. See also Stigers' "Retreat from the Male: Catullus 62 and Sappho's Erotic Flowers," *Ramus* 6 (1977), 92–93, and "Sappho's Private World," *Women's Studies* 8 (1981), 47–65. This entire issue is devoted to women in antiquity and serves as a sequel to two issues of the classical journal *Arethusa* (vol. 6, no. 1 [Spring 1973] and vol. 11, nos. 1 and 2 [Spring and Fall 1978]), devoted to the same topic. Monique Wittig's *Le Corps lesbien* (Paris: Minuit, 1973; trans. William Morrow, 1975) is an invocation to Sappho which combines Sappho's lyrical power, sensuousness, and sexuality in a haunting and innovative work. With its enumeration of the female body—from the cervix to the esophagus to the heart—this eloquent text might well be described as an anatomy of desire.

40. D. L. Page, *Sappho and Alcaeus: An Introduction to the Study of Ancient Lesbian Poetry* (Oxford: Clarendon Press, 1955), p. 30. For translations of Sappho, I consulted Page as well as Campbell. See also Lefkowitz, chap. 9.

which transmit delight to the very foundation of the soul will always be lacking from women's writings. They are all cold and pretty like their authors."[41] Women adorn their writing, in short, with the same calculated eye toward effect with which they apply makeup. Such attitudes mark rhetoric, too, as a "harlot." The underlying assumption of Rousseau's prejudices, as well as Page's, is that there is something real, natural, unartificial in speech, beneath or behind writing, beyond the illusions rhetoric creates. The same dichotomy has been applied since Plato to poetry and rhetoric: poetry is associated with mimesis, clarity, and high seriousness; rhetoric, with illusion, deception, ornament, frivolity. The *Heroides*, as verse epistles that are yet commonly viewed as the most rhetorical of Ovid's works, disrupt this dichotomy. Western literature's premises derive from Platonic models of the self as coherent and unified, but the Ovidian self is capricious and changeable, and Ovid constantly subverts the Platonic values of consistency, clarity, and unity. The Ovidian conception of knowledge, of self, of style, indeed marks a radical departure, for rather than seeing illusion as veiling a central reality or a fixed truth, Ovid celebrates illusion for its own sake.[42] Particularly where love is concerned, Ovid recognizes how large a role artifice plays in arousing and sustaining desire. Roland Barthes's motto in his modern amorous discourse could well have come from Ovid: "*Larvatus prodeo:* I advance pointing to my mask: I set a mask upon my passion, but with a discreet (and wily) finger I designate this mask."[43] Ovid not only relishes the masks, poses, adornments of the "harlot" rhetoric; he goes so far as to write a treatise full of advice to women on how to embellish their beauty by using cosmetics. In *The Art of Love*, indeed, he exhorts women to cultivate their bodies, caring for their good looks with the same dedication artists devote to beauty (3:101–28). (Yeats's poem "Adam's Curse" comes to mind.) "Art counterfeits chance," Ovid observes; "your looks are aided by dissembled art" (3:155, 210). For Ovid, therefore, style makes the woman, and the *Heroides* enables us to reassess rhetoric, the female lover, and the relation between them.

Because Sappho is both a historical figure and a character in the

<hr>

41. Jean-Jacques Rousseau, *La Lettre à d'Alembert sur les spectacles* (Amsterdam: Marc Michel Rey, 1758), note k, pp. 193–94, trans. Peggy Kamuf, "Writing Like a Woman," in *Women and Language in Literature and Society*, ed. Sally McConnell-Ginet, Ruth Borker, and Nelly Furman (New York: Praeger, 1980), p. 290.

42. Lanham, chaps. 1 and 2.

43. Barthes, *A Lover's Discourse*, p. 43.

Heroides, Ovid's treatment is doubly provocative, particularly since scholars have relied on Ovid's epistle for biographical information about Sappho. Sappho's is the most discussed of all Ovid's epistles, largely because, in Jacobson's words, "the hazards of transmission have afflicted this poem with ambiguous paternity and the result has been a long-standing dispute as to its authenticity."[44] Paternity is at issue within the epistle as well, for Ovid's Sappho refers to her orphanhood by lamenting, "Six natal days had passed for me, when I gathered the bones of my parent" (15:61–62). Scholars commonly interpret this as a reference to Sappho's father, but in Latin the sex of the parent is ambiguous; *parens* is sometimes used interchangeably and often stands for the *female* parent.[45]

Also at issue is Sappho as a parent to Ovid. His allusions to her poetry are so conscious and so direct that, according to Jacobson, "It seems safe to say that Ovid's direct use of Sappho is now consensus opinion. . . . when he writes, '*Lesbia quid docuit Sappho, nisi amare, puellas?*' (Tr. 2.365), one almost senses that he considers her his female counterpart."[46] The passage Jacobson cites from the *Tristia* is worth quoting more fully. Ovid laments, "Not I alone have written tales of tender love, but for writing of love I alone have been punished. . . . What did Lesbian Sappho teach the girls if not love? Yet Sappho was secure" (2:361–66). Not only does he consciously identify with Sappho in these lines, but he could have drawn even stronger parallels had he been willing to risk alienating Augustus, for Ovid is well aware that Sappho herself was exiled to Sicily, since he refers to it in the *Heroides,* and her exile, like his, was for political reasons.

Another link between Ovid and Sappho involves music. Indeed, the analogies between music and amorous discourses will resonate throughout my book, for music is another expression of dialogism. Like a duet, it is dialogic in the sense of being a dialogue, and it persuades by means of an alternative logic, positing an alternative structure that is related to the body's gesture, to dance, to movement. In *A Lover's Discourse,* Barthes writes: "These fragments of discourse can be called *figures.* The word is to be understood, not in its rhetorical sense, but rather in its gymnastic or choreographic acceptation . . . [as] the body's gesture. . . . The figure is a kind of opera aria; just as this aria is identified, memorized, and manipulated through its

44. Jacobson, p. 277.
45. Ibid., p. 279.
46. Ibid., p. 281.

incipit . . . so the figure takes its departure from a turn of phrase, a kind of verse, refrain, or cantillation which articulates it in the darkness."[47] The relation to music, of course, is crucial in Sappho, for not only did she write lyrics, she invented a kind of lyre on which to play them. Some scholars believe that Ovid, imitating Sappho, designed the *Heroides* to be sung as well. In the *Tristia,* indeed, Ovid describes his poetry as mimes for the stage and boasts, "My poems too have often been presented to the people with dancing" (2:515–18). The words that echo Sappho's are those related to music. Like Sappho, Ovid uses the words describing musical instruments βάρβιτος and χέλυς. The former is an instrument used by Sappho and Alcaeus, which differs little from the lyre except in having a lower pitch; the latter—*chelyn* (l. 181)—is a lyre whose strings are stretched on a tortoise's shell. *Chelyn* is a word that has not been found in any Latin poetry before *Heroides* 15. (Elsewhere, Ovid's Sappho tells the Lesbian daughters to "cease thronging to me more to hear my shell!" [15:201–2]).

Yet another decisive parallel to Ovid involves Sappho's reference to the headband she has not been able to procure for her daughter (5:75–76). These lines bring us back to the ways in which style makes the woman and to the relation of adornments—lyric and physical—to creativity, for Ovid's Sappho laments: "Lo, see, my hair lies scattered in disorder about my neck, my fingers are laden with no sparkling gems; I am clad in garment mean, no gold is in the strands of my hair, my locks are scented with no gifts of Araby. For whom should I adorn myself, or whom should I strive to please? He, the one cause for my adornment, is gone. . . . Thalia, mistress of my art, is making my nature soft" (15:72–84).[48] The shared emphases on speech, on music, on love as the adornments that enable one to adorn one's lyrics are thus among the many legacies from Sappho to Ovid.

47. Barthes, *A Lover's Discourse,* pp. 3–5. Julia Kristeva also explores the relation of music to experimental novels like Philippe Sollers' *H* in "The Novel as Polylogue," in *Desire in Language: A Semiotic Approach to Literature and Art,* ed. Leon S. Roudiez, trans. Thomas Gora, Alice Jardine, and Leon S. Roudiez (New York: Columbia Univ. Press, 1980), pp. 159–209. In contrast to Kristeva's semiotic approach, Jean Hagstrum's is thematic; see *Sex and Sensibility: Ideal and Erotic Love from Milton to Mozart* (Chicago: Univ. of Chicago Press, 1980), chap. 11.

48. Jacobson (pp. 281–85) enumerates in detail the striking parallels between Sapphic lyrics and the *Heroides.* Campbell, in *Greek Lyric* (p. x) has this to say about Sappho's musical inventions: "Writers . . . attributed to her the invention of the plectrum and . . . a type of lyre. . . . writers on music were certain that Sappho . . . had a place in the history of music."

In the *Heroides* Ovid is faced with the problem of inventing a female persona whose desire differs from the customary male construction of desire, and in Sappho he found clues to alternative models. The letters from men to women that he added later highlight the contrast: where the men view love as penetration and domination, in Sappho's lyrics love is a forgetfulness of self, a delight in mutuality, in mirroring, and in giving pleasure to the beloved. As Eva Stehle Stigers explains:

> The formal problem facing Sappho was to find a way of presenting the female persona as an erotic subject. Culturally acceptable models presumably did not include woman's pursuing man. . . . The narrator . . . recalls a whole range of shared experience, including but not limited to the erotic. The intimacy, she suggests, engages two complete personalities. . . . Sappho dramatizes her absorption with the other woman, the lapse of her separate self-consciousness as she is caught up in the other's sensuousness. The other woman's happiness is in turn a reflection of her closeness to Sappho, since memory of it serves as the token of warmth that Sappho would have the girl carry away with her.[49]

Another of Sappho's legacies involves the intensity of her focus on the moment of parting—with all the longing it brings and with the awareness of the insistent elusiveness of desire. Says Stigers, "Sappho uses the moment of parting as the frame for the picture of intimacy, for intimacy seems most precious, union most complete in the face of imminent loneliness."[50] In such situations, the power of the letter to bridge the gap between lovers is particularly important, as in Julian's *Letter to Iamblichus*, written after Sappho, which begins by rejoicing: "You came, yes, you did; for thanks to your letter you came even although you were absent" (1:95). As Chrysippus points out in *Negatives*, the emphasis on the extremity of love's madness, on the crazed and divided heart ("I do not know what I am to do: I am in two minds" [1:97]) is another of Sappho's trademarks. In the one complete poem we have, the narrator addresses Aphrodite as "wile-weaving" and recalls how Aphrodite "asked what was the matter with me this time and why I was calling this time and what in my maddened heart I most wished to happen for myself." The narrator beseeches Aphrodite to "deliver me from oppressive anxieties; fulfill all that my heart longs to fulfill, and you yourself be my fellow-fighter" (1:53–

---

49. Stigers, "Sappho's Private World," pp. 49, 55.
50. Ibid., pp. 57–58.

55). There is a similar appeal to a deity of desire in every subsequent discourse of desire, from the *Heroides* to Heloise's letters, from *Clarissa* to Jane Eyre's appeal to a Universal Mother. As Longinus observes, Sappho always focuses on the most excessive traits and the extremities of passion in such passages as: "A subtle fire has stolen beneath my flesh, I see nothing with my eyes, my ears hum, sweat pours from me, a trembling seizes me all over, I am greener than grass, and it seems to me that I am little short of dying" (1:81). Longinus goes on to marvel at the vividness of sensory impressions in this passage, at the startlingly detailed combination of bodily sensations, emotional intensity, and contradictory feelings. The traits he praises later become characteristic of amorous epistolary discourse, which runs the gamut of contradictory emotions and sensory stimuli:

> Are you not amazed how at one and the same moment she seeks out soul, body, hearing, tongue, sight, complexion as though they had all left her and were external, and how in contradiction she both freezes and burns, is irrational and sane, is afraid and nearly dead, so that we observe in her not one single emotion but a concourse of emotions? All this of course happens to people in love; but . . . it is her selection of the most important details and her combination of them into a single whole that have produced the excellence of the poem.[51]

It is Sappho who invented such words as *bittersweet*, contributing to the language an oxymoron that encapsulates the contradictory impulses of desire. At other points, she contrasts those who find beauty in fanfare and warfare with those who find beauty in love: "Some say a host of cavalry, others of infantry, and others of ships, is the most beautiful thing on the black earth, but I say it is whatsoever a person loves" (1:67). War or love, glory or passion: the same contrast between men going to war and women warring with their passions recurs in all the amorous discourses in this book—from the nun's passion for the French chevalier stationed in Portugal, to Rosa Coldfield's passion for the Confederate Colonel Sutpen, to the three Marias' account of centuries of men's war and women's desire in *New Portuguese Letters*. Historically, as Barthes reflects, "The discourse of absence is carried on by the Woman: . . . Woman is faithful (she waits), man is fickle (he sails away, he cruises). It is Woman who gives shape to absence, elaborates its fiction, for she has time to do so; she weaves and she sings; the Spinning Songs express both immobility . . . and absence (far

---

51. Longinus, *On Sublimity*, cited in *Greek Lyric*, p. 81.

away, rhythms of travel, sea surges, cavalcades)."[52] To weave and to sing: the heroines frequently weave wool or webs as well as discourses of desire. Sappho, for instance, explicitly compares her poetry to weaving when she laments that she cannot compose a lyric: "I cannot weave my web, for I am overcome with desire for a boy" (1:127). Much later, when Maximus of Tyre contrasts Socrates' view of Eros with Sappho's, he notes, "Socrates says Eros is a Sophist; Sappho calls him a weaver of tales. Socrates is driven mad for Phaedrus by Eros, while Sappho's heart is shaken by Eros like a wind falling on oaks on a mountain."[53] Thus Eros affects Socrates' intellect, Sappho's heart. Where Socrates wants literal truth and logical arguments, Sappho sees Eros' relation to art and artifice; she recognizes that love has as many forms, faces, and threads as the labyrinth of fiction. The inscription on the Cretan labyrinth reads:

> This is the labyrinth which the Cretan Dedalus built,
> Out of which nobody could get who was inside,
> Except Theseus; nor could he have done it, unless he had
> been helped with a thread by Ariadne, all of love.

Ariadne's thread—like Arachne's web—has become a focal point for poststructuralist and feminist critics who draw attention to the relation of text to *textus*—something woven or made—what Derrida calls a tissue of grafts. Elsewhere, it is Derrida who relates the word web (*erion*) to wool, fleece, and the ring of pubic hair. Throughout this book, whether one thinks of Ariadne's thread or Medea's fleece or Sappho's lyrics or of the conflation of Ariadne in Arachne, the weaving of webs and tales is intimately related to Eros in discourses of desire.[54]

In Sappho's letter in the *Heroides*, the oral and oracular merge, for it is at a naiad's command that Sappho proposes to leap from the Leucadian cliff. Suicide has a double function in Ovid and in subsequent amorous epistles: it is a potent threat and a rhetorical strategy

---

52. Barthes, *A Lover's Discourse*, p. 14.

53. Sappho's lament is reported by Hephaestion, *Handbook on Metres;* Maximus of Tyre's comparison of Socrates and Sappho is in his *Orations.* Both quotations are cited in *Greek Lyric*, pp. 127 and 93, respectively.

54. In "Ariadne's Thread: Repetition and the Narrative Line," *Critical Inquiry* 3 (Autumn 1976), 57–77, J. Hillis Miller discusses the inscription in the Cretan labyrinth and Derrida's allusion to *erion*, as well the conflation of Ariadne/Arachne. See also "Ariachne's Broken Woof." See also Nancy K. Miller, "Arachnologies: The Woman, the Text, and the Critic," in *Poetics of Gender* (New York: Columbia Univ. Press, 1986).

of persuasion. Heroine after heroine imagines the misery the beloved will feel at having caused her death, and each woman prophesies that his name will be blackened for all time. As Sappho asks Phaon, "Why do you send me to the shores of Actium . . . when you yourself could turn back your wandering steps? . . . If I perish, O more savage than any cliff or wave, can you endure the name of causing my death?" (15:185–90). To make sure the beloved realizes the enormity of his crime, the heroine's threat of suicide alternates with the threat of publicity. She will make sure the world knows who caused her death by inscribing his name on her tomb.

Yet the act of inscribing is an act of absolute isolation, for the beloved's indifference renders all threats, all strategies, all persuasive ploys futile. Suicide is omnipresent but unfulfilled in the text, for the act of writing is a continual deferral of death. Phyllis, for instance, imagines drowning, poisoning, stabbing, hanging herself: "In the choosing of my death there shall be but small delay" (2:143–45). But the very act of first imagining, then spelling out all the different ways to die is itself a delay, a deferral of the act, a detour that keeps the narrative alive. Phyllis goes on to imagine how she will inscribe her own tomb, warning Demophoon that he will be

> inscribed as the hateful cause of my death. By this, or by some similar verse shall you be known:
>
> DEMOPHOON 'TWAS SENT PHYLLIS TO HER DOOM;
> HER GUEST WAS HE, SHE LOVED HIM WELL.
> HE WAS THE CAUSE THAT BROUGHT HER DEATH TO PASS;
> HER OWN THE HAND BY WHICH SHE FELL. (2:147–48)

The clue is "some similar verse," which reveals that Phyllis either has not yet decided which verse to use or has not yet composed it; therefore, neither her letter nor her fate are sealed at the end.

Like Phyllis, Dido identifies the man as the cause of her doom, the hand as her own. But if one hand holds the sword, the other holds a pen. The narrative depends on the tension between the two impulses, death and writing. Canace makes the juxtaposition most vivid: "If aught of what I write is yet blotted deep and escapes your eye, 'twill be because the little roll has been stained by its mistress' blood. My right hand holds the pen, a drawn blade the other holds, and the paper lies unrolled in my lap" (11:1–5). Her life will last, one senses, as long as the roll does, but the precise duration is something that remains indeterminate. Canace's words here demonstrate the metaphoric substitution of pen for sword, paper for body, ink for blood, the textual for the corporeal—all are inscribed in Ovid's text. Poised between the sword that pierces the body and the pen that writes the discourse, Canace's pose points to the sources of desire, for the needs of the body are articulated in language. We need because we are in the flesh, we demand because we are in language; desire lies in the lap, signifying the gap between need and demand, flesh and language.[55]

As a character in the *Heroides*, Sappho demonstrates that desire is the dynamic impetus of narrative; for she is highly self-conscious and self-reflexive; she draws attention to writing in her opening address and takes great pride in her artistic power, confronting Phaon by asking him, "Unless you had read their author's name, Sappho, would you fail to know whence these brief words come?" (15:3–4). The question is a loaded one, implying, on the one hand, that perhaps scores of wronged women have written Phaon and, on the other, that he recognizes neither Sappho's penmanship nor her consummate artistry, a sin all the more grievous since it was her poetry rather than her person that first aroused Phaon's ardor. She justifies her rejection of the lyric on the grounds of Phaon's rejection of her: "You may ask why my verses alternate, when I am better suited to the lyric mode. I must weep, for my love—and elegy is the weeping strain; no lyre is suited to my tears" (15:5–8). She thus reveals her identification of her art with her body and expresses her desire that the act of reading stimulate him as much as writing stimulates her.

Ovid's characterization of Sappho has sometimes been dismissed by scholars who felt that Ovid was merely mocking the lover-poet as a type or using Sappho for self-parody in order to speak glibly about himself, but Ovid had ample opportunity in his other works to play the parodist. Here, he explores modes of expression that he ignores in other texts, the whole concourse of contradictory emotions that Longinus praises. In view of his obsession with the gap at the center, with the lack of interiority, the *Heroides* enabled him to experiment with contradictory combinations, to circumvent the conventional dichotomies of epistle and verse, history and myth, narrative and discourse, masculine and feminine. That circumvention is his motive for adopting so many female personae in the *Heroides*, a motive illumi-

---

55. See Jacques Lacan, *Ecrits: A Selection*, trans. Alan Sheridan (New York: W. W. Norton, 1977); and *The Language of the Self*, pp. 91–100.

nated by Barthes's confession that "in any man who utters the other's absence *something feminine* is declared: this man who waits and who suffers from his waiting is miraculously feminized. . . . (Myth and utopia: the origins have belonged, the future will belong to the subjects *in whom there is something feminine.)*"[56] Devereux, remember, defined Sappho as an "inverted female," but Barthes makes it clear that homosexuality (male or female) is not the "culprit" by explaining that "a man is not feminized because he is inverted, but because he is in love." Love is the ultimate transgression, and therefore love is relegated to the realms of myth and utopia. Yet the aim of all amorous discourses is to inscribe what has been relegated to the margins of the conceptual universe, to explore a theory of knowledge based on the senses—loving as a way of knowing. The exploration of this ancient analogy is the legacy passed down from Sappho to Ovid to Barthes. Amorous epistolary discourse defies the logic of idealists, the exaltation of *episteme,* and substitutes "an unheardof" language of the body as sign, as figure, as alphabet, as style.[57] Sappho's brilliant originality lies in the ways her lyrics break free from institutional contexts and poetic traditions to speak in an astonishingly intense mode of individual emotion.[58]

Inspired by Sappho, Ovid offers a poetics that links the female body to style, postures and poses to composition, and sexual to textual pleasure. As Lanham observes, Western literature has assumed that language "first tried to be clear and only later degenerated into self-pleasing rituals. Why not the other way round—pleasure first?"[59] Pleasure—the paradoxical pleasure of remembering past sorrows, the pleasure of the rituals of sexual pursuit and consummation, the pleasures of language, the lover's pleasure in posing and composing—is certainly primary among Ovid's heroines. *Discourse,* after all, suggests the vacillation between extremes (*dis:* apart, from; *currere:* to

56. Barthes, *A Lover's Discourse,* p. 14.

57. Ulmer, pp. 61–64. Ulmer explains the theoretical implications of what he calls "the *schema* of a new genre" and "a significant contribution to the 'new rhetoric'" in Barthes's *A Lover's Discourse,* without recognizing Barthes's debt to Sappho, Ovid, and the generic tradition of amorous epistolary discourse.

58. See Stigers, "Sappho's Private World," p. 61, nn. 5 and 6. See also *Les Choeurs de jeunes filles en Grece archaïque* (Rome: Edizioni dell'Ateneo & Bizzarri, 1977), 1: 430–31, by Claude Calame, who sees Sappho's poetry as portraying great personal sensitivity; Paul Friedrich, similarly, emphasizes Sappho's distinctiveness from male poets and all earlier poets on the same grounds in *The Meaning of Aphrodite* (Chicago: Univ. of Chicago Press, 1978), pp. 112–23.

59. Lanham, p. 21.

run to and fro). The pen of the female lover races from the rhetorical to the serious, from duplicity to lucidity, from passion to threats of punishment, from the pleasures of the body to the pleasures of the text. The *Heroides* thus defies textual limits, purposely subverting traditional dichotomies and blurring the boundaries between the fictional and the authentic, rhetoric and poetry, narrative and speech. Ovid challenges the values of Augustan Rome by rejecting the officially endorsed genre of epic, experimenting instead with one that is by definition transgressive, for to write like a woman is to challenge conventional notions of tradition, of origins, of fathers, of paternity, of authority, of identity. Since doubleness and duplicity, as we have seen, are the characteristic Ovidian strategies, Ovid simultaneously boasts of his generic inventiveness and subverts the search for paternal origins with myriad allusions to and borrowings from Sappho, whose letter may have concluded the original text of the *Heroides*. Thus, the search for the lost father of an art form ends inconclusively, as does each heroine's letter. Ovid, by refusing to glorify a mythical past of omnipotent patriarchs, breaks "the law of the genre."[60] Instead, he posits an identity *and* a difference between the feminine and masculine genre and gender, encoding in amorous epistolary discourse—with all its erotic, emotional, and sensuous intensity—the indelible trace of Sappho.

60. The phrase is Jacques Derrida's in "La Loi du genre / The Law of Genre," *Glyph* 7 (Spring 1980), trans. Avital Ronell, *Critical Inquiry* 7 (Autumn 1980), 55–81. Grant Showerman notes in his translation of the *Heroides* (pp. 180–81) that "the Sappho-Phaon story seems to have been well known by the fourth century B.C. The authorship of this letter has been disputed, but it is generally conceded to be Ovid's."

Yet write, oh write me all, that I may join
Griefs to thy griefs, and echo sighs to thine.

   . . .

Ere such a soul regains its peaceful state,
How often must it love, how often hate!
Conceal, disdain,—do all things but forget.

ALEXANDER POPE, "Eloisa to Abelard"

2

The Irremediable:
Heloise to Abelard

Eloisa. 1779. This engraving by William W. Ryland, after
Angelica Kauffmann, appeared in Charlotte Charrier's *Héloïse
dans l'histoire et dans la légende* (Paris: Librairie ancienne Honoré
Champion, 1933).

The Forms of Tyranny, the Tyranny of Forms

> For me . . . this story has already taken place. . . .
> Amorous seduction takes place *before* discourse and
> *behind* the proscenium of consciousness: the amorous
> "event" . . . is my own local legend, my little sacred
> history that I declaim to myself, and this declamation
> of a *fait accompli* (frozen, embalmed, removed from
> any *praxis*) is the lover's discourse.
>
> ROLAND BARTHES, *A Lover's Discourse*

The story is over when Heloise writes her first letter to Abelard.
He had seduced her long before, in the house where her uncle
Fulbert had hired him to tutor his brilliant niece. Instead, the tutor
initiated her in the arts of passion. From the outset, the seduction and
subsequent affair were sustained by letters that were calculated to
inflame her. He confesses, "Knowing the girl's knowledge and love of
letters I thought she would be all the more ready to consent, and that
even when separated we could enjoy each other's presence by exchange of written messages in which we could speak more openly
than in person, and so need never lack the pleasures of conversation."
Only in writing can they speak openly; this equation of writing with
sexual freedom, transgression, and seduction is reiterated throughout Heloise's correspondence, as if she never forgot the lessons
Abelard taught her. They met between 1117 and 1119, when she was
about seventeen and he was about thirty-eight; by 1119 she had borne
a son, Abelard had been castrated by Fulbert's men, and Heloise had
renounced sex and the world at Abelard's command. With his castration an accomplished fact, her motive for writing is removed from any
praxis. For him, all desire has been forsaken or frozen or forgotten,
but hers remains sacred, searing, unsated. Prompted by discovering
his *Historia calamitatum* (The story of his misfortunes), Heloise writes
to him between 1132 and 1135, after a silence of some ten years.[1]

---

1. *The Letters of Abelard and Heloise*, trans., ed., and introd. Betty Radice (Baltimore:
Penguin, 1974), p. 66, hereinafter cited parenthetically in the text by page number

64

Many forms of tyranny precede the beginning of the correspondence. Fulbert had given Abelard the authority to beat Heloise if she proved a recalcitrant student; Abelard had indulged in beatings as a form of sex play and later had sex with Heloise in the convent, forcing her with threats and blows when she resisted him. Perhaps the greatest tyranny is his command that she take religious orders before him; the fact that he did not trust her to take vows voluntarily greatly embitters her in retrospect. These tyrannies are revealed in Abelard's *Historia calamitatum* and in the personal letters he and Heloise exchange. Despite the scandalous content, the epistolary forms are those of the *epistola consolatoria* and the *epistola deprecatoria*. The *consolatoria's* rhetorical purpose—what Abelard accomplishes in the *Historia*—is to convince the reader that the writer's woes have been much worse than the reader's own. The rules of the *deprecatoria* require that Heloise first state the request that leads her to write to Abelard, then demonstrate its merit and Abelard's ability to grant it. She must then explain why she deserves to have her request granted.[2] Despite the vehemence of her passion, the vehicle for its expression is thus a rigid one that Heloise follows to the letter. She requests that Abelard grant her the same consolation that he has extended to the recipient of the *Historia:* "I beg you, then, as you set about tending the wounds which others have dealt, heal the wounds you have yourself inflicted" (111). This one sentence amply demonstrates the rhetorical strategy that recurs repeatedly in Heloise's letters, for although she appears to submit to the tyranny of formal rhetoric, every letter contains many ambiguities and multiple meanings that veil a subtle rebellion. Here, for instance, her phrasing suggests that while tending to the wounds others dealt by castrating him, Abelard should heal the psychic wounds he inflicted by abandoning her, who should mean far more to him than anyone, since "a greater debt . . . binds you in obligation . . . [which] needs neither proof nor witness, were it in any doubt; if the whole world kept silent, the facts themselves would cry out" (111).

Heloise's use of the plural in her opening address is another ostensible sign of her submission to the tyranny of forms. She writes as one

---

only. See also Enid McLeod, *Heloise: A Biography* (London: Chatto and Windus, 1971); Charlotte Charrier, *Héloïse dans l'histoire et dans la légende* (Paris: Librairie ancienne Honoré Champion, 1933); Etienne Gilson, *Heloise and Abelard* (Ann Arbor: Univ. of Michigan Press, 1960).

2. R. W. Southern, *Medieval Humanism* (New York: Harper and Row, 1970), pp. 86–96.

nun among many, veiling in language how absolutely her relation to
Abelard differs from that of other nuns, yet leaving it visible for him
to surmise beneath the habit of epistolary tradition. She goes on in
this passage to refer to him as "sole founder of this place, the sole
builder of this oratory, the sole creator of this community. You have
built nothing here upon another man's foundation. Everything here
is your own creation" (111). The literal meaning is that Abelard is
responsible for founding the order of nuns at Paraclete, but one need
not strain to read it as a confession of the state of Heloise's heart: no
other man has ever had a place in it; Abelard created the tumultuous
emotions that divide it; and he alone has provoked the oratory that is
her discourse of desire. She goes on to speak of the wildness of the
place, the need for the careful cultivation of the land as well as the
spirit, especially in view of the "weak, feminine nature" of the planta-
tion; from here she moves logically to the image of Abelard as the first
planter of a seed, which could be interpreted as an allusion to her
pregnancy or to the seed of desire. By the end of this one paragraph,
Heloise forsakes all pretense and speaks directly of herself: "Apart
from everything else, consider the close tie by which you have bound
yourself to me, and repay the debt you owe a whole community of
women dedicated to God by discharging it the more dutifully to her
who is yours alone" (112).

Having thus broken through the tyranny of forms, Heloise goes
on to recite the forms of tyranny that she has endured. She describes
herself—now as then—as being utterly and irrevocably in Abelard's
power; he is the owner and arbiter of every emotion in her heart.
"You are the sole cause of my sorrow, and you alone can grant me the
grace of consolation. You alone have the power to make me sad, to
bring me happiness or comfort" (113). As a literary motif, the sentiment is as old as Sappho, but Heloise's thralldom is so great that she
would willingly have embraced annihilation had Abelard commanded. She quite explicitly dedicates body and soul to him alone,
despite the heresy of doing so. "You alone," she writes, "have so great
a debt to repay me, particularly now when I have carried out all your
orders so implicitly that when I was powerless to oppose you in anything, I found strength at your command to destroy myself. . . . immediately at your bidding I changed my clothing along with my mind,
in order to prove you the sole possessor of my body and my will alike"
(113). Since her act of taking the veil comes after his castration, the
idea of Abelard as sole possessor of her body memorializes what is

now an absence; never shall another possess what Abelard himself can never possess. Beneath the restrictions of her new clothing, however, Heloise's desire remains unbound. When Abelard reports with approval that at the moment she took the veil, Heloise quoted Cornelia's last words before committing suicide over the corpse of Pompey, his interpretation casts him in the light of the transcendent and unjustly victimized Pompey. Here is Abelard's translation:

> O noble husband,
> Too great for me to wed, was it my fate
> To bend that lofty head? What prompted me
> To marry you and bring about your fall?
> Now claim your due, and see me gladly pay.
> (Lucan, *Pharsalia*, 8:94)

An alternative interpretation is at least possible—particularly in light of the fact that witnesses were horrified by Heloise's action and tried to stop her—Heloise may have quoted Cornelia because she identified the act of taking religious orders with a form of self-annihilation. Her letters reveal her rage at his insistence that she take vows before he did; her anger at this sign of his possessiveness and mistrust remains undiminished years later. Abelard maintains that she refused to listen to those "who in pity for her youth had tried to dissuade her from submitting to the yoke of monastic rule as a penance too hard to bear" (22, 76). Audaciously, she equates the act with madness as well as with self-destruction. She first seems to be acquiescing to the conventional (and conventual) view of love as madness when she recalls, "My love rose to such heights of madness." But the rest of the sentence rebels against that conventional wisdom, for what was mad was not her love but that her love "robbed itself of what is most desired beyond hope of recovery" (113). Taking the veil is thus synonymous, for Heloise, with self-annihilation. She characterizes her love as an independent entity. Sometimes it submits to tyranny; sometimes it doesn't. In any case, it rarely acts in what she considers her own best interest, and frequently either it is betrayed or it betrays her. (*The Portuguese Letters* begin on precisely the same note.)

The reply is a cunningly constructed testament to the tyranny of formal argument. Abelard excuses himself for his silence by saying that Heloise's exemplary behavior makes any advice or consolation from him superfluous. If, however, her humility makes her think differently, he is willing to instruct her, but he abdicates personal involvement and emotion, saying that he can only answer "as God permits me." By the next sentence he has utterly forgotten her need and her torment, burying it amid "thanksgiving" that God "has filled *all* your hearts with anxiety for my desperate, unceasing perils, and made you share in my affliction" (119, my italics). He thus refuses to acknowledge her in any terms other than as one nun among many. The rest of the letter is simply a variation on this theme of Abelard's self-absorption with his own misery. The last sentence illustrates the tone of the whole, for rather than saying that in thinking of Abelard the nuns should be mindful of Christ, Abelard inverts the order: "Live, but I pray, in Christ be mindful of me" (126). Rhetorically, the letter shrewdly deflects a dangerous level of discourse, while as an *epistola consolatoria* it is a skillful exercise, to which—going by the rules—Heloise would be unable to reply.

But in her next letter, Heloise breaks the rules, bursts through the forms of acceptable correspondence, and shatters the refuge Abelard had taken in treatises, authorities, conventions. R. W. Southern says that this "letter can be fitted into no rhetorical category," but it belongs quite clearly to the genre of amorous discourse.[3] Significantly, Heloise begins by rebuking Abelard for breaking the rules of address by placing her name first; she calls this placement a disruption of both the epistolary and the natural order. After this demonstration that she knows the rules well, however, Heloise proceeds to disregard them. By this strategy, she fosters the illusion of submissiveness, while the letter itself stages a rebellion. She again commences by speaking of herself as merely one among many nuns, although she is really talking solely about herself. When she says, for instance, that the nuns would all wish to die before Abelard, she means that *she* could not bear to remain alive without him; her meaning becomes clear when she goes on first to implore him not to speak of dying before her: "spare us—spare her at least, who is yours alone" (128). The very thought not only makes her frantic, but precipitates her rage against God, and that rage results in an escalation of explicitly sexual discourse. By the next paragraph she has once again dropped the pretense of speaking for her sisters and frankly addresses her real subject: how much she misses him. In contrast to his utter self-absorption, "a pity beyond all telling" underlies her logic, for when all else is lost, the one consolation left her in life is merely to know that Abelard is alive,

3. Southern, p. 97.

somewhere in the world: "If I lose you, what is left for me to hope for? What reason for continuing on life's pilgrimage, for which I have no support but you, and none in you save the knowledge that you are alive, now that I am forbidden all other pleasures in you and denied even the joy of your presence which from time to time could restore me to myself?" (129). Heloise here repeats the fundamental motif of amorous epistolary discourse by situating her identity absolutely in the absent beloved. Her question focuses on lack, but she is also reproaching him when she tells him that the only support he gives her is by remaining alive. Abelard, in contrast, can find absolutely nothing to live for. It never occurs to him to live for Heloise. He thinks nothing of telling her frankly that he often longs for death. He goes so far as to rebuke her for her complaints:

> At least you must know that whoever frees me from life will deliver me from the greatest suffering. What I may afterwards incur is uncertain, but from what I shall be set free is not in question. Every unhappy life is happy in its ending, and those who feel true sympathy and pain for the anxieties of others want to see these ended, even to their own loss, if they really love those they see suffer and think more of their friends' advantage than of their own. . . . I cannot see why you should prefer me to live on in great misery rather than be happier in death. If you see your advantage in prolonging my miseries, you are proved an enemy, not a friend. (143)

The harshness of this rebuke demonstrates how little Abelard understands passion, how little he feels "sympathy and pain for the anxieties" of *Heloise,* and how little he cherishes her love. Perhaps she is selfish to want him to live, as he maintains here, but it is certainly a selfishness that is forgivable, particularly in view of her selflessness in so many other ways.

Just as Ovid's heroines place the beloved above their fathers and their fatherland, Heloise single-mindedly focuses on Abelard as her sole judge and jury. He is an idol who completely displaces God the Father. She tells him boldly that everything she has done has been for his love: "At every stage of my life . . . as God knows, I have feared to offend you rather than God, and tried to please you more than him. It was your command, not love of God which made me take the veil" (134). She cannot bring herself to do anything for God because she has not forgiven Him; on the contrary, she repeatedly and blasphemously accuses God of the greatest cruelty toward her and Abelard. Her unrepentant view of God's malevolence could not be

more dissimilar from Abelard's belief in God's benevolence; all
Heloise sees is the violence of her fall from supreme happiness to
unutterable woe:

> O God—if I dare say it—cruel to me in everything! O merciless mercy!
> O Fortune who is only ill-fortune, who has already spent on me so many
> of the shafts she uses in her battle against mankind that she has none
> left with which to vent her anger on others. She has emptied a full
> quiver on me, so that henceforth no one else need fear her onslaughts,
> and if she still had a single arrow she could find no place in me to take a
> wound. Her only dread is that through my many wounds death may
> end my sufferings; and though she does not cease to destroy me, she
> still fears the destruction which she hurries on. (129)

In her suffering and in her sense of the uniqueness of her situation, Heloise looks back to Hypsipyle and forward to the Portuguese
nun:

> Of all wretched women I am the most wretched, and amongst the
> unhappy I am unhappiest. The higher I was exalted when you pre-
> ferred me to all other women, the greater my suffering over my own
> fall and yours, when I was flung down; for the higher the ascent, the
> heavier the fall. Has Fortune ever set any great or noble woman above
> me or made her my equal, only to be similarly cast down and crushed
> with grief? What glory she gave me in you, what ruin she brought upon
> me through you! Violent in either extreme, she showed no moderation
> in good or evil. To make me the saddest of all women she first made me
> blessed above all, so that when I thought how much I had lost, my
> consuming grief would match my crushing loss, and my sorrow for
> what was taken from me would be the greater for the fuller joy of
> possession which had gone before; and so that the happiness of su-
> preme ecstasy would end in the supreme bitterness of sorrow. (129–30)

Just as Ovid's Ariadne ponders what all women are doomed to suffer,
Heloise casts about in her mind for other examples of great women
who have suffered, but she can think of none more wretched than
herself, because she holds herself responsible for causing her lover's
ruin as well as her own. Rhetorically, the passage oscillates between
two laments across a relentlessly antithetical syntax: Fortune was not
moderate but granted supreme ecstasy at the price of extravagant
sorrow. This idea alternates from sentence to sentence with a second
idée fixe: that Abelard's love was the sole source of her glory and her
blessedness. Thus in losing him, she lost herself.

Her double loss explains why, throughout her letters, Heloise is far more obsessed with Abelard's castration than he is. He repeatedly refers to it as an act of mercy, for it freed him from the compulsions of the flesh that still torment Heloise. Her obsession is clearly revealed when he rebukes her for her "old perpetual complaint against God concerning the manner of our entry into religious life and the cruelty of the act of treachery performed on me" (137). Heloise cannot forget Abelard's castration, not merely because of what it denies her but also because she is tormented by guilt at being the cause of her uncle's heinous act. Her sense of responsibility marks a radical departure from Ovid's heroines, who see men as treacherous. Instead, Heloise laments: "What misery for me—born as I was to be the cause of such a crime! Is it the general lot of women to bring total ruin on great men?" (130) She sees herself as Eve, as Delilah, as Bathsheba. She does, however, distinguish between the women who consciously seduced men to their destruction and herself, guilty without malice. As in the *Heroides,* no repetition is exactly the same, yet Heloise broods obsessively over both the trauma of repetition and the interpretation of a trauma. She is, moreover, outraged at the imbalance between the punishment and the crime, for castration would be fitting for an adulterer, but Abelard's punishment came after marriage (130).

Another aspect of the experience that she interprets and reinterprets ceaselessly concerns the unjust timing of God's vengeance against them. Her outrage against the tyranny of forms is most pronounced on the issue of marriage, which she equates with hypocrisy, enslavement, and legalized prostitution. What kind of God, she wonders, would reverse "all the laws of equity. . . . For while we enjoyed the pleasures of an uneasy love and abandoned ourselves to fornication (if I may use an ugly but expressive word) we were spared God's severity. But when we amended our unlawful conduct by what was lawful, and atoned for the shame of fornication by an honourable marriage, then the Lord in his anger laid his hand heavily upon us, and would not permit a chaste union though he had long tolerated one which was unchaste" (130). As so often in her letters, Heloise's questions are heretical, unrepentant, sharply critical of both the tyrannies of language and the enslavement of formal appearances, which make marriage a condition of respectability. In one of her most famous transgressions, she corrects the account he has given in the *Historia calamitatum* of her reasons for refusing to marry him and rebukes him for remaining silent about the most important of her arguments: "You kept silent about most of my arguments for preferring love to wedlock and freedom to chains. God is my witness that if Augustus, Emperor of the whole world, thought fit to honour me with marriage and conferred all the earth on me to possess for ever, it would be dearer and more honourable to me to be called not his Empress but your whore" (114). Abelard's version is significant for its omissions and inversions; he had written, "The name of mistress instead of wife would be dearer to her and more honourable to me (*sibi carius existeret mihique honestius*)."[4] He completely ignores what Heloise exalts: her love, her free choice, her *own* honor.

Her defense of her own honor represents a significant departure from the common view that Abelard was castrated because he insulted not Heloise's honor but her uncle's; he betrayed Fulbert and soiled his property. (Because Heloise may have been illegitimate, scholars have long speculated that she was Fulbert's natural daughter and that his possessiveness was—consciously or unconsciously—sexually motivated.)[5] Abelard repeats the world's assessment in the *Historia* when he refers to Fulbert as "the man whose honour was most involved" (68). Heloise, however, in effect refuses to be viewed as a damaged object of exchange between her uncle and Abelard; what is most scandalous about her assertion is not that she prefers to be a whore (which is what most commentators find scandalous) but that her motive revolves around what would be "more honourable to me." The Portuguese nun, Clarissa, and the three Marias will repeat this transgression, declaring the primacy of their individual worth and honor over the property rights of fathers, husbands, and guardians.

Every single letter that Heloise writes is similarly marked by an assertion of values that Abelard's logic excludes, by an inscription of desire, within the form of the *epistola deprecatoria*, that he deflects or depreciates. She recollects every episode of her seduction and sexual abandon. She flatters his pride and assesses her own susceptibility by reminding him of the many other women who desired him and envied her; wives would even break their marriage vows to have him: "Every wife, every young girl desired you in absence and was on fire in your presence; queens and great ladies envied me my joys and my bed" (115).

Her second letter is Heloise's most flagrant transgression of epis-

4. See Peggy Kamuf, *Fictions of Feminine Desire: Disclosures of Heloise* (Lincoln: Univ. of Nebraska Press, 1982), pp. 14–15. I am indebted to Kamuf's analysis of the entire correspondence.

5. Radice, Introduction to *The Letters*, p. 16. See also McLeod, pp. 10–12.

tolary conventions and the most erotic evocation of her desire. Even
at mass, even while sleeping, she longs for Abelard. She asks him
frankly what point there is in praying for forgiveness as long as she
still yearns for lost pleasure. The kind of doubleness that she describes between her flesh and her mind, between outward show of
piety and inner unrepentance, between fleshly mortification and
fleshly pleasure resembles the characteristic strategy of doubleness
traced in the *Heroides:* "How can it be called repentance for sins,
however great the mortification of the flesh, if the mind still retains
the will to sin and is on fire with its old desires? It is easy enough for
anyone to confess his sins, to accuse himself, or even to mortify his
body in outward show of penance, but it is very difficult to tear the
heart away from hankering after its dearest pleasures" (132). This
doubleness has not gone unnoticed by scholars, but rather than relating it to the genre of amorous discourse, they have cited it as proof
that Heloise's letters could not be authentic. The Basilian monk
Joseph Muckle, for instance, maintains that

> her letters picture Heloise as leading a double life: that of a religious
> superior bound by vows, and as a woman of sensual mind, serving
> Abelard and not God, or as she herself puts it, being such a hypocrite as
> to fool even Abelard himself. On the other hand, Heloise enjoyed a
> good reputation among the religious leaders of the time from the Pope
> down . . . which was that of a sincere, able and holy religious and a
> worthy abbess.
>   In view of the evidence, I am inclined to think that the first two
> letters of Heloise, at any rate, were worked over and perhaps expanded
> to some extent.[6]

Yet there is every reason to believe that it is Heloise herself who
provides the evidence of her double life, that she is the one making a
conscious effort to expose it. The device of drawing attention to her
own duplicity is itself a strategy of doubleness, for on the one hand
she writes as abbess seeking spiritual guidance, but at the same time
she wants to combat Abelard's apparent indifference, to end the silence of ten years, and to engage him actively in amorous correspondence.

As we saw in the first chapter, Sappho's lyrics provide a legacy that

6. Fr. Joseph Muckle, "The Personal Letters between Abelard and Heloise," *Mediaeval Studies* 15 (1953), 47–94, cited in Peter Dronke, *Abelard and Heloise in Medieval
Testimonies* (Glasgow: Univ. of Glasgow Press, 1976), pp. 9, 32, n. 2.

is musical as well as amorous in discourses of desire. Not only was Heloise wooed by songs and verse, but her letters have certain affinities with medieval lyric genres. The tensions Paul Zumthor discovers in the *fine amor* songs parallel the tensions between Heloise and Abelard. His remarks are particularly relevant in view of my comments below on Heloise's enthrallment and on the ways in which her opening address may encapsulate the entire history of the affair:

> Fundamentally, what constitutes the utterance . . . is the endlessly repeated expression of both a desire enthralled by its own fantasies and an intellectual response that denies their reality. The sometimes chaotic textual surface is summarily put together according to a latent narrative scheme: first visual encounter, the actual meeting, the request, a waiting period, abandonment or rejection; and each one of these terms serves as a mnemonic reference, external to the text, to one of the propositions set forth in the story. This pattern explicitly underlies Dante's *Vita nuova*.[7]

The same pattern structures the entire genre of amorous discourse; it certainly underlies Heloise's letters, for she proclaims, "Everything we did and also the time and places are stamped on my heart along with your image, so that I live through it all again with you" (133). The time, the date, the scene of their sexual encounters are stamped on her heart, as one might stamp and date a letter. She consecrates her memories and her image of the beloved in a scene that she can review ceaselessly. Zumthor further relates the voice to the human body when he addresses the issues of memory and authenticity in

7. Paul Zumthor, "The Text and the Voice," *New Literary History* 16 (Autumn 1984), 67–92. See also James E. Wellington, ed., *"Eloisa to Abelard,"* Univ. of Miami Critical Studies, 5 (Coral Gables, Fla.: Univ. of Miami Press, 1965), pp. 29–30. In discussing the reaccentuation of Heloise's letters by Pope, Wellington notes: "It has been insufficiently remarked that a genre comparable to the heroic epistle in poetry enjoyed a distinguished parallel existence in music during the seventeenth and eighteenth centuries, and that Pope, in 1717, was writing in the midst of a musical tradition already well established throughout Europe and destined to continue unabated for the remainder of the century." The music Wellington cites as stylistically related to the heroic epistle includes the preclassical trio sonatas and *concerti grossi* in which composers portrayed the anguish of abandoned women, including Pietro Locatelli's (1693–1764) *Il Pianto d'Arianna* ("Ariadne's lament"), a *concerto a quattro* (op. 7, no. 6; published at Leyden, 1741); and Giuseppe Tartini's (1692–1770) G minor sonata, subtitled *Didone abbandonata*. Another critical study that considers the close relation of the literary to the musical tradition of passion in the seventeenth and eighteenth centuries is Jean Hagstrum's *Sex and Sensibility: Ideal and Erotic Love from Milton to Mozart* (Chicago: Univ. of Chicago Press, 1980).

medieval texts. "Let us agree then," he writes, "that 'orality' is the historical authenticity of a voice. . . . There is no doubt that poetic voice carries the imprint of some 'arche-writing,' but this imprinted trace is inscribed there in a specific manner, since voiced discourse given aloud has its roots more clearly in the human body . . . and lends itself better to the inflections of memory."[8] Not only is Heloise's a historically authentic voice, but her discourse specifically commemorates her body's desires. The duplicitousness of her motives is everywhere apparent; while ostensibly soliciting advice, she savors her memories of pleasure with Abelard and reminds him of his past ardor. In the private theaters of all the heroines who write amorous discourses, the same process, the same consecration of memory, image, and scene will be rehearsed again and again.

Scholars who dispute the authenticity of the letters argue that the entire correspondence is a fictional account of a conversion experience. They view the oppositions Heloise poses in her second letter between flesh and mind, pure prayers and lewd visions, as merely conventional variations on the theme of good versus evil, but Heloise subverts traditional dichotomies in a variety of ways. Her opening address in her first letter is a purposeful interweaving of the complex web of relations that underlie those of man and woman: "To her master, or rather her father, husband, or rather brother; his handmaid, or rather his daughter, wife, or rather sister; to Abelard, Heloise" (109). The ordering in the sentence suspends the logical dichotomization of master–servant, father–daughter, husband–wife, brother–sister, forcing the reader's attention on disruption and transgression and perhaps signaling to Abelard the whole history of their affair in miniature, from his initial role as tutor, to that of guardian once he took her from Fulbert's house, to their secret marriage, and last, to the celibacy of siblings. There is no question that this is a conscious rhetorical strategy on Heloise's part, for it is in her next letter that she reprimands Abelard for disregarding the rhetorical rules of salutation in his reply. In her second letter, similarly, Heloise again disrupts conventional dichotomies by blasphemously valorizing the second term in each pair, by cherishing the very thing she is supposed to be repenting. The letter is thus the opposite of a conversion; it is a declaration of unrepentance, a lament for what she has lost:

8. Zumthor, p. 69.

The pleasures of lovers which we shared have been too sweet—they can never displease me, and can scarcely be banished from my thoughts. Wherever I turn they are always there before my eyes, bringing with them awakened longings and fantasies which will not even let me sleep. Even during the celebration of the Mass, when our prayers should be purer, lewd visions of those pleasures take such a hold upon my unhappy soul that my thoughts are on their wantonness instead of on prayers. I should be groaning over the sins I have committed, but I can only sigh for what I have lost. . . . Even in sleep I know no respite. Sometimes my thoughts are betrayed in a movement of my body, or they break out in an unguarded word. . . . But for me, youth and passion and experience of pleasures which were so delightful intensify the torments of the flesh and longings of desire. (133)

One must keep in mind that, while Abelard is in his mid-forties when he receives this letter, Heloise is only in her mid-twenties. Yet her youth is already a thing of the past, as she reveals in this last sentence, and this loss is a vital part of her lament: her imagination is fixed in retrospective fascination not just on Abelard but on the self she sacrificed for him. Her own innocence, youth, and intensity can be evoked solely in writing. Heloise reveals quite explicitly that her writing is directly related to the desires of her body, to all the thoughts that the body's movements betray, to all the "longings and fantasies which will not even let me sleep." R. W. Southern has argued that Heloise "was not moved by lust, but by a fixation of her will towards Abelard. It was this that made her voluntarily submit to his will, to his obscenities, to his commands, to his lusts, to anything that he cared to put on her."[9] I think the distinction Southern is trying to make, however, relies on a conception of Heloise's ability to compartmentalize mind from body that goes against the evidence of the sexual dynamics at work. It also goes against the explicit evidence of this letter, because her insistence that she yearns for their past pleasures is an assertion of her own will, not Abelard's. Southern's assessment is an astute analysis of Abelard's motives, not Heloise's, for Abelard demanded Heloise's absolute subjection. He robs her of youth, innocence, and freedom, but what he seems most to desire is something far more extreme: her self-willed enslavement. Of the many forms of tyranny encoded in the letters, this is perhaps the subtlest. Sartre has explained it in the following terms: "The lover does not desire to possess the beloved as

9. Southern, p. 94.

one possesses a thing; he demands a special type of appropriation. He wants to possess a freedom as freedom. . . . He wants to be loved by a freedom but demands that this freedom as freedom should no longer be free. . . . He wants this freedom to be captured by itself, to turn back upon itself, as in madness, as in a dream, so as to will its own captivity. This captivity must be a resignation that is both free and yet chained in our hands."[10] Thus when Heloise speaks of the madness of relinquishing what she most desires, she is giving Abelard precisely what he wants, without reservation. To the horror of all onlookers, she explicitly wills her own captivity by taking the veil, as she implicitly did earlier by submitting to his sexual perversions. I think Abelard's motive was the same before and after his castration, for whether he wants Heloise to submit to him or to God, his desire is to appropriate her freedom and her consciousness. He confesses that he married her because "at the time I desired to keep you whom I loved beyond measure for myself alone. . . . Had you not been previously joined to me in wedlock, you might easily have clung to the world when I withdrew from it, either at the suggestion of your relatives or in enjoyment of carnal delights" (149). This is an astounding statement, for the very things he prides himself on saving her from are the things she misses most. What he interprets as salvation she interprets as deprivation and eternal punishment.

We saw in the previous chapter how Ovid's *Heroides* may have combined the rhetorical exercises of *suasoriae* and *ethopoiiae*, while far surpassing their limits. The relation of *suasoriae*, which persuade by logic, and *ethopoiiae*, which emphasize character and emotion, to legal oratory and trial literature is particularly pronounced in Heloise's letters, for hers is a discourse of pathos that relies on the presentation of evidence as if she were staging a courtroom trial. In her dialogue with Abelard she not only debates rhetorical rules and epistolary conventions; she also acts as her own defense and presents powerful evidence of her submission to the trials he devised for her. Thus she mentions "proof" again and again, offering substantial evidence of the justice of her lament, of the injuries she has sustained, of her absolute devotion and obedience to Abelard. She speaks in one letter of striving to "prove you the sole possessor of my body and my will";

10. Jean-Paul Sartre, *Being and Nothingness*, trans. Hazel E. Barnes (New York: Philosophical Library, 1956), p. 367.

in another she dismisses the charge that her passion was mere lust (which is how Abelard describes his love for her). As evidence, she proclaims that "the end is proof of the beginning. I have finally denied myself every pleasure in obedience to your will, kept nothing for myself except to prove that now, even more, I am yours" (117). The more Heloise renounces, the more she belongs to Abelard. The paradox is that, contrary to Abelard's design, renunciation keeps the circuit of desire open rather than closing it, for as Sartre explains, "pleasure is the death and the failure of desire. It is the death of desire because it is not only its fulfillment but its limit and its end."[11] By denying herself every pleasure, Heloise insures that pleasure has no limit. The result is that in the act of obeying Abelard (by her denial) Heloise simultaneously defies his command that she cease to desire.

Many scholars see Heloise's last letter as a radical departure from her earlier ones; they cite the resignation in her tone and the neutrality of her emphasis on church matters.[12] But the fifth letter begins with a discussion of the difference between speech and writing, the body and the pen. Heloise thus draws attention once again to the forms Abelard would have her observe; that she chooses to obey does not mean that she does not recognize the tyranny of his injunction. "I would not," she writes, "want to give you cause for finding me disobedient in anything, so I have set the bridle of your injunction on the words which issue from my unbounded grief; thus in writing at least I may moderate what it is difficult or rather impossible to forestall in speech. For nothing is less under our control than the heart—having no power to command it we are forced to obey" (159). Although Heloise here connects the heart with spontaneity and the pen with restraint, she finds the means through the act of writing to reproach Abelard in ways that would be impossible if they confronted each other. That writing itself is erotic is revealed by Heloise's confession that she was seduced specifically by Abelard's artful wooing in verse and in song; these gifts, she reflects, would have won the heart of any woman. Not only was she won by words, but writing kept both her and Abelard aflame: "When in the past you sought me out for sinful pleasures your letters came to me thick and fast, and your many songs put your Heloise on everyone's lips, so that every street and house echoed with my name" (117–18).

11. Ibid., p. 397.
12. See, for example, Radice, Introduction to *The Letters*, p. 29; McLeod, pp. 168–71.

The multiple implications here are all significant: first, the discourse of others (Heloise's name is on everyone's lips) precedes her amorous discourse in the letters. (And as we shall see presently in Faulkner's "A Rose for Emily" and Rosa Coldfield's narrative in *Absalom, Absalom!* the story the town tells about Heloise does not always correspond to the story she tells about herself.) Second, Heloise's letters are encoded with the discourse of the other, for just as Bakhtin noted that "novelistic pathos . . . must borrow the discourses of others," Heloise borrows from many literary sources to describe her pathos. The fame of Abelard and Heloise in their own time has been discussed at great length; what interests me here is how that fame led them to fictionalize themselves. I mentioned earlier that in taking the veil, Heloise quotes Lucan's Cornelia, and Abelard clearly sees himself as Pompey—fatally undone by a woman—but their allusions to the same texts often work at cross-purposes, for Heloise frequently quotes such defiant passages from *Pharsalia* as Lucan's plea to God: "May it be sudden, whatever your plan for us; may man's mind / Be blind to the future. Let him hope on in his fears."[13] Moreover, even when she compares herself to legendary temptresses who have caused the ruin of great men, it is important to note that such analogies involve making a fiction not just of herself but of Abelard as well. Thus, in order to come to terms with the decision to enslave her will to Abelard, Heloise must maintain the fiction of his greatness and of his mastery over her.[14] I think, actually, that she refers repeatedly to the necessity of making reparation to him, of demonstrating how obedient she has been, of giving him proof after proof of her fidelity, to maintain the fiction that she is still as much an obsession with him as he is with her.

Abelard's letters, however, tell a different story, for his sole obsession seems to be himself and his own suffering. He sees himself as weak, as powerless, as a martyr and a victim. He wants Heloise to play Magdalene to his Christ.[15] He has been punished more than she, he tells her, because he is the weaker; he needs her prayers far more than she needs his. Where Heloise maintains that all they have suffered has been for love, he deprives her of even this consolation:

13. Lucan, *The Civil War*, books 1–10 (*Pharsalia*), trans. J. D. Duff, Loeb Classical Library (Cambridge: Harvard Univ. Press, 1928), book 2, ll. 14–15, p. 129.

14. Kamuf, *Fictions*, pp. 17–19, 32.

15. Peter Dronke, "Héloise and Marianne: Some Reconsiderations," *Romanische Forschungen* 72:3–4 (1960), 223–56.

"You say I suffered for you, and perhaps that is true, but it was really through you, and even this, unwillingly; not for love of you but under compulsion, and to bring you not salvation but sorrow" (153). He even goes so far as to tell her, totally unaware of his own arrogance and self-absorption, that her sole purpose in being born was to aid in his martyrdom: "You should not grieve because you are the cause of so great a good, for which you must not doubt you were specially created by God. Nor should you weep because I have to bear this, except when our blessings through the martyrs in their sufferings and the Lord's death sadden you" (145). Thus in trying to persuade her of the virtue of her situation, he relies on a fictional metamorphosis, transforming her from sinful Eve into saintly Mary. Significantly, he tries to persuade her that what is most attractive about her fate is that it differs from that of a "mere" woman's. It would have been a "hateful loss and grievous misfortune if you had abandoned yourself to the defilement of carnal pleasures only to bear in suffering a few children for the world, when now you are delivered in exultation of numerous progeny for heaven! Nor would you have been more than a woman, whereas now you rise even above men, and have turned the curse of Eve into the blessing of Mary. How unseemly for those holy hands which now turn the pages of sacred books to have to perform degrading services in women's concerns!" (150). Abelard's hierarchy of values bears close analysis. The curse visited on Eve for her sin is to bring forth children in pain; thus, one supposed consolation of Heloise's barrenness is to be spared that pain. Another is that she has many spiritual daughters in the sisterhood. Third, her barrenness frees her from the degradation of "women's concerns," which in context seem to be sexual intercourse, pregnancy, and childbirth, since he goes on to speak of "contamination," "filth," and "mire." Abelard thus relegates the entire life of the body and its life-giving capacity to the realm of degradation and defilement. Heloise has been spared involvement in the cycle of birth and life; her "consolation" is that she gets to handle sacred books. But the ancient *topos* of the *envoi*—the author delivering his book to the world as a woman delivers a child—cannot be invoked, for Heloise is not allowed to write, to "deliver" the sacred books; she can only turn the pages of those written by holy men! Finally, what Abelard thinks should most console Heloise is that the barrenness and sterility of her existence (which is how she herself describes it) have given her the opportunity to be like a man; she has,

moreover, risen "even above men." The "even" is the telling detail
that reveals Abelard's deepest desire: to strip her of sexuality as he
has been stripped and, what is more, to reconcile her to that condition.[16] Abelard unquestionably views himself as barren, but rather
than sympathizing with Heloise's plight or trying to spare her the
same fate, he falls into self-pity: she has borne spiritual daughters, but
"I remain totally barren and labour in vain amongst the sons of perdi-
tion!" (150).

Thus, just as Abelard once relied on letters to seduce Heloise, he
now uses letters to seduce her with the logic of his argument and to
reconcile her to her barrenness. As self-conscious practitioners of the
art of letter writing, they know which learned authorities from antiquity and the Bible should provide consolation, but Heloise derives
scant solace either from these sources or from Abelard. On the contrary, as he points out, their skill in writing letters can never be a
source of comfort because it is this skill that has led to their punishment. Their crime was to use literary skill to inflame each other rather
than to glorify God, who became, according to Abelard, "indignant or
grieved because our knowledge of letters, the talents which he had
entrusted to us, were not being used to glorify his name. . . . God
himself has thought fit to raise us up from the contamination of this
filth and the pleasures of this mire and draw us to him by force . . .
and by our example perhaps to deter from our audacity others who
are also trained in letters" (149–50). Heloise's aim in writing is to
reassure herself that she has sacrificed her life because of the greatness of his love, but he denies her that reassurance uncategorically.
Again and again, she asks him if it was lust rather than love that
moved him, as the entire world believes. Instead of denying it,
Abelard affirms it: "My love, which brought us both to sin, should be
called lust, not love. I took my fill of my wretched pleasures in you,
and this was the sum total of my love" (153). He took her and forgot
her; she writes to fill the void he has left, finally rebelling against his
injunction to silence and submission. She rebels even in the last letter
both against the tyranny of formal writing and against the multiple
forms of tyranny he would impose.

If amorous discourses are dialogic in the sense of positing an
alternative logic, one model for such an alternative, as we have seen,

16. Cf. Kamuf, *Fictions*, pp. 35–36.

comes from music. Paul Zumthor points out that medieval texts also had notable musical qualities; he even suggests that we "*consider on principle every text* earlier than the thirteenth century . . . *as a dance*."[17] The idea is particularly provocative in Heloise's discourse of desire, as are Zumthor's comments about the orality of medieval discourse: "Every medieval 'literary' text, whatever its mode of composition and transmission, was designed to be communicated aloud to the individuals who constituted its audience. . . . The 'enclosure' of the text . . . breaks apart, and through the breach comes something else that is no longer discourse and which crosses over the boundary lines of ordinary language."[18] Zumthor's idea is particularly relevant when we recall one of the primary characteristics of amorous discourse: whether or not it is spoken in fact, it is written as if it were going to be spoken to the beloved. Bakhtin, remember, argues that "language when it means, is someone talking to someone else. . . . All rhetorical forms . . . are oriented toward the listener and his answer."[19]

One of the most painful discoveries Heloise makes by writing to Abelard and reading his responses is that despite the closeness of their intimacy in the past, nothing could be more dissimilar than their feelings in the present. If Abelard was indeed enslaved by lust, perhaps castration is as liberating as he claims it to be. But the heart cannot be castrated, and Heloise sustains her faith in the primacy of the heart's desires to the end. In her final letter, she continues to break through the boundaries Abelard has set for her by arguing for the fundamental integrity of the heart. She does so by posing the same dichotomy that Ovid posed in Phaedra's letter between writing and speech: "When the [heart's] impulses move us, none of us can stop their sudden promptings from easily breaking out, and even more easily overflowing into words which are the ever-ready indications of the heart's emotions: as it is written, 'A man's words are spoken from the overflowing of the heart.' I will therefore hold my hand from writing words which I cannot restrain my tongue from speaking; would that a grieving heart would be as ready to obey as a writer's hand!" (159). By means of this strategy, Heloise draws attention to the difficulty of obedience and then declares that she will obey nevertheless. The evidence of the letter itself, however, is at odds with her declaration, for in this letter she once

17. Zumthor, p. 89 (Zumthor's italics).
18. Ibid., pp. 67, 75.
19. Mikhail Bakhtin, *The Dialogic Imagination: Four Essays*, trans. Michael Holquist and Caryl Emerson (Austin: Univ. of Texas Press, 1981), pp. xvi, 28, 352.

again encodes her erotic desire. All her allusions are transgressions. She cites the banquet scenes of fornication in Ovid's *Art of Love*, for instance; although she dismisses Ovid as "that master of sensuality and shame," the parallels between him and another past master of sensuality are perhaps implied. (It is likely, moreover, that Ovid was one of the authors Heloise studied with *her* master, Abelard, who cites several of his works both in the *Historia* and in his letters and describes how he and Heloise were discovered in bed together by alluding to Ovid's description in *The Art of Love* [2:561ff.] and in *Metamorphoses* [4:169ff.] of the same fate befalling Mars and Venus.) Since Ovid describes Vulcan's skill in forging delicate chains, nets, and snares thinner than the "thinnest threads spun on the loom, or cobwebs hanging from the rafters," which entangled the lovers in the very act of embracing in bed, Heloise may have the same story (as well as the Bible) in mind when she refers to woman as a "snare, her heart a net, her arms are chains" (131). Heloise goes so far as to draw Abelard's attention to the openings in a woman's body, ostensibly inquiring about women's consumption of wine; one wonders if her words inevitably make him remember his enjoyment of her body—and the outlet it provided him—when she cites the allusion in *Saturnalia* to the frequent purgations "a woman's body is . . . destined for [since it] is pierced with several holes, so that it opens into channels and provides outlets for the moisture draining away to be dispersed. . . . By contrast, in old men the body is dry, as is shown by their rough and wrinkled skin" (166). Beneath the surface texture of the dutiful quotation from Macrobius Theodosius, the subtext draws a sharp distinction between the dry body of Abelard and the vibrant body of Heloise. Although the literal meaning of her letter is a plea for advice about the numerous dangers that beset the flesh, her allusions, her images, her emphases all point to a struggle at the scene of writing. It is precisely this struggle that she draws attention to in the opening of this last letter, for she simultaneously declares obedience and draws attention to the tyranny to which she is submitting: she bridles her grief, she moderates her writing, she forestalls her speech.

Still, something remains uncircumscribed. Only in writing, she claims, can she obey his injunction to discuss neutral matters, but— veiled in neutrality and obedience—she uncovers numerous opportunities to continue her erotic discourse. She finds the occasion to mention scores of sexual issues relevant to herself and to their past as lovers: the smoothness and glossiness of a woman's skin, the difficulty of continence, sexual intercourse, the rashness of vows taken by young women. Writing gives her the occasion to continue to lament her own rashness in agreeing to foresake love, eros, Abelard.

Ovid uses precisely the same strategy in the *Tristia*—mentioning *The Art of Love* while swearing never to mention it again and pretending to repent for having written it. Zumthor points out the paradoxes when he observes, "Uttering the spoken word thereby takes on within itself the value of a symbolic act: by reason of the voice, it is exhibition and gift, aggression, conquest, and hope for victory over its adversary; manifest internalization overcome by the necessity to physically invade the object of its desire: the vocalized sound goes from the inside out and, without any other mediation, links together two lives."[20] The notion—far from limited to medieval texts—will reappear in the Brontës, for the uncanny cry that carries over the hills from the maimed Rochester to Jane Eyre is a perfect example of vocalized sound that reunites two lives. The idea of utterance as symbolic act points to an intrinsic characteristic of amorous discourse; Roland Barthes describes the dedication in such discourse, for instance, as an "episode of language which accompanies any amorous gift, whether real or projected; and more generally, every gesture, whether actual or interior, by which the subject dedicates something to the loved being."[21]

The Literary History of the Letters

The subsequent history of Heloise's letters, like the letters themselves, is marked by transgressions, transformations, duplicitous transcriptions of illicit desire. The first French translation is Jean de Meun's at the end of the thirteenth century, but it is limited to Abelard's *Historia calamitatum*. Roger de Rabutin, Comte de Bussy, sent his cousin Mme de Sévigné a paraphrase of Heloise's first two letters and Abelard's first reply in 1687; he published them in 1697. Two years earlier a composite volume had appeared, which included an account of the lovers' history by Jacques Alluis (first published in 1675); F. N. Du Bois's 1695 paraphrase includes this history as well as the three Bussy-Rabutin letters, which had been plagiarized and trans-

20. Zumthor, pp. 75, 78.
21. Roland Barthes, *A Lover's Discourse: Fragments*, trans. Richard Howard (New York: Hill and Wang, 1978), p. 75.

formed by another author. In later editions, Du Bois drew on *Bayle's Dictionary*, first published in 1697.[22] In England, John Hughes's translated paraphrase of the letters, "extracted chiefly from Monsieur Bayle" appeared in 1714; it is in fact a direct translation of Du Bois's 1695 patchwork. It is Hughes's version and not Richard Rawlinson's Latin version that influenced Alexander Pope's "Eloisa to Abelard," which was published in 1717, a year before the Rawlinson text even appeared. Hughes's translation, indeed, continued to be popular long after the definitive English translation by the Reverend Joseph Berington appeared in 1787.[23]

As it passed from history into legend, Heloise's character, like Sappho's before her, underwent a momentous metamorphosis. Sometime between the appearance of her Latin letters in France in 1616 and Bussy-Rabutin's passionate paraphrase in 1687, the learned medieval philosopher who acted on high ethical principles was transformed into a fictional *grande amoureuse*. What happened was that *The Letters of a Portuguese Nun* appeared anonymously in Paris in 1669. Although it is unlikely that Heloise's original letters directly affected Guilleragues' conception of the *Portuguese Letters*, the latter certainly had a profound influence on all the subsequent versions, imitations, sequels, and paraphrases of Heloise's letters. Robert Adams Day

22. McLeod, pp. 302–5.
23. Ibid. See also Wellington, ed., *"Eloisa to Abelard,"* pp. 1–61. The text includes the John Hughes translation of three of Heloise's letters. Wellington discusses Hughes's friendship with Pope and notes that among major English poets, only John Donne, Michael Drayton, and John Dryden took up the genre of the heroic epistle, despite the fact that George Turberville translated the *Heroides* in 1567. Dryden translated three of the *Heroides*—Dido's, Helen's, and Canace's—and wrote the preface in a translation by several hands (London: Jacob Tonson, 1680). He praised Ovid in his *Essay of Dramatic Poesy*—as Longinus before him had praised Sappho—for showing "the various movements of a soul combating betwixt two different passions."
The critical reception of Pope's "Eloisa" demonstrates once again that amorous epistolary discourse is a genre relegated to the margins of critical comprehension and drawn from an alien area of discourse. Critics failed to recognize the link between Pope's epistle and the genre of amorous epistolary discourse, despite the fact that the only other heroic epistle Pope ever wrote was a translation of Ovid's "Sappho to Phaon." Of Pope's translation, Joseph Warton remarks, "This species of writing, beautiful as it is, has not been much cultivated among us" (*An Essay on the Genius and Writings of Pope*, 5th ed., 2 vols. [London: W. J. and J. Richardson, 1806], 1:292). Those preromantic and romantic critics, including William Bowles and William Hazlitt, who admired "Eloisa" disliked most of Pope's work—so different from this poem in every way. Conversely, admirers of the majority of Pope's work had no idea how to classify "Eloisa to Abelard." Says Wellington: "[It] may be said to rank as the finest poem ever written in a classification which admittedly offers little by way of competition" (p. 29).

maintains that "there is little doubt that Bussy was influenced in his treatment of [Heloise's] letters by the 'Portuguese' manner. He made many adaptations large and small, ranging from the suppression of phrases to the insertion of scenes."[24] Bussy-Rabutin was not the only adapter to fall under the spell of *la Portugaise,* for John Hughes's English translation of Heloise's letters bears all the marks of the same enchantment. Says Day: "The similarity between the . . . book in English (which was more like a work of epistolary fiction than anything else) and the *Portuguese Letters* is remarkable. . . . the vacillating emotions and frantic accents of passion, the disjointed utterances, are much the same as the Nun's."[25] In his preface, Hughes draws explicit parallels to the *Portuguese Letters,* which he deems inferior to those of Heloise and Abelard because the latter are genuine, "truly written by the persons themselves, whose names they bear."[26]

Peter Dronke has documented the slow transformation of Heloise in the seventeenth and eighteenth centuries from selfless lover into self-absorbed coquette, but he exempts the *Portuguese Letters* from the general trend of imitative works to trivialize Heloise. (The Portuguese nun in her turn undergoes the same transformation in scores of imitations.) Dronke concludes that, in contrast to such "elegant Cartesian analysts of the passions" as Bussy-Rabutin, Hughes, and Pope, the Portuguese nun, like Heloise, must have been an authentic woman because her passion is so "natural" and "her resemblances to an *héroïne de roman* are surface merely; in essence she belongs to the world of Héloïse."[27] Dronke's view of woman as artist relies on such notions of woman's "essence"; the underlying assumption of this essentialist argument is that woman can write only what she feels; she is incapable of "*mere* literary construction."[28] Subsequent scholarship has revealed that Dronke was probably wrong about Mariane's identity, but no one has noticed that he is also wrong in equating writing with inauthenticity and in his implicit assumption that writing is a "mere" substitute for something beneath, beyond language. On the contrary, as in Sappho and Ovid, writing becomes the whole point in

24. Robert Adams Day, *Told in Letters: Epistolary Fiction before Richardson* (Ann Arbor: Univ. of Michigan Press, 1966), p. 38.

25. Ibid.

26. Cited ibid., p. 101.

27. Dronke, "Héloïse and Marianne," p. 256. Charlotte Charrier also charts the literary history of Heloise's transformation from transcendental lover to trivial coquette, pt. 2, chap. 2.

28. Ibid., p. 252.

both texts. The tone of outrage and despair, the stylistic shifts from elegy to pathos to tragic tirade, the ability to portray "the whole contradictory concourse of emotions" that Longinus so admired in Sappho—these become the "ever-fixéd mark" toward which both nuns aim in their discourses of desire.

The literary history of Heloise's letters thus demonstrates the dialogic dynamism of amorous epistolary discourse from Latin to French to English, stretching back to the *Heroides* and forward to the *Portuguese Letters*. It is a dialogue staged between lovers, between texts, between languages, between authentic and fictional correspondents, between definitive translations, spurious paraphrases, and a patchwork of other sources. As in Ovid, the search for origins, for the lost father, and for the definitive text becomes as entangled as threads in a labyrinth or the narrative line.[29] While such writers as Bussy-Rabutin were transforming Heloise from philosopher to coquette, medieval scholars were busy dismantling her claims to authorship of her own correspondence. One scholar's theory—complete with forgeries, thefts, and conspiracies—resembles the plot twists of Umberto Eco's *The Name of the Rose*. John F. Benton notes that "fictional letters written under the name of famous people were a common form of literary activity." That fact leads him to a hypothesis that involves multiple forgeries. In the late thirteeth century, a forger wrote a long treatise, Epistle VIII in *The Letters of Abelard and Heloise*, in order to introduce male dominance in the convent. To authenticate his work, he persuaded a second forger to compose the *Historia* and the personal letters by plagiarizing a twelfth-century work of fiction based on Abelard's life. (Three forgers are thus involved so far.) The initial forger, moreover, may have enlisted a fourth forger with literary skill to embellish the final product with "literariness."[30]

Literature as a letter, the letter as literature: the issues of authorship, authenticity, and paternity are crucial in defining the "literariness" of this correspondence. Those who believe that the letters are literature argue that their composition is too unified, their moral too exemplary to be anything but a fictional conversion experience. But what if the moral exemplum was not intrinsic in the text but instead

29. See J. Hillis Miller, "Ariadne's Thread: Repetition and the Narrative Line," *Critical Inquiry* 3 (Autumn 1976), 57–77.

30. John F. Benton, "Fraud, Fiction, and Borrowing in the Correspondence of Abelard and Heloise," in *Pierre Abélard—Pierre le Vénérable,* Colloques internationaux du Centre National de la Recherche scientifique, 546 (Paris, 1975), pp. 469–511.

was applied to it later, in the interpretations of late medieval moralists? Furthermore, if an exemplary conversion is the didactic purpose of this work of "literature," why is that conversion so well disguised? Why does Heloise never explicitly say that she repents or that she is converted? Some medievalists have overlooked this omission; others have "solved" the dilemma by erasing Heloise as an author altogether. According to John Benton, since "her letters . . . may have been composed by a thirteenth-century author who wanted to put women in their place, we need not imagine [Heloise] as so . . . tortured by sensuality as she appears in the correspondence. . . . we are now free to see these two great figures (Abelard and Heloise) in more positive terms."[31] Benton believes that a man wrote Heloise's letters "to put women in their place," yet he sees nothing incongruous in his own assumption that " 'more positive' means 'less sensual' "[32] or in the fact that, by attributing Heloise's letters to a male author, he writes her out of her own correspondence! Just as some classicists discredit Sappho's discourse of the body, some medievalists utterly discredit Heloise's. They also argue that modern readers should not approach Abelard and Heloise as if they held twentieth-century views of love, sex, and passion. D. W. Robertson leads the group of medieval scholars who believe that all medieval texts must be approached in what he calls Augustinian terms. Thus, he argues, medieval readers would have viewed as "sentimental" the notion that there was anything tragic or romantic about the fate of the lovers. Robertson insists that their love is a "sordid affair" and that Abelard wrote all the letters to demonstrate how Heloise developed "from a vain and amusingly unreasonable young girl into a mature and respected abbess."[33] Other scholars have made similar arguments: being put in her place is precisely what Heloise needed, and Abelard performed a valuable service by curing her of her "unreasonable" passion. Father Muckle, for instance, comments: "One would expect that Abelard would have chided her and tried to set her right in regard to such extravagant and sinful dispositions. . . . One might expect some word of disapproval of such impassioned and sinful protestations of love."[34] Such criticism is itself as subjective as the classicist's condemnation of Sappho's lesbianism cited

31. Ibid., p. 501.
32. Dronke, *Abelard and Heloise*, p. 13.
33. D. W. Robertson, Jr., *Abelard and Heloise* (New York: Dial Press, 1972), p. 97, cited in Dronke, *Abelard and Héloise*, pp. 13–14.
34. Muckle, p. 59, cited in Dronke, *Abelard and Héloise*, p. 8.

in the last chapter; it illuminates little in the letters but exposes a strong critical bias that repeatedly recurs in scholarly assessments of Heloise and of other discourses of desire.

Peter Dronke, in contrast, has convincingly argued that there is no evidence in medieval testimonies to suggest that contemporaries saw this love as sordid, nor do any of these testimonies suggest that Heloise ever repented or ever ceased to love Abelard. He demonstrates how large a role the sexual element plays even in the consolation Peter the Venerable offers Heloise when Abelard dies. Peter the Venerable, the abbot of Cluny, tells her that she will join her lover in heaven and that their reunion will combine divine with sexual love. Dronke notes that Peter the Venerable

> does not shun a language rich in erotic connotations. At this solemn moment he uses sexual expressions consciously and daringly: . . . *carnalis copula, vinculum, adherere, gremium, confovere.* . . . Not a word about their being washed clean of the foulness of earthly lust: there is not a phrase in Peter's letter such as the twentieth-century moralistic scholars delight in using, and delight in thinking makes them more truly medieval in outlook than the rest of us. . . . the majority of contemporaries of whom we have evidence . . . up to the time of Jean de Meun, were convinced of the uniqueness and stature of Abelard's and Heloise's love, and regarded their tragedy with wonderment and compassion. And no one in the twelfth or thirteenth century . . . ever suggests that Heloise came to see the error of her ways in loving Abelard. Of what many of our modern judges so confidently affirm, the medieval evidence shows no trace.[35]

Despite the tyranny of Abelard's logic and rhetorical forms, despite the efforts of scholars from de Meun forward to degrade Heloise's desire or to erase her from her own correspondence, despite the forgeries, the thefts, the labyrinthine windings of literary history, Heloise's letters endure—a defiant transgression of the tyrannies of logic and abstinence, an affirmation of all that remains uncircumscribed, unrepented, and, alas, irremediable in the realm of desire.

35. Dronke, *Abelard and Héloise*, pp. 23, 30–31.

How we squander our sorrows
     gazing beyond them
               into the sad
wastes of duration
     to see if maybe
               they have a limit.
But they are
     our winter foliage
     our dark evergreens
one of the seasons
     of our secret year
               —and not only a season

they are situation,
     settlement, lair,
          soil, home.

RAINER MARIA RILKE, *Duino Elegies*

3
Disorder and Early Sorrow:
The Letters of a Portuguese Nun

The Portuguese Nun. 1808. Mackenzie's engraving was published
in *Letters from a Portuguese Nun to an Officer in the French Army,*
trans. W. R. Bowles, 2d ed. (London: Sherwood, Neely, and
Jones, 1817). It is reproduced courtesy of the William Andrews
Clark Memorial Library, University of California, Los Angeles.

Writing under Erasure

Who does the Portuguese nun belong to? Why are all her letters unsigned? Who signs *The Letters of a Portuguese Nun?* The letters appeared anonymously in French in 1669, ostensibly translated from the Portuguese. For three hundred years, scholars have tried to identify the translator, the nun, and the chevalier to whom she writes, who seduced her while he was stationed in Portugal with the forces of Louis XIV. In 1669 the lover was identified as Noël Bouton, the Chevalier de Chamilly, who later became marshal of France. Guilleragues was identified as the man who translated the letters from Portuguese into French. In 1810 a scholar named Boissonade discovered a handwritten note in his first edition of the letters, which identified the nun as Mariana Alcoforada. Her existence was confirmed in 1876. A Maria Ana Alcoforado had become a nun at the age of sixteen at the Convent of the Conception in Béja, Portugal, in 1656; between 1665 and 1667 when this affair would have taken place, she would have been about twenty-five, he thirty. In 1709 Maria Ana became mother superior; in 1723 she died. The discovery of Maria Ana led Portuguese scholars to translate the letters "back" into Portuguese; this reconstructed version was then hailed as a masterpiece of Portuguese literature. (In libraries around the world to this day, the text is still listed under Portuguese literature.)

In 1926 a number of discrepancies between the text and the life of Maria Ana Alcoforado were examined by F. C. Green. The real nun was a member of an old, distinguished family, for example, but the fictional nun complains of "la médiocrité de ma condition." In 1962 Frédéric Deloffre and J. Rougeot presented evidence to prove that Gabriel-Joseph de Lavergne de Guilleragues was not the translator but the author of the letters. These scholars have not eliminated all skepticism, however; some still maintain that the work was at least inspired by some authentic letters written by a Portuguese woman; others believe that they belong to Portugal, although no Portuguese original has ever been found. Peter Dronke, for instance, maintains that the entire issue "remains . . . wide open," and Yves Florenne, in a recent edition of the letters, argues for "a woman's voice." Jean-Pierre and Thérèse LaSalle, moreover, recently discovered seven additional letters, which clearly precede the five extant letters chronologically and form a coherent whole. All twelve letters appear to be the work of one author, but the editors do not draw definite conclusions in favor of either the nun's or Guilleragues' authorship.[1]

Both the duration and the vehemence of this controversy have a surprisingly sustained intensity. What is at stake is national pride in a literary classic, for one thing. One Portuguese critic sees the letters as the only beautiful work produced by his country in the seventeenth century.[2] A solution to the ancient dispute over art versus *génie* is also at stake. Critics on one side cite the letters as proof that natural genius—the spontaneous overflow of powerful feelings—is sufficient to produce great art. One of the ironies of the dispute, as Deloffre points out, is that many of the artists who are the most self-conscious in their own work—including La Bruyère, Laclos, Stendhal, Sainte-Beuve, and Rilke—endorsed the view that these letters were the product of *génie*. (Rilke translated *Lettres portugaises* into German in

1. For a discussion of the history of the letters, see Frédéric Deloffre and J. Rougeot, "L'Enigme des *Lettres portugaises*," in *Lettres portugaises, Valentins, et autres oeuvres de Guilleragues* (Paris: Garnier, 1962), pp. v–xxiii. The English translation of the French *Lettres portugaises* by Donald Ericson is in Maria Isabel Barreño, Maria Teresa Horta, Maria Velho da Costa, *The Three Marias: New Portuguese Letters*, trans. from the Portuguese by Helen R. Lane (New York: Bantam, 1976), pp. 339–62. Since Ericson's arrangement of the letters follows a discredited chronology, and since his translation is sometimes inadequate, I occasionally make minor changes, which are noted parenthetically in the text, along with page numbers to this edition. When I quote the French version along with the English, Deloffre and Rougeot's page numbers are cited parenthetically. See also F. C. Green, "Who Was the Author of the 'Lettres portugaises'?" *Modern Language Review* 21 (1926), 159–67. Luciano Cordeiro, in "*Soror Marianna: A freira portugueza*," (Lisbon: Livaria Ferin, 1888), argues that Guilleragues based his fictional letters on authentic Portuguese originals by the celebrated nun. More recently, the entire debate was rehearsed in the *Times Literary Supplement* by Margaret C. Weitz, 15 Oct. 1976, p. 1306, and Peter Dronke, 5 Nov. 1976, p. 1397. See also Yves Florenne, Introduction, *Lettres de la religieuse portugaise* (Paris: Librairie générale française, 1979), p. 77; Jean-Pierre LaSalle and Thérèse LaSalle, *Un Manuscrit des lettres d'un religieuse portugaise: Leçons, interrogations, hypothèses*, Papers on French Seventeenth-Century Literature 6 (Paris: Biblio 17, 1982).

2. Theophilo Braga, cited in Edgar Prestage, trans., Introduction, *The Letters of a Portuguese Nun* (London: D. Nutt, 1897), p. xxvii. D. Nutt's edition is a reprint of an 1893 edition printed by Constable Press and limited to 500 copies; it was reprinted again in 1900 in Portland, Me., by Thos. Mosher.

1913; their influence on the *Duino Elegies* has often been remarked.)[3]
The opposite view holds that the letters are too carefully constructed,
with too many allusions to classical texts and Racinian tragedy to be
the work of an unworldly and wholly uneducated nun. But perhaps
an altogether different issue has given the debate its lasting ferocity,
for many have cited these letters to demonstrate the difference between feminine writing and masculine writing. Those who maintain
that the letters are the authentic work of a woman cite the disorder,
the passion, the vehemence of her emotion as evidence. Sainte-Beuve,
for instance, "gives a large place to 'la Portugaise' among the female
authors of letters written at the moment of passion, with a particular
charm in their disorder."[4] In *Les Liaisons dangereuses*, similarly, the
vicomte de Valmont confesses to the marquise de Merteuil that he has
taken pains with his letters to give them the appearance of disorder,
because "sans déraisonnement, point de tendresse"; that emotional
abandon, that irrationality, he argues, is what makes women superior
writers of love letters.[5] One of the few dissenters from this dominant
view of woman's superiority where either love or writing is concerned
is Rousseau, who reasoned:

> Women, in general, show neither appreciation nor proficiency nor ge-
> nius in any part. They can succeed in certain short works which de-
> mand only lightness, taste, grace, sometimes even philosophy and rea-
> soning. They can acquire scientific knowledge, erudition, talents and
> anything which can be acquired through hard work. . . . They may
> show great wit but never any soul. They are a hundred times more
> reasonable than they are passionate. Women know neither how to de-
> scribe nor experience love itself. Only Sappho and one other deserve to

---

3. Rilke, like Goethe before him, was much impressed by the *Portuguese Letters;*
among the many critics who have cited the influence of the letters on Rilke, see Deloffre
and Rougeot, "L'Enigme des *Lettres portugaises*," p. vi; and Barreño et al., *The Three
Marias: New Portuguese Letters*, p. xi. What Rilke may have found particularly resonant
in the *Portuguese Letters* is the renunciation of any claim to extratextual authority. In the
Duino Elegies, as Paul de Man points out, Rilke converts personal destinies or subjective
experiences into figures by focusing on a void or a lack: "Hence the prevalence of a
thematics of negative experiences . . . the insatiability of desire, the powerlessness of
love, death of the unfulfilled or the innocent . . . the alienation of consciousness." See
Allegories of Reading: Figural Language in Rousseau, Nietzsche, Rilke, and Proust (New
Haven: Yale Univ. Press, 1979), pp. 49–50.
    4. Charles-Augustin Sainte-Beuve, "Du roman intime; ou, Mademoiselle de
Liron," in *Portraits des femmes* (Paris: Didier, 1852), cited in Deloffre and Rougeot, p. vi.
    5. Pierre-Ambroise-François Choderlos de Laclos, *Les Liaisons dangereuses*, 2 vols.
(Amsterdam: Durand Neveu, 1782), letter 70, 1:71.

be counted as exceptions. I would bet everything I have that the *Portuguese Letters* were written by a man.[6]

Thus, the very qualities that led previous critics to define the letters as feminine writing—the transports, the intensity, the anguish—led Rousseau to wager that a man wrote them. He identifies the female with mind rather than with heart, with cold calculation rather than burning passion. Ironically, although his view of women is diametrically opposed to that of other critics, it is just as negative, for where the others maintain that women can only write what they feel, Rousseau asserts that they are incapable of creation because they are incapable of feeling.

The *Portuguese Letters* are perhaps the most dramatic example in the genre of the dynamic process of dialogism—between texts and languages—and of reaccentuation. They indeed had such a phenomenal impact on both sides of the English Channel that to write "à la portugaise" became a veritable code for a certain style—written at the height of passion in a moment of disorder and distress. In July of 1671, for instance, two years after the letters were published, Mme de Sévigné could write her daughter and mention, "Brancas has, at last, wrote me a letter, crouded with expressions of such tenderness, that it makes ample amends for all his past forgetfulness and neglect. He talks amain to me of his heart in almost every line. Were I to answer him in the same strain, I should make a true Portuguese epistle of it." ("Si je le faisois réponse sur le même ton, *ce seroit une portugaise.*")[7] The scores of sequels to and imitations and translations of the letters attest to their continuing popularity: before 1740 the English translation of the letters went through ten printings; the imitative *Seven Portuguese Letters*, through five printings; eight verse versions and a bilingual edition were published; and Sir Roger L'Estrange's *Five Love-Letters, from a Nun to a Cavalier, with the Cavalier's Answers* went through four print-

---

6. Jean-Jacques Rousseau, *La Lettre à d'Alembert sur les spectacles* (Amsterdam: Marc Michel Rey, 1758), note k, pp. 193–94, trans. Peggy Kamuf, "Writing like a Woman," in *Women and Language in Literature and Society*, ed. Sally McConnell-Ginet, Ruth Borker, Nelly Furman (New York: Praeger, 1980), p. 290. I am indebted to her analysis of the correspondence in this article.

7. Mme de Sévigné, *Court Secrets: or, The Lady's Chronicle. Historical and Gallant. Extracted from the Letters of Madam de Sévigné, which have been suppressed at Paris* (London: Henry Curll, 1727), p. 31. Mme de Sévigné's letter to Mme de Grignan, dated 19 July 1671, is cited in Max von Waldberg, *Der empfindsame Roman in Frankreich* (Strasbourg and Berlin: Verlag von Karl J. Trubner, 1906), pp. 45–122.

ings. Aphra Behn, Mary de la Rivière Manley, Jane Barker, Mary Davys, and Eliza Haywood all wrote enormously popular versions of the letters, imitations of them, or sequels to the originals.[8] The cultural assumptions underlying the code of the Portuguese style deserve mention, for Portugal was commonly viewed as the land of passion and the nun's sexuality, sensuality, and sensibility were attributed to the extremes of heat, intensity, and mystery in her environment. Until quite recently these assumptions, which so influence the assessment of feminine writing "à la portugaise," had never been examined, although a great deal of ink was spilled trying to reach a definitive conclusion about the letters' origin and authenticity and about the genius and gender of the author. Godfrey Singer, for instance, struggles valiantly with the problem:

> The . . . letters are a long complaint of the Nun for what she calls, after the fashion of the abandoned Ariadne, "my Inconsiderate, Improvident, and most unfortunate Love." Incidentally, the woman berates her lover in good round terms that are occasionally reminiscent of the writing of a

8. Robert Adams Day, *Told in Letters: Epistolary Fiction before Richardson* (Ann Arbor: Univ. of Michigan Press, 1966), pp. 32–37, 112. See also Day's appendixes, which provide chronological lists of English letter fiction, 1660–1740, notes on epistolary miscellanies, and letter fiction in periodicals. See also Jean Rousset's "Une Forme littéraire: Le Roman par lettres," in *Forme et signification: essais sur les structures littéraires de Corneille à Claudel* (Paris: Corti, 1962), chap. 4; and François Jost, "Le Roman épistolaire et la technique narrative au XVIIIe siècle," *Comparative Literature Studies* 3 (1966), 397–427, revised and reprinted as "L'Evolution d'un genre: Le Roman épistolaire dans les lettres occidentales," in *Essais de littérature comparée* (Fribourg, Switz.: Editions universitaires, 1968), 2:89–179, 380–402. Among Jost's six basic types of epistolary novels, one is the "type portugais"; another is the "type Abélard"; a third (relevant in terms of Barthes's reaccentuation in *A Lover's Discourse*) is the "type Werther." Each of Jost's classifications revolves around one significant work that spawned scores of imitations and sequels; my focus has been on generic transformations and the formal and thematic similarities in amorous discourse.
To cite but a partial list of the imitations and sequels in which the influence of *Lettres portugaises* is most pronounced: Aphra Behn, *Love Letters between a Nobleman and His Sister* (part I, 1683; part II, 1685; part III, 1687). Mary de la Rivière Manley, *Letters Written by Mrs. Manley. To Which Is Added a Letter from a Supposed Nun in Portugal, to a Gentleman in France, in Imitation of the Nun's Five Letters in Print*, by Colonel Pack (1696). *Memoirs of the Fair Eloisa, a Nun, and Abelard, a Monk*, said to be by Sir Roger L'Estrange and included in *Familiar Letters of Love, Gallantry, and Several Occasions* (1694; six editions by 1724). Eliza Haywood, *Love in Excess* (1719); *Letters from a Lady of Quality to a Chevalier* (1721); *Love-Letters on All Occasions* (1730). Mrs. Jane Barker, *A Patchwork Screen for the Ladies; or, Love and Virtue* (1723) and *The Lining of the Patchwork Screen* (1726). Mrs. Mary Davys, *The Works of Mrs. Davys*, including *Familiar Letters betwixt a Gentleman and a Lady* (1725).

man rather than of a woman. Not that there is present any suggestion of indelicacy, but rather that the tone of much of the writing is possessed of a masculine vigor. Perhaps this is due to the fact that the translation is the work of a man, Sir Roger L'Estrange. . . . It is difficult to say with any degree of finality whether the difference between the English and the French versions is that of the writing of man and woman or the natural difference between the more masculine English timbre and the less masculine French. . . . We might wish to avoid the original Nun as a dangerous individual in her just anger.[9]

Singer traps himself in a tangled web of definitions here. Men's writing is indelicate; women's writing lacks vigor; the entire English language is "more masculine" than French. Significantly, Singer seems unaware of the fact that he is taking the man's point of view as he writes; like the chevalier, "we" might wish to avoid the nun, assuming "we" are men. Furthermore, the note of unease with anger is one that will sound again and again, for whether the male critic is speaking of Clarissa or Rosa Coldfield, he will expose the same fear and dread of female rage. Singer follows the tendency of most critics of the *Portuguese Letters*, who use the letters to support preconceived notions about the difference between masculine and feminine, between artifice and natural creativity, between Portugal and France, France and England. As the letters are thus made to encode and enclose difference, what frequently gets lost in translation is the woman, as Mariane gets lost between Singer's sympathy for the object of her rage and the translation of Roger L'Estrange.

Leo Spitzer, writing twenty years later, also takes the man's side. In "Les *Lettres portugaises*," Spitzer concludes that the correspondence of Heloise and Abelard was entirely rewritten by Abelard. Furthermore, since the letters were reprinted in seventeenth-century France, they must have been the models for the *Portuguese Letters*, which he believes were also written by a man. Of Mariane, he says: "It is . . . characteristic that Mariana never tells us the name of her lover, she who does identify her own role in the drama under the name of Mariana. She never thinks of putting him before her and giving him a reality outside of herself. We are in the presence of a 'narcissistic' love." Like

9. Godfrey Frank Singer, *The Epistolary Novel: Its Origin, Development, Decline, and Residuary Influence* (Philadelphia: Univ. of Pennsylvania Press, 1933), pp. 46–47. On the myth of Portuguese passion, see for example, Prestage, Introduction, *The Letters of a Portuguese Nun*, p. xxviii. On cultural assumptions about feminine writing, see Kamuf, "Writing like a Woman," pp. 284–99.

Singer, Spitzer uses his role as critic to defend the man's position; he quite arbitrarily decides that the chevalier is a "brilliant French officer . . . a well-balanced nobleman who cannot be impolite to a woman. He's a ladies' man. . . . But what of it? Isn't it natural for a young and ebullient officer of aristocratic birth, 'likeable,' unmarried . . . ? It is not the infrequent and cold responses of the lover but the narrowness of her image of him that killed Mariana's passion."[10] (Saint-Simon, incidentally, offers a quite different view; he confesses in his memoirs that no one, after seeing or hearing the dullard Chamilly, could understand how he had inspired the kind of unparalleled passion that is revealed in the famous *Lettres portugaises*.)[11] Spitzer implies that the man is the woman's opposite in everything. He is brilliant, she is untutored; he is well-balanced, she is unbalanced; he is likable, she is narcissistic, a killer of love. Thus, after erasing Heloise as an author in Abelard's correspondence, Spitzer proceeds to erase the Portuguese nun's predicament, her pathos, and the power of her discourse.[12]

Barbin's *Avis*

When the *Portuguese Letters* first appeared in Paris, the publisher, Claude Barbin, attached the following *avis au lecteur:*

With much care and difficulty I found the means to recover an accurate copy of the translation of five Portuguese letters which were written to a gentleman of high quality who was serving in Portugal. I envisioned with such eagerness all those who are well versed in matters of passion—either knowing how to extol it or how to seek it out—that I believed I would be doing them a special favor in publishing them. I do not at all know the name of the one to whom they were written or of the one who made the translation of them. However, it seemed to me that I would probably not be displeasing either of them by making the letters public. It is hard to believe that [had I not published them] they would

10. Leo Spitzer, "Les *Lettres portugaises*," *Romanische Forschungen* 65:1–2 (1954), 94–135, trans. Kamuf, "Writing like a Woman," p. 296.
11. Duc de Saint-Simon, *Memoires*, ed. A. de Boislisle, 45 vols., Edit. des Grands Ecrivains de la France (Paris: Hachette, 1879–1930), 11:10–11, cited in Deloffre and Rougeot, "L'Enigme des *Lettres portugaises*," p. viii.
12. Kamuf, "Writing like a Woman," pp. 295–98. See also Nancy K. Miller, "The Text's Heroine: A Feminist Critic and Her Fictions," *Diacritics* 12 (Summer 1982), 48–53, and "I's in Drag: The Sex of Recollection," *Eighteenth Century* 22:1(1981), 47–57.

not eventually have been published [by someone else] with misprints
that would have blemished them [my translation].

It is a strange message. If the letters were indeed written by Guilleragues, then the author must have conspired with Barbin (a shrewd
judge of literary taste who was also the first to publish Mme de
Lafayette's *La Princesse de Clèves* and the first French edition of *Don
Quixote*). By pretending that the letters were authentic, Barbin pan-
dered to the public taste for "found letters"; he knew well how seventeenth-century audiences disliked fiction. He was also aware of how
the claim of authenticity would enhance the scandalous appeal of the
letters. His *avis* is thus a guarantee of authenticity and a certification
of his own authority, for he recounts the trouble he has taken to print
the letters and to secure a correct copy of the translation. The last line
is both a justification and a validation; the implication is that if Barbin
had not published the letters, someone else would have botched the
job. He highlights his authority again when he points out that neither
the male to whom the letters are addressed nor the translator will be
displeased to see these letters in print.

Barbin has neglected to mention the most crucial element in the
text: the woman. Amid his efforts to validate his own authority, Barbin never once mentions the author—the Portuguese nun. In decid-
ing to publish the letters, he takes the displeasure of the seducer and
the translator into consideration, but he never considers whether or
not the nun might be displeased. It is as if the possibility of her
displeasure or her dishonor are of no consequence. Paradoxically, the
authenticity of the text depends on its illegitimacy; what makes it authentic is that it does not have a father. Barbin's role thus resembles
that of the midwife; he "delivers" an illegitimate text to readers who
will be well pleased to receive it, precisely because it is a "natural"
product. Barbin further buttresses his authority by defining in advance the sort of readers he has in mind; he subtly flatters their pride,
sensibility, and exclusiveness, for he has published the letters as a
"special favor" to only those who worship or pursue passion. Since the
glorious emotions to which his readers will respond are the nun's, it
seems all the more curious that Barbin erases her from this preface,
particularly since by making her prominent he would have further
substantiated his claim of authenticity for the letters. That Barbin
would thus work against his own purposes is the first of many paradoxes in this enigmatic text. While trying to create the illusion that the

letters came from the nun's pen, he in effect erases as he writes, for—
as in the criticism of Singer and Spitzer—what gets lost in Barbin's
emphasis on the translation from Portuguese to French is the woman
who writes. Regardless of whether we view the nun as fictional or
authentic, she is disenfranchised in Barbin's preface. What the preface erases, the letters restore: the erotic scene of writing.[13]

The Metamorphosis of Rhetoric

Disenfranchisement is at the margins of the plot in the *Portuguese
Letters,* for Mariane's seducer comes to Portugal to expand his king's
conquests. The chevalier makes a conquest of Mariane, then sails
home to France, leaving her without resources to recover, to escape
from the convent, or to confront the family and the church she has
defied. He has as little concern for the woman as for the colony and
loses interest after her first letter, for she complains in her second of
hearing nothing from him in six months. When he writes again, he
has nothing to say; the nun notices how difficult it is for him to fill
half the page. In his final letter, he vows eternal friendship; in response the nun pours out her rage and bitterness at his hypocrisy and
treachery.

The nun's first words, "Considère, mon amour," reveal the characteristic doubleness of amorous discourse, for they are addressed
both to the chevalier and to herself. She maintains that ambiguity
throughout her letters, oscillating between the pathos of an interior
monologue and the fury of a tragic tirade. "Consider, my love, how
extremely lacking you have been in foresight. You have been betrayed, miserable one, and you have betrayed me with false hopes. A
passion on which you have built so many prospects for pleasure can
give you now nothing but mortal despair, equalled only by the cruelty
of the separation which causes it" (339, minor changes). As happens
so often in amorous discourse, the heart acts as a separate entity that
sometimes obeys and sometimes betrays the heroine. The heart is the
organ of all the nun's diverse *mouvements;* this one word recurs more

13. Kamuf discusses the erotic scene of writing in Heloise's letters in *Fictions of
Feminine Desire: Disclosures of Heloise* (Lincoln: Univ. of Nebraska Press, 1982); Roland
Barthes describes the consecration of the amorous scene in *A Lover's Discourse: Frag-
ments,* trans. Richard Howard (New York: Hill and Wang, 1978), pp. 192–93, 216–17.

frequently than any other in her letters. In the restricted vocabulary of seventeenth-century France, it designated the passions, the spontaneous impulses, the ecstasies, the desires that escape the control of the will and even the conscious mind.[14] The act of writing about these *mouvements*, therefore, is a conscious attempt to relive and recover spontaneous desires that were initially unconscious. Mariane speaks of *mouvements* again when she records her response as reader after receiving the chevalier's letter. "Your last letter has left my heart in a strange state; its agitation was so strong that it seemed to be trying to separate itself from me to go in search of you" (340). ("Votre dernière lettre le réduisit en un étrange état: il eut des mouvements si sensibles qu'il fit, ce semble, des efforts pour se séparer de moi, et pour vous aller trouver" [40].)

As Heloise does with Abelard, the Portuguese nun makes an idol of the chevalier and then consecrates herself to the idol. In retrospect, she establishes a beginning, middle, and end to the affair: it becomes a story. She declares, "From the first moment I saw you my life was yours, and somehow I take pleasure in sacrificing it to you" (339). The nun has turned her first view of the chevalier into an event, a scene that is "fiction" in both senses of the word, a story and a lie, for a few pages later she contradicts herself by noting that, although she was charmed when she first saw the chevalier, the "first stirrings of . . . passion" came not on that first day but later (345). Thus the phenomenon of love at first sight is an invention after the fact; what we first love is a scene, and this scene consecrates the object we are going to love. The structure of the nun's narrative thus repeats the same pattern Paul Zumthor relates to medieval texts—the latent narrative scheme proceeds from first sight of the beloved to the first meeting, and from the waiting period before the lovers fall in love to the aftermath of abandonment.[15] So eager is the nun to enshrine the scene in her memory that she slips into the imperfect tense, which in amorous discourse, Barthes observes, is "the tense of fascination. . . . From the start, greedy to play a role, scenes take their position in memory: often I feel this, I foresee this, at the very moment when these scenes are forming."[16] The nun recollects the birth of her passion in the imperfect tense:

14. Deloffre and Rougeot, Glossaire of *Lettres portugaises*, pp. 265–66.
15. Paul Zumthor, "The Text and the Voice," *New Literary History* 16 (Autumn 1984), 67–92.
16. Barthes, *A Lover's Discourse*, p. 217.

It was on this balcony that, charmed by your bearing, I so often watched you ride by; and I stood on this balcony on that fateful day when I felt the first stirrings of my unhappy passion. It seemed to me that you wanted to please me, although you did not know me. I convinced myself that you had noticed me among all of those who were with me. I imagined to myself that when you stopped, you wanted me to see you better so that I might admire the skill and grace with which you handled your horse. I was seized with fear when you took him over a difficult spot. In a word, I took a secret interest in all your actions. I felt that you were not indifferent to me and I understood everything you did to be for me. (345, minor changes)

The tenses in French reinforce the fictiveness of the process: je me *persuadai*, je *m'imaginai*, je *m'intéressais*, je *sentais*, je *prenais* pour moi tout ce que vous *faisiez*. This last phrase can also mean "I took everything you did for myself"; the chevalier's actions, his looks, his emotions were appropriated by the nun, who invented a meaning for them that could have absolutely no basis in reality, since she had not yet even met him.[17] From the outset, then, the chevalier is the object of a desire that thrives on imagination, roles, scenes, theater.

This passage is one of the most direct allusions to the *Heroides*, for Phaedra's avowal of love for Hippolytus is nearly identical; there is even the same distinction drawn between first being charmed and later feeling "piercing love lodged in my deepest bones." Phaedra confesses that she is enamored of Hippolytus' "hardness of feature. . . . Whether you draw rein and curb the resisting neck of your spirited steed, I look with wonder at your turning his feet in circle so slight; whether with strong arm you hurl the pliant shaft, your gallant arm draws my regard upon itself. . . . To say no more, my eyes delight in whatso'er you do" (4:77–84). In both passages the heroines admire the beloved's mobility; the nun's lover, after all is a chevalier, an expert rider. The three Marias will make the connection of women to horses explicit, referring frequently to their pleasure in passages that are not very different from Phaedra's lust for Hippolytus. Elsewhere, the Portuguese women defy men to try to "break our spirits with the bridle and a tight rein." They go so far as to reverse the traditional paradigm of the immobility of the woman weaving with the mobility of the chevalier in this passage:

17. On the lover as rider and the double entendre of "je prenais tout ce que vous faisiez," see Kamuf, *Fictions*, pp. 62–63.

They wanted the three of us to sit in parlors, patiently embroidering our days with the many silences, the many soft words and gestures that custom dictates. But . . . we have refused to be cloistered, we are quietly or brazenly stripping ourselves of our habits all of a sudden. . . . The three of us will weave even more webs if necessary—cunning spiders spinning out of our own selves our art, our advantage, our freedom, or our order.[18]

The shift from woman as spinner (and spinster) to woman as spider is worth noting, since it resembles the conflation of Arachne in Ariadne that, as we have seen, is a repeated motif from Sappho onward. The Marias similarly oscillate between images of webs as imprisoning or creative; what unites Phaedra, the Portuguese nun, and the Marias, what enables them to escape the immobility that would otherwise imprison them, is the inscription of desire in the act of writing.

Time is perhaps the most flexible prop in the theater of the nun's emotions, for she moves from the imperfect tense of fascination to the future tense of incertitude, and the past tense of nostalgia. Since her letters have no date, no time, no salutation, no signature, they indeed seem removed from praxis. Being dateless, they seem ageless; they exemplify the temporal autonomy of narrative.

In the nun's reverie on the balcony, the use of the imperfect tense is sustained by repetition: the nun often watched the chevalier ride by, and every time she would engage in the same process of fiction making. Her ritual reenactment whenever he appeared establishes a link between repetitive event and narrative inspiration that, significantly, depends on an absence. They did not yet know one another, but the nun fills in the gaps by narrating what she felt, imagined, persuaded herself to believe. This moment marks the birth of her vocation, the vocation of iterative narrative.[19] All amorous discourses are iterative. The heroine ceaselessly evokes a beloved who no longer cares (or never did) and reiterates events (such as lovemaking) long since past, as if she can discover some law of recurrence that either will make the lover reappear or will sustain her reveries by focusing on quantity and reciprocity. "A *thousand* times *a day I send* my sighs to you; *everywhere* they seek you out, but all they *bring* me *in return* for *so*

18. Barreño et al., *The Three Marias*, pp. 17, 34, hereinafter cited parenthetically in the text.

19. See Gérard Genette, *Narrative Discourse: An Essay in Method*, trans. Jane E. Lewin (Ithaca: Cornell Univ. Press, 1980), chap. 3.

much anguish is the warning voice of my sad fate, which will not let me console myself, which *keeps whispering,* 'Stop, Mariane, *stop torturing* yourself *in vain; stop seeking* a lover whom you will never see *again*'" (339–40, my italics). All the italicized words reveal the nun's obsession with repeated utterance, with two moments at the same time, with the duration and frequency of iterative narrative.[20] The mere act of standing on the balcony, on the site where she first consecrated her love, has such cumulative force as a result of iteration that the nun is overwhelmed with painful memories for the rest of the day; everything reminds her of when she used to see him—all objects, all sights, all words. The nun is obsessed with questions of motive, cause and effect, repetition and return. What made the chevalier keep riding by her balcony? What made him keep coming to her room? What made him leave her on certain occasions and not on others? What aroused him then and what might arouse him now? Why did he write initially, then remain silent for six months? How can she get him to write frequently? How can she sustain her own passion by writing?

The answer to the latter question lies in the technique of the letters. Critics have long been puzzled by the apparent masochism of Mariane's many confessions of "affection for this misery which you alone have brought upon me" and her exhortations to the chevalier to "continue to make me suffer" (339, 341). After contemplating the happiness she would feel if she could join him in France, she demurs, "I will not nourish a hope that is so sure to give me pleasure; I wish to have only feelings of sorrow" (341). By nourishing her sorrow, she thus sustains her passion in a variety of remarkably subtle ways. First, she takes pleasure in justifying his actions, despite all the evidence of his treachery. As in the *Heroides,* the process of retrospection begins with denial and disbelief. It is inconceivable that the chevalier will not return, will not write, that she will never see him again, that he seduced and abandoned her. She tries to imagine this possibility, then rejects it: "But no, I cannot bring myself to think so harshly of you; I am too deeply interested in justifying you. I do not wish to believe that you have forgotten me. Am I not unhappy enough without tormenting myself with false suspicions? And why should I force myself to forget all the efforts you made to convince me of your love?" (340). Just as Hypsipyle justifies Jason by saying that "Love is quick to believe; may it prove that I am hasty, and have brought a groundless

20. Ibid., pp. 116, 138–43.

charge against my lord!" (*Heroides*, 6:21–22), the nun quickly replaces her doubts with remorse for having doubted in the first place. This posture becomes increasingly untenable as time goes by, but the nun's commitment to it intensifies rather than diminishes. Not only does she exhort the chevalier to increase her suffering, but after thanking him for the "despair you cause me," she confesses in the third letter, "I despise the tranquillity in which I lived before knowing you. Adieu . . . my love grows with every moment. How many things I still have to say to you . . ." (352). The three sentences have a logic characteristic of amorous discourse. Having made the lover the repository of all identity and desire, the heroine memorializes everything that is related to the image of the beloved and despises everything else. The very confession (which is not unlike Heloise's audacious claim that she would rather be Abelard's whore than Augustus' empress), not only proclaims but augments desire. The act of writing, in other words, arouses desire, and the more she desires, the more she has to say.

Another reason that the nun holds so tenaciously to her suffering is that it enables her to sustain the illusion of the chevalier's active engagement with her, for she prefers anything—even his active hatred—to his indifference. She bombards him with questions concerning his wishes, his desires, his demands of her, when the sad fact is that he wants nothing because he no longer cares for her. To ward off recognition of this fact she stages confrontations, as in her third letter: "What will become of me; what would you have me do? I find myself so far from everything I had once anticipated. I imagined that you would write me from all the places through which you passed, and that your letters would be very long; that you would sustain my passion with the hope of seeing you again" (349). Frequently in iterative narrative, the heroine is forced to recognize that when the future becomes present, it seldom resembles the vision she had of it in the past. The sense of distance and detachment is particularly notable here, for it is marked by paralysis as well as disappointment. The nun recognizes that some action must be taken to remedy her situation, but she is incapable of initiating it. Rather than doing, she asks, "What is to be done?" She appeals to the lover, invokes action, threatens vengeance, vacillates between alternatives from sentence to sentence, but does nothing. Her questions echo those of Ovid's Ariadne, lamenting her exile from her lover, her father, and her homeland ("What am I to do? Whither shall I take myself. . . . where am I to go?" [10:59, 64]). Deloffre and Rougeot cite many examples of the persistent pattern of such resemblances between the *Heroides* and the *Portuguese Letters*. They do the same thing with Racine's heroines (Phaedra, Hermione, Medea), citing Guilleragues' many Racinian allusions and his friendship with Racine as evidence that Guilleragues wrote the letters. But while meticulously accounting for these allusions to the *Heroides* and to Racine, the two scholars make no attempt to place the letters in the context of amorous discourse. What Guilleragues and Racine took specifically from Ovid was a conception of erotic desire fueled by absence, by memory and retrospective recital, by the violent vacillation between love and hate, thoroughly removed from exterior scenes and action.[21]

In her first letter, Mariane still believes that the chevalier may send for her or at least write to her, but subsequent letters chart her slowly dawning awareness of utter abandonment and betrayal. She nevertheless continues to proclaim her fidelity and to defy those who would make her repent. In her second letter, she reveals the increasingly fictive nature of her project when she poignantly confesses:

> I could content myself with your remembering me, but I dare not be sure even of that. When I saw you every day I did not limit my hopes to this, but you have made me understand that I must submit to your will in everything. And yet I do not regret having adored you. . . . I am even glad to have been betrayed by you. All the harshness of your absence— eternal though it may prove to be—in no way diminishes the strength of my love. I want the whole world to know of it. I make no secret of it, and I am delighted to have done all that I did for you alone and in defiance of all propriety. It was my honor, my religion, to love you desperately for the rest of my life once I had begun to love you. (354– 55)

Since the nun speaks elsewhere of the risks she has taken by outraging the morals of her church, country, and family, each of whom could exact vengeance for her transgressions, it is particularly notable that

---

21. See Deloffre and Rougeot, "Analyse d'un chef-d'oeuvre," pp. 3–33. The editors discuss the literary circle in which Guilleragues moved, which included La Rochefoucauld, Mme de Lafayette, Mme de Sévigné, Racine, and Bussy-Rabutin (paraphraser of Heloise's letters). My comments on the nun's inaction are indebted to Roland Barthes's discussion of Racinian Eros in *On Racine*, trans. Richard Howard (New York: Hill and Wang, 1964). Barthes, too, fails to place the *Portuguese Letters* within the genre, a failure that seems all the more paradoxical since he was later to make his own contribution to the genre, *A Lover's Discourse: Fragments* (1977). There is no question that he was thoroughly familiar both with the *Heroides* and with the *Portuguese Letters*, although he makes no direct reference to either in his *Lover's Discourse*.

she, like Heloise before her, takes an audacious stand here in defense of her own honor. From this self-assertion, however, she goes to the other extreme of absolute submission to her lover's will: in this, too, her motive is identical to Heloise's, for the fiction of the lover's mastery and command over her is necessary to sustain the illusion of his abiding interest. It is, in short, yet another strategy to circumvent the reality of his indifference.

The nun has a variety of other such strategies at her disposal, which have long puzzled the critics. They are scandalized, for instance, by her desire to become the chevalier's servant; she tells him that she would have served him with far more zeal than his two Portuguese servants, whose happiness she envies (45). When she goes so far as to speculate about waiting on the chevalier's new mistress, critics cite the passage as evidence of her madness, her degradation, her masochism.[22] The nun's suggestion does not appear unusual, however, when it is placed within the context of amorous discourse. Ovid's Briseis, we may recall, suggests that Achilles let her "be a lowly slave of yours. . . . Only let not your lady be harsh with me, I pray . . . and suffer her not to tear my hair before your eyes, while you lightly say of me: 'She, too, once was mine.' Or, suffer it even so, if only I am not despised and left behind—this is the fear, ah woe is wretched me, that shakes my very bones!" (3:75–82). The passage illustrates the heroine's characteristic desperation in negotiating with her lover; Briseis offers herself on the condition that the new mistress not abuse her, then immediately reverses herself and confesses that she would rather endure anything than abandonment. What most critics of the *Portuguese Letters* have overlooked, moreover, is that the suggestion to serve her rival is a strategy calculated to keep all possibilities, all desire, and all writing open—to exclude, to conclude nothing. In her fourth letter, the nun recalls that the chevalier once confessed that he loved a woman in Paris; she urges him: "Write me everything she says to you. Perhaps I will find in them some reason to console myself or to make me more inconsolable. . . . Everything that means something to you is very dear to me, for I am completely devoted to all that interests you. I have no interest left in my own life. Often I think I have

---

22. E.g., Spitzer, pp. 121–22; Peter Dronke, "Héloise and Marianne: Some Reconsiderations," *Romanische Forschungen* 72:3–4 (1960), 223–56. Deloffre and Rougeot discover a parallel in Catullus' Ariadne, who similarly suggests to Theseus that he take her along as his slave. See "Analyse d'un chef-d'oeuvre," p. 6.

enough humility to serve her whom you love" (347). The French makes even clearer the speculative nature of her thought here. ("J'y trouverais, peut-être, des raisons de me consoler, ou de m'affliger davantage. . . . Il y a des moments où il me semble que j'aurais assez de soumission pour servir celle que vous aimez" [57].) It also reveals the close alliance of sorrow and joy, hatred and love. By her fourth letter the nun has reached the point where her vocation can be sustained equally by consoling or by tormenting herself—with the emphasis on *herself*. The chevalier has become increasingly irrelevant to the emotions she seeks to nurture. Indeed, by the end of this letter she has made the astonishing discovery that the chevalier is irrelevant even as a correspondent; rather than send her letter, she keeps it to continue writing.

This remarkable process of fiction making is launched in the very first paragraph of the first letter, when the nun refers to "this separation, to which my grief, imaginative as it is, can give no name poignant enough" (339) ("cette absence, à laquelle ma douleur, toute ingénieuse qu'elle est, ne peut donner un nom assez funeste" [39]). *Ingénieuse* means not only "ingenious" but "gifted," "clever," "inspired," "imaginative"; *ingénier*, moreover, means "to strain one's ingenuity, to exercise one's wits." These nuances of ingenuity and exercise are highlighted in the three Marias' response to the nun's letters when they confess that their main interest, like Mariane's is "not so much the object of our passion, which is a mere pretext, but passion itself . . . not so much passion itself, which is a mere pretext, but its exercise" (1). As with *ingénier*, the word *funeste* has nuances not captured by "poignant," including connotations of fatality and death. It thus reinforces the nun's declaration in the next sentence: "Alas, my eyes have lost the only light that gave them life; they have nothing now but tears, and I use them only in incessant weeping since I have learned that you are determined upon this separation which I cannot bear, which will yet be my death" (339).

Even death, which is one of Mariane's major obsessions, has a fictive quality that becomes more pronounced as the chevalier becomes more remote, although as early as her first letter she confesses that her memories are so overwhelming that "I flattered myself with the thought that I was dying of love" (340). In subsequent letters, the fantasy escalates. She imagines that the chevalier wants her to die of love, which she not only is willing to do but anticipates with great voluptuousness. If the chevalier desires her death, his feelings are still volatile; hatred is far better than indifference. In one tumultuous paragraph in her third letter, the nun's thoughts move swiftly from her lover's ingratitude for all she has sacrificed, to remorse, then defiance. She concludes by revealing the fictive nature of despair:

> I have lost my reputation. . . . But I am well aware that my remorse is not so real; that with all my heart I should gladly have wished to risk greater dangers for love of you; and that I take a fatal pleasure in having put life and honor at stake. . . . It even seems to me that I am not so completely satisfied either with my grief or the excess of my love. . . . I live, a faithless creature, and do just as much to preserve my life as to destroy it. Ah, I die of shame! My despair exists only in my letters! (350–51)

The source of Mariane's dissatisfaction with her grief and her love is that neither is excessive enough; she concludes with the speculation that writing not only augments despair but creates it. "If I love you as much as I have told you a thousand times," she reasons, "should I not have died long ago? I have deceived you; it is for you to reproach me. . . . Treat me harshly, reproach me that my emotions are not ardent enough; be more difficult to please; let me hear that you wish me to die of love; I entreat you to help me in this way so that I may overcome the weakness of my sex and put an end to my irresolution by genuine despair" (351). By thus distinguishing the despair writing creates from a "genuine" (*véritable*) despair, the nun signals once again that she is straining her ingenuity, and that—as with her *ingénieuse* sorrow—her project is illusory, fictive, tied more to her letters than to her lover. By the end of this letter, her imagination has leapt forward to envision the effect her suicide would have on him; she perceives that he would probably boast of having inspired such a desperate passion and would exploit it to seduce other women. Ovid's heroines, we may recall, engaged in precisely the same anticipatory process; Briseis, for example, tells Achilles, "If your love for me has turned to weariness, compel the death of her whom you compel to live without you!" (3:139).[23] The repetition and parallelism emphasizes the cause-and-effect relation between his abandonment and her death; it is a rhetorical strategy that fixes responsibility on the se-

---

23. Cited in Deloffre and Rougeot, "Analyse d'un chef-d'oeuvre," p. 5.

ducer, compelling him to take the consequences and pursue them to their logical conclusion. Thus, as with Ovid's heroines, the Portuguese nun's threats of suicide are designed to make the seducer feel guilty; they are a last-ditch effort to see if death will evoke a response from the man unmoved by love. The only act that postpones her suicide is writing.

Writing is the gesture by which the nun simultaneously effaces the possibility of suicide and keeps it legible. She does the same thing to the chevalier by diminishing him and elevating her passion. The doubleness of the project is characteristic of amorous epistolary discourse: the erotic scene of writing is also the site of exorcism. Far from recollecting the chevalier in tranquillity, the nun dwells on his treachery, his baseness, his ingratitude, his selfishness. Even his lovemaking was grossly inept. Her greatest moments of happiness, she now remembers, were always spoiled by doubts of his fidelity, and fears of abandonment. Whereas she treasured every moment they spent together, he frequently chose to squander his time hunting or gambling. He is, she finally realizes, unworthy of her passion, and she warns him to be aware that she now sees all his despicable qualities: "Sachez que je m'aperçois que vous êtes indigne de tous mes sentiments, et que je connais toutes vos méchantes qualités" (63). Lest he take too much pride in his conquest, she reminds him that she was young, credulous, sheltered in the convent since childhood and that everyone had spoken well of him. She is particularly embittered by the realization that the conquest was carefully calculated from the outset and that even his passion was feigned:

> I am all alone in my unhappiness. This is what crushes me, and I shudder at the thought that in all our pleasures, your deepest feelings were never really engaged. I realize now the deceitfulness of all your acts. You deceived me every time you said that it made you happy to be alone with me. Your ardors and transports were due only to my importunity; you had calculatingly planned to kindle my passion; you looked upon it only as another conquest and your heart was never really moved by my love. (349)

Initially, the nun occupies herself in trying to understand why the chevalier is in a "frenzy" to make her unhappy. By her last letter, however, she is forced to recognize that she has not mattered enough for either passionate love or violent hatred, although she has attributed both extremes to him from the outset. The nun prefers even enmity to ennui, because it would necessitate the chevalier's active involvement and his remembrance of her. She, similarly, prefers feeling jealousy to confronting a void. In her last letter she says: "I would have endured your hatred and even all the pangs of jealousy which your affection for another woman might have aroused in me. Then, at least, I would have had some passion to combat, but your indifference to me is insupportable" (357, minor changes).

Like Ovid's heroines and Heloise, Mariane is obsessed with the paradoxical relation of spontaneity and calculation. The nun discovers that, even in abandoning oneself to passion, one must remain aloof, suspicious, and one must learn to suspect man's motives, sincerity, engagement. Passion, she learns, inevitably involves some measure of calculation and artifice; in both love and letter writing, spontaneity is a carefully nurtured illusion that relies on artifice. Love, moreover, is seldom reciprocal, never symmetrical; one cannot make oneself loved, however volatile the force of one's own feelings are, as the nun reflects poignantly:

> Why must I learn from you the imperfection and pain of an attachment that is not lasting . . . the whole bitter course of a passionate love that is not mutual? What blind and malicious fate is it that drives us irresistibly to those who have feelings only for others? . . .
> From the very beginning, all too openly, I made you aware of my deep passion; one should use more subtle art to make oneself loved. One must be ingenious in finding means to inflame a lover. Love alone is not enough to arouse love. [Il faut de l'artifice pour se faire aimer; il faut chercher avec quelque adresse les moyens d'enflammer, et l'amour tout seul ne donne point de l'amour (67).] (358, 361)

The French *adresse* has a particular pointedness here, since it is related to the body and to love as well as to letters. The first meaning refers to the body's movements; physical activities demanding *l'adresse*, require skill and dexterity; in context then, the nun means that one must be sexually expert to inflame a lover. The second connotation involves finesse, savoir-faire, delicacy of spirit; and the third—an address on a letter—relates to the letter the nun is writing. Finally, *l'adresse* is also an appeal to the lover. Therefore, if love is inseparable from artifice, so are letters. That this correspondence becomes a veritable vocation for the nun is made abundantly clear when she contrasts his indifference to her absorption in her project; she pities his inability to love, to feel, to be deeply involved, maliciously hinting at one point that perhaps he is only aroused by ill-treatment from his mistresses. Like Ovid's heroines and Heloise, she explores the distinction between heart and pen, between feelings and writing, when she reflects: "It seems to me that I am doing the greatest possible wrong to the feelings of my heart in trying to make them clear in writing to you. How happy I should be if you could guess them by the violence of your own!" (353). Writing inevitably falsifies passion by spelling it out; hearts that are truly in sympathy do not need writing—or even words. This compulsion to express the inexpressible is a characteristic paradox of amorous epistolary discourse, as is the heroine's complaint that she has been consigned to a medium of expression antipathetic to feeling. Yet she is already reconciling herself to the only medium she has; as early as this second letter, indeed, her focus begins to shift from the lover's absence to the process of composition. Furthermore, although this letter begins with an assertion that writing distorts passion and does violence to the purity and depth of feeling, Mariane goes on to comment on the transitory nature of "fleeting desire, coming and going with the pleasure of the moment" (354). Writing, in contrast, endures. Even its falsifications are advantages, for instead of having to dwell on the chevalier's new mistresses, the nun instead can defy him "to forget me utterly; I flatter myself that I have brought you to such a point that your pleasures must be imperfect without me; and I am much happier than you because I am much busier" (354). Only in her letters can the nun dispense with the unpleasant facts about the chevalier's present pleasures by persuading herself, flattering herself, that she is indispensable; such defiance of the facts would not be possible if he were present. As a nun, relieved of distractions from the world outside the convent, only one thing keeps Mariane so busy: the vocation of writing, the relentless rearrangement of past, present, and future.

By the end of this second letter, the nun's desire has become more and more detached from the actual object; she ends by remarking, "My love no longer depends upon the way in which you treat me" (355). As Barthes observes, "The subject lives the scene without being . . . deceived by it. Classical rhetoric possessed a figure of speech to express this imagination of the past, hypotyposis . . . the image takes the place of the thing."[24] By the fourth letter the nun no longer needs even to mail what she writes; she allows the lieutenant to leave without delivering her letter and recognizes that "I write more for myself than for you. I want only to release myself" (348, minor changes). ("J'écris plus pour moi que pour vous, je ne cherche qu'à me soulager" [58].) *Soulager* signifies the easing of burdens, pressures, feelings, the release of pent-up frustrations. She effaces the chevalier by focusing increasingly on her motives for writing and on a retrospective recital of her involvement with him. He did not seduce her, she now maintains; instead, "the violence of my own desire seduced me" (342).

By her fifth letter, she has so exorcised him that Mariane can clearly distinguish between the chevalier and her passion: "I realized the whole terrible power of my love only when I exerted all my efforts to rid myself of it! . . . I discovered that it was not so much you as my own passion to which I was attached; it was remarkable how I suffered while struggling with it even after you had become despicable to me through your wretched behavior" (357). He is odious, but her desire remains intact; she recognizes by her fifth letter how completely the actual lover is a mere pretext for her passion. Her last letter, indeed, is a mixture of cold rage and the lucidity that comes with repudiation; it is written in response to the cold, curt, hypocritical note she has just received from him, in which he swears eternal friendship. This response lets her know that he has received all her previous letters and that they left him unmoved. She is filled with fury: "I detest your frankness and easy-going attitude. Did I ever sincerely beg you to tell me the truth? You needed only never to write; I would never have searched to be disburdened of my illusions" (357, minor changes). The question is convincing evidence that she has been conscious of the fictiveness of her endeavor from the outset. But this realization nurtures rather than nullifies her desire. What she dismantles is not her passion but its object: "I realize now that you are not worthy of my love; too clearly now I see all your despicable qualities" (357, minor changes).

Critics have frequently compared the nun to the Princess of Clèves, criticizing both heroines for their renunciation of the world

---

24. Barthes, *On Racine*, p. 18.

for the cloister. Few have understood that the Portuguese nun, like the princess, acts not to renounce but to preserve her passion.[25] For Mariane, as for Heloise and Ovid's heroines, passion is not the consolation prize after the real man departs but, instead, the mark—the goal, the objective, the distinction. The act of writing becomes the proof of the distinction between the man and the desire; this vocation enables the nun to proclaim, "J'ai éprouvé que vous m'étiez moins cher que ma passion" (62). The word *éprouvé* is perhaps the most crucial in this letter; it signifies the attempt to test, to verify certain qualities; it also refers to what one learns from experience, as well as one's trials, what makes one suffer. All three meanings should be considered simultaneously both here and in another crucial passage, which begins with the words *N'éprouvé-je:*

> Have I not proved that a heart is never more deeply affected than when first it is made aware of the depths of feeling of which it is capable? All its emotions are centered upon the idol which it builds for itself. Its first wounds are neither to be healed nor to be effaced. The passions which come freely to the heart's aid and give it power to express and satisfy itself afford it a profound emotion that is never to be recaptured. All the pleasures which it seeks, *though without true desire to find them,* serve only to show that nothing is so dear to it as the remembrance of past sorrows. (358, my italics)

The italics point up the underlying impulse of amorous discourse: to make the past present without ceasing to cherish it as memory. The erotic scene can be evoked endlessly through repetition and rehearsal; therefore the heart does not even desire to find the pleasures it seeks.[26] Mariane memorializes what she loves most, which is what she herself has created: her desire and her discourse.

   Her fifth letter commences with the declared aim of writing for the last time, in obedience to the chevalier. But the letter displays the same transgression of the beloved's injunction that Heloise's last letter to Abelard contained, for the nun contradicts herself near the end when she says: "I shall write you just one more letter to show you that in time I shall perhaps be more composed. What pleasure I shall take

25. On the Princess of Clèves, see Nancy K. Miller, "Emphasis Added: Plots and Plausibilities in Women's Fiction," *PMLA* 96 (Jan. 1981), 36–48.
   26. Barthes, *On Racine*, pp. 17–18.

in reproaching you for your wickedness when it no longer touches me
so deeply; and when I have come so far as to tell you that I despise
you, that I am able to speak with complete indifference of how you
deceived me, that I have forgotten both pleasures and sorrows . . .
how then I shall rejoice!" (361). The passage reveals yet another rhetorical strategy characteristic of amorous discourse: the resolution to
express the indifference that lies ahead. Paradoxically, the anticipation of such indifference enables the writing to go forward, since it
necessitates still another letter, which will demonstrate that indifference. Ironically, if the nun were ever to become truly indifferent,
she would have no interest in writing to the chevalier. Her situation is
the opposite of the one Proust will later describe in *Remembrance of
Things Past:* "[Swann] had made a vow that if ever he ceased to love
[Odette] . . . he would implacably exhibit to her an indifference that
would at length be sincere . . . [but] with his love had vanished the
desire to show that he was in love no longer."[27] The Portuguese nun,
in contrast, consumed with the desire to show that she no longer
loves, demonstrates that she is through neither desiring nor writing.
Her last words reveal that writing is always inaugural, always in the
process of becoming. "I am a fool to keep repeating the same things
over and over again. . . . But I will write no more. Am I obliged to give
you an exact account of all my diverse impulses and feelings?" (362,
minor changes) ("Je suis une folle de redire les mêmes choses si sou-
vent. . . . je crois même que je ne vous écrirai plus; suis-je obligée de
vous rendre un compte exact de tous mes divers mouvements?" [69]).

The question marks a radical departure from the premise of the
nun's early letters, which was that the chevalier was withholding the
thing she most needed and that he owed it to her to meet her needs
and her demands. Here, she in a sense turns the tables, by implying
that it is the chevalier who needs, who is making demands on her. The
word *compte* is particularly evocative, since it suggests the evaluation of
a quantity (like the amount of love the nun gave him). It can also
signify a profit, an advantage; the profitable advantage the nun has

27. Cited by Genette, pp. 80–81. Genette cites the same impulse in *Jean Santeuil:*
"Sometimes passing in front of the hotel he remembered the rainy days when he used
to bring his nursemaid that far. . . . But he remembered them without the melancholy
that he then thought he would surely some day savor on feeling that he no longer loved
her. For this melancholy, projected in anticipation prior to the indifference that lay
ahead, came from his love. And this love existed no more (p. 38)."

discovered is the act of writing. *Rendre un compte* means "to analyze, to expose, to explicate"; the nun's five letters are themselves an *explication de texte* in which she simultaneously analyzes and exposes her desire. Amorous discourses frequently revolve around such confrontations couched in economic terms. The heroine feels that the seducer owes her something; she wants to settle accounts, to make him pay. In all amorous discourse, the heart is the gift that the lover imagines giving away; it is what the lover values above all, and every time it is "returned," it is all that remains.[28] Thus, the nun demands payment for having given away her heart—and with it her identity, for the chevalier's abandonment initially made the nun feel annihilated; she reflects in her last letter that he had filled her with a passion that drove her out of her mind. She now sees that he stole her being when he stole her heart. He first created her out of nothingness, then capriciously plunged her back into nothingness, reducing her to a sense of utter nullification.[29] She recalls, "Never before had I heard such charming things as you were continually saying to me. It seemed to me that I owed to you the attractions and beauties which you discovered in me, and of which you first made me conscious" (362).

The nun's fifth letter thus represents an escape from annihilation, from nullification. She finally discovers that he did not invent her or her beauty; he possessed her, but the traits he found in her were there all along. With the realization that they are her possessions, not his, she regains her self-possession. Writing is thus a strategy of recuperation, in the senses both of healing and of reparation. (Again, the significance of the chevalier as colonist and of the nun's disenfranchisement as conquest comes to mind.) In the process of self-reparation, Mariane simultaneously achieves her desire for recognition and recognizes her desire. All her *divers mouvements*—her various transports, impulses, emotions, passions—will continue to be the subjects of and motives for her discourse. At the end, by effacing the chevalier, yet keeping him legible, she keeps the circuit of desire open. The nun inaugurates her true vocation of writing by the "end" of her letters; Roland Barthes's amorous fragments similarly help to illuminate the paradoxes—as well as the strategy of recuperation—at play in all discourses of desire: "To know that one does not write for the other, to know that these things I am going to write will never

28. Barthes, *A Lover's Discourse*, p. 52.
29. See Barthes, *On Racine*, pp. 27–28.

cause me to be loved by the one I love (the other) . . . that it is precisely *there where you are not*—this is the beginning of writing."[30] In confronting this characteristic paradox, the Portuguese nun becomes one of the elect, canonized not just by passion but by the art that makes her letters a pivotal document in the canon of amorous discourse.

30. Barthes, *A Lover's Discourse,* p. 100.

There seem to be two kinds of imagination:
1. Keen, impetuous . . . imagination, leading instantly
to action, chafing and languishing at a delay of even
twenty-four hours. . . . characterized by impatience, [it]
flares into anger against what it cannot obtain. It
perceives external objects but these merely add fuel to
its fire; it assimilates them and at once converts them
to increase the passion.
2. Imagination which kindles only slowly, but which
after a time no longer perceives external objects and
succeeds in becoming exclusively concerned with, and
dependent on, its own passion.

STENDHAL, *On Love*

4
Passion as Suffering: The Composition of Clarissa Harlowe

Clarissa Writing, Arabella Playing. Louis Michel Halbou made this engraving from a drawing by Clément Pierre Marillier (1740–1808), in *The Novels of Samuel Richardson* (New York: Crowscup and Sterling, 1901).

Forward, Backward, and Belfour

In the multilingual meanderings of amorous discourse, *Clarissa* comes at a critical crossroads. From this point forward, the generic path from Ovid to Heloise to the Portuguese nun seems to detour, for the solitary heroine writing cloistered in a cell or a convent gives way to multiple correspondents, myriad topics, numerous subplots, scores of characters—a vastly expanded textual *topos*. There is absolutely no question that the genre I am charting becomes assimilated into the novel, like a footpath joining a highway; my aim is to show that its trace nevertheless remains vital not only in Richardson's novel but in subsequent fiction. *Clarissa* has been variously treated as a central document in the rise of the bourgeoisie, as a revelation of the Puritan character, as a Derridean exercise in the struggles of interpretation.[1] My focus is on Clarissa's writing as a discourse of pathos, for it is this strain that connects Clarissa to Ovid's heroines, to Heloise, to the Portuguese nun. Following Bakhtin's observation that the discourse of pathos in the novel "almost always works to restore some *other* genre . . . that, in [its] own unmediated and pure form, [has] lost [its] own base in reality,"[2] my aim in this chapter is to demonstrate that the specific genre invoked is that of amorous epistolary discourse. If the *Heroides* and the letters of Heloise and Mariane mark the "unmediated and pure form" of amorous epistolary discourse, Clarissa's letters, insofar as they are a discourse of pathos, keep the ancient Ovidian genre alive. In subsequent chapters we shall see the further assimilation of the ancient genre in Brontë, James, and Faulkner, but in their texts too, it never entirely disappears. With *The Three Marias*,

1. Christopher Hill, "Clarissa Harlowe and Her Times," *Essays in Criticism* 5 (1955), 315–40, and Ian Watt, *The Rise of the Novel* (Berkeley: Univ. of California Press, 1957), relate the novel to the rise of the bourgeoisie; Cynthia Griffin Wolff relates it to Puritanism in *Samuel Richardson and the Eighteenth-Century Puritan Character* (Hamden, Connecticut: Archon Books, 1972), and William Beatty Warner draws on Derrida in *Reading "Clarissa": The Struggles of Interpretation* (New Haven: Yale Univ. Press, 1979).
2. Mikhail Bakhtin, *The Dialogic Imagination: Four Essays*, ed. Michael Holquist, trans. Caryl Emerson and Michael Holquist (Austin: Univ. of Texas Press, 1981), p. 394.

the original genre once again reemerges in a form closest to its generic model; that text will demonstrate how a genre can simultaneously
be assimilated and restored.

The Portuguese Letters, long credited with establishing the foundations of the epistolary novel, mark the pivotal transition from the
Ovidian amorous epistle to the Richardsonian epistolary novel. What
is most significant about this critical commonplace is the consensus
among scholars through the ages that the unique contribution of
these letters involves the authenticity of the emotion conveyed—the
nun's passion and pathos. With these letters, "distress" becomes a
fictional technique that sustains the illusion of writing-to-the-moment
in a state of acute anxiety and passionate intensity. Charlotte Morgan
calls the letters "perhaps the greatest single influence of the century . . . the first example of realism of emotional detail." Margaret
Doody, in her study of the evolution of Richardson's fiction, notes,
"Since the Lettres Portugaises the letter had been recognized as the true
voice of feeling." F. C. Green says that the nun's "disjointed utterances, hailed as proof of the genuineness of the letters by credulous
writers, are an early manifestation of the sentimental novel." Thus,
long before the rise of the novel, which Ian Watt attributed to Defoe,
Richardson, and Fielding, the Portuguese Letters heralded the revolt
against classicism and the emergence of sentiment in an intensely
realistic form. Yet realism is a word as suspect as femininity; what
emerges in tracing the generic influence of the Portuguese Letters is not
so much an authentic portrayal of feminine passion as a representation dependent on the codes of literature that have come before. The
influence of the Portuguese Letters on the English novel, as well as the
French, was nevertheless enormous; indeed, Robert Adams Day
maintains that Richardson gave the novel but its second great impetus; its first came from the Portuguese Letters.[3] Although it is thus

3. Charlotte Morgan, The Rise of the Novel of Manners: A Study of English Prose Fiction
between 1600 and 1740 (New York: Columbia Univ. Press, 1911; rpr. New York: Russell
and Russell, 1963), pp. 70–75; Margaret Doody, A Natural Passion: A Study of the Novels
of Samuel Richardson (Oxford: Clarendon Press, 1974), p. 23; F. C. Green, "Who Was
the Author of the 'Lettres portugaises'?" Modern Language Review 21 (1926), 159–67;
Ian Watt, The Rise of the Novel (Berkeley: Univ. of California Press, 1957); Robert
Adams Day, Told in Letters: Epistolary Fiction before Richardson (Ann Arbor: Univ. of
Michigan Press, 1966), pp. 113, 116. See also Max von Waldberg, Der empfindsame
Roman in Frankreich (Strasbourg and Berlin: Verlag von Karl J. Trubner, 1906), chap.
2; and F. C. Green, French Novelists, Manners, and Ideas: From the Renaissance to the
Revolution (London: J. M. Dent, 1928), pp. 54–56.

difficult to overestimate the effect of these celebrated letters, a forward look at their profound influence on the development of the epistolary novel must be balanced with a backward look, for a recognition of their relation to the *Heroides*, as well as to Heloise, reveals a far older generic pattern of pathos and desire.[4]

Janus-like, *Clarissa* thus looks two ways: backward to Mariane, whose unique contribution to the development of the novel was precisely the stylistic intensity of her passion and her pathos; and forward to Rosa Coldfield, whose pathos marks the trace of amorous discourse in first-person narratives long after epistolarity ceases to be central. In *Clarissa*, then, amorous epistolary discourse is assimilated into the epistolary novel, but that does not mean it disappears. Quite the contrary: Clarissa's correspondence highlights it. Many of the essential motifs—the rebellion against the tyranny of fathers and lovers; their control of women and speech; the heroine's critique of the distorted representations of women; the conflicts between art and nature, calculation and spontaneity—remain intact. Clarissa combines the tragic grandeur of Ovid's heroines, the high ethical principles of Heloise, and the pathos of the Portuguese nun. The combination of *suasoriae* and *ethopoiiae*—as well as the elegant Ovidian refinements of those ancient rhetorical exercises—reemerge here, for Clarissa's discourse is on the one hand a sustained, logical, legal argument that culminates in a legal document, her will. On the other hand, it is a plea for pity, a testament to the sincerity of her sentiments, and an inscription of desire. In my view, most critics have paid far too little attention to that desire. It has been overlooked because Clarissa's desire takes the form of a funeral elegy, and it is as such that her discourse looks forward specifically to Rosa Coldfield's, which is another elegy of desire.

Thus, at this critical crossroads, two things happen to the genre of

---

4. Frédéric Deloffre and J. Rougeot, "Analyse d'un chef-d'oeuvre," in *Lettres portugaises, Valentins, et autres oeuvres de Guilleragues* (Paris: Garnier, 1962), compare the *Heroides* to *Lettres portugaises;* Leo Spitzer, in "Les *Lettres portugaises,*" *Romanische Forschungen* 65:1–2 (1954), 94–135, and Peter Dronke in "Héloïse and Marianne: Some Reconsiderations," *Romanische Forschungen* 72:3–4 (1960), 223–56, compare Heloise and Mariane, as does Peggy Kamuf, *Fictions of Feminine Desire: Disclosures of Heloise* (Lincoln: Univ. of Nebraska Press, 1982). François Jost discusses the differences between the *type portugais* and the *type Abélard* in his study of epistolary evolution ("L'Evolution d'un genre: le roman épistolaire dans les lettres occidentales," in *Essais de littérature comparée* [Fribourg, Switz.: Editions universitaires, 1968], 2:89–179, 380–402). No one, to my knowledge, discusses the *Heroides*, Heloise, and Mariane in the context of the generic development of amorous epistolary discourse which I am tracing here.

amorous epistolary discourse. While it is being assimilated into the genre of the epistolary novel, its trace is being illuminated, for the ancient genre loses neither its amatory, epistolary, and discursive distinctiveness, nor its capacity to generate authentic letters that directly influence the shape, direction, and meaning of the fictional correspondence. Just as the *Portuguese Letters* were imitated by fashionable letter writers in the salons of European capitals, generating replies and sequels for decades, Richardson's correspondence with Lady Bradshaigh had a profound effect on the shape of *Clarissa*. Her responses to the novel affected the final installment and led Richardson in later editions to add an increasingly unwieldy editorial apparatus to "clarify" his meaning and intention.[5] One can measure the extent of her influence by noting that in the definitive biography of Richardson, the editors devote an entire chapter to her; she shares equal billing with Clarissa in the chapter's title, "The Composition of *Clarissa:* Lady Bradshaigh."[6] Their correspondence is thus another provocative example of the transgressions of the boundaries of fiction, of the letter as literature, literature as a letter.

Lady Bradshaigh first writes to Richardson on 10 October 1748; the second installment of the novel had appeared in April of that year; the third and final one was due that fall. It is specifically Clarissa's discourse of pathos to which Lady Bradshaigh responds. She is moved to write because of rumors that Clarissa was to die in the final installment, and she beseeches Richardson to spare his heroine's life with all the vehemence of someone pleading for her own. The intrusion of fictiveness even in these authentic letters is evident in this close identification with Richardson's heroine and in Lady Bradshaigh's adoption of a penname, Belfour. She asks, "Is it possible, that he who has the art to please in softness, in the most natural, easy, humorous, and sensible manner, can resolve to give joy only to the ill-natured reader, and heave the compassionate breast with tears for irremediable woes?" Her plea thus concentrates on central issues in the entire novel: the conflict between art and nature, the response to pathos, and the difficulty of assessing the motives of the letter writer. On the one hand, reading his novel has, she believes, made her intimate with the workings of his heart: "I pretend to know your heart so well, that you must think it a crime, never to be forgiven, to leave vice tri-

5. See Warner, *Reading "Clarissa,"* chaps. 5 and 6.
6. T. C. Duncan Eaves and Ben D. Kimpel, *Samuel Richardson: A Biography* (Oxford: Clarendon Press, 1971), chap. 10.

umphant, and virtue depressed." She blames Richardson's advisers, who, she believes, "delight in horror, (detestable wretches!) insisted upon rapes, ruin, and destruction." She urges Richardson not to yield to them by killing off the heroine. Just as Clarissa suffers her father's curse both here and in the hereafter, Belfour usurps the authority of the father-author, Richardson, by warning him, "If you disappoint me, attend to my curse:—May the hatred of all the young, beautiful, and virtuous, for ever be your portion! and may your eyes never behold any thing but age and deformity! may you meet with applause only from envious old maids, surly bachelors, and tyrannical parents! may you be doomed to the company of such! and, after death, may their ugly souls haunt you!" She goes on to assure him that she is not merely a giddy girl of sixteen, but a mature matron, "past my romantic time of life, though young enough to wish two lovers happy in a married state." Lady Bradshaigh writes him again almost immediately (the letter is undated), again begging him to save his heroine's life and apologizing for "the incoherence of this tedious epistle; but write I must, or die, for I can neither eat or sleep till I am disburdened of my load."[7] Richardson's response on 26 October 1748 demonstrates his involvement with his impassioned reader and his active encouragement of the correspondence:

> I am pained for your apprehended pain, were you to read to the end; and the more so, I own, that I have lost my aim, and judge wrongly from my own heart and eyes, if there are not scenes to come that will affect so tender a heart as yours. . . .
> It would be difficult in me to deny myself the hope of such a correspondent to the end of my life. I love Miss Howe next to Clarissa; and I see very evidently in your letters that you are the twin-sister of that lady. And indeed I adore your spirit and your earnestness.[8]

Particularly notable about Richardson's words here is the appeal to the authority of the heart as a register of the sincerity and authenticity of emotion: if his reader's heart is not moved, he has misjudged his own. The relation of heart to eyes, of feeling to perception and to judgment are primary motifs in all amorous discourses. When Richardson describes his theory of epistolarity (Lovelace's etymology of

7. Lady Bradshaigh to Samuel Richardson, 10 Oct. 1748, in *The Correspondence of Samuel Richardson*, ed. Anna Laetitia Barbauld, 6 vols. (London: Richard Phillips, 1804), 4:177–83. On the dating of her second letter, see note 11 below.
8. Samuel Richardson to Lady Bradshaigh, 26 Oct. 1748, in *The Correspondence*, 4:193–94.

the word *correspondence* will be discussed presently), he reverses the customary hierarchy of speaking over writing; writing, he maintains, is "more pure" and "more ardent" precisely because of the "deliberation it allows, from the very preparation to, and action of writing"; it is free of interruption. He repeats yet another of the primary motifs of amorous discourse when he reflects that the pen "makes distance, presence; and brings back to sweet remembrance all the delights of presence; which makes even presence but body, while absence becomes the soul."[9]

Belfour responds to Richardson's encouragement by making a bargain with the author: she will read the next volume "if I find the dreaded horrid act is not perpetrated." Her close identification with the heroine is further evidence of the blurring of the boundaries between the fictional letters of Clarissa and her own authentic correspondence, for she concludes this letter by telling Richardson that she thought his story "would have torn my heart in a thousand pieces. . . . my hand trembles, for I can scarce hold my pen. I am as mad as the poor injured Clarissa; and am afraid I cannot help hating you, if you alter not your scheme." From this point forward she becomes an increasingly active participant in the text. Arguing from an alternative logic, she proposes an alternative ending to Richardson's. The happy ending she envisions in her first letters is fleshed into a full-fledged plot in her third letter: Lovelace, taken with a fever, repents on his deathbed; Clarissa marries him out of charity and compassion, after which he miraculously recovers to live blessedly as her husband.[10]

In her next letter, Belfour has read the next installment, in which Richardson has indeed killed off his heroine. Belfour consciously compares Richardson to Lovelace for this action: "The deadly blow is struck, as Lovelace says, after the most villainous of acts; you now can go no farther; my dear Clarissa is gone!—adieu my joys! and there drops a tear!"[11] In murdering his heroine, the author "can go no

---

9. Richardson's reflections on epistolarity are in a letter to Miss Westcomb [1746?], in *The Correspondence*, 3:245–46. See also John Carroll, ed., "Epistolary Theory and Practice," in *The Selected Letters of Samuel Richardson* (London: Oxford Univ. Press, 1964), pp. 31–35.

10. The first two quotations are from an undated letter Bradshaigh to Richardson, ca. 17 Nov. 1748, in *The Correspondence*, 4:200–201 (see note 11 below); her alternative plot for *Clarissa* is contained in a letter of 20 Nov. 1748, 4:202–206.

11. Bradshaigh to Richardson, n.d., in *The Correspondence*, 4:207. Eaves and Kimpel tentatively date the letter 17 Nov. 1748 because she mentions a letter of the 17th of the previous month in her early December letter. See *Samuel Richardson*, app., p. 643.

farther"; he has done his worst not only to his character but to the correspondent who feels betrayed and who cites her tears as evidence of her anguish.

The authentic correspondence thus contains all the essential elements of amorous epistolary discourse. Lady Bradshaigh inscribes her heart's desires in these letters, describing her alternative plot as "my own heart's wish" and confessing that it "came into my wild head; and, for my life, I could not help transmitting it to paper. Every thought relating to this affair takes possession of me like infatuation; for I am drawn from one thing to another, spite of all resistance."[12] The entire correspondence, indeed, draws repeatedly on the rhetoric of seduction: as early as his first response to Belfour, Richardson sends her the fifth volume and hopes that "you will favour me with a letter upon it—yet you must take care how you favour me too—men are naturally incroachers."[13]

Among the many fascinating aspects of this correspondence, the reversal of roles is one of the most intriguing. William Warner describes Belfour's seductiveness; her role is that "of a solicitous advisor who sees that Richardson has a 'noble' design 'within' him but fears he is in danger of losing it. She tempts and woos Richardson towards a revised ending."[14] They exchange tales about their early lives and loves and engage in debates about love and marriage as spirited as those of Abelard and Heloise. Says Lady Bradshaigh, echoing Clarissa's sentiments, "The laws are severe, at least in practice; but they were made by men, to justify their tyranny." When Richardson invokes the authority of the Patriarchs, Lady Bradshaigh retorts: "What do I care for the Patriarchs! If they took it into their heads to be tyrants, why should we allow them to be worthy examples to imitate?" He sees an element of fear as necessary in love; she argues that such elements—far from necessary—should never be a part of love.[15] Her arguments are thus frequently based on a logic at odds with Richardson's, and the correspondence is another demonstration of the dialogic dynamism we have been tracing.

---

12. Bradshaigh to Richardson, 10 Oct. 1748 and 20 Nov. 1748, in *The Correspondence*, 4:180, 202–3.
    13. Richardson to Bradshaigh, 26 Oct. 1748, in *The Correspondence*, 4:193.
    14. William Beatty Warner, "Proposal and Habitation: The Temporality and Authority of Interpretation in and about a Scene of Richardson's *Clarissa*," *boundary 2: 7* (1979), 169–99.
    15. Bradshaigh to Richardson, 28 July 1752, in *The Correspondence*, 6:193–95.

The famous story of their reluctance to meet face to face and the amount of ink spilled in negotiating such a meeting and deferring it[16] reveal the same underlying tensions about presence and absence, speech and writing, the letter as literature—in short, all the same highly charged issues in the fictional amorous correspondences of the genre. Indeed, on the one hand, Richardson argues that Belfour should be glad Clarissa was released from this miserable world into the bliss of the hereafter.[17] Yet, as Lady Bradshaigh reports, in trying to cajole her into meeting him, he asks "if [she] would choose to refer [her] knowledge of [him] to another world," to which the lady wittily responds, "*If* I was sure of our acquaintance there, I should be very indifferent as to our meeting in this; but if different places are allotted for higher and lower degrees of merit, I am very apprehensive your apartment and mine will be far distant from each other!"[18]

Again the stereotypical sex roles are reversed when Richardson confesses his diffidence, modesty, and shyness upon finally meeting her in person, and his relief that these qualities did not make him sink in her Ladyship's favor, noting that it is only "in writing, I own, I was always an impudent Man."[19] On the other hand, Lady Bradshaigh's mischievous wit, her love of pranks, raillery, and badinage are positively Lovelacean. "I shall frighten you with another letter so soon after my last," she writes on 20 November 1748. "Methinks I hear you say, 'What! every post! No respite! No quiet! No hopes of being relieved from the persecutions of this troublesome woman!' . . . I am impertinent, rude, tiresome, and every thing you can think of."[20] As so often happens in amorous discourse, she thus not only writes her part in it but invents dialogues and imagines the effect she has on her beloved Reader. Much later, she writes, "I *will* call you names . . . for you are . . . the most indulgent, unprejudiced, humblest, bearing, and forebearing correspondent that ever saucy woman was favoured with." She shares Richardson's view of *Tom Jones*'s immorality but laughs at it nevertheless, and at *Tristram Shandy* as well, while conceding that the latter possesses a "mean, *dirty* Wit." She frequently refers to her "wild youth," her pranks, sauciness, impudence, and humor.

16. The story of their meeting is in Eaves and Kimpel, *Samuel Richardson*, chap. 10.
17. Richardson to Bradshaigh, 26 Oct. 1748, in *The Correspondence*, 4:187–93.
18. Bradshaigh to Richardson, n.d., in *The Correspondence*, 4:265–66. Eaves and Kimpel tentatively date the letter early November 1749; see Eaves and Kimpel, *Samuel Richardson*, app., p. 648.
19. Richardson to Bradshaigh, 13 Aug. 1755, in *The Selected Letters*, pp. 318–19.
20. Bradshaigh to Richardson, 20 Nov. 1748, in *The Correspondence*, 4:202.

Actually, as Belfour, the female equivalent of Belford, Lady Bradshaigh serves the same function in relation to Richardson that Belford serves with Clarissa: she becomes a textual compiler, editor, and commentator practically up to the moment of Richardson's death, for in one of his last letters he asks to see the comments she made in the margins of "her" *Pamela* and *Clarissa*.[21] Anna Barbauld cites evidence that Lady Bradshaigh subsequently became the model for Charlotte Grandison, for Richardson writes to her sister, Lady Echlin, that certain faults in Charlotte's character were thrown in "on Lady Bradshaigh's account. . . . How hard is it to rein in lively imaginations, especially when blessed with health and spirits!"[22] Thus, the entire correspondence is an astonishing revelation of the fluidity of all sorts of boundaries: between authentic and fictional correspondence, author and reader, male and female, gender and genre.

Lady Bradshaigh's direct identification with Richardson's heroine unquestionably seems naïve to modern readers, but we are no less afflicted than she with a mixture of blindness and insight, for what now strikes us as an alien area of discourse in *Clarissa* is a discourse of pathos that was immediately recognizable to Lady Bradshaigh. Modern criticism has nearly obliterated not just the pathos of Clarissa's predicament but pathos as a discursive mode. Just as critics condemned Sappho's lesbianism, Heloise's blasphemy, and the Portuguese nun's narcissism, they have condemned Clarissa for longing for "self-immolation," for her will to power, her narcissism, and her hysteria. John Dussinger's catalogue of her sins includes a "clitoral assertion of self," "a lesbian contempt for men," "hysteria," "penis envy," castration fantasies, and a desire to return to the "primal womb."[23] Warner is representative of those critics who maintain that Clarissa sees herself as a paragon of virtue; Ian Watt makes her into one: "She is the heroic representative of all that is free and positive in the new individualism, and especially of the spiritual independence

---

21. Bradshaigh to Richardson, 25 Sept. 1753, 14 Jan. 1754, and Richardson's request for her marginalia [March 1761], all in the Forster Collection of the Victoria and Albert Museum, XI, ff. 25–28, 62–67, 270, cited in Eaves and Kimpel, 233–34, and in Warner, *Reading "Clarissa,"* pp. 131–32, 145, 147.

22. Richardson to Lady Echlin, 12 Sept. 1754, in *The Correspondence*, 5:26. Barbauld suggests the parallels between Lady Bradshaigh and Charlotte Grandison, 6:290 and 1:cciv–ccx; Doody makes a similar suggestion, p. 363, n. 2.

23. John A. Dussinger, *The Discourse of the Mind in Eighteenth-Century Fiction* (The Hague: Mouton, 1974), pp. 93, 101, 103, 104, 115, 126.

which was associated with Puritanism."[24] Leslie Fiedler, similarly, makes Clarissa too much of an abstraction as virtue embodied, but he does offer an astute assessment of her strength when he notes that she captured the novelistic imagination for two hundred years because she embodied strength and power. With time, however, she came to embody "Woman as weakness rather than strength, thus standing the Clarissa-archetype on its head. The original point was, of course, that Clarissa needed the intervention of no hero to save either herself or Lovelace; for she was conceived as spirit, and spirit as the only force capable of defeating evil."[25] The concept of Clarissa's strength is crucial to the understanding of her passion, which, rather than being passive, is an active *agon*. The critical devaluation of Clarissa, like that of Heloise and Mariane, is related to the devaluation of the discourse of pathos. One can examine the discourse of pathos without resorting to the "referential fallacy" by recognizing that Richardson's constructions of gender are as literary as his construction of genre, indebted to Ovid, Heloise, Guilleragues, and many other sources before him. Unexamined assumptions about sexuality, about novelistic realism, and about the representation of women in literature have helped to disguise Clarissa's elegy of desire. Sue Warrick Doederlein suggests a multivalent approach to the text, one that combines an analysis of its linguistic and textual ambiguities with an examination of spatial, temporal, and physical images that define and circumscribe the bounds of the "feminine."[26] I turn now to the Ovidian traces and transgressions of those boundaries and definitions.

The Lady's Legacy: The Trace of Ovid

Clarissa's correspondence looks forward not just to Rosa Coldfield's elegy of desire but to *The Three Marias*, for letters between women who love each other, like those between Clarissa and Anna Howe, do more in these texts than merely supplement those to the

24. Watt, p. 222.

25. Leslie Fiedler, *Love and Death in the American Novel* (New York: Criterion Books, 1960), p. 37.

26. Sue Warrick Doederlein, "Clarissa in the Hands of the Critics," *Eighteenth-Century Studies* 16 (Summer 1983), 401–14. I am grateful to my colleague James Thompson for bringing this essay to my attention. My own argument was written long before but had not yet gone to press.

absent male; they are focal points for exploring the origins of human misunderstanding. What are those origins? From the title page on-ward, the issues of paternity, authority, obedience, property rights, and legal documents lead to volatile speculations (as in *Paradise Lost*) about first causes, first crimes, the first disobedience. What authority in the novel allows the crimes to become so monstrous? Who are the authors of evil in *Clarissa*? Clarissa's parents are described first as "authors" of her existence and later as "authors of . . . [her] persecu-tion." Clarissa writes in the aftermath of abandonment, but whereas in previous texts it is the lover who abandons the heroine, Clarissa is abandoned by her father, who persecutes her before she leaves home, repudiates her afterwards, and curses her in the hereafter. Lovelace and her father are, in important respects, interchangeable agents of persecution, for like Lovelace, Mr. Harlowe is obsessed with power and revenge, with legacies and legalities. (Richardson's original title was *The Lady's Legacy*.)[27] The novel subverts attempts to locate origins, to fix either blame or interpretation for all time, and readers "out-side" the text are drawn into the circle of readers within the novel whose interpretations are necessarily limited to partial explanations, fragmentary revelations, correspondences that contradict rather than cohere. From the first letter forward, we find ourselves engaged in a search for the origins of actions that have already taken place, origins of the conflict, of legalistic evidence, of suffering and aggression. Anna Howe writes to Clarissa on 10 January:

> I am extremely concerned, my dearest Friend, for the disturbances that have happened in your Family. I know how it must hurt you to become the subject of the public talk: And yet upon an occasion so generally known, it is impossible but that whatever relates to a young Lady whose distinguished merits have made her the public care, should engage every-body's attention. I long to have the particulars from yourself; and of the usage I am told you receive upon an accident you could not help; and in which, as far as I can learn, the Sufferer was the Aggressor.[28]

Anna's exhortation to Clarissa to set the record straight, to clear her name, immediately establishes the generic link to amorous epis-tolary discourse, with its emphasis on accusations, confrontations, evi-

27. Hill, p. 315.
28. Samuel Richardson, *Clarissa; or, The History of a Young Lady*, Shakespeare Head Edition (Oxford: Basil Blackwell, 1930), vol. 1, letter 1, p. 1, hereinafter cited paren-thetically in the text by volume, letter number, and page.

dence, trials, injunctions, and self-justification. Bakhtin points out that the kind of discourse that is written in response to "alien discourses, alien points of view . . . is the kind . . . associated with justification (self-justification) and accusation"; such a discourse, which "continually senses the resistance" to its logic and motives, is defined by Bakhtin as a discourse of pathos.[29] This resistance is expressed in *Clarissa* as well. The heroine reluctantly begins a correspondence with Lovelace, with the Harlowe family's "general approbation" (1:3:18), yet she is prohibited from writing to anyone when they discover that he has enclosed private letters to her along with those meant for the entire family's eyes. Thus the same polarities between art and nature, calculation and spontaneity, woman and man that we have seen in previous texts of the ancient genre reappear here. Lovelace's linguistic facility is seen as a sign of his merit (the Harlowes themselves praise his "reading, judgement and taste" [1:3:18] on the basis of his writing style), but Clarissa's powers of expression are interpreted as deeply devious. Once she leaves her father's house, writing is her only means of communication, but because of her skill, this is the mode they find most insincere and thus have the greatest resistance to. When Clarissa beseeches her Aunt Hervey to help, for instance, Aunt replies, "O my dear! how Art produces Art!" (3:48:271). The family's suspicion remains to the very last; even as Clarissa nears death, her pleas for justice, forgiveness, and mercy are given no credence but are instead attributed merely to her eloquent command of language.[30] Of her last farewell to Anna, for example, James asks scornfully, "What was there . . . in what was read, but the result of the talent [she] had of moving the passions?" (7:90:393). Lovelace, moreover, is abundantly aware of the family's suspicion of Clarissa's eloquence and exploits it to his advantage; he refers to her as "Mistress of our passions: No one ever had to so much perfection the Art of moveing. This all her family know, and have equally feared and revered her for it" (4:5:22). Clarissa's discourse is continually tested and

---

29. Bakhtin, *The Dialogic Imagination*, pp. 388, 394. Jean Hagstrum examines the linguistic and thematic transformations of the word *pathetic* between the seventeeth and the eighteenth centuries. Initially linked to passivity in pain and passion, its connotations changed from violence to delicacy. (The contrast between the Portuguese nun and Clarissa is illustrative.) See *Sex and Sensibility: Ideal and Erotic Love from Milton to Mozart* (Chicago: Univ. of Chicago Press, 1980), pp. 6–7.

30. William Beatty Warner's recent deconstruction of Richardson's novel likewise praises Lovelace's writing virtuosity while condemning Clarissa's skillful use of the pen as aggressive and devious. See *Reading "Clarissa,"* pp. 3–27.

found wanting precisely because it is too persuasive, too moving, too eloquent. She is castigated as a harlot because she uses "the harlot rhetoric"—and the rhetorical exercises of *suasoriae* and *ethopoiiae*—with such skill.

Writing is both Clarissa's crime and her punishment, imposed upon her by the severe silence and physical absence of her family. Her transgression lies not only in defying her father's authority but in being an author herself, attempting to name, to define herself to others. Her writing, indeed, from first to last is an exercise in self-definition and an analysis of the meaning, definition, and nature of authority, which her brother not only inherits as his birthright but usurps from her father. Her brother resents her because she "is in a fair way to *out-uncle*, as she has already *out-grandfather'd*" him (1:13:85); she resents both his lord-liness in taking over as head of the house long before her father is dead and his attempt to solidify the family fortune by sacrificing her in marriage to Solmes. Clarissa has too many fathers; she is as surfeited with father figures—her parent, grandparents, uncles, brother, and cousins—as Lovelace is with sexual partners. The irony is that these "fathers" ought to be her protectors, but instead, they want only to coerce and nullify her. The law, too, makes women (supposedly for their own "protection") invisible; they are quite literally a legal fiction. William Blackstone, whose *Commentaries* were later to become the foundation of common law, notes: "The very being or legal existence of the woman is suspended during marriage, or at least is incorporated and consolidated into that of the husband; under whose wing, protection, and cover, she performs everthing; and is therefore . . . a *femme covert* . . . and is said to be *covert-baron* or under the protection and influence of her husband, her *baron*, or lord; and her condition during her marriage is called her *coverture*."[31] Clarissa would have been not only covered but smothered by this legal code had not one thing intervened: her grandfather's will. By endowing her with a handsome legacy, her grandfather transformed her from a legal fiction into a powerful force, one whose discourse is a continual challenge to the assumptions of her society. Why, she asks, should women be invisible in the eyes of the law? Why must oppression be part of the social and legal code? She goes further, actually identifying the very authors of those

---

31. Cited by Norma Basch, "Invisible Women: The Legal Fiction of Marital Unity in Nineteenth-Century America," *Feminist Studies* 5 (Summer 1976), 346–66. Leo Braudy mentions Edward Gibbon's discussion of Blackstone. See Braudy, "Penetration and Impenetrability in *Clarissa*," in *New Approaches to Eighteenth-Century Literature*, ed. Phillip Harth (New York: Columbia Univ. Press, 1974), pp. 187–88.

codes, challenging their authority to issue and enforce decrees. The law of matrimony, for example, which subordinates woman to man, has not been handed down by God, as Clarissa points out: "The men were the framers of the Matrimonial Office, and made *obedience* a part of the woman's vow" (1:40:292).

Clarissa's use of *suasoriae*, or persuasions through logic, closely resembles Ovid's use of the same technique in the *Heroides*, as well as Heloise's *epistola deprecatoria*. Moreover, her discourse, like theirs, posits a logic based on the integrity of the body and the supremacy of the heart, which is antithetical to the logic enforced by men. Initially, Clarissa sees no deception in language, no schism between word and deed, writing and feeling, inner and outer realities. To her, the body is the visible sign of the heart's desires; Solmes disgusts her because his revolting character is revealed in every line of his phlegmatic face. An even more egregious error is that she uses her own emotions as a standard for judging the emotions of others; she sees an identity where there is only a difference. Long after she has been disabused of her folly, she thinks back on her initial impressions of Lovelace in terms that are nearly identical to the retrospective analyses of Heloise and Mariane. Just as the two nuns recall their initial attraction to their seducers and their own innocence and credulity, Clarissa writes to Lovelace: "At first, I saw something in your Air and Person that displeased me not. Your Birth and Fortunes were no small advantages to you.—You acted not ignobly by my passionate Brother. Every-body said you were brave: Every-body said you were generous" (5:36:331). In retrospect, Clarissa sees the folly of believing that what "everybody said" must be true. She recognizes not only the treachery of appearances but the corrupt values upon which society's approbation is based. In what is perhaps the profoundest parallel to Heloise and Mariane, however, Clarissa reserves the most merciless scrutiny for herself. Like them, she is not content to see herself merely as a victim but instead frankly assesses the large role her own imagination played in making Lovelace attractive, in attributing virtues to him that he never possessed. The word *possession* reverberates through the novel because of its sexual and proprietary overtones and because *self-possession* is what everyone denies Clarissa. But Clarissa herself confesses that she confused self-possession with preconceived preju-dices—with *prepossession*—in matters of the heart:

A *brave* man, I thought, could not be a *base* man: A *generous* man could not, I believed, be *ungenerous*, where he acknowledged *obligation*. Thus prepossessed, all the rest that my soul loved and wished for in your Reformation, I hoped!—I knew not, but by report, any flagrant instances of your vileness. You seemed frank, as well as generous: Frankness and Generosity ever attracted me: Whoever kept up those appearances, I judged of their hearts by my own; and whatever qualities I *wished* to find in them, I was *ready* to find; and *when* found, I believed them to be natives of the soil. (5:36:331–32)

The last words reveal how fundamental the idea of man's natural goodness is to Clarissa's morality; what she fails to see is that there are no "natives of the soil" in the heart of man; the organic metaphor is utterly sterile in the society around her. Nor does she realize the extent to which appearances depend on such fictions as that of the Rake's Reform, which she relies upon in responding to Lovelace. She mistakenly judges other hearts by her own without realizing that nothing is alien—or organic—in the heart of man. In short, she mistakes the figure for the thing itself. As Terry Castle explains, Clarissa

> holds implicitly to a myth of language, which she applies first to her own discourse, and then by extension to the speech of others. Utterance, she assumes, is grounded in being and truth. Words come from within and express the soul. They have a "natural" or privileged relation to the actual; they have an exact correspondence to the inner person. Typically Clarissa uses a body metaphor to register this belief: language flows from the "heart." The "dictating heart" is the image she uses to account for signification itself. Her own speech, she imagines, is both motivated and constrained by the "authority" of the heart. And hence the message clothed in language must needs be as clear, as translucent, as the heart itself. When her family distort her words, they distort the core of her being . . . Richardson's—and Lovelace's—fanciful etymological linking of "cor-respondence" with the communication of "hearts" is to the point here: Clarissa's figure of the dictating heart reveals her desire to "naturalize" discourse—to invest it with a kind of absolute truthfulness, the truth of human presence.[32]

One of the fundamental characteristics of heroines who write amorous discourses is precisely this desire to establish an equivalence be-

32. Terry Castle, *Clarissa's Ciphers: Meaning and Disruption in Richardson's "Clarissa"* (Ithaca: Cornell Univ. Press, 1982), pp. 67, 70. In the 1985 spy trial of Svetlana Ogorodnikova, convicted of passing documents to the Soviet Union by seducing former FBI agent Richard W. Miller, Miller testified that she had "stolen" his heart. She responded that it was her "business" to know Miller's heart. To make her response sound less cold-blooded, her attorneys argued that she was merely referring to a class in cardiac resuscitation that their client had completed. Her attorneys' cleverness perhaps saved her from a life sentence; she is now serving an eighteen-year prison term. *Los Angeles Times*, 16 July 1985, pt. 2, pp. 1, 6.

tween what is natural and what is written, between the heart's authority and the hand's penmanship. (Heloise, remember, begins her
second letter by rebuking Abelard for placing her name before his
own; he has disrupted not just the epistolary but the natural order.)
The soul as signified, the heart as signifier, the body as alphabet:
from the *Heroides* to Heloise, from the *Portuguese Letters* to *Clarissa*, the
same essential value system is reiterated ceaselessly in amorous discourse and is ceaselessly betrayed.

Yet Clarissa does not maintain that she is a paragon of virtue,
despite the claims of some critics and the attempts of others to reduce
her to one. Her letters relentlessly reexamine the relation of art to
nature to see what that relation can reveal about her own actions. The
discourse of pathos, with its many elements of trial rhetoric, is particularly notable in Richardson's novel because Clarissa puts herself on
trial, cross-examines herself, revealing her own errors, poor judgment, and pride. She exposes her own complicity in her betrayal by
Lovelace, even after he has raped her. In Paper III, Clarissa's parable
of the lady who raises and tames a bear, which eventually turns on her
and tears her to pieces, is a scathing self-indictment, for the lady acted
against nature, while the bear remained true to its character. (Lovelace, significantly, repeatedly boasts of remaining "in character" while
tormenting Clarissa, asking Belford at one point, "What! wouldst
thou not have me act in character?") Yet nature itself is problematical
in the novel. Goodness is not a "native of the soil," and the parallels
between the animal kingdom and the human belie the same kind of
savagery as does the parable of the lady and the bear. Lovelace justifies his persecution of Clarissa, for instance, by conceding:

> There may possibly be some *cruelty* necessary: But there may be
> *consent in struggle;* there may be *yielding in resistance.* But the first conflict
> over, whether the following may not be weaker and weaker, till *willing-
> ness* ensue, is the point to be tried. I will illustrate what I have said by the
> Simile of a Bird new-caught. We begin, when Boys, with Birds; and,
> when grown up, go on to Women; and both, perhaps, in turn, experi-
> ence our sportive cruelty.
>
> Hast thou not observed the charming gradations by which the en-
> snared Volatile has been brought to bear with its new condition? How,
> at first, refusing all sustenance, it beats and bruises itself against its
> wires, till it makes its gay plumage fly about, and overspread its well-
> secured cage. . . .
>
> Now, let me tell thee, that I have known a Bird actually starve itself,
> and die with grief, at its being caught and caged. But never did I meet

with a Woman, who was so silly. . . . And, yet we must all own, that it is more difficult to catch a *Bird* than a *Lady.* . . .

She will even refuse her sustenance for some time. . . . Then she comes to eat and drink, to oblige you. . . .

Now, Belford, were I to go no further than I have gone with my beloved Miss Harlowe, how shall I know the difference between *her* and *another* bird? . . . How do I know, except I try, whether she may not be brought to sing me a fine song, and to be as well contented as I have brought other birds to be, and very shy ones too? (4:4:12–14)

This ominous passage reveals the savagery in nature and in man, exposes how much of Lovelace's cruelty is pure sport, and fore-shadows Clarissa's self-starvation. In earlier amorous discourses, woman was compared to a horse mounted by a chevalier; here a *volatile* refers to any flying creature; in my subsequent chapters the metaphor of woman as bird will again take on tragic significance. Lovelace's argument here epitomizes the alien discourse that Clarissa's discourse of pathos must resist and refute by presenting an alternative logic. Lovelace's seemingly inexorable logic relies on false assumptions about identity and difference; he must know the exact extent of Clarissa's similarity to and difference from other women. (Abelard, remember, "consoles" Heloise by telling her how different she is from other women; how close she comes to being "even above men" in her cloistered condition.)

Lovelace's specious logic serves his all-consuming passion not for Clarissa but for novelty. The fact that we first learn of his obsession from a bailiff suggests yet another trace of the legal strain of *suasoriae* in amorous discourse. The bailiff reports that Lovelace is "a sad gentleman . . . as to women:—If his tenants had pretty daughters, they chose to keep them out of his sight. [The bailiff] believed [Lovelace] kept no particular mistress; for he had heard *newelty,* that was the man's word, was every-thing with him" (1:4:24). While underlining Lovelace's obsession with *newelty,* Richardson undermines it by invariably linking it to repetition. The very report of his obsession with *newelty* comes to us in the form of repetition: the bailiff repeats it to James, who repeats it to his uncles, who repeat it to Aunt Hervey, who repeats it to Clarissa. The reader learns of it in Clarissa's letter to Anna Howe.

Newelty means novelty, newness, but it also connotes food that is a delicacy, as in the *Oxford English Dictionary*'s example: "I ain't had a bit of pig-meat so long, it's quite a *newalty!*" Delicacy, of course, is also crucial in the novel. In one sense Clarissa is a delicacy Lovelace would like to consume; in another sense her delicacy, her concern with punctilio, is the main obstacle to the consummation he so devoutly wishes. The understanding that Lovelace's underlying compulsion is not his desire to possess Clarissa but his need for *newelty* dramatically changes one's conception of his potential ever to have loved Clarissa. This is his doom: since he so freely indulges his appetite for women, he is constantly looking for some delicate morsel to refresh his surfeited palate. Yet it is precisely the inevitable repetition of all physical acts that he most wants to escape. He does so by negating the body, as when he rapes Clarissa. Thus he seeks the very thing his experience denies him; he wants life to be a series of firsts, from birth to death. His is a perennial quest for the new, for first experiences, for "rosebuds." Therefore he rejects women whom he has been the first to despoil; to return to them would be merely to repeat. His distaste for them is more complex than the cliché of the double standard, for he is a sexual explorer who sees woman as the undiscovered country, and he is "always aiming at the merit of a first discoverer" (4:43:283).

This trait returns us once again to Ovid, for just as Lovelace blithely describes the "sportive cruelty" of predatory men, Ovid in *The Art of Love* advises: "First let assurance come to your minds, that all women can be caught; spread but your nets and you will catch them. Sooner would birds be silent in spring . . . than a woman persuasively wooed resist a lover: nay, even she, whom you will think cruel, will be kind. And as stolen love is pleasant to a man, so is it also to a woman; the man dissembles badly: she conceals desire better."[33] If pathos is the dominant tone of the *Heroides*, the peripatetic lover in *The Art of Love* is driven by the same search for novelty that is such a compulsion with Lovelace. The whole aim of approaching love as an art, a technique, is to provide infinite variety—at all costs to avoid the tedium that might come with familiarity. Novelty itself is the attraction; the woman merely the vehicle for obtaining it. Ovid even provides the identical stratagem by which Lovelace first ensnares Clarissa, for Ovid advises the seducer to try to win the woman without any cost to himself:

Let a letter speed, traced with persuasive words, and explore her feelings, and be the first to try the path. . . . Suppose she has read, but will not write back: compel her not; only see that she is ever reading your

33. Ovid, *The Art of Love and Other Poems*, trans. J. H. Mozley, Loeb Classical Library (Cambridge: Harvard Univ. Press, 1929), book I, ll. 269–76, pp. 31–32, hereinafter cited parenthetically in the text by book and line number.

flatteries. She who has consented to read will consent to answer what she has read; that will come by its own stages and degrees. Perhaps even an angry letter will first come to you, asking you to be pleased not to vex her. What she asks, she fears; what she does not ask, she desires—that you will continue; press on, then, and soon you will have gained your wish. (1:455–56, 479–86)

There almost seem to be two Ovids at play in Richardson's novel: Lovelace reflects the jaunty tone, the glib attitude, the calculated approach of the Ovid of *The Art of Love,* while Clarissa's discourse of pathos links her to the heroines of the *Heroides.* Yet such a division is too schematic, for the *Heroides* itself contains male correspondents who can clearly be seen as Lovelace's predecessors. After publishing the original fifteen letters from the heroines, which focused on the aftermath of seduction, Ovid later added six more letters—the so-called double letters of Paris to Helen, Acontius to Cydippe, and Leander to Hero, along with the heroines' replies. The disputes over legitimacy and authority—so frequent in the genre of amorous epistolary discourse—recur with these letters, for doubts of their authenticity existed as early as the Renaissance. Certainly the men's letters, as W. S. Anderson notes, mark an entirely new development in literature, as original in their way as the first fifteen were before them. Anderson describes the shift in focus between the first fifteen and the last six letters.[34] Ovid continues to experiment with the idea of writing like a woman as opposed to writing like a man, radically subverting the categories of genre and gender. In these six letters, however, he explores a different phase of love—not betrayal but the initial stages of attraction, exploration, and passion—from the man's as well as the woman's point of view, just as Richardson would later do. Paris, for instance, is one of Lovelace's predecessors, for he reveals the same arrogance as Lovelace when he boasts of his vast sexual experience and reminds Helen that he is a prize coveted by many other women: "As I long for you, so women have longed for me; alone, you can possess the object of many women's prayers! And not only have the daughters of princes and chieftains sought me, but even the nymphs have felt for me

34. W. S. Anderson, *"The Heroides,"* in *Ovid,* ed. J. W. Binns (London: Routledge and Kegan Paul, 1973). Scholars who maintain that the double letters are authentic include: Albert R. Baca, "Ovid's Epistle from Sappho to Phaon," *Transactions of the American Philological Association* 102 (1971), 29–38; and Sereno Burton Clark, "The Authorship and the Date of the Double Letters in Ovid's *Heroides,*" *Harvard Studies in Classical Philology* 19 (1908), 121–55.

the cares of love. . . . But I am weary of all of them . . . since hope was made mine of winning you" (16:93–96, 99–100).

If Paris anticipates Lovelace's conceit, Acontius anticipates his trickery. The correspondence of Acontius and Cydippe, indeed, bears the strongest "family resemblance" to Lovelace and Clarissa's, for like Lovelace, Acontius tricked his beloved into a relationship with him by writing to her. He threw an apple to her in the temple of Diana, on which he had carved the words, "By Artemis I swear I will marry Acontius." Cydippe's nurse picked it up, but being illiterate, she passed it to her mistress who read it aloud, thus inadvertently making a sacred vow in a holy temple and pledging herself to Acontius. Cydippe's parents try, as do Clarissa's, to marry her to someone else, but the girl falls ill each time, and after the third deathly illness, her parents learn from the oracle of Apollo that her sickness is the result of an unfulfilled vow—the one to Acontius. Like Lovelace, Acontius vows to rape Cydippe if he cannot win her lawfully; like Lovelace, he invokes the law to justify his actions:

> In words dictated by [Love] I made our betrothal bond; Love was the lawyer that taught me knavery. . . . May the gods give me power to lay more bonds on you, so that your pledge may nowhere leave you free! A thousand wiles remain—I am only perspiring at the foot of the steep; my ardour will leave nothing unessayed. Grant 'tis doubtful whether you can be taken; the taking shall at least be tried. . . . You may evade a part, but you will not escape all the nets which Love, in greater number than you think, has stretched for you. If art will not serve, I shall resort to arms, and you will be seized and borne away in the embrace that longs for you. . . . Allow that death is fit punishment for this theft of you, it will be less than not to have possessed you. (20:29–30, 39–43, 45–48, 51–52)

Love here is a lawyer; Acontius' inexorable logic reduces love to prosecution and persecution, to contractual codes and legal strategies. The same associative process, significantly, recurs repeatedly in amorous discourse, for from Acontius to Rochester, from Lovelace to Thomas Sutpen, the male invokes the law to secure his desires and protect his interests. Love as a lawyer teaches the male what bonds he may impose, what sanctions he may have to face, what force he may use, what laws will come to his aid. Like Acontius, Lovelace "resorts to arms" when art fails, and he, too, refers to rape as theft; he calls himself a "villainous burglar, felon, thief" (7:84:348), yet coolly calculates the legal extent of the damage he causes. If he marries his victim, the law will exonerate him. Lovelace's very name underlines the same impulse that Acontius reveals in the passage above. If Love is a lawyer, it promises maximum security for the male, while lacing the woman, binding her in nets from which there is no escape. Cydippe wastes away while Acontius threatens rape; the fundamental schism in *Clarissa* as in Ovid is that the female's last resort is only self-destruction, while the male has the resources to act out his fantasies of power and revenge. Indeed, what Acontius threatens, Lovelace enacts, for he repeatedly proclaims that either Clarissa will be his or she will be dead, and he turns out to be right. Elsewhere, Lovelace invokes the same legalistic nihilism by proclaiming that it does not matter if Clarissa dies in childbirth (as a result of his raping her), so long as she produces a son before she dies. Thus, if Love is a lawyer, he enforces bonds based on power and oppression rather than affection and freedom. Lovelace maintains that he is torn between two impulses—love and revenge—but his actions show that revenge is by far the stronger force. By juxtaposing two particular letters, one sees how little Lovelace changes in the course of the novel, how this seeker after novelty is instead circumscribed by repetition and circularity. In his first letter, he writes, "[I have] written . . . upon Something; upon Nothing; upon REVENGE, which I love; upon LOVE, which I hate, heartily hate, because 'tis my master: And upon the devil knows what besides" (1:31:221–22). Much, much later, even after he has discovered novelty after novelty in Clarissa, he repeats: "The Rage of Love, the Rage of Revenge, is upon me! By turns they tear me!" (5:31:311). By the next letter, he has raped Clarissa.

"When Honor's at the Stake": Clarissa's Elegy of Desire

The rape is not an act of passion by a man in love but a vicious act of violence by a man bent on revenge. It marks the turning point in Clarissa's disintegration, the point where the danger of annihilation is greatest, for rape tears not only the hymen but the veil of reality, revealing that male authority is based solely on physical force and that women—from Mrs. Harlowe to Mrs. Sinclair—merely aid and abet their masters. Clarissa lies, "moping, dozing, weeping, raving, scribbling, tearing"; her illusions are in shreds. This tearing is another trace of the genre of amorous epistolary discourse, for Clarissa's identification of her body with her letters is one of the trademarks of the genre. But here the analogy becomes a source of horror as Clarissa explicitly tries to tear, to shred, to blot out the existence of both her body and letters. In earlier texts in the genre, as we have seen, weaving is an analogue for the narrative line; here, tearing represents the opposite impulse toward silence and annihilation. Many of Sappho's sisters are weavers of fiction who confront this temptation to cut the thread of life, of narrative: Emma Bovary, after her failed affairs, furiously unstitches her petticoats before the fire; Rosa Coldfield sews clumsily while she listens to the slow unraveling of the South in the Civil War; and in Doris Lessing's *Golden Notebook,* Anna Wulf compulsively cuts up newspaper stories and defaces her notebooks with black slashes. As a portrait of a mind in distress, torn by a thousand contradictions and vacillations, Clarissa's fragments resemble nothing so much as the *Portuguese Letters;* the dashes, ellipses, repetition, violent shifts in tone and syntax from sentence to sentence convey unbearable disorder and despair. Thus Mariane laments, "I know neither who I am nor what I do nor what I desire; I am torn by a thousand conflicting emotions," and Clarissa, torn in a thousand fragments, writes of her weariness with the world and herself in a torn letter to Anna:

> I am tired of myself. . . . But how I ramble!
> I sat down to say a great deal—My heart was full—I did not know what to say first—And thought, and grief, and confusion, and (O my poor head!) I cannot tell what—And thought, and grief, and confusion, came crouding so thick upon me; *one* would be first, *another* would be first, *all* would be first; so I can write nothing at all.—Only that, whatever they have done to me, I cannot tell; but I am no longer what I was in any one thing. (5:36:327)

The passage is painful to read; the fragmentation of the style corresponds to the fragmentation of the writer, who can no longer make the narrative line cohere or progress, much less express in any but an oblique way the enormity of the crimes, the anguish of the effects of what she has suffered. The last line is ambiguous: perhaps she "cannot tell" what they have done because her writing is censored or because she is not certain precisely what has happened to her or because it lies beyond her powers of expression to convey the hideousness of her deflowering. Thought competes with feeling. She aches physically, not just from a headache but from the rupture of maidenhead; she tries confusedly to separate thought about the future from grief about the past, but sequential logic and chronology have been obliterated. Time, indeed, begins to go very fast from this point. Once the processes of her body's natural development have been brutally disrupted, weeks become as days; days as hours, and Clarissa passes from virginity to premature death without ever knowing love, pleasure, or sexual fulfillment. The same phenomenon occurs when the Portuguese nun compresses the whole chronology of her seduction, her defloration, and her abandonment in the phrase "my shame, my confusion, my disorder" and confesses, "I am tortured by the unlikelihood of my ever being myself again." Clarissa echoes this lament: "My name is—I don't know what my name is! . . . . But I shall never be what I was. My head is gone. I have wept away all my brain. . . . [Lovelace] has killed my head" (5:36:328,334–37).

By dismissing Clarissa's pain after the rape as a "mere notional violation," Lovelace negates the body, holding rigidly to dichotomies in which mind can triumph over matter, intellect over the senses. But in lamenting that Lovelace "killed her head," Clarissa is asserting that intellect cannot be separated from the body. Her mind is devastated when her maidenhead is destroyed; both are united in unspeakable pain that is well-nigh unbearable precisely because it is both psychic and physical.

Lovelace's reaction to these heartbreaking fragments is to obliterate any consciousness of Clarissa's psychic and physical suffering and to concentrate instead on a purely aesthetic reaction, as when he comments on her artifice to Belford: "This eloquent nonsense . . . rather shews a raised, than a quenched, imagination" (5:36:328). He reveals once again that his true obsession is not with Clarissa but with novelty when he finally tells his friend that he will copy a few of these fragments "for the novelty of the thing, and to shew thee how her mind works now she is in this whimsical way" (5:36:326). Later, his remarks on writing-to-the-moment point directly to the same evaluation of epistolary technique that made *The Letters of a Portuguese Nun* famous:

> As she is always writing, what a melancholy pleasure will the perusal . . . of her papers afford me! Such a sweetness of temper, so much patience and resignation, as she seems to be mistress of; yet writing of and in the midst of *present* distresses! How *much more* lively and affecting, for that reason, must her style be; her mind tortured by the pangs of uncertainty (the events then hidden in the womb of Fate) *than* the dry, narrative, unanimated style of persons, relating difficulties and dangers sur-

mounted; the relator perfectly at ease; and if himself unmoved by his
own Story, not likely greatly to affect the Reader! (7:22:77)

Lovelace's tastes are representative of those cultivated by the reading
public ever since the appearance of the *Portuguese Letters.* The public's
avidity for epistolary texts that exalt distress as an epistolary technique is but one of the points to notice. Lovelace's anticipation of the
pleasures of reading, after all, are related in the context of being
made Clarissa's executor; he is as cheerful here, faced with the prospect of her death, as he was after her rape. He plays the connoisseur
of style while evading his responsibility for causing the distresses that
have made her writing affecting, taking refuge in such metaphors (a
particularly revealing one in view of the possibility that the rape resulted in pregnancy) as Fate's womb. In short, he anticipates being
Clarissa's legal executor, when in fact he is her literal executor. Since
his mode of response is so consistently based on aesthetic imitation,
divorced from the reality of physical suffering, it is significant that his
entire existence is summarized at his death as "a cursed still-life"—
which is to say, an imitation of an imitation.

Clarissa's existence, however, is not static, for in moving from
despair to overcome nihilism and the temptation to annihilate herself,
her discourse becomes an elegy of desire that illuminates the etymological meaning of passion as suffering. She is no mere passive
victim; instead she makes the radical determination to fight for her
own honor. It is this defiant gesture of self-definition that marks
Heloise as her ancestor and Jane Eyre and the three Marias as her
heirs. As in previous texts in the genre of amorous discourse, what is
at stake is honor, yet the source of the dispute lies in defining precisely whose honor must be avenged. The Harlowes' rage for revenge
is based on the damage to their "goods" and the insult to the family
name ("The Honour of the house . . . is all the cry!"). Lovelace shares
this view, thoroughly dismissing the notion that either Clarissa's body
or her honor are injured when he argues that since he plans to take
legal possession of the very "merchandise" he has damaged, "Whom
but myself shall I have injured?" (4:35:217). "Whose property, I pray
thee, shall I invade?" (4:57:377). He believes that he can rectify the
rape by marriage, which "is an atonement for all we can do [to wom-
en] . . . A true dramatic recompense."

Clarissa, indeed, is besieged on all sides by those who irrationally
demand that she either marry her rapist or prosecute him; this alien

discourse that her own must address helps to explain why *suasoriae* are as crucial as *ethopoiiae* in her rhetoric. Clarissa's conception of honor closely resembles Heloise's; she invokes the same ethic of intention that underlies Heloise's assertion that she finds more honor as Abelard's whore than she would as Augustus' empress. Clarissa says, similarly, "Let me wrap myself about in the mantle of my own Integrity, and take comfort in my unfaulty intention! Since it is now too late to look back, let me collect all my Fortitude, and endeavour to stand those shafts of angry Providence, which it will not permit me to shun! That, whatever the trials may be, which I am destined to undergo, I may not behave unworthily in them; and may come out amended by them" (3:51:280). Clarissa's words directly echo those of Heloise, who laments, "Fortune . . . has already spent on me so many of the shafts she uses in her battle against mankind that she has none left with which to vent her anger on others."[35]

One sees what Clarissa is up against by comparing Abelard's logic to Lovelace's. For Abelard, Heloise could only be "sinful Eve or saintly Mary"; for Lovelace, Clarissa must be either angel or whore. Just as Abelard's idea of consolation was to assure Heloise that all her suffering would make him a glorious martyr, Clarissa similarly says of Lovelace, "I am but a *cypher,* to give *him* significance, and *myself* pain" (4:8:40). Her role is to hold the mirror up not to nature but to Lovelace, to let him luxuriate in narcissism; toward this end he bombards her with his definitions, making himself her judge, jury, and executioner. Even when his compulsions have resulted in her death, he is still obsessively defining her either as a heavenly mediator or as perversely self-destructive. As Castle observes:

> Lovelace is supremely happy in his self-appointed role as Clarissa's exegete. In her, he finds the subject for his own compulsively manic discourse. . . . "I never had a more illustrious subject to exercise my pen upon" (III, 26). . . . Lovelace tends to merge the subject of interpretation with the political subject—again suggesting the fundamental link between them in the world of the novel. The bombastic imagery of conquest and empire, tyrants and subjects which he uses to encode his treatment of Clarissa points back to the more intimate, rhetorical subjugation going on in his letters themselves. Inverting the famous metaphor of Frantz Fanon, one might say that she is colonized by his writing. . . .

35. *The Letters of Abelard and Heloise,* trans., ed., and introd. Betty Radice (Baltimore: Penguin, 1974), p. 129.

> . . . [He] is busy circumscribing Clarissa's very body with the marks
> of "Woman"—the quintessentially empty sign of Western patriarchal
> discourse. . . . his goal is domination; his means is systematic alteration
> of the systems of order through which she tries to understand herself
> and the world.[36]

Here again, as in previous amorous epistles, those who can define
are the masters, and the male once again defines himself as the arbiter
of reason, speech, and discourse, while the female is relegated to
madness, silence, self-destruction. As in *The Portuguese Letters,* woman
is the colony, the conquest, the undiscovered country that must be
charted and circumscribed. Lovelace wants not just Clarissa's obedience, but the same willing self-enslavement that Abelard demanded
from Heloise. Abelard defines and corrects what Heloise reads,
writes, and studies; Lovelace tries to exercise the same tyranny, telling
Belford that he has prohibited Clarissa from reading, since "What
Books can tell her more than she knows? But *I* can. So she had better
study *me*" (3:9:62). If Clarissa thus looks back to Heloise, she also
looks forward to Jane Eyre, who will undergo similar trials at the
hands of two other "Judas-protectors," two other menacing mentors:
Rochester and St. John Rivers.

Clarissa reverses the authorities in her will, which marks the
culmination of the dual strains of *suasoriae* and *ethopoiiae* that connect
her letters to the ancient Ovidian rhetorical tradition. From being
subject to the authority of a family unfit to rule, Clarissa progresses to
the invocation of a higher authority in the authorship of her will,
which marks the final stage of her journey from disintegration to
recomposition. The will is far more than a distribution of material
possessions; it is the final testimony for the defense. As such, it is
based on a radically different logic, for although Clarissa writes in
self-defense, she writes with the knowledge that she will secure no
clemency, undo no injustice, and certainly save no life—least of all
her own. The power and poignancy of this discourse thus derives
from Clarissa's awareness that her point of view has diverged so far
from those of her readers: their minds are fixed on the present and
the past, while hers is fixed on the relation of time to eternity. Where
her family sought to obliterate her by systematically removing her
drawings, clothes, portraits, books, money, and jewels, as if neither
they nor she had ever existed, in her will Clarissa reinstates the identi-

36. Castle, pp. 89–90.

ty her family stripped from her point by point, in bequest after bequest of pictures, plates, books, needlework, and art. She writes:

> I have heard of so many instances of confusion and disagreement in families, and so much doubt and difficulty, for want of absolute clearness in the Testaments of departed persons, that I have often concluded . . . that this Last Act as to its designation and operation, ought not to be the Last in its composition or making; but should be the result of cool deliberation; and (as is more *frequently* than *justly* said) of a *sound mind* and *memory;* which too seldom are met with, but in *sound health*. All pretences of insanity of mind are likewise prevented, when a testator gives reasons for what he wills; all cavils about words are obviated; the obliged are assured; and They enjoy the benefit for whom the benefit was intended. Hence have I for some time past employed myself in penning down heads of such a disposition; which, as reasons offered, I have altered and added to; so that I never was absolutely destitute of a *Will*, had I been taken off ever so suddenly. These minutes and imperfect sketches enabled me, as God has graciously given me time and sedateness, to digest them into the form in which they appear. (8:105–6)

As Lovelace's prisoner, she was subjected to his alteration of the systems of order that made the world comprehensible. In her will, she turns the tables, trying to communicate to an uncomprehending audience her vision of an order in which time in one sense is "of the essence," since she has so little time left, but in a larger sense has absolutely ceased to matter. The pun on *minutes* encapsulates her project: since the years allotted her have been reduced to minutes, she passes them in writing up the minutes of her will, with minute attention to the details of her dispensations. Yet time, and even eternity, always consisted of minutes; one only becomes aware of them when they are numbered. Clarissa's will, therefore, is not a plea to be freed, for she realizes that she has already been freed. What she tries to do in her will is not to castigate her persecutors but to convey the remarkable exhilaration that this epiphany brings, a joy she also reveals in closing each of her last letters with an affirmation that she is at last happy. Clarissa's will is thus less a protest against the death sentence that has been imposed upon her, than a response to it. In each line of her will, she is literally composing a death sentence of indeterminate length, since she cannot know exactly when she will die. She thus argues by no logic that is comprehensible to her posthumous readers, for her logic is based on a radically different conception of time, of eternity, of suffering that perhaps only the dying perceive, and perceiving, die.

Other motifs in her testament involve the meaning of language and the origins of human misunderstanding. She demonstrates in her will as nowhere else that words have meaning; she suits the word to the deed by giving each person his due dispensation. She illustrates that black cannot simply be made white, as Lovelace liked to boast, that acts like rape are more than mere "notional violations"; as in so many previous amorous discourses, Clarissa enunciates the reality of the body. The rape was related to the disintegration of Clarissa's mind and body and to her text in images of cutting, ripping, and tearing, but in her will she specifically provides for the preservation of her letters and her corpse. In these provisions she resists Lovelace's underlying logic. She prevents him from having her body "opened and embalmed" and from seizing her papers, for she knows he will think that he owns the corpse because he raped the woman.[37] That that is precisely what he *does* think is revealed in his letter to Belford:

> I will take her papers. And as no one can do her memory justice equal to myself, and I will not spare myself, Who can better shew the world what she was, and what a villain he, that could use her ill? And the world shall also see, what implacable and unworthy parents she had. . . . For as I shall make the worst figure in it myself, and have a right to treat myself as nobody else shall; who will controul me? Who dare call me to account? (8:17:50)

Clarissa dares, by anticipating this demand and bequeathing all her papers to Anna Howe. She subverts his logic and thwarts his desires by committing both her corpse and her corpus to the care of women. She has ceased to be a "cypher" and has turned the tables by becoming the one whose writing, like the emblems on her coffin, has to be deciphered by others, for she writes knowing that what is luminous to her is absolutely enigmatic to her readers. The letter about meeting Lovelace in her Father's House is a good example of the radical difference between Clarissa's conception of time and that of her readers. In a posthumous letter to Lovelace, she reflects on the potential life he has denied her:

37. Janet Todd, *Women's Friendship in Literature* (New York: Columbia Univ. Press, 1980), p. 20. On the relation of death to language, see Garrett Stewart, *Death Sentences: Styles of Dying in British Fiction* (Cambridge: Harvard Univ. Press, 1984).

You have only robbed me of what once were my favorite expectations in the transient life I shall have quitted when you receive this. . . . to say I once respected you with a preference, is what I ought to blush to own, since at the very time, I was far from thinking you even a moral man; tho' I little thought that you, or indeed that any man breathing could be—what you have proved yourself to be. But, indeed, Sir, I have long been greatly above you: For from my heart I have despised you, and all your ways ever since I saw what manner of man you were. (8:137)

Thus readers of the novel participate in the same process of perceiving time as partial, fragmentary, discontinuous, which is the folly of characters *in* the novel, for this letter comes near the end of the eight volumes, but Clarissa wrote it just two days after writing Lovelace about meeting her in her Father's House. The proximity of the two letters shows how long Clarissa has ceased to think in terms of human time, while Lovelace continues to scheme and to deceive, and while readers like Belfour, moved by the pathos of Clarissa's rhetoric, continue to plead for her life.

Instead, for Clarissa the "hours now are days, nay years" (7:97:406). Her logic is diametrically opposed to Lovelace's legalistic machinations, for he plots to "procure for myself a Legal Right to [Clarissa's] favour" (6:4:14). If, like Acontius, one conceives of Love as a lawyer, then he is also a procurer whose legalities reduce love to prostitution. Nowhere is the nullification of the female that the legal code facilitates clearer than in the arrangements Lovelace makes after having sex with one mistress after another. After satisfying himself sexually, he quickly reverts to the letter of the law to dispense with such nuisances as pregnancies. His practice is "To marry off a former mistress, if possible, before I took to a new one: To maintain a Lady handsomely in her lying-in: To provide for the Little one, if it lived, according to the degree of its mother: To go into mourning for the mother, if she died. And the promise of this was a great comfort to the pretty dears, as they grew near their times" (3:44:250).

Some critics have castigated Clarissa as morbid for equating sex with death.[38] Yet it is clear that intercourse led directly from pregnancy to death often enough to necessitate the kind of contractual arrangement that Lovelace routinely keeps at hand. The entire letter, indeed, is a justification for the death of a previous mistress, and he refers, in the course of congratulating himself, to other "worthy crea-

38. E.g., Watt, pp. 232–38.

tures who died in Childbed by me" (3:44:250). The image of the
captive bird is emblematic of the opposition between the man's attitude toward sex and the woman's. Lovelace believes that the "ensnared Volatile" must be subject to his "sportive cruelty"; all consequences of that cruelty—forcible rape, pregnancy, even death—can
be settled by legal contracts. He explains how the act of paying women
off "could acquit my conscience" and goes on to protest that while
"rapes are unnatural things" they are also "more *rare* than are imagined" (3:44:251). Given the power of Clarissa's discourse of pathos,
one of the shocking things about Richardson's novel—what perhaps
most shocked Belfour—is how little efficacy pathos has to mitigate the
severity of the legal code. In nullifying the female, that code makes a
mockery of all sanctuaries, for the Harlowe House, like the Sinclair
House, is interchangeable with brothels, prisons, and tombs.[39]

The caged bird is also a traditional emblem of the soul in captivity,
awaiting its release, as Clarissa is finally released from all earthly
enclosures that buried her alive. One of the many complexities of
Richardson's novel, however, is that, while celebrating her release
from this life, she simultaneously inscribes a discourse of desire for
what Rosa Coldfield will later call the "might-have-been." Clarissa is
conscious of all the natural processes of development that Lovelace
has thwarted, from love to sex, from marriage to childbirth. The final
correspondence to the genre of amorous epistolary discourse is that
she, too, writes a discourse of desire, but it takes the form of an elegy.
Sappho, we may recall, writes of her desire, "I am greener than grass,
and it seems to me that I am little short of dying."[40] Clarissa uses
similar images, but hers offer a stark contrast in contexts between
desire and literal death, for she draws on the Book of Job to lament all
that has been thwarted—her life, her womanly development, her
desire: "Let not *her* that is deceived trust in vanity; for vanity shall be
her recompence. *She* shall be accomplished before *her* time; and *her*
branch shall not be green. *She* shall shake off *her* unripe grape as the
vine, and shall cast off *her* flower as the olive" (8:123). Clarissa's letters
record not her sense of her superiority, as Warner and others have
maintained, but her tragic sense of aborted natural processes of development. Her allusions to the unripe grape, the vine, and being

39. Doody, p. 214.
40. "Sappho" in *Greek Lyric*, 4 vols., trans. David A. Campbell, Loeb Classical Library (Cambridge: Harvard Univ. Press, 1932), vol. 1, p. 199.

"accomplished before her time," take on even more tragic significance when one keeps in mind that she may be pregnant as a result of
the rape. She writes, as we have seen, with a radically different conception of time and eternity in mind; but she may also be writing with
the awareness of having conceived a child who will never be born.[41]
She writes in her will, "You have only been the cause that I have been
cut off in the bloom of youth, *and of curtailing a life, that might have been
agreeable to myself*, or otherwise, as had suited the designs and ends of
Providence" (8:137, my italics). This is one of the passages where she
ponders the "might-have-been," as Rosa Coldfield does later. The
italicized lines can be read as simply an elaboration of the first clause:
Lovelace has cut off her life in its bloom, has curtailed an existence
that might have been agreeable. But while referring in the first clause
to her own life, Clarissa may be referring obliquely in the second
clause to the life within her—to a child whom she might have found
agreeable, depending on Providence. In any case, her letters elegize
all the desires that, like the fetus (if it exists), will die without ever
having lived. That life may be growing in her body while she wastes
away is thus one of the unspeakable—and unspoken—horrors the
novel forces us to contemplate. The extent of that horror cannot be
mitigated by the word-play of critics such as Warner, who remarks,
"Clarissa and Lovelace bear no children but their union is not unfruit-
ful. For Lovelace's violence against Clarissa plants the seed for a more
insidious will to power over others: Clarissa's idea for a book that will
tell her story."[42] (Abelard's specious consolation that Heloise gets to
turn the pages of holy books instead of bearing children comes to
mind.) What Warner overlooks is that "the book" is an elegy of desire,
and that it is precisely for writing that Clarissa receives calumny;
writing is her crime and her punishment in the eyes of certain characters and critics alike. That writing is "a more insidious will to power"

41. In "He Could Go No Farther: A Modest Proposal about Lovelace and Clarissa,"
PMLA 92 (1977), 19–32, Judith Wilt suggests that, because Lovelace is impotent, Mrs.
Sinclair and her women actually carry out Clarissa's violation. Although R. Schmitz
disputes Wilt (*PMLA* 92 [1977], 1005–6), the inconclusiveness of textual evidence
makes her proposal possible. Although I disagree with it, Wilt's reading is particularly
provocative because it highlights the transformations of gender in the text by contrasting the "man-woman" Sinclair with the "woman-man" Lovelace. Morris Golden also
discusses these fluid and ambiguous gender boundaries in *Richardson's Characters* (Ann
Arbor: Univ. of Michigan Press, 1963). I see the doubleness and duplicity of these
transformations of gender as yet another remnant of Ovidian stylistics in the genre of
amorous epistolary discourse, closely related to the doubling of genres discussed in
note 48 below.
42. Warner, *Reading "Clarissa,"* p. 75.

than rape and the death rape brings about is but another turn of the screw in the old story of the nullification of the female in nature and in culture.[43]

Thus, what nature and culture would nullify, Clarissa's discourse of desire reinscribes. Her will is a decree that supplements an inadequate and injust social code; such supplements, as Derrida has shown, become necessary when there are lacks in nature and culture.[44] Some critics have dismissed the last third of Richardson's novel as merely a morbid compendium of Puritan death literature, without recognizing that the real significance of the length of the supplement is the enormity of the gap Clarissa is trying to fill. It is no more perverse of Clarissa to write a discourse of desire on her deathbed than for Heloise to inscribe her desire after Abelard has been castrated. If, moreover, it seems unnatural that Clarissa composes her own eulogy, it is even more unnatural that no relatives mourn for her as she lies dying. She is aware that she writes to supplement this lack, for she apologizes by saying: "If any necessary matter be omitted in this my Will . . . [it is because] I am now . . . very weak and ill; having put off the finishing hand a little too long, in hopes of obtaining the last forgiveness of my honoured friends; in which case I should have acknowledged the favour with a suitable warmth of duty, and *filled up some blanks* which I left to the very last, in a more agreeable manner to myself, than now I have been enabled to do" (8:123–24, my italics). "To myself" is a telling detail here; since it parallels the Portuguese nun's confession that she writes for herself rather than for the chevalier, it again drives home the point that all amorous discourses are written in the extremity of solitude, without the satisfaction of an answer.

These words reveal yet another generic trace of amorous episto-

---

43. The sexual politics of Warner's argument are examined by Castle, pp. 189–96, and by Terry Eagleton, *The Rape of Clarissa: Writing, Sexuality, and Class Struggle in Samuel Richardson* (Minneapolis: Univ. of Minnesota Press, 1982). In his review of Castle and Eagleton, Warner shifts the grounds of argument by criticizing those who approach critical theory as something to be applied ("Reading Rape: Marxist-Feminist Figurations of the Literal," *Diacritics* 13 [Winter 1983], 12–32). He argues that new French theory, which critiques the modes of idealization, is now being used by critics like Castle and Eagleton to idealize Clarissa. Warner fails to recognize that one can undermine the mimetic assumptions made about the text and analyze its sexual-political implications at the same time, as some of the best poststructuralist feminist criticism is now doing. In addition to Terry Castle, see Peggy Kamuf, *Fictions of Feminine Desire: Disclosures of Heloise* (Lincoln: Univ. of Nebraska Press, 1982).

44. Jacques Derrida, *Of Grammatology*, trans. Gayatri Chakravorty Spivak (Baltimore: Johns Hopkins Univ. Press, 1976), pp. 141–64.

lary discourse and its twin obsessions with death and writing. Clarissa's apologetic tone, indeed, recalls that of Ovid in the *Tristia* and Canace in the *Heroides;* where Clarissa begs forgiveness for the blanks, Canace apologizes for the blots that stain the paper—as Ovid and Ovid's book apologize in the *Tristia.* Where Canace holds pen in one hand and sword in the other, Clarissa's penknife conflates the two functions, as does her use of her coffin as a writing desk. (The frontispiece of a seventeenth-century English translation of Ovid's *Tristia* portrays the whole course of Ovid's life from his fame in Rome to his banishment in Tomos. On one side stands a pyramid built on the books that are monuments to his fame; on the other side is the pyramid of his ruin, the sole foundation of which is *The Art of Love.* In the foreground, Ovid himself lies with an open book, writing implements, and a bay leaf laurel: he is using his coffin as a writing desk.)[45] The obsession with inscription—with writing-to-the-moment taken up to the mouth of the grave—leads directly back to such Ovidian heroines as Phyllis, who testifies against the man who "brought her death to pass / Her own the hand by which she fell" (2:147–48). In Richardson's *History of a Young Lady,* writing is an act that simultaneously makes history while recording it, yet few acts are more isolating than the act of inscription. Clarissa's inscription, like those of Ovid's heroines, is her testimony; her coffin, indeed, becomes a complex code to be deciphered, inviting exhaustive exegesis but subverting all attempts to fix the meaning as unalterably as Clarissa's fate is fixed. In many ways, the coffin is a microcosm of the entire project of epistolarity: the obsession with deadlines, dates, dreaded days, and destinations that mark the genre are compressed here in three enigmatic numbers: the year, the date, April 10, and "aetat xix." The numbers themselves are a confession of all that is unknowable, for while wondering whether she has "Ten days?—A week?" to live, Clarissa must finally inscribe a date without knowing what her closing day will be; by the time she does know, moreover, time has become utterly irrelevant to her. (This irrelevance is what makes her grandfather's attempt to hoard the family's possessions "to the end of time" so ironically futile.)[46] Her way of signing (of signing off, one might say) is another manifestation of epistolarity; like her signatures in previous letters, the way she decorates her coffin situates her on an emotional map.

45. Ovid, *Tristia*, trans. W. Saltonstall (London: Mary Clarke, 5th edition, 1681). On death and writing, see Stewart, especially "Afterwords: Death Bequeathed," pp. 313–56.

46. Doody, p. 186.

Where previous letters sounded every note on the emotional register from "your ever-sorrowful" to "your now happy daughter," the coffin registers her final recognition of the relation of time to eternity and her anticipation of her psychic journey home.

The coffin as a writing desk signifies not only the relation of death to writing, but of writing to the body: the same container that supports her paper while she writes will cradle her body—and perhaps her child—in death. The two realities that have eluded representation time out of mind—death and the female body—are thus joined in one container: Clarissa's coffin. Clarissa's body, moreover, is finally as cryptic as her coffin, for though it has been pierced by Lovelace's rape, he never penetrates the mystery of what he ravishes. Thus, Clarissa writes: "O Lovelace! if you could be sorry for yourself, I would be sorry too—But when all my doors are fast, and nothing but the key-hole open, and the key of late put into that, to be where you are, in a manner without opening any of them . . ." (5:36:335). This crucial passage is yet another of Clarissa's enigmatic laments, drawn from that "alien area of discourse" that is the legacy of the genre of amorous epistolary discourse. If only Lovelace could feel something for himself, Clarissa could feel something for him too; it is in this sense that her letters are an elegy of desire. Her pity and compassion are for her persecutor as well as for herself, but that empathy is blocked, thwarted by the qualifier "if." What she recognizes is not only that he can feel nothing for her but that he is so self-alienated that he feels nothing at all. Clarissa's awareness is a repeated motif—a going out of herself to imagine the other, even in her moments of greatest extremity. Even on her deathbed when she repudiates him for cutting her off in the bloom of her youth, she continues to reflect on what it must be like to be Lovelace: "I have reason to be thankful, for being taken away from the evil of supporting my part of a yoke with a man so *unhappy*" (8:137). Mark Kinkead-Weekes maintains that Lovelace will ever be present at the center of Clarissa's personality, since he has penetrated her innermost core, but the reverse is true. *She* understands *his* innermost core.[47] Her words here, actually, explicitly refute the notion that he has penetrated to her "center," for the rape is an act of savagery that excludes Lovelace more than ever before.

The dialogism that is one of the trademarks of the genre of amo-

47. Mark Kinkead-Weekes, *Samuel Richardson: Dramatic Novelist* (Ithaca: Cornell Univ. Press, 1973), pp. 253–59.

rous epistolary discourse is multifaceted in *Clarissa*. First, as we have seen, Clarissa's use of an alternative logic in conflict with Lovelace's makes the novel dialogic, but the novel is also the site of a multilingual dialogue between texts, for Richardsonian eros looks back to Racine and forward to de Sade. Eros in this novel is an ordeal of fascination: Clarissa's ordeal, Lovelace's fascination. Racine's subject is not so much eros as the use of force in an erotic situation. Eros is therefore closely allied to hatred, for when sexuality is conceived of as power, then eros can only take the form of conflict between strong and weak, tyrant and captive.[48] This view of love illuminates Lovelace's treatment of Clarissa, his impulses toward destruction and revenge, dominance and submission. Like Racine's lover-tyrants, notably, Lovelace is simultaneously an actor and a spectator in the drama. That doubling lies at the heart of Richardsonian eros, for it reveals that Lovelace is compelled not by desire but by alienation. Clarissa's words are an explicit recognition of this profound paradox. Despite the fact that she has just been raped, she makes an imaginative leap from self to other, which is the more extraordinary because it comes at precisely the moment of her greatest extremity and disintegration. In an instant when her own physical state is ghastly, the words "If you could be sorry for yourself, I would be sorry too" are an epiphany about Lovelace's self-hatred, his utter self-alienation. Terry Eagleton remarks on Lovelace's "own terrible lack of being. . . . thoroughly narcissistic and regressive, Lovelace's 'rakishness,' for all its virile panache, is nothing less than a crippling incapacity for adult sexual relationship. His misogyny and infantile sadism achieve their appropriate expression in the virulently anti-sexual act of rape. It is this pathetic character who has been celebrated by the critics as Byronic hero, Satanic vitalist or post-modernist artist."[49] Such critical myopia

48. See Roland Barthes's discussion of Racinian eros in *On Racine*, trans. Richard Howard (New York: Hill and Wang, 1964), pp. 12, 22–25. Doody (chaps. 5 and 6) compares Lovelace to the rakes of Restoration comedy and the lover-tyrants who come to Restoration tragedy by way of Racine and Corneille. Although I trace Lovelace's predecessors to Ovid, Doody's argument in many ways supports my own, for the parallels she draws reveal the dialogic dynamism I am charting. Doody further demonstrates that the conflict between the principals is related to a conflict of genres. Lovelace defines himself as a rake in a comedy of seduction, which Richardson juxtaposes with the tragedy of Clarissa's death (pp. 113–14). Such generic doubleness is of course one of the distinguishing characteristics of Ovidian stylistics, paralleling the doubling of genders.

49. Eagleton, *The Rape of Clarissa*, pp. 63–64.

has obscured not just Lovelace's lack but the elegy of desire in Clarissa's discourse.

Just as Heloise inscribes her desire within the rigid form of the *epistola deprecatoria,* Clarissa's desire lies encrypted in her will. The same ambiguous relation of love and hate, inside and outside, art and nature relates to Clarissa's crypt as well as her body, for a crypt, as Derrida suggests, disguises and hides a body but simultaneously disguises the act of hiding and hides a disguise. Like the writing in amorous discourses, death in this novel partakes of both presence and absence, nature and art. Anna Howe praises her dead friend's artistry in decorating her coffin by lamenting, "In this, as in every-thing else, *Nature* was her *Art,* her *Art* was *Nature*" (8:232). Yet it is possible that Anna is seeing an identity where there is a difference, for a crypt is, as Derrida reflects,

> carved out of nature. . . . these grounds are not natural. A crypt is never natural through and through, and if, as is well known, *physis* has a tendency to encrypt (itself), that is because it overflows its own bounds and encloses, naturally, its others, all others. The crypt is thus not a natural place, but the striking history of an artifice, an *architecture,* an artifact: of a place *comprehended* within another but rigorously separate from it, isolated from general space by partitions, an enclosure, an enclave.[50]

In *Clarissa; or, The History of a Young Lady,* the heroine is treated like an artifact; locked up like the silver plate, she returns home in a silver coffin. Denied all significance on her own terms, she can only be comprehended within other systems of signification: her father tells her he'll never speak to her again except as Mrs. Solmes; her rapist tells her she'll die a Lovelace.[51] Yet her letters overflow all bounds. The traces of amorous epistolary discourse can be seen in the defiant transgression her letters represent, for her adaptation of the Book of Job is a remarkable transgression of the boundaries of gender, of language, of prophecy, of lamentation. By transforming all the biblical references from *he* and *him* to *she* and *her,* she encloses an alternative sign system in a testament of radical feminism. Her discourse is a sustained critique of language, for her substitutions expose the limitations of language, the partitions that separate woman as other.

50. Jacques Derrida, "Fors," trans. Barbara Johnson, *Georgia Review* 31 (Spring 1977), 64–116.
51. Doody, p. 186. See also Castle, chaps. 4 and 5.

Language turns women into fictions, making them invisible not only in the law books but in the book of life. The ways in which her imagery in her revision of the Book of Job departs from the original is a crucial deformation, signaling her isolation and the sterility by which she is partitioned. The lack of fertility and fruition—the unripe grape, the cast-off flower—dramatize how thoroughly her attention is fixed on the interruption of natural processes and on the conspiracy of nature and culture in the nullification of the female. Her writing stages a revolt against all such scriptures and strictures. She discovers the duplicity of all dichotomies—victory and defeat, love and hate, life and death—for these fictions of man's language have nothing to do with the heart's desires or the body's experience.

Thus, as in the *Heroides* and in the letters of Heloise and Mariane, desire lies encrypted but not enclosed in Clarissa's coffin, the final container of her body, her desire, and her text. The impending death of the heroine gives birth to the reader, Lady Bradshaigh, who in turn pleads with Richardson, the only author with the authority to save Clarissa's life, although Belfour provides him with multiple alternatives to forestall both the heroine's death and the cessation of writing. Like Clarissa's, Belfour's correspondence is the inscription of *différance;* Belfour differs with the authorities and defers death. This dialogic dynamic is multidimensional, for her correspondence with the author becomes entangled in the narrative line, making the production of meaning a complex transference of desire. The desires that are transferred are not identical in all ages, however, as the contrast between Lady Bradshaigh's response and that of Freudian critics like John Dussinger makes clear. Freud at the beginning of the century helped to unlock our sexual responses; it is perhaps time at the end of the century to unlock our affectional responses.[52] Experiments like Barthes's *Lover's Discourse: Fragments* and *The Three Marias* are just such conscious attempts at unlocking—attempts which are neither naïve nor nostalgic nor blithely sentimental. They are based

52. Mark Spilka, "On the Enrichment of Poor Monkeys by Myth and Dream; or, How Dickens Rousseauisticized and Pre-Freudianized Victorian Views of Childhood," *Sexuality and Victorian Literature,* ed. Don Richard Cox, Tennessee Studies in Literature 27 (Knoxville: Univ. of Tennessee Press, 1984), p. 177. Lawrence Stone maintains in his controversial study, *The Family, Sex and Marriage in England, 1500–1800* (London: Weidenfeld and Nicolson, 1977), that the eighteenth century saw the rise of "affective individualism," which led to a new acceptance of romantic love and a new role for the novel: "The growth of literacy . . . created a literature of self-exploration, from the novel to the love letter," p. 226.

not on character identification but on writing. By writing to certain lovers (Werther, the Portuguese nun), Barthes and the Marias re-inscribe the discourse of pathos central in each classic text. This kind of writing is an encoding of desire that, in Barthes's words, destroys "every point of origin. . . . Writing is that neutral, composite, oblique space where our subject slips away, the negative where all identity is lost, starting with the very identity of the body writing. . . . In the multiplicity of writing, everything is to be disentangled, nothing de-ciphered."[53] Because Clarissa refuses to be constituted as Lovelace's subject or to subject herself to the authority of a family unfit to rule, with her death Lovelace laments, "I have lost the only subject worth writing on." The final rebellion Clarissa's writing stages lies in slip-ping away with the words, "I am Nobody's." It also lies in leaving the living with a clearly inscribed record of what might have been, for the legalistic logic of Lovelace and the Harlowes is far from inexorable. Arguing eloquently by an alternative logic, Clarissa demonstrates that love, honor, and fulfillment were all possible; this understanding is what her elegy of desire inscribes. From Ariadne's thread we come full circle to Clarissa's emblem of the serpent with its tail in its mouth, for amorous discourse subverts all searches for origins and all strat-egies to reduce, sum up, or contain the space of desire. Richardson's novel thus simultaneously assimilates the genre of amorous epistolary discourse and highlights it, for by combining the ancient rhetorical exercises of *suasoriae* and *ethopoiiae* in a discourse of pathos, Clarissa looks back to Ovid's heroines, to Heloise, and to the Portuguese nun. In her quest for integrity of text and body, she transforms the ordeal of abandonment into a testament of passion. In her search for a home, Clarissa resembles another outcast thrown back on her own resources. Like Clarissa, Jane Eyre is a writer striving to control her ire and compose herself, searching for a Universal Parent who, rather than cursing her, will claim and embrace her.

53. Roland Barthes, "The Death of the Author," in *Image-Music-Text*, trans. Ste-phen Heath (New York: Hill and Wang, 1977), p. 142. See also Castle, pp. 146–47.

Love is a shadow.
How you lie and cry after it
Listen: these are its hooves: it has gone off, like a
horse.
       . . .
I am inhabited by a cry.
Nightly it flaps out
Looking, with its hooks, for something to love.

SYLVIA PLATH, "Elm"

5

Jane Eyre:
The Ties That Blind

The Letter Writer. This color chalk drawing by Achille Deveria (1800–1857) is reproduced courtesy of the Cooper-Hewitt Museum, The Smithsonian Institution's National Museum of Design, New York.

Charlotte Brontë's Letters to M. Heger

In Charlotte Brontë's letters to Constantin Heger, the Belgian schoolmaster whom she loved hopelessly, amorous epistolary discourse resurfaces with all the passionate intensity of unrequited love. Her letters have all the rhetorical power of Heloise's, all the desperation and despair of the Portuguese nun's. Where Lady Bradshaigh is transformed from Richardson's correspondent into collaborator in the composition of *Clarissa*, Charlotte Brontë is transformed from Heger's correspondent into the novelist of *Jane Eyre*. Rather than psychoanalyze Charlotte or reduce the art to the life, I aim to examine the rhetorical strategies that link these particular letters to this particular novel, to explore once more the fluid boundaries between the letter as literature, literature as a letter. In turning from Richardson's epistolary novel to Brontë's first-person narrative, the genre of amorous epistolary discourse takes another detour, and Charlotte's love letters are the signpost of that detour, the means by which we can trace the metamorphosis of the rhetoric of passion from an authentic to a fictional discourse.

The facts, briefly, are these: Charlotte and Emily set out for Brussels in February 1842, determined to further their education in order to free themselves from the slavery of being governesses for the rest of their lives. They both returned to England upon their aunt's death; Charlotte went back to Brussels alone in February 1843, "prompted by what then seemed an irresistible impulse"[1]—her passionate infatuation with the married man who was first her teacher, then her employer. Long before either Heger or Charlotte was fully conscious of the situation, Mme Heger assessed its implications; relations between the Hegers and Charlotte cooled, and she went home in

---

1. Charlotte Brontë to Ellen Nussey, 14 Oct. 1846, in Clement K. Shorter, *The Brontës: Life and Letters* (London: Hodder Press, 1908), 1:339. I have also consulted Shorter's *The Brontës and Their Circle* (London: Dent, 1914); and T. J. Wise and J. A. Symington, eds., *The Brontës: Their Lives, Friendships, and Correspondence*, Shakespeare Head Edition, 4 vols. (Oxford: Basil Blackwell, 1932). Further references in parenthesis in the text are to *SLL*, *SBC*, and *W & S*, respectively.

January 1844, "the biggest single experience of her life . . . over."[2] Charlotte, however, hoped to return to Brussels and wanted to correspond frequently and intimately with her beloved master in the interim. Between January and July 1844, they did correspond, and Mlle Louise Heger, the professor's daughter, maintained that Charlotte wrote many more letters than the four that survive.[3] What seems to have happened is that Charlotte's letters became increasingly personal, passionate, intense, for she writes on 24 July 1844: "Ah, Monsieur! I once wrote you a letter that was less than reasonable, because sorrow was at my heart; but I shall do so no more.—I shall try to be selfish no longer; and even while I look upon your letters as one of the greatest felicities known to me, I shall await the receipt of them in patience until it pleases you and suits you to send me any. Meanwhile, I may well send you a little letter from time to time:—you have authorised me to do so" (*W & S*, 2:12). From the first letter forward, all the distinguishing characteristics of amorous epistolary discourse are present: the denial of the reality of separation, the desire for contact, despair at the master's silence, and finally, resigned desolation. As is so often the case in amorous epistles, the story is over when the curtain rises, for this letter gives a tantalizing glimpse of prior events that remain enigmatic. In this letter, the first extant evidence of the extent of Charlotte's passion, she is as submissive as Heloise was initially. The emphasis on having been given the authority to write is important, for it demonstrates once again the master's control over speech, his authority to impose silence. As in the *Portuguese Letters*, it reflects a naïve belief in reciprocity. So long as the beloved writes, one can sustain the illusion of a relationship, nurture the hope of reunion, and not be too sad. Despite Charlotte's conciliatory tone of apology for previous "excesses" (whatever they might have been), Heger responds by reprimanding her for extravagant feelings and morbid outlook, and commands her to confine herself to such neutral matters as her health, her activities, her family—not, in other words, to write out of turn.[4] Just as Heloise rebelled against the tyranny of forms in her second letter to Abelard, Charlotte's conciliatory tone shifts after his rebuke. Instead of submitting to this injunction, she escalates the passionate tone of her letters; she becomes more outspoken, more

2. Winifred Gérin, *Charlotte Brontë: The Evolution of Genius* (Oxford: Oxford Univ. Press, 1967), p. 255. The whole tale is recounted in Chapters 12–14.
3. See *Brontë Society Transactions* 11:4 (1949), p. 260; Gérin, p. 260.
4. Gérin, pp. 259–60.

indignant, less submissive. She imagines that Mme Heger has poisoned her husband's mind against her and becomes convinced that she intercepts Charlotte's letters; she therefore devises means to insure that friends carry her letters to him directly. Still he does not respond. By January 1845, exactly one year after she left Brussels, she writes to him without salutation, lamenting his silence and telling herself, "You must be resigned, and above all do not grieve at a misfortune which you have not deserved" (*W & S*, 2:23). Like so much of amorous epistolary discourse, the letter is addressed to the self as well as the beloved. Charlotte situates herself emotionally, spatially, and temporally vis-à-vis Heger; she imagines the letter as a dialogue with him. She tries to convey the effect his silence has on her and at the same time to imagine what his response as reader will be: "I know that you will be irritated when you read this letter. You will say once more that I am hysterical [or neurotic]—that I have black thoughts, etc. So be it, Monsieur; I do not seek to justify myself; I submit to every sort of reproach" (*W & S*, 2:23).

Her words recall Mariane's proclamation that she would rather suffer than forget her beloved, for Charlotte continues, "I would rather suffer the greatest physical pain than always have my heart lacerated by smarting regrets." Like the Portuguese nun, she beseeches Heger to help her understand her experience and her emotions; what torments her more than anything are her doubts about his feelings. Did she imagine that he ever cared for her? Whatever her feelings, her outward behavior was irreproachable; why is she being persecuted when she is innocent? How could such an astute observer as she have miscalculated the behavior of one she had watched with such intense interest? How could he take such an interest in her in Brussels and abandon her so utterly now? In his silence, she imagines in this same letter his side of the correspondence:

> If my master withdraws his friendship from me entirely I shall be altogether without hope; if he gives me a little—just a little—I shall be satisfied—happy; I shall have a reason for living on, for working. . . .
>
> Nor do I, either, need much affection from those I love. I should not know what to do with a friendship entire and complete—I am not used to it. But you showed me of yore a *little* interest, when I was your pupil in Brussels, and I hold on to the maintenance of that *little* interest—I hold on to it as I would hold on to life. . . .
>
> You will tell me perhaps—"I take not the slightest interest in you, Mademoiselle Charlotte. You are no longer an inmate of my House; I have forgotten you."

Well, Monsieur, tell me so frankly. It will be a shock to me. It matters
not. It would be less dreadful than uncertainty. (*W & S*, 2:23–24)

Charlotte's plea resembles that of the Portuguese nun, who first
begged the chevalier to end her doubt, then castigated him when he
destroyed her illusions. Like all amorous epistolary discourses, Charlotte's letters are demands, pleas, threats, and confrontations, filled
with the same marks of internal tension, contradiction, self-division,
and torment. Like Heloise, she is acutely aware of her emotions as they
arise and has the same power to articulate them.

Although Mrs. Gaskell refers to "poor Charlotte," as if her passion
for Heger had absolutely no basis in reality, the real situation was far
more ambiguous, for she is a "threshold figure" whose very role as
student-governess-teacher makes her status ambiguous sexually, economically, and emotionally. She is simultaneously a family intimate
and a family employee; the boundaries between belonging to and
being excluded from the family are constantly shifting ones. Brontë
returns repeatedly to this double bind by focusing on the figure of the
governess. On the one hand, the governess is dependent upon her
employers; on the other hand, her superior education separates her
from the servants, who frequently view her with some suspicion. In
short, she is a lady in every sense except in the economic sense. As
Elizabeth Rigby points out in a review of *Vanity Fair* and *Jane Eyre*,
which includes a report on the status of governesses:

> The real definition of a governess, in the English sense, is a being who is
> our equal in birth, manners, and education, but our inferior in worldly
> wealth. . . . There is no class which so cruelly requires its members to be,
> in birth, mind, and manners, above their station, in order to fit them for
> their station. . . . She is a bore to almost any gentleman, as a tabooed
> woman, to whom he is interdicted from granting the usual privileges of
> the sex, and yet who is perpetually crossing his path. She is a bore to
> most ladies by the same rule, and a reproach, too—for her dull, fag-
> ging, bread-and-water life is perpetually putting their pampered list-
> lessness to shame. The servants invariably detest her, for she is a depen-
> dent like themselves, and yet, for all that, as much their superior in
> other respects as the family they both serve. Her pupils may love her,
> and she may take the deepest interest in them, but they cannot be her
> friends.[5]

5. Elizabeth Rigby, "*Vanity Fair, Jane Eyre*, and the Governesses' Benevolent Institution—Report for 1847," *Quarterly Review* 84 (Dec. 1848), 153–85. See also Elizabeth Gaskell, *The Life of Charlotte Brontë*, 2 vols. (London: Smith, Elder, and Co., 1857),
chaps. 11 and 12.

The ambiguity of the governess' status helps to explain Blanche Ingram's attempt to humiliate Jane Eyre. The Ingrams recall how they "sermonised [their governess] on the presumption of attempting to teach such clever blades as we were, when she was herself so ignorant."[6] (James's heroine in *The Turn of the Screw* is similarly preoccupied with the contrast between her own "small, smothered life" and the children's need of a large "education for the world."[7] She alternates between asserting her superiority over the illiterate Mrs. Grose, and hiding her sense of inferiority and insecurity from the children.) Blanche Ingram recalls getting revenge on one poor governess by "prosecuting (or persecuting)" the tutor and the governess for falling in love, for "there are a thousand reasons why liaisons between governesses and tutors should never be tolerated a moment in any well-regulated house . . . danger of bad example to innocence of childhood—distractions and consequent neglect of duty on the part of the attached—mutual alliance and reliance; confidence thence resulting—insolence accompanying—mutiny and general blow-up" (156). Many of her earlier letters testify to Charlotte's deep sense of humiliation at what she calls "the slavery of governessing"; she complains in one letter that tutoring "dolts" drains her of energy for writing, and she continually feels acutely compromised. When she served as governess for the Sidgwicks in 1839, for instance, one cousin reported that if Charlotte was "invited to walk to church with them, she thought she was being ordered about like a slave; if she was not invited, she imagined she was excluded from the family circle" (*W & S*, 1:177).[8] Charlotte was as sensitive to injustices related to sex as to class status. In Brussels, for example, she was acutely aware of the unfairness of her situation as a single woman; she was deeply disturbed when a fellow teacher confessed her desperation to marry, else she'd have no choice but to become a sister of charity when her employment with the Hegers ended.[9]

From Ovid onward, orphanhood, solitude, and exile are the major

6. Charlotte Brontë, *Jane Eyre: An Autobiography*, ed. Richard J. Dunn (New York: W. W. Norton, 1971), p. 156, hereinafter cited parenthetically in the text by page number.

7. Henry James, *The Turn of the Screw*, ed. Robert Kimbrough (New York: W. W. Norton, 1966), p. 15.

8. See also Tom Winnifrith, *The Brontës and Their Background: Romance and Reality* (New York: Barnes and Noble, 1973), p. 153; Terry Eagleton, *Myths of Power: A Marxist Study of the Brontës* (London: Macmillan, 1975), p. 10.

9. Gérin, pp. 229–30.

themes in amorous epistolary discourse; these traumas form the core of Charlotte's Brussels experience and are ceaselessly reiterated in her subsequent letters to Heger. On the basis of these letters, her biographer Winifred Gérin concludes:

> The more she fed upon the pleasure of [Heger's] company and friendship, the more she realized what little claim she had to either. . . .
> The more she tasted it the more she craved, and soon *not* to be in his company was torment. To be relegated to the secondary role of employee, when at times she could be the confidante of his expansive moods, was almost too bitter to be borne—however absurd the claim. But she knew that it was absurd. It was this that made her forgo the Heger's sitting room in the evening, rather than any feeling of delicacy about encroaching on the family privacy.
> The sight of his absorption in family-life could rouse feelings so rebellious and searing that she would rather endure loneliness than provoke them . . . [but] their suppression almost unhinged her.[10]

The sentences in Charlotte's letters are as contradictory as her emotions. At one point, she beseeches Heger to "speak to me a little of yourself"; she asks for news of his children, the school, and his travels. But the neutral tone shifts suddenly to desperation when she adds, "Tell me, in short, my master, what you will, but tell me something. To write to an ex-assistant-governess (No! I refuse to remember my employment as assistant-governess—I repudiate it)—anyhow, to write to an old pupil cannot be a very interesting occupation for you, I know; but for me it is life. Your last letter was stay and prop to me—nourishment to me for half a year" (*W & S*, 2:70). The letter thus testifies to the tensions of status as well as sex; if she seems in these lines to regain her composure by regarding herself as a pupil rather than an ex-governess, she loses it again in trying to make Heger see how much she needs to hear from him. The emphasis on emotional starvation, indeed, is a repeated motif in all of her poems and letters; she asks him for nourishment and concludes this letter by confessing that she has no appetite. In an earlier letter, similarly, she tries to convince him to write to her by remarking that "the poor have not need of much to sustain them—they ask only for the crumbs that fall from the rich men's table. But if they are refused the crumbs they die of hunger" (*W & S*, 2:23).

The plea, like all her pleas, is painful to read, but it was met with

---

10. Ibid., p. 226 and see app. A, "Mrs. Gaskell and M. Heger," pp. 568–75.

silence. The letters testify to Charlotte's struggle to reconcile her memory of her master's warmth to his present coldness. In Brussels with the Heger family, she struggled with the ambiguity of her role as both an insider and an outsider, but the subtler struggle to decipher the signs of sexual attraction on her part—and encouragement on Heger's—is more difficult to assess. Despite Mrs. Gaskell's attempts to exonerate Heger, it seems unlikely that Charlotte's response to him was sheer fantasy. Instead, as with Abelard and Heloise, the relation of male professor and female student was sexually charged, and Charlotte may well have responded intuitively to a charisma that was sexual as well as intellectual. Heger, moreover, could exploit that charged atmosphere without actually seducing any students. None of his letters to Charlotte survive, but his letters to other students reveal passionate and intense—albeit platonic—relationships. To Meta Mossman, a student who, like Charlotte, "adored" him, he wrote: "I have only to think of you to see you . . . with a hearty will I evoke your image. . . . I see you, I talk with you . . . just as I knew you, my dear M—— as I have esteemed and loved you." He goes on—in words that seem uncannily to foreshadow Rochester's psychic communication with Jane Eyre—to speak of her as always close to him by means of "communication between two distant hearts, instantaneous, without paper, without pen, or words, or messenger," a method of correspondence he finds "precious . . . spiritual, magnetic."[11] Ironically, this is just the sort of exchange Charlotte yearned for. That Heger's own personality was powerfully magnetic can be seen in other letters, as well as in Brontë's portraits of him in *Jane Eyre* and *Villette*. Indeed, critical assessments of the Brontë-Heger relationship bear a remarkable resemblance to Abelard and Heloise's. Helene Moglen, for example, describes Heger as "both father and lover: she is mistress and daughter. . . . A domineering man, possessed of a quick temper, he used his position and his personality as weapons: substitutes for reason, excuses for petty tyrannies. . . . He exploited the teacher-student relationship, with its undisputed hierarchy of power, its always latent sexuality, its allowance for dependence—even idolatry. . . . All of this provided a channeling of psychosexual forces acceptable within the Victorian culture."[12] If Moglen is even partially right, then one must

11. Translation of original letter from M. Heger to Meta Mossman, 21 Nov. 1887, by courtesy of Walter Cunliffe, Esq., cited in Gérin, pp. 262–63.
12. Helene Moglen, *Charlotte Brontë: The Self Conceived* (New York: W. W. Norton, 1976), pp. 63, 83.

shift one's perception of the relationship from the fantasies of "poor Charlotte" to a response to Heger's power as employer, professor, and master; if his dynamism was sexual as well as intellectual, then Charlotte's "expulsion" from the Pensionnat Heger may have been the result of her too explicit response to the underlying realities of the situation and his character. Since her letters home invariably concentrate on those underlying realities of her Brussels experience, rather than mere superficialities, it seems plausible that in the lost love letters as well she would address the "deep structure" rather than the surface experience. In Moglen's view, Heger rebukes her and ends the correspondence precisely because she "blasted the surface of 'conventional interaction' [and] grasped implication by the throat."[13] Thus, in addition to suffering the sense of exclusion that plagues the lovers in amorous discourse, Charlotte's humiliation was inextricably linked to the social code that made a single woman a symbolic threat to the society around her—to the class system that exploited her ambiguous status, to the school's reputation, to the family, to monogamy. No wonder Mme Heger got rid of her. How deep a threat she was conceived to be is perhaps revealed in the fact that the very name Brontë was taboo at the school for many years after her departure.[14]

As master, Heger's authority to impose silence cannot be overestimated. It is this authority that has the most profound effect on Charlotte's writing, for she returns to its tyrannies again and again in her letters and in *Jane Eyre*. What is perhaps most striking is her own capacity for self-denial and abject submission; in her yearning for his approval and her desire to win his heart by lacerating her own, she resembles the Portuguese nun. She imposes a silence of six months upon herself, just to show Heger that the tone of her letters will never again be so passionate and explicit. Like so many amorous writers before her, she reveals her obsession with times, dates, deadlines, for she writes to him on the exact date that the six-month sentence ends:

The six months of silence have run their course. It is now the 18th of Novr.; my last letter was dated . . . the 18th of May. I may therefore write to you without failing in my promise.
The summer and autumn seemed very long to me; truth to tell, it has needed painful efforts on my part to bear hitherto the self-denial which I have imposed on myself. . . . I tell you frankly that I have tried

13. Ibid., p. 70.
14. Gérin, p. 263.

meanwhile to forget you, for the remembrance of a person whom one thinks never to see again and whom, nevertheless, one greatly esteems, frets too much the mind; and when one has suffered that kind of anxiety for a year or two, one is ready to do anything to find peace once more. I have done everything; I have sought occupations; I have denied myself absolutely the pleasure of speaking about you—even to Emily; but I have been able to conquer neither my regrets nor my impatience. That, indeed, is humiliating—to be unable to control one's own thoughts, to be a slave of a regret, of a memory, the slave of a fixed and dominant idea which lords it over the mind. Why cannot I have just as much friendship for you, as you for me—neither more nor less? Then should I be so tranquil, so free—I could keep silence then for ten years without an effort. . . .

To forbid me to write to you, to refuse to answer me, would be to tear from me my only joy on earth, to deprive me of my last privilege—a privilege I never shall consent willingly to surrender. Believe me, my master, in writing to me it is a good deed that you will do. So long as I believe you are pleased with me, so long as I have hope of receiving news from you, I can be at rest and not too sad. But when a prolonged and gloomy silence seems to threaten me with the estrangement of my master—when day by day I await a letter, and when day by day disappointment comes to fling me back into overwhelming sorrow, and the sweet delight of seeing your handwriting . . . escapes me as a vision that is vain, then fever claims me—I lose appetite and sleep—I pine away.

May I write to you again next May? I would rather wait a year, but it is impossible—it is too long. (18 Nov. 1845, *W & S*, 2:69–71)

This one letter reiterates many of the distinguishing characteristics of the genre I have been tracing, demonstrating just how fluid are the boundaries between fictional and authentic correspondence. The subdued tone is nearly identical to that in the Portuguese nun's last letter; it is a resigned effort to come to grips with the beloved's indifference. Just as the nun wonders what blind and malicious fate drives us to love those who only love others, Charlotte wonders why she cannot feel mere friendship for Heger. Both letters similarly testify to a desire for tranquillity. Like Heloise, Charlotte is an articulate recorder of her suffering, an intelligent observer of her own powerlessness, acutely aware of her inability to substitute "correct" thoughts for those of her implacable idée fixe. Like Heloise, she is aware of all the tyrannies to which she is subjected and openly defies them when she says that she will never willingly surrender the privilege of writing. The letter is an extraordinary record of the tension between submission and rebellion; she asks permission to write again, thus keeping the circuit of desire open, and tries to be dutiful by postponing the pleasure of writing for six months, but she finally refuses to wait that long. The letter is an attempt to negotiate some kind of correspondence with Heger that he will not find objectionable; all she dares hope for is an occasional word to let her know that he is "pleased" with her. Like other amorous epistles, her letter is a masterpiece of rhetorical persuasion; she tries to convince him that writing to her will be an act of Christian charity, a good deed. Sadly, she is not able to negotiate even the kind of impersonal correspondence Heloise eventually secures from Abelard, for Heger never responds and she never writes to him again.

In her fiction as well as her letters, therefore, silence is not just a theme but an obsession. Brontë makes it clear in her letters that she would have relinquished all the joys of creative expression—in fiction writing as well as letter writing—to win his approval. Not only does she torture herself by imposing a six-month silence in a correspondence that she calls "her only source of joy," but she is even willing to abandon writing altogether in obedience to Heger's counsel. Gérin points out that "she had sacrificed, under M. Heger's influence, her ambition to become a writer; she was self-condemned to the teaching profession, and if she had opened a school now her dedication to it would have been complete. That she had confided to M. Heger her youthful ambitions to become an author, and had, moreover, on returning to Brussels in 1843, taken back with her a sample of her juvenilia, has come to light."[15] Heger advised her to forsake writing and stick to teaching. So completely does she accept his evaluation of her talent—despite the encouragement of Southey and Coleridge—that she wistfully refers to her writing only as something that might have been:

> There is nothing I fear so much as idleness, the want of occupation . . . the lethargy of the faculties. . . . I should not know this lethargy if I could write. Formerly I passed whole days and weeks and months in writing, not wholly without result, for Southey and Coleridge . . . to whom I sent certain manuscripts—were good enough to express their approval. . . . I should write a book, and I should dedicate it to . . . the only master I ever had—to you, Monsieur. . . . But that cannot be—it is not to be thought of. The career of letters is closed to me—only that of teaching is open. It does not offer the same attractions, never mind, I shall enter it. (*W & S*, 2:13)

15. Ibid., p. 259.

Heger thus had an enormous effect on Charlotte's identity, her vocation, her vision of the world. For her, abandonment meant only one thing: Heger's utter rejection, his unremitting silence. In her letters, poems, and novels Charlotte continued all her life to portray the intense misery of loneliness, exile, and unrequited love. She speaks in one poem from this period of love as a "thin illusion . . . a hollow dream," and laments that she never even understood what caused his changed attitude towards her, "why my lover's eye . . . grew cold and clouded, proud and stern."[16] What is remarkable is how much she suffered and how long it lasted. Her father's near blindness, her own fear of going blind, Branwell's breakdown, the deaths one after the other of her sisters, and the unremitting isolation of Haworth exacerbated her grief over Heger. The circle is a vicious one: if she could write, she could break out of it; if she could break out of it, she could write. In Manchester for her father's cataract operation, she begins *Jane Eyre* "almost as a gesture of despair." This novel is thus a direct response to her obsession, a last refuge from the ordeal of consciousness that made her a "slave to sorrow."[17] I have chosen to focus on *Jane Eyre* precisely because of its rhetorically close connection to Charlotte's love letters to Heger. There are, of course, many more obvious parallels between Charlotte's Brussels experience and her novel *Villette* (1853), particularly the well-known similarities between Heger and Paul Emmanuel. My focus, however, is not on his characterization but on the metamorphosis of the rhetoric of passion from an authentic amorous epistolary discourse into the work of fiction with the closest parallels to that genre. Since Heger's silence nearly silenced her, causing her to forsake her fiction, it is not surprising that in the novel the master has the supreme authority to impose silence on all the women of Thornfield (Mrs. Fairfax, Grace Poole, Bertha Mason, and Jane herself). Like Abelard, he is the authority whose definitions revolve around dichotomies: sanity and madness, speech and silence, freedom and imprisonment. The novel enables us to trace the metamorphosis of the rhetoric of passion from Charlotte's authentic amorous epistolary discourse to a first-person narrative she defines as an autobiography. With *Jane Eyre,* an astute analysis of blind idolatry and solitary suffering in the life and letters of Charlotte Brontë is transformed into a sustained fiction of unsurpassed intensity and power.

16. *The Poems of Charlotte Brontë and Patrick Branwell Brontë,* ed. T. J. Wise and J. A. Symington (Oxford: Shakespeare Head Press, 1934), pp. 239–40. Further references in parenthesis in the text are to *PCB*.

17. Gérin, p. 328.

Blind Mouths: Critics of Gender and *Jane Eyre*

What is the difference between writing *like* a woman and being a woman writing? In *Jane Eyre*, Charlotte Brontë tries to focus her readers' attention on the tale rather than the teller, but the ruse had precisely the opposite effect, stimulating a rage of speculation about the identity, sex, circumstances, morality of the author of *Jane Eyre*. Charlotte tried, like Guilleragues and Richardson, to place an editor in the gap between author and text, but contemporary readers were more than a little preoccupied with the enigma of a title page that read *"Jane Eyre, An Autobiography,* Edited by Currer Bell." As had happened upon publication of the *Portuguese Letters,* theories demonstrating why the novel could only have been written by a woman and others insisting just as adamantly on male authorship proliferated. With Ovid, Guilleragues, and Richardson, we have explored some of the implications of writing *like* a woman, but to be a woman writing is apparently a far more volatile matter, for as Charlotte suggests, the woman writer faces *ad feminam* attacks on her character and personality. Writing as Currer Bell in the "Biographical Notice of Ellis and Acton Bell" that appears in *Wuthering Heights* and *Agnes Grey* (1850), she explains:

> Averse to personal publicity, we *veiled* our own names under those of Currer, Ellis, and Acton Bell; the *ambiguous* choice being dictated by a sort of conscientious scruple at assuming Christian names positively masculine, while we did not like to declare ourselves women, because— without at that time suspecting that our mode of *writing and thinking* was not what is called *"feminine"*—we had a vague impression that authoresses are liable to be looked on with prejudice; we had noticed how critics sometimes used for their chastisement the weapon of *personality*, and for their reward, a flattery, which is not true praise. (*W & S*, 2:79–80, my italics)

Despite the novel's popular and critical success, certain critical assessments dredge up all the stereotypical dichotomies associated with masculine and feminine: intellect versus emotion, head versus heart, hard versus soft, reason versus passion.

In addition, *Jane Eyre* is testimony to the same blurring of boundaries between art and life that figures so prominently in Lady Bradshaigh's correspondence with Richardson. The Mayfair crowd became convinced not only that Currer Bell was a woman but that she was William Thackeray's mistress and governess to his two children; gossips believed that the governess had written the novel in revenge for being jilted. The assumption that *governess* is synonymous with *mistress* reveals once again the extent to which a governess is a threshold figure, a sexual threat to family stability. Thackeray's wife, unfortunately, had been incarcerated for mental illness, and this circumstance further fueled the rumors. None of this society gossip reached Charlotte, who unwittingly added to Thackeray's discomfort by dedicating the second edition of the novel to him.[18]

Ironically, some critics thought they were demonstrating an enlightened, modern attitude of emancipation in concluding that the novelist was male. The reviewer for *Era,* for instance, proclaims that *Jane Eyre* "is no woman's writing. Although ladies have written histories, and travels, and warlike novels, to say nothing of books upon the different arts and sciences, no woman could have penned the 'Autobiography of Jane Eyre.'" Why not? Because it demonstrates the masculine "victory of mind over matter; the mastery of reason over feeling. . . . The writer dives deep into human life, and possesses the gift of being able to write as he thinks and feels. There is a vigour in all he says."[19] What it means to be human is thus relegated to masculine mastery, masculine vigor, masculine clarity and comprehension; other reviewers repeated the same praise in similar terms. One even congratulated the author for his "bold and skilful soldiership," his courage in "the front of the battle, as the champion of the weaker party."[20]

Critics who believed the author was a woman did not praise her boldness, vigor, and intellect. Instead, many found both the character and her creator *deficient* as women. James Lorimer, for example, says there is too much about Jane that is "hard, and angular, and indelicate as a woman. . . . We feel that she is a creature more of the intellect than of the affections." Thus, what is praiseworthy in a male is a shortcoming in a female. The novel, says Lorimer, is a "vigorous dwarf; in whose misshapen limbs the idea of the same powerful nature is still to be traced. . . . [its] fault is deformity." Not only does the critic evoke the medieval image of woman as a defective man, but he extends the monster metaphor from heroine to novelist. If *Jane Eyre* is the product "of a woman, she must be a woman pretty nearly

18. The same gossips speculated that Thackeray got even with his discarded mistress-turned-authoress by portraying her as Becky Sharp. See Rigby, pp. 174–75.

19. Unsigned review, *Era,* 14 Nov. 1847, in Miriam Allott, ed., *The Brontës: The Critical Heritage* (London: Routledge and Kegan Paul, 1974), p. 74.

20. A. W. Fonblanque, *Examiner,* 27 Nov. 1847, pp. 756–57, in Allott, p. 79.

unsexed; and Jane Eyre strikes us as a personage much more likely to have sprung ready armed from the head of a man, and that head a pretty hard one, than to have experienced, in any shape, the softening influence of female creation."[21] One of the most ingenious reviewers, E. P. Whipple, suggests that the novel was the joint effort of a man and a woman writer; since he knew for a "fact" that Ellis Bell had written *Wuthering Heights,* he concludes that one of the Bell sisters must have contributed the novel's feminine elements, but in other respects, "we observe the mind of the [male] author of *Wuthering Heights* at work in the text." He attributes the "clear, distinct, decisive style of its representation of character, manners, and scenery" to a male mind; the parts that he attributes to a female, significantly, are consistently described as peculiar. The novel contains some "unconscious feminine peculiarities," and the early chapters convey "a powerful and peculiar female intellect." Ultimately, however, the reviewer is too "gallant" to believe any female could have written the scenes of "mere animal appetite . . . of passion so hot, emphatic, and condensed in expression and so sternly masculine in feeling." He concludes by revealing the bias that underlies so many of these criticisms: "From the masculine tone of *Jane Eyre,* it might pass altogether as the composition of a man, were it not for some unconscious feminine peculiarities, which the strongest-minded woman that *ever aspired after manhood* cannot suppress" (my italics). Whipple's words here recall those of the Sappho scholar who referred to Sappho as a man manqué, who "experiences her 'defect' with violent and crushing intensity [because] . . . a man . . . has what she does not have and which she would give her life to have."[22]

Women reviewers seldom showed greater insight. Such passages as Brontë's famous plea for women's independence in Chapter 12 were seen as evidence that a "restless and vagrant imagination, though owned by woman, can have no sympathy of insight into the *really* feminine nature. . . . It is in the daily round of simple duties . . . that its

21. James Lorimer, *North British Review* 11 (Aug. 1849), 455–93, in Allott, p. 116. Lorimer concludes his review of *Wuthering Heights, The Tenant of Wildfellhall,* and *Jane Eyre* by confessing that he refused to read *Wuthering Heights* to the end: "The only consolation which we have in reflecting upon [all three books], arises from the conviction that they will never be very generally read."

22. Edwin Percy Whipple, "Novels of the Season," *North American Review* 141 (Oct. 1848), 354–69, in Allott, p. 98. Sappho's "defects" are analyzed by George Devereux, "The Nature of Sappho's Seizure in Fr. 31 LP as Evidence of Her Inversion," *Classical Quarterly,* n.s. 20 (1970), 22.

true happiness and satisfaction lie."[23] Elizabeth Rigby, similarly, shares the notion that only a deficient woman, unsexed in some way, could have written *Jane Eyre*. She criticizes the novelist's "horrid taste," "sheer rudeness and vulgarity," and Jane's "unregenerate and un-disciplined spirit." Rigby concludes that "if we ascribe the book to a woman at all, we have no alternative but to ascribe it to one who has, for some sufficient reason, long forfeited the society of her sex. And if by no woman, it is certainly also by no artist."[24]

It is Rigby who points out the deeply transgressive nature of Brontë's novel; it is not just the unlawful passion that she finds alarm-ing but the threat that passion poses to patriarchal structures—legal, religious, and economic. She sees *Jane Eyre* as inciting rebellion and transgression; the novel is as dangerous as is the threshold figure of the governess herself to class divisions and family unity. "Altogether," she understands,

> the auto-biography of *Jane Eyre* is preeminently an anti-Christian dis-course. There is throughout it a murmuring against the comforts of the rich and against the privations of the poor, which, as far as each indi-vidual is concerned, is a murmuring against God's appointment . . . for which we find no authority either in God's word or in God's provi-dence. . . . ungodly discontent . . . is . . . the most subtle evil which the law and the pulpit, which all civilized society in fact has at the present day to contend with. We do not hesitate to say that the tone of mind and thought which has overthrown authority and violated every code human and divine abroad, and fostered Chartism and rebellion at home, is the same which has also written *Jane Eyre*.[25]

What these reviews collectively reveal is just how shocking critics find feminine desire—what they refer to as the novel's coarseness and vulgarity. Equally objectionable is Brontë's inclusion of rage, not just love, in her depiction of passion. The enigmatic title, *Jane Eyre: An Autobiography*, may merely refer to Brontë's use of such factual details of her life as Cowan Bridge school, transformed into Lowood, or Maria, become Helen Burns. But the deep structure of autobiography, I believe, lies elsewhere. As Matthew Arnold comments of *Villette*, "The writer's mind contains nothing but hunger, rebellion, and rage, and therefore that is all she can, in fact, put into her book."[26] Yet could it

23. Anne Mozley, *Christian Remembrancer* 25 (April 1853), 401–43, in Allott, pp. 202–8.
24. Rigby, p. 176.
25. Ibid., pp. 173–74.
26. Matthew Arnold to Mrs. Foster, 14 April 1853, in Allott, p. 201.

not be precisely *because* Charlotte perceived other possibilities—saw the potential for far more happiness than she ever found—that she is full of hunger and rage? Virginia Woolf's assessment also focuses on rage: "The woman who wrote those pages . . . will write in a rage where she should write calmly . . . she will write of herself where she should write of her characters. She is at war with her lot."[27] Heger also criticized Brontë for the passion in her writing and commanded her to write "calmly"; yet the brutality of his silence resulted in years of anguish for Charlotte. In my view, this rage and desire constitute the deep structure of autobiography in the novel and illuminate the critics' preoccupation with what is variously termed its rebelliousness, competitiveness, envy, violence, or intensity.

Apparently, then, the critics can approve of men who adopt a so-called feminine style of writing, for they have praised such male authors as Ovid, Guilleragues, Richardson, and James for writing "like a woman." A woman writing, however, is an entirely different matter. If one judges from the critics cited above, one might conclude that *there is no such thing* as a woman writer: if she writes as Brontë does, she is condemned as "not *really feminine*," for a "real woman" would be incapable of writing with such rebelliousness, violence, and anger. A real woman, these critics seem to agree, is "calm" where Brontë rages; she expresses the "true happiness and satisfaction" that comes from doing her duty, where Brontë rebels. The structure of repression is triangular: (1) Charlotte's love letters resulted in Heger's rebuke for "writing out of turn." In an attempt to penetrate his indifference and break his silence, she forsakes her ambition to write and imposes a sentence of silence upon herself. (2) Within the novel, men criticize Jane as "violent and unfeminine" for having "an unfortunate state of mind." (3) Charlotte Brontë, the novelist, is rebuked for not writing like a woman. "The softening influence of female creation" is said to be lacking, and she is found too intellectual, too rational, too much the *master* of feeling, or others criticize her for excessive emotion. It is a classic example of a double bind. When a woman writing is perceived as a contradiction in terms, what woman writer, one wonders, would not be at war?[28]

27. Virginia Woolf, *A Room of One's Own* (New York: Harcourt, Brace, and World, 1929, 1957), p. 104.

28. In "The Difference of View," Mary Jacobus demonstrates how Virginia Woolf edits into her writing (in *A Room of One's Own*) the outburst edited out of Charlotte Brontë's, in *Women Writing and Writing about Women* (London: Croom Helm, 1979), pp. 16–17.

Critics have placed *Jane Eyre* in several novelistic traditions, ranging in focus from the governess novel to the Gothic. Thus Jerome
Beaty sees the genre of the governess novel as "a more appropriate
generic context" than has previously been noticed.[29] Robert Heilman,
however, defines the novel as "new Gothic," tracing its line of descent
from Richardson. Provocatively, in defining *new Gothic*, Heilman describes exactly those characteristics we have traced from the *Heroides*:

> When this line of descent [from Richardson] continues in the Brontës,
> the vital feeling moves toward an intensity, a freedom, and even an
> abandon virtually non-existent in historical Gothic. . . . Charlotte's
> women vibrate with passions . . . [with] an almost violent devotedness
> that has in it at once a fire of independence, a spiritual energy, a vivid
> sexual responsiveness, and, along with this, self-righteousness, a sense
> of power, sometimes self-pity and envious competitiveness. To an ex-
> tent the heroines are "unheroined," unsweetened. Into them there has
> come a new sense of the dark side of feeling and personality.[30]

The traits that Heilman identifies as new, however, are actually as
old as Ovid. Intensity, freedom, abandon, sexuality, power, rivalry,
envy, self-pity, and self-righteousness—the traits that make amorous
epistolary discourse distinctive are all here. Long before Jane Eyre,
unsweetened heroines—from Hermione to Helen, Hero to Hypermnestra—were writing discourses of desire. Both Heilman's and
Beaty's categories contain provocative elements of the tradition I am
tracing; in my view, the genre of amorous epistolary discourse includes elements of both the Gothic and the governess novel that they
see as generically definitive.

The precise relation between Charlotte's fiction and her love letters to Heger is enigmatic; one can only speculate on the extent to
which the power of her prose sprang from the repression of her
passion. If it is true, as Virginia Woolf suggests, that Charlotte wrote
of herself rather than of her characters, then Charlotte was Bertha
Mason as well as Jane Eyre, enraged at being cast out and shut up.
The novel, like the letters, defies the injunction of silence, recording
passionate anger as well as desire. As Woolf remarks of Charlotte,
"All her force, and it is the more tremendous for being constricted,

29. Jerome Beaty, *"Jane Eyre* and Genre," *Genre* 10 (Winter 1977), 619–53.
30. Robert B. Heilman, "Charlotte Brontë's 'New' Gothic," in *From Jane Austen to
Joseph Conrad*, ed. Robert Rathburn and Martin Steinmann, Jr. (Minneapolis: Univ. of
Minnesota Press, 1958), pp. 118–32, rpr. in Brontë, *Jane Eyre*, ed. Dunn, pp. 458–62.

goes into the assertion, 'I love,' 'I hate,' 'I suffer.'. . . . There is in [her] some untamed ferocity perpetually at war with the accepted order of things which makes [her] desire to create instantly rather than to observe patiently. This very ardour . . . allies itself with [her] more inarticulate passions."[31]

From Ovid's *Heroides* to *Clarissa*, all the texts examined thus far have been clearly related to the epistolary genre. Theorists of epistolarity have divided the genre into two major categories: the erotic and the educational. Janet Altman suggests that the letters of Heloise and Abelard may be the prototype for both strains, since Heloise's love letters are juxtaposed with Abelard's letters of direction.[32] (My own view is that both strains can be traced to Ovid, whose *Heroides* embodies the erotic strain and whose *Art of Love* embodies the educational.) The erotic impulse generates such epistolary seduction novels as the *Portuguese Letters*, which are addressed to the lover-seducer. Epistolary novels that follow the educational impulse are addressed to the mentor-guide. Altman identifies three forms of the educational impulse in epistolary fiction: (1) The letter writer is a teacher and the letter is primer, as in Richardson's *Familiar Letters*. (2) The writer is guide and the novel is a travelogue or essay on such topics as society, science, or the arts, as in Tobias Smollett's *Humphry Clinker*. (3) The mentor competes with other teachers for influence over a pupil; he is a corruptor-debaucher, often called "my dear mentor" by his pupil; the novels of Restif de la Bretonne fall into this category.[33] In my view, *Jane Eyre* combines both the erotic and the educational impulses of epistolary discourse in a first-person retrospective narrative. Furthermore, it contains elements of all three subcategories of the educational impulse. Jane is literally a teacher, whose narrative has been defined as a female version of the penultimate primer, *Pilgrim's Progress*. Rochester, moreover, is the "dear master" who is both a lover-seducer and a mentor-guide. His bigamous design makes him a corruptor; he even presents the history of his debaucheries in the form of a travelogue from the West Indies to France, Italy, and Germany.

31. Virginia Woolf, *The Common Reader* (New York: Harcourt Brace Jovanovich, 1925), pp. 222, 223–24.
32. See Janet Gurkin Altman, *Epistolarity: Approaches to a Form* (Columbus: Ohio State Univ. Press, 1983), pp. 190–200. See also François Jost, "L'Evolution d'un genre: Le Roman épistolaire dans les lettres occidentales," in *Essais de littérature comparée* (Fribourg, Switz.: Editions universitaires, 1968), 2:89–179, 380–402.
33. Altman, p. 196.

Finally, near the end of the novel he sees St. John Rivers at his rival; Rivers is indeed another teacher who exerts considerable influence over Jane. Jane's education consists in sorting out the various temptations these teacher-rivals represent. To have yielded to Rochester, she realizes, would have been an error of principle; to have yielded to Rivers, an error in judgment (368).

My aim in placing *Jane Eyre* in a study of amorous epistolary discourse is thus to examine the further assimilation of epistolary traits in first-person narrative, purposely to present another transgression of the generic boundaries with which I began. Since Heger combines the roles of lover and mentor in Charlotte's imagination, one reason she calls the novel an autobiography is that it transforms her love letters into literature. The novel she began in despair reinscribes her one-sided correspondence with her beloved master—with a difference. The boundaries between the ancient Ovidian genre and this particular first-person narrative are thus far more fluid than fixed, for Jane writes retrospectively, after the drama is over; she highlights the acts of writing and reading in recording her blindness and insight; and she defers the revelation that her narrative is addressed to her beloved until the final page.

Jane Eyre's Blind Idolatry

Self-address, a distinctive characteristic of amorous discourse, recurs throughout Brontë's novel. Chapter 16 contains this typical passage:

> "*You*," I said, "a favorite with Mr. Rochester? *You* gifted with the power of pleasing him? . . . He said something in praise of your eyes, did he? Blind puppy! Open their bleared lids and look on your own accursed senselessness! It does good to no woman to be flattered by her superior, who cannot possibly intend to marry her; and it is madness in all women to let a secret love kindle within them, which, if unreturned and unknown, must devour the life that feeds it; and, if discovered and responded to, must lead, *ignis-fatuus*-like, into miry wilds, whence there is no extrication." (140–41)

But which self is being addressed? One self is the child within, the blind puppy who naïvely believes in her attractions. Another is the self who fancies that love, conquering all, can overcome class biases. Another is the self suffering from unrequited love. Many selves are summoned simultaneously; many allusions—and illusions—fill the space of desire. Both the fictional and the authentic amorous discourse reveal Charlotte's obsession with blind idolatry, duplicity, delusion, and folly. As in her love letters, in the novel her heroine vacillates between blindness and insight, partially deciphering her experience yet returning to its enigmas again and again. In view of Brontë's unrequited love for Heger, the passage above has a particular poignancy, for it points to an awareness of the madness and futility of her passion, yet at the same time reveals the futility of her efforts to extricate herself. Writing later to Ellen Nussey, in response to Ellen's suggestion that she leave home, Charlotte recalls that the result of her impulsive decision to return to Brussels—and the aftermath of the experience—was that "I was punished for my selfish folly by a total withdrawal for more than two years of happiness and peace of mind—I could hardly expect success if I were to err again in the same way" (14 Oct. 1846, *W & S*, 2:114–15). Since she went on to compose a novel about an erring heroine, Charlotte's words demonstrate that writing never makes desire cease. If anything, the opposite is true: writing is desiring. It is not necessary to resort to a naïve mimeticism to trace the correspondences in the language of desire from Charlotte's letters and poems to the novel.

One paradox is immediately apparent in the passage above: Charlotte writes in the consciousness of her failure with Heger, but she reverses her heroine's situation. Jane writes retrospectively of her failure at this particular moment in the narrative while she is conscious of her ultimate success. Brontë repeatedly draws attention to her juxtaposition of Jane as *focus* (in her development from child to adult) and Jane as *voice*, the retrospective narrator who, unlike the reader, knows that, however mad her desire seemed, she eventually prevailed. It is precisely for this reason that the novel seems not to belong in the genre of amorous epistolary discourse. Jane, after all, not only writes in the presence of her beloved, she marries him. Yet she devotes a scant two pages to her wedded bliss; the rest of the narrative focuses on the pain and pressure of her prior existence. Furthermore, although no one doubts that Rochester is redeemed through his suffering, he is no longer the same figure whom Jane initially idolized. In my view, she writes not to exorcise her passion but to resurrect it. In fact, her motives for writing are myriad, contradictory, and duplicitous; Jane's narrative is both an evocation of her idol and an expiation. Jane is, after all, "the instrument of evil to what [she] wholly loves." If Rochester's first wife was the instrument of his disappearance, however, his second is the instrument of his return. And indeed Jane's expiation involves yet another doubling, for it is addressed to Bertha too, in recognition that the happiness of one woman is frequently built on the misery of others.

Jane writes, then, not to exorcise but to resurrect the unreformed Rochester—the charismatic, careless, calculating man with whom she originally fell in love. It is *he,* the former Rochester, who remains absent when Jane begins to write. In writing she brings to life all she felt before of Rochester's power and her desire, for writing is not only recollection but re-vision, repetition, reliving, anticipating all over again. In passages of self-address like the one above, Brontë purposely distracts the reader from the retrospective focus of the narrative, but she highlights it in many other passages. This technique of temporal prolepsis is one of the strategies by which the first-person narrator derives her authority. As Gérard Genette explains: "The 'first-person' narrative lends itself better than any other to anticipation, by the very fact of its avowedly retrospective character, which *authorizes* the narrator to allude to the future and in particular to his present situation. . . . Prolepses . . . are testimonies to the intensity of the present memory, and to some extent *authenticate* the narrative of the past."[34] Temporal prolepsis is one of the distinguishing characteristics of amorous epistolary discourse from the *Heroides* forward.

Jane Eyre reveals one of her motives for writing her narrative in one such proleptic passage when she describes Rochester's guests playing charades; in recollecting the scene, she makes the beloved present in her mind's eye and authenticates the memory's intensity and veracity: "I still see the consultation which followed each scene: I see Mr. Rochester turn to Miss Ingram, and Miss Ingram to him; I see her incline her head towards him till the jetty curls almost touch his shoulder . . . I hear their mutual whisperings; I recall their interchanged glances; and something even of the feeling roused by the spectacle returns in memory at this moment" (162). It is a memory of exclusion from the magic circle of the beloved, one of those scenes

34. Gérard Genette, *Narrative Discourse: An Essay in Method,* trans. Jane E. Lewin (Ithaca: Cornell Univ. Press, 1980), pp. 67, 69, my italics.

that is supposed to remind Jane of the folly of loving her superior when he could marry such beauties as Blanche Ingram. Only a second reading of the novel enables one to imagine Jane writing triumphantly, since she writes knowing that she later married her master. Until the last two pages, however, the fundamental psychic trauma reenacted again and again is rejection. In writing retrospectively, what novelist and heroine reinscribe is the despair of an impossible love. The memory of that trauma, moreover, is at least as intense as the happy ending that eventually replaces it, for—as we have seen in earlier amorous discourses—love may replace but can never erase the trauma of abandonment. This particular scene, which many critics dismiss as awkward,[35] is thus central in the novel, for in it Jane simultaneously recognizes her desire and desires recognition. She confesses, "I had not intended to love him. . . . he made me love him without looking at me" (153). Throughout the scene, the sensation of humiliation is as intense as that of pleasure; they play equal roles in the intensity of both the moment and the memory. When Blanche tries to humiliate Jane by speaking scornfully of governesses, Jane thinks, "I feared—or should I say, hoped—the allusion to me would make Mr. Rochester glance my way; and I involuntarily shrank further into the shade; but he never turned his eyes" (155).

As a focal point of desire, the scene is also important as an analysis of the qualities that attract Jane to Rochester. She is attracted by his haughtiness, his indifference, his harshness, his sarcasm; watching him with other women, she notes that his manner, "if careless and choosing rather to be sought than to seek, was yet, in its very carelessness, captivating, and in its very pride, irresistible" (163). From Ariadne to Rosa Coldfield, the heroine's desire is aroused by the beloved's aloofness and arrogance; precisely because he is unattainable, the heroine desires him. The entire scene is a masterful portrayal of the acute anxiety that arouses Jane. Only in oxymorons can she describe the intensity of the moment. "I had," she writes, "an acute pleasure in

35. E.g., Charles Burkhart, *Charlotte Brontë: A Psychosexual Study of Her Novels* (London: Victor Gollancz, 1973), p. 66. See also Rigby, p. 168, and Mrs. Humphry Ward, Introduction to *Jane Eyre*, Haworth edition (London: Smith, Elder, 1905–6), 1:xiv. Margot Peters, in contrast, argues that this "scene which has often been decreed blatantly awkward is subtly laced with the theme of trial: Jane is judged . . . by the guests; Rochester is trying her emotional fidelity, at the same time, Blanche's temperament; Blanche is testing her power over Rochester; and throughout, Jane is judging [everyone else]." *Charlotte Brontë: Style in the Novel* (Madison: Univ. of Wisconsin Press, 1973), p. 140.

looking—a precious, yet poignant pleasure; pure gold, with a steelly point of agony: a pleasure like what the thirst-perishing man might feel who knows the well to which he has crept is poisoned, yet stoops and drinks divine draughts nevertheless" (153). The same images of hunger, eating, drinking, devouring, engulfing that dominate Brontë's letters to Heger can be seen here, for Jane confesses, "The sarcasm that had repelled, the harshness that had startled . . . were only like keen condiments in a choice dish: their presence was pungent, but their absence would be felt as comparatively insipid" (165). Read with a sense of the so-called happy ending in mind, this is an audacious confession, for it implies that Jane finds her redeemed husband rather insipid, compared to the unredeemed rake who had been potent as well as pungent! Carelessness, pride, harshness, and sarcasm, after all, are the very traits that, after the fire at Thornfield, are either subdued in Rochester or extinguished altogether. At the very least, the possible implication here suggests motives for Jane's writing that, so far as I know, have never been acknowledged.

In this scene within a scene, Jane's desires are aroused by anxiety and by the absolute impenetrability of the beloved; she casts about to comprehend him and comes up with not too few but too many answers, with multiple explanations for his moods, his actions, his unpredictable behavior. The personality of the beloved is an unsolvable mystery that the narrator, viewed within the confines of internal focalization, cannot resolve.[36] Yet one of Jane's deepest desires is to satisfy her curiosity and resolve the mystery of Rochester's personality. She envies her rival, Blanche, whose familiarity with Rochester enables her to

> fathom the strange depth partially disclosed; that something which used to make me fear and shrink, as if I had been wandering amongst volcanic-looking hills, and had suddenly felt the ground quiver, and seen it gape; that something I at intervals beheld still, and with throbbing heart, but not with palsied nerves. Instead of wishing to shun, I longed only to dare—to divine it; and I thought Miss Ingram happy, because one day she might look into the abyss at her leisure, explore its secrets, and analyse their nature. (165)

What Jane initially fails to recognize is that her ignorance is also her freedom, for the abyss in Rochester entails manipulation, mastery, a

36. See Genette, pp. 198–211.

will to power. Jane recognizes that Blanche lacks the powers of observation she herself has; she notes that Blanche's "pride and self-complacency repelled further and further what she wished to allure"; but what Jane fails to comprehend is that Blanche would in some ways be a perfect match for Rochester precisely because she is so unconscious, for his terror of intimacy makes him distance himself from emotion and equate vulnerability with exposure. The images of devouring, engulfing, and burning imply that love poses certain threats to self-mastery, to the "armor of the I." Rochester devises many tests and trials for Jane to keep her from penetrating that armor. His remoteness in this scene, for instance, astounds Jane, since she has just saved him from burning to death. His changed demeanor is incomprehensible, for minutes earlier he had "revealed a heart full and eager to overflow; in whose emotions I had a part. How near had I approached him at that moment! What had occurred since, calculated to change his and my relative positions? Yet now, how distant, how far estranged we were! So far estranged, that I did not expect him to come and speak to me" (153).

A thorough analysis of the multiple resemblances of Rochester to his predecessor Lovelace lies beyond the scope of this book, but certainly they share a desire for confession and release that neither is able to reconcile with the drive for power and control.[37] The conflict informs Rochester's actions in this chapter and the next; he repeats the same pattern of approaching, then rejecting Jane, of coming close to self-revelation and intimacy, then resorting to cruelty. He almost confesses that he wants Jane to be "the instrument of my cure" but instead becomes harshly sarcastic, taunting Jane with Blanche's beauty. As so often happens in amorous discourse, the heroine becomes obsessed with securing what the beloved denies. She submits herself to a relentless examination of her own inadequacies, rather than attribute any flaws to the beloved. Jane, for example, can see intellectually that she is superior to Blanche, yet she remains as obsessed with her as Bertha Mason is with Jane. Rochester's charmed circle, indeed,

37. Sandra M. Gilbert and Susan Gubar identify Rochester's other predecessors as the Earl of Rochester, Byron, and Bluebeard. See *The Madwoman in the Attic: The Woman Writer and the Nineteenth-Century Literary Imagination* (New Haven: Yale Univ. Press, 1979), p. 354. The Earl of Rochester's deathbed confessions served as a model of reformed rakehood for Lovelace as well as for Rochester here. In keeping with the generic intertexuality of amorous discourse that I have been tracing, it is worth noting that Sutpen, whom I compare to Rochester later in this chapter, is also compared to Bluebeard in *Absalom, Absalom!*

contains a pride of brides. The first charade he performs with Blanche, entitled Bridewell, foreshadows the charade he will later attempt in trying to marry Jane. Each potential bride occupies the same place in the structure of the beloved: behind Jane stands Blanche; behind Blanche stands Bertha. Jane illogically believes that if only she were different, Rochester would love her; she does not see that Rochester uses each of the women as an obstacle to intimacy with any of the others.

The result is that the heroine must repeatedly reenact her repudiation. Of her single-minded obsession, Jane writes, "I thought only of my master and his future bride—saw only them, heard only their discourse, and considered only their movements of importance" (165). Jane, moreover, seems to fulfill the very desires Lovelace had of Clarissa; he wanted to be "the subject of her dreams" and hoped she would "think every moment lost, that is not passed with me" (4:41:265). Jane dreams morning and night of her rival, her exclusion, and her beloved's repudiation of her: "I dreamt of Miss Ingram all the night: in a vivid morning dream I saw her closing the gates of Thornfield against me and pointing me out another road; and Mr. Rochester looked on with his arms folded—smiling sardonically, as it seemed, at both her and me" (213). This passage echoes the terms of Brontë's own suffering; she writes to Heger: "Day and night I find neither rest nor peace. If I sleep I am disturbed by tormenting dreams in which I see you, always severe, always grave, always incensed against me" (8 Jan. 1845, W & S, 2:23). Heger, like Rochester, was surrounded by women over whom he exercised considerable power and authority, the schoolgirls and teachers who vied for his attention and affection. If, as some critics argue, *Jane Eyre* were mere wish fulfillment, the novel would not focus so unremittingly on suffering. Instead, what Brontë reinscribes in her letters, poems, and novels is the powerlessness, the abjection, the misery of the ordeal of abandonment, which no success can compensate, no eventual happiness utterly assuage.[38] For Jane, writing retrospectively, that awareness is so vivid, the memory of abandonment is still so painful, that when she tries to describe her physical suffering and degradation after she flees from Thornfield the narrative breaks down. She

38. Faulkner presents the same idea of the ineradicability of rejection in his characterization of Charles Bon, whom, after Sutpen's repudiation, "revenge could not compensate him nor love assuage." *Absalom, Absalom!* (New York: Random House, 1964), p. 343.

writes: "At this day I can scarcely bear to review the times to which I allude: the moral degradation, blent with the physical suffering, form too distressing a recollection ever to be willingly dwelt on. . . . Let me condense now. I am sick of the subject" (289). Like the Portuguese nun's lament that she wrongs her feelings by trying to describe them in writing, this passage is an example of narration under duress, of the heroine's compulsion to remember what she wishes to repress and to describe the unspeakable.

Yet before this point Jane expresses another compulsion—to spend every moment before he marries Blanche Ingram with Rochester. Just as Charlotte put off her impending departure from Brussels from day to day, despite the chilly atmosphere Mme Heger created, Jane is distraught at the impending separation and longs to be with Rochester continually: "Hasten! hasten! be with him while you may: but a few more days or weeks, at most, and you are parted with him for ever!" (214). In her desperation, she even fantasizes that he will, "Even after his marriage, keep us [Adele and herself] together somewhere under the shelter of his protection, and not quite exiled from the sunshine of his presence" (216). Jane shares with Ovid's heroines and the Portuguese nun the desperate desire to be a servant to her rival if she can so remain close to the beloved.

Ironically, the one who is actually "sheltered by Rochester's protection" never sees the sun; to be "protected" by Rochester is to be imprisoned in the attic. Although Jane does not realize it yet, he is a seducer-guide, a Judas-protector; like Lovelace, he devotes all his wealth, status, and power to repressing those he should protect. When Richard Mason is attacked by Bertha, Jane gets a chance to experience the "abyss" of Rochester's nature, for she too is locked in the attic and forbidden to speak. Here, Thornfield is revealed as a false paradise, Rochester as Judas; as shadows flicker over the panels of the cabinet, next to a crucifix of thorn-crowned Christ, "the devilish face of Judas" seems to jump out of the panel, "gathering life and threatening a revelation of the arch-traitor—of Satan himself—in his subordinate's form" (185). Jane turns all her questions inward since Rochester has sworn her to silence. "What crime was this," she wonders, "that lived incarnate in this sequestered mansion, and could neither be expelled nor subdued by the owner?—What mystery, that broke out, now in fire and now in blood, at the deadest hours of night? What creature was it, that, masked in the ordinary woman's face and shape, uttered the voice, now of a mocking demon, and anon

of a carrion-seeking bird of prey?" (185). Rochester's command of
silence is so absolute that Jane is paralyzed; even though she fears
Richard Mason is dying, "I might not even speak to him" (186).

Significantly, in moments of extreme anxiety, Jane's thoughts re-
vert to the many women in Rochester's life, although she identifies
not Bertha but Grace Poole as her rival. It is almost as if Jane is
imagining how she herself will appear when she becomes matronly; if
her plainness is no longer offset by her youth, she will have only her
character to recommend her:

> Had Grace been young and handsome, I should have been tempted to
> think that tenderer feelings than prudence or fear influenced Mr.
> Rochester in her behalf; but, hard-favored and matronly as she was, the
> idea could not be admitted. "Yet," I reflected, "she has been young
> once; her youth would be contemporary with her master's. Mrs. Fairfax
> told me once she had lived here many years. I don't think she can ever
> have been pretty; but, for aught I know, she may possess originality and
> strength of character to compensate for the want of personal advan-
> tages. (137)

The idea leads Jane logically to compare her own disadvantages and
plainness to Grace's, but ultimately, objectivity breaks down and Jane
becomes disgusted with her train of thought. In her disgust, she
makes a revealing statement that exposes a far-reaching strategy of
denial at work. What finally distinguishes her from Grace, she decides, is that "Bessie Leaven had said I was quite a lady; and she spoke
truth: I was a lady. And now I looked much better than I did when
Bessie saw me: I had more colour and more flesh; more life, more
vivacity; because I had brighter hopes and keener enjoyments" (137).
Not only will Jane shortly be supplanted by a *genuine* lady, Blanche
Ingram, but it will be Rochester himself who marks for Jane the
contrast between her own fancies and Blanche's ample endow-
ments—of beauty as well as wealth. Significantly, the governess in *The
Turn of the Screw* has identical fantasies, particularly after she learns
that her predecessor, Miss Jessel, was "a real lady." Moreover, just as
Jane contrasts herself to Grace Poole, James's governess takes pride in
the difference between herself and Mrs. Grose. Like Mrs. Fairfax,
Mrs. Grose not only keeps the house; she keeps the master's silence
and secrets from the governess. *Jane Eyre*, as we shall see presently,
thus demonstrates once again the dialogism of amorous discourse, for
it is a veritable subtext throughout James's tale.

In previous chapters, I have discussed the alternative logic that heroines argue by; Heloise, for example, defies the injunctions that the master logician Abelard attempts to impose upon her. Like Abelard and Lovelace, Rochester seems to be the eminently rational man. Jane Eyre, like Clarissa before her, is subjected to the systematic alteration of the sign systems by which she makes her world coherent. One must look first at the ways in which that world is rendered incoherent by Rochester's machinations in order to see how and why Jane comes close to madness, then eventually manages to posit an alternative logic based on feeling. Here again, it helps to keep the temporal duality of the narrative in mind; Jane as *voice* can look back retrospectively on the specious logic that swayed her, but Jane the *focus* does not see how Rochester redefines words, principles, realities that he finds inconvenient. *Bigamy*, for instance, is dismissed by Rochester as nothing more than "an ugly word." He knows that Jane's principles will be an insurmountable obstacle to the bigamy he proposes, so he reduces them to mere stubbornness on her part—her "early instilled prejudice" (277). His quest for the ideal woman (which resembles Lovelace's compulsion always to be "the first discoverer") takes him from France to Italy to Germany; it is in these peregrinations that the erotic epistolary strains merge with the educational, for the lover-seducer merges with the mentor-guide, the man of the world. "I had determined, and was convinced," he says, "that I could and ought [to marry]. It was not my original intention to deceive, as I have deceived you. I meant to tell my tale plainly, and make my proposals openly: and it appeared to me so absolutely rational that I should be considered free to love and be loved, I never doubted some woman might be found willing and able to understand my case and accept me, in spite of the curse with which I was burdened" (273). This scheme, which he presents to Jane as "absolutely rational," reveals that Brontë's narrative relies on the same doubleness and duplicity that has characterized amorous discourse since Ovid. The flaw in Rochester's logic is that any woman who would accept him under such conditions could not, by definition, fit his conception of the ideal. The women he finds are instead only mistresses, inferiors with whom Rochester finds it humiliating to live. He later describes these humiliations to Jane, although he is proposing to enter precisely the same relationship with her. (One is reminded of Abelard's frank confession that, since he could not hope for a lady and would be demeaned by a whore, he chose Heloise, his easiest prey.) Despite

Rochester's flawed logic, there is something inexorable in his cause-and-effect analysis of Bertha's incarceration: "Since the medical men had pronounced her mad she had of course been shut up" (270). *Shut up* signifies that she is silenced as well as imprisoned; she is a mute symbol of how disobedient women are silenced and driven mad under the supervision of so-called rational men. As Shosana Felman argues, "Women . . . are associated both with madness and with silence, whereas men are identified with prerogatives of discourse and reason. In fact, men appear not only as the possessors, but also as the dispensers, of reason, which they can at will mete out to—or take away from—others."[39] Bertha is "*pronounced* mad." Rochester is first supported by the medical men; later he appeals to the representatives of law and religion. If they fail him, he can always resort to physical violence, as when he threatens, "Jane! will you hear reason? . . . because if you won't, I'll try violence!" (266). Like Lovelace, he can back up the pretense of rationality with brute force if all else fails.

To see how Jane's very sanity is undermined by Rochester, another facet of his flawed logic must be examined, for again and again what he presents as rationality is narcissism. He uses himself as a standard for his definitions of sanity and madness, confessing that he once contemplated suicide in the West Indies. But he says, since he was not "insane, the crisis of exquisite and unalloyed despair which had originated the wish and design of self-destruction was past in a second" (271). When he reports this to Jane, she has just arisen after "longing to be dead" (261); it thus seems clear that Rochester would define her as mad. He does so in fact when he redefines her resolution to leave him: "I pass over the *madness* about parting from me. You mean you must become a part of me" (267, my italics). To be defined as sane, woman must first recognize, then idolize, and finally become part and parcel of Rochester's possessions and his identity. He repeats this fundamental pattern in all his relations with women; for instance, he confesses that his "grande passion" for Céline arose because "he thought himself her idol . . . he believed . . . that she preferred his 'taille d'athlète' to the elegance of the Apollo Belvidere [*sic*]" (123). Rochester's narcissism underlies his attraction to Bertha, to his mistresses, and initially, to Jane. He loves Céline because the passion he feels is returned "with even superior ardor" (123). When

39. Shoshana Felman, "Women and Madness: The Critical Phallacy," *Diacritics* 5:4 (Winter 1975), 2–10.

he first met Bertha, similarly, she "flattered me, and lavishly displayed for my pleasure her charms and accomplishments. All the men in her circle seemed to admire her and envy me" (268). He wants to transform Jane into a beauty so that men will envy him, as they did when Bertha enhanced his status by being "the boast of Spanish Town for her beauty" (268).

The maxim attributed to Virginia Woolf about male narcissism comes to mind: "Women have served all these centuries as looking-glasses possessing the magic and delicious power of reflecting the figure of man at twice its natural size." The description of Rochester as a Byronic hero has become a critical commonplace that, it seems to me, excludes more than it includes, for Rochester has other predecessors who illuminate such aspects as the relation of male narcissism to female madness. One obvious predecessor, as we have seen, is Lovelace; like Lovelace's definition of himself as rake in a comedy of seduction, Rochester's narrative of his past suggests that he wants Jane to "read" his life story as a reformed rake's tale, not unlike that of his namesake, the Earl of Rochester. A more immediate predecessor is the hero of Balzac's 1830 story, "Adieu," another tale about male narcissism and female madness. Philippe's mistress, Stéphanie, is driven mad during the Napoleonic Wars; her last sane utterance to her lover is the word, "Adieu." Philippe first tries to cure her by taming her—like an animal, like a shrew—just as Rochester tries to tame Bertha. Philippe believes that Stéphanie's sanity is inextricably bound to her ability to recognize and adore *him*. What makes her madness so terrible to him is that she can no longer function as looking glass, whereas in the past she had been "the glory of her lover." (Rochester, similarly, defines Jane as "the desire of his eyes." Jane says, "My heart was with my eyes; and both seemed migrated into Mr. Rochester's frame" [253].) Philippe concocts a violent scheme—an act as forcible as rape—that insures him her recognition and adoration, whereupon the countess is "cured," bids him adieu, and dies.[40]

Like Philippe, Rochester equates sanity in the female with recognition of the male. When Jane reproaches him for hating Bertha, he reassures her by saying that he would love Jane even if she were mad: "I could hang over you with untiring tenderness, though you gave me no smile in return; and never weary of gazing into your eyes, though they had no longer a ray of recognition for me" (265). (In view of his

40. Ibid., pp. 4–10.

consistent inability to really "see" Jane, his vow is particularly ironic.) What is crucial about this scene is that Jane defends Bertha, speaking out on her behalf and articulating the injustice of male definitions of sanity and madness. In *The Turn of the Screw*, a similar recognition scene between the governess and *her* predecessor, Miss Jessel, hinges on her refusal to pity the tormented woman she resembles; her repudiation leads to utterly different consequences that are avoided here by Jane's act of identification.

In the genre of the amorous epistle, trials and tests, courtroom rhetoric and legal imagery are consistent marks of generic development from Ovid's refinements of rhetorical exercises like *suasoriae* and *ethopoiiae* to Clarissa's will. These generic elements are particularly vivid in *Jane Eyre*, for trials and tests recur throughout the novel. From the opening scene, we see the consequences of Jane's having been found guilty of disobedience. Even the scene of the guests playing charades is a series of trials and tests; Rochester is testing both Blanche and Jane, and the charades enacted concern the trials of Rebecca and the prison of Bridewell.[41] Marriage as a bride's prison is to the point here, for Rochester marshals his defense of having made his first bride a prisoner, and uses the language of legal transcripts: "Imagine yourself in a remote foreign land; conceive that you there commit a capital error. . . . Mind, I don't say a *crime*; I am not speaking of shedding of blood or any other guilty act, which might make the perpetrator amenable to the law: my word is *error*. The results of what you have done become in time to you utterly insupportable; you take measures to obtain relief: unusual measures, but neither unlawful nor culpable" (191).

To glance ahead for a moment at the persistence of this particular strain of the genre in modern literature, compare Sutpen's speech in *Absalom, Absalom!* when he solicits the "trained legal mind" of Grandfather Compson to help him find a legal rationalization for abandoning his first wife and son, an unconscionable action he tries to justify according to what is ironically referred to as "his code of logic and morality, his formula and recipe of fact and deduction":

"I was faced with condoning a fact which had been foisted upon me without my knowledge during the process of building toward my de-

41. For an analysis of the legal language in the novel, see Margot Peters, *Charlotte Bronte*, pp. 131–54. Peters demonstrates that the novel is "bound more firmly to the real world than has often been supposed" by those who overemphasize the elements of gothic horror, fairy tale, and romance.

sign, which meant the absolute and irrevocable negation of the design; or in holding to my original plan for the design in pursuit of which I had incurred this negation. I chose, and I made to the fullest what atonement lay in my power for whatever injury I might have done in choosing, paying even more for the privilege of choosing as I chose than I might have been expected to, or even (by law) required."[42]

Ironically, like Rochester, Sutpen is trying to justify his treatment of a Creole wife from the West Indies, whose heritage is "tainted" not by madness but (allegedly) by Negro blood.

From Paris' invocation of Love as a lawyer to the spurious defense of indefensible actions by Lovelace, Rochester, and Sutpen, the logic that the heroines must combat consists of the same narrowly legalistic mode of thought. It continually reduces the spiritual to the literal, morality to legality, compassion to contracts and codes. When Rochester promises to explain all the mysteries of Thornfield to Jane in one year and one day, his morality is narrowly legalistic; he follows not the spirit but the letter of the law, and even this promise is only extracted after he has come close to making Jane as mad as Bertha is.[43] He undermines Jane's ability to trust her own judgment by systematically dismissing the eerie events at Thornfield as mere fantasies. He swears the servants to secrecy regarding Bertha's existence and categorically denies that any of the events Bertha causes are real. When Jane relates her fears, her feelings, her dreams to him, he ridicules her; after she relates her prophetic dream of Thornfield's destruction, for example, he first calls her a hypochondriac, then a witch (246–47). Even before she has a chance to articulate her fears, he dismisses her and her dream: "I will not believe it to be anything important. I warn you of incredulity beforehand" (248). When Jane proceeds to describe Bertha's visit to her room, Rochester ascribes it to Jane's overstimulated brain, her delicate nerves. He thus invalidates her terror while keeping his private knowledge of Bertha secret. He prefers to make Jane doubt her own sanity, rather than reveal his duplicity. Furthermore, he demonstrates that he has the power and authority to determine what is real and what is not, for when Jane argues that the reality of the incident is confirmed by Rochester's inability to explain it, he dismisses her forebodings and argues that it is precisely because

---

42. William Faulkner, *Absalom, Absalom!* (New York: Modern Library, 1966), p. 273.
43. In another example of the dialogic dynamism of *Jane Eyre*, Jean Rhys demonstrates just how responsible Rochester might have been for Bertha's madness in her novel, *Wide Sargasso Sea* (New York: Popular Library, 1966).

he cannot explain the mystery that "it must have been unreal." As in the gypsy scene, he insists on holding all the cards. Like Lovelace, he will employ every trick, every disguise, every artifice to win the game; ironically, artifice, which is what he finds most objectionable in women, is what he practices in spades. The impulse to disguise himself as an old woman recalls Lovelace's dream of being an old bawd sleeping in the same bed with Clarissa. The disguise reveals the depth of Rochester's desire to penetrate the secrets of Jane's heart; she wonders "what unseen spirit had been sitting for weeks by my heart watching its workings and taking record of every pulse" (175). He not only wants to foretell her destiny; he wants to be its sole arbiter.

Feminist critics may object to my emphasis on heroines whose lovers so clearly epitomize patriarchal values. I have discussed Rochester's logic at length here to demonstrate precisely what Jane Eyre is up against, for however specious his logic, Rochester has the weight of civil and ecclesiastical authority on his side in his cruel repudiation and inhumane incarceration of Bertha, his taking of mistresses, his courtship (if not marriage) of Jane. Jane's severest test comes in the tense scene after Bertha's existence is revealed, for when Jane comes nearest to capitulating to Rochester, she is nearest to madness as well. He has no compunction about using all the power, the authority, even the force he can command to make Jane his mistress, yet he maintains that nothing could be further from the truth: "Never fear that I wish to lure you into error—to make you my mistress." Nothing, he insists, is more reasonable, more necessary, more *natural* than his desire. When she resists, he resorts to all the snobbery of his class, cruelly questioning her motives for loving him and attacking her for loving only "my station and the rank of wife." Just as Lovelace argues that Clarissa's rape is "a mere notional violation," Rochester argues that Jane's resistance is "a distortion in your judgment . . . a perversity in your ideas. . . . Is it better to drive a fellow-creature to despair than to transgress a mere human law—no man being injured by the breach? for you have neither relatives nor acquaintances whom you need fear to offend by living with me" (279). Brontë's critique is quite subtle here, for what is at stake once again is female honor. Underlying Rochester's logic is the implicit assumption that he will not be damaging the honor of fathers, uncles, or brothers if Jane becomes his mistress. It is the logic of Abelard, of Lovelace, and of the Harlowes: honor is the exclusive property of the male. His wording further reveals that in language as well as life the female half of humankind is invisible, for while it is true that no *man* would be injured by Jane's misconduct, one *woman* would be: Jane herself. In this scene the effect of Rochester's systematic subversion of the signs by which Jane makes the world comprehensible culminates in her own madness, for she protests, "I will hold to the principles received by me when I was sane, and not mad—as I am now. Laws and principles . . . have a worth . . . and if I cannot believe it now, it is because I am insane—quite insane" (279).

Most remarkable about this astonishing scene is the degree to which Jane is swayed by Rochester's logic. She finds his suffering more compelling than her own self-preservation as she thinks of "his misery . . . danger. . . . look at his state when left alone. . . . soothe him; save him; love him; who in the world cares about *you*? or will be injured by what you do?" One is reminded of Charlotte's reluctance to leave M. Heger in Brussels: "However long I live, I shall not forget what the parting . . . cost me; it grieved me so much to grieve him" (*W & S*, 2:3). However, Charlotte subsequently discovers that the pain of parting was all on her side; this realization may explain why she attributes to Rochester the wildness of grief lacking in Heger. Jane eventually learns to answer the question "Who in the world cares about *you*?" by declaring, "I care for myself. The more solitary, the more friendless, the more unsustained I am, the more I will respect myself" (279). Her words echo those of Clarissa: "To despond would be to add sin to sin. And whom have I to raise me up, whom to comfort me, if I desert *myself*?" (4:34:210). Jane does, therefore, leave, and the chapter of her flight is the culmination of the imagery that has linked her to Bertha ever since John Reed called her a "mad cat." What she shares with Bertha from the outset, indeed, is the impulse toward disobedience. Jane's very existence, after all, springs from her mother's disobedience to Jane's grandfather. Despite the fact that the subject itself is a forbidden one, Jane overhears Bessie and discovers "that my father had been a poor clergyman; that my mother had married him against the wishes of her friends, who considered the match beneath her; that my grandfather Reed was so irritated at her disobedience, he cut her off without a shilling; that after my mother and father had been married a year, the latter caught typhus fever . . . that my mother took the infection from him, and both died within a month of each other" (21). Curiously, what is omitted from that narrative is Jane's own birth; Jane is the fruit of her mother's disobedience. The novel opens, moreover, on a day that began with wandering. "That day" is marked in Jane's memory because she has been set apart and commanded to silence "until [she] can speak pleasantly." The day is memorable for one other reason: it is her first rebellion against the tyranny and sadism of John Reed; it is the day of Jane's first disobedience. She rebels specifically against the injunction of silence and against the negative ways in which the Reeds define her. Yet, like Bertha, who howls execrations at Rochester from her prison-bedroom, Jane discovers that the result of speaking out at the Reeds' is imprisonment in the red room. Thus by the time she discovers Bertha's imprisonment, she comes to see just how pervasive the connection between disobedience and nullification can become. She flees Thornfield "like one delirious," nurturing "some fear—or hope—that here I should die: but I was soon up; crawling forwards on my hands and knees" (283). This humbling posture is the culmination of all her own previous experiences—of John Reed's persecution, of Brocklehurst's sadism, of Rochester's manipulation. At this moment, in my view, she comes closest not just to imagining but to experiencing what it has felt like to be Bertha Mason, to endure "moral degradation, blent with physical suffering" (289). She comes to know Bertha by feeling what she felt, just as Rochester will finally *see* Jane's suffering by feeling it. Thus, it is only in the retrospective focalization that Jane fully sees herself as Bertha's voice; her narrative is an expiation, an attempt to "speak the silence that is woman," a testimony to Bertha's mute suffering as well as to Jane's blind idolatry.

The sense of utter exile is yet another characteristic that links Brontë's novel to amorous epistolary discourse, for like so many of Ovid's heroines, she loses everything—home, friend, lover, master, idol. Her faith and trust in her judgment and her heart are utterly destroyed; just as Clarissa had "judged of [Lovelace's] heart by my own," Jane sees her "faith . . . blighted—confidence destroyed! Mr. Rochester was not what I had thought him. . . . the attribute of stainless truth was gone from his idea" (260). Like so many heroines who write amorous discourses, what Jane mourns for is not only the beloved but the loss of the innocence that enabled her to love. The child who haunts her dreams is the symbol of that innocence, for it appears in every crisis of faith: after Rochester disguises himself as a gypsy and penetrates her secrets; after he taunts her about Blanche's greater beauty; after Bertha rips her wedding veil. All the facets of that child come into focus when she contemplates her shattered love; it *is* the child: "I looked at my love: . . . it shivered in my heart, like a suffering child in a cold cradle; sickness and anguish had seized it; it could not seek Mr. Rochester's arms, it could not derive warmth from his breast" (260). Jane's entire emotional life, indeed, is imaged in that child, with its desperate need of nurturing, protection, reassurance; its utter defenselessness; its unquestioning trust, faith, and naïveté. That childlike naïveté precludes intellectual analysis, puts her mind to sleep in a sense, suspends critical judgment so that Rochester becomes "my whole world . . . almost my hope of heaven . . . as an eclipse intervenes between man and the broad sun. I could not . . . see God for his creature: of whom I had made an idol" (241). Brontë's depiction of a woman in love is a favorite motif in amorous discourses; from Sappho forward, love generates faith rather than thought, and only in retrospect does the heroine begin to think.[44] The child of Jane's dreams thus reveals yet another motive for Jane's narrative. By writing she resurrects all the facets of her own passionate nature that are related to this child. Her name suggests not only *err*, *ire*, and *heir*, but *ere*, as in Shakespeare's "to love that well which thou must leave ere long." *Ere* is *before*; Jane writes to record how she felt and what she was before her idol was destroyed. Paradoxically, she writes nostalgically and penitentially for the fallen idol, lamenting, like the Portuguese nun, "A heart is never more deeply affected than when first it is made aware of the depths of feeling of which it is capable. All its emotions are centered upon the idol which it builds for itself."[45] If, as Mary Jacobus suggests, the moment of desire is "the moment when the writer most clearly installs herself in her writing,"[46] then Brontë's desire, like her suffering, lasted long. Years later she is still inscribing the moment of desire, still reiterating her anguish over Heger's silence and her blind idolatry:

44. Compare Doris Lessing's heroine, Anna Wulf, whose fictional alter ego Ella reflects on her separation from her lover Paul: "Any intelligent person could have foreseen the end of this affair from its beginning. And yet I . . . refused to see it. Paul gave birth to Ella, the naive Ella. He destroyed in her the knowing, doubting, sophisticated Ella and again and again he put her intelligence to sleep, and with her willing connivance, so that she floated darkly on her love for him, on her naivety, which is another word for a spontaneous creative faith. And when his own distrust of himself destroyed this woman-in-love, so that she began thinking, she would fight to return to naivety. Now, when I am drawn to a man, I can assess the depth of a possible relationship with him by the degree to which the naive Anna is re-created in me." *The Golden Notebook* (New York: Bantam Books, 1973), pp. 211–12.
45. Frédéric Deloffre and J. Rougeot, eds., *Lettres portugaises, Valentins, et autres oeuvres de Guilleragues* (Paris: Garnier, 1962), p. 64.
46. Jacobus, pp. 16–17.

He saw my heart's woe, discerned my soul's anguish
How in fever, in thirst, in atrophy it pined;
Knew he could heal, yet looked and let it languish,
To its moans spirit-deaf, to its pangs spirit-blind.

. . . . .

He was mute as is the grave, he stood stirless as a tower,
At last I looked up, and saw I prayed to stone;
I asked help of that which to help had no power,
I sought love where love was utterly unknown.
Idolater I kneeled to an idol cut in rock,
I might have slashed my flesh and drawn my heart's best blood,
The Granite God had felt no tenderness, no shock;
My Baal had not seen nor heard nor understood.

(*PCB*, 240–41)

The violence of the passion, the impulse toward self-destruction, the solitariness of Charlotte's suffering all make the poem nearly unbearable. In contrast to the tone of abject pleading in her letters to Heger, by the time Charlotte writes this poem that abjection has turned to rage at Heger's injustice and indifference. The poem testifies to the duration of Charlotte's obsession and the extent to which she was writing her desire for years afterward. It records the same shattering discovery that the Portuguese nun makes: love alone does not arouse love; nor does a fine composition arouse compassion. It is devastating to discover that those who can *cause* such suffering haven't the power to heal the sufferer or, worse yet, that they are capable of ignoring such heart-wrenching appeals for solace.

This is a poem of enigmatic contradictions, for on the one hand the beloved is endowed with the power of a God—as strong as stone, as tall as a tower—yet he is also described as powerless. One meaning is simply that he has no power to love her, but a further implication is that he is helpless, as Heger was helpless to prevent his wife from banishing his favorite student. (Charlotte may thus have been doubly damned: by the wife as a threat to the family and by the husband for exposing his fundamental weakness and cowardice.) Without resorting to speculations about authorial intention, I simply wish to suggest the possibility that Charlotte eventually recognized the folly of seeing men as superior beings, that she outgrew the attitudes she expressed in a youthful letter to Ellen Nussey, in which she proclaims that she rejected Ellen's brother as a suitor because "I had not, and could not have, that intense attachment which would make me willing to die for him; and if ever I marry, it must be in that light of adoration that I will regard my husband" (12 March 1839, *W & S*, 1:174). Charlotte's marriage to Arthur Bell Nicolls certainly suggests that she had put such notions behind her. The theme of idolatry thus helps us to situate certain feminist issues, for not only is it dehumanizing for women to see men as repositories of strength and power who must either be idolized as beloved masters or resisted as oppressors, but it is also dehumanizing for men. Perhaps Rochester's maiming is not a punishment of him but a gift to Jane, for it allows her to see him realistically, rather than as the embodiment of ideal manhood. Thus, although feminist critics may take exception to my emphasis on the abject devotion of Charlotte to Heger and of Jane Eyre to Rochester, it seems possible that Charlotte's own example provides a more profound feminist insight than has heretofore been acknowledged. A pedestal, after all, is as uncomfortable for men as for women; blind idolatry oppresses not only the lover but the beloved; and the idolatry of male power is as much a form of objectification as the idolatry of female sexuality.

Despite her merciless self-scrutiny once she is no longer blinded by her love for Rochester, Jane continues to mourn for her lost innocence and fallen idol long after she meets the Rivers family. It is precisely because she is still so tormented herself that she recognizes St. John's "troubling impulses of insatiable yearnings and disquieting aspirations," his utter lack of inner peace: "He had no more found it than had I; with my concealed and racking regrets for my broken idol and lost elysium—to which I have latterly avoided referring; but which possessed me and tyrannised over me ruthlessly" (310). Like the Portuguese nun and Clarissa, Jane cogently analyzes Rochester's character and her attraction once she leaves him, assessing her complicity in her own betrayal and sadly condemning her folly. In view of that analysis, it seems incredible that she repeats the very same pattern of idolatry with St. John Rivers. Yet the repetition connects the first-person narrative to that particular strain of the educational epistolary genre that focuses on the rivalry of the mentor-guides; at stake is the mind and affection of the student-wanderer, Jane. Although Jane feels no passion for St. John, her compulsion to submit to his instruction, to win his approval, to pass the tests he devises demonstrate the undiminished intensity of her need. If Rochester's predecessor is Lovelace, St. John Rivers' is Abelard. In the narrowness of his principles, in his repudiation of desire, in his stern mastery of the feelings and the flesh, he seeks Jane's absolute submission, her willing self-enslavement. Rivers is clearly the wrong object of desire, yet he is as magnetic in his way as Rochester was in his. Their similarities, though less obvious than their differences, are no less important. Both exercise the same male prerogatives where speech and silence, reason and madness are concerned. For example, where Rochester praised Jane's "pliancy," St. John composes certain tests that Jane dutifully passes by being "docile, diligent . . . and gentle"; like Rochester, he imposes certain definitions as if Jane were nothing more than a blank page, a text: "I have made you my study for ten months" (355). Because of the enormity of the trauma at Thornfield, Jane no longer speaks confidently of her emotions; when St. John asks her to "speak her heart" concerning his suit, she replies, "My heart is mute." He, however, is all too willing to dominate and articulate: "Then I will speak for it." Just as Rochester repudiated her doubts and terrors, St. John utterly denies her deepest feelings. She senses instinctively that "If I were to marry you, you would kill me. You are killing me now." Yet he responds to this fear, this plea, by casting doubt on her femininity and silencing her: "Your words are such as ought not to be used: violent, unfeminine, and untrue. They betray an unfortunate state of mind: they merit severe reproof" (363). St. John sounds exactly like Abelard here. Heloise, remember, beseeched Abelard to send her "some sweet semblance of himself in a letter"; instead he held up the mirror of castration.[47] St. John offers Jane even less than Abelard offers Heloise: the prospect of a life of hardship, utterly devoid of warmth and affection—much less passion—and an early death under the Indian sun. Jane comprehends the danger that St. John represents, but she nevertheless comes dangerously close to self-annihilation through some overreach of despair. Intellectually, she sees his coldness and inflexibility clearly, yet she believes that if she married him, she would conceive an "inevitable, strange, torturing kind of love for him" (366). In her awareness of the masochism of that love, of the rejection she would suffer, of the impossibility of ever finding affection with someone incapable of loving, Brontë inscribes yet another aspect of her own capacity for idolatry with Heger. As Gérin points out, for Charlotte, "the dedication of

47. See Peggy Kamuf, *Fictions of Feminine Desire: Disclosures of Heloise* (Lincoln: Univ. of Nebraska Press, 1982), p. 35.

[her] heart contained an element of religion. . . . worship and love were one."[48]

In the aftermath of abandonment, heroines from the *Heroides* forward mercilessly examine their lovers' fallibilities, once they are liberated from that kind of adoration. This exorcism is evident in *Jane Eyre*, for the temptation of self-annihilation is followed by a clearsighted assessment of St. John's shortcomings. To succumb to St. John, as to Rochester, is to be engulfed. Her will paralyzed, Jane nearly puts her mind to sleep: "I was tempted to cease struggling with him—to rush down the torrent of his will into the gulf of his existence and there lose my own" (368). In conquering this impulse, Jane regains her power—power that, as we have seen in previous examples of the genre, is directly related to the power of speech. She turns the tables, demanding both obedience and silence from St. John: "It was *my* time to assume ascendancy. *My* powers were in play and in force. I told him to forbear question or remark; I desired him to leave me: I must, and would be alone. He obeyed at once. Where there is energy to command well enough, obedience never fails" (370). Perhaps what is most significant about this scene is that in it Jane is not guided by her intellect but by a profoundly passionate and intuitive conviction, the "inexpressible feeling" that Rochester's summons evokes. Since the disproportion of passion and judgment is one obsession in amorous discourse, the relation of feeling to judgment—a primary theme in all Brontë's writing—has a particular relevance here. St. John is a cold, hard man; he can judge but not feel. Rochester errs in the opposite direction, using ill-judgment about Bertha because of his passionate desire to bind Jane to him. As Brontë remarks, "Feeling without judgement is a washy draught indeed; but judgement untempered by feeling is too bitter and husky a morsel for human deglutition." The relation of feeling to judgment, in my view, is the only way to make sense of Rochester's maiming, for when the lovers are reunited, all the same passionate emotions—jealousy, insecurity, unworthiness, and helplessness—are reenacted, but this time it is Rochester who experiences them. Therefore, when Jane reveals her involvement with St. John, Rochester discovers how much his involve-

48. Gérin, p. 286. Patricia Beer compares Jane's idolatry of Rochester and St. John Rivers to Charlotte's idolatry of Branwell and Patrick Brontë, in *Reader, I Married Him: A Study of Women Characters in Austen, Brontë, Gaskell, and Eliot* (New York: Barnes and Noble, 1974), p. 100.

ment with Blanche Ingram must have pierced her to the heart. Just as Jane once bitterly exclaimed, "If I had wealth and beauty, I would make it hard for you to leave me," in this scene, when Jane says she does not care about marriage, all the bitterness is Rochester's: "If I were what I once was, I would try to make you care" (383). Richard Chase and other critics have ridiculed Brontë for "castrating" Rochester.[49] Her real achievement, however, is to transform him from someone terrified of intimacy, armed against vulnerability, into someone who because he is "unarmed," is no longer crippled emotionally. Seen in this light, his maiming is not a punishment but a gift that enables him to depend on others, to relinquish power, to feel. For the first time, actually, Rochester tries to "see" Jane—Jane herself rather than a mere reflection of himself. He "sees" a face rather than a mirror, finally recognizing what it must have felt like to be Jane—dependent, unloved, bereft of prospects and hope. Where previously he longed to hear his name on her lips, what restores her to him is *her* name on *his* lips. Rather than longing for blind adoration, he longs to feel: "I *cannot* see, but I must feel, or my heart will stop and my brain burst" (381).

To dismiss Jane's achievement as the reward of "a patient and practical woman," as Chase does, is to ignore the enormous role that silence played in the life and art of Charlotte Brontë. Jane's real achievement is neither her ability to support herself independently nor even her marriage to Rochester. The roots of her true triumph can be found in the famous passage in Chapter 12 where she speaks of the millions of women "condemned to a stiller doom . . . in silent revolt against their lot." At this point Jane is one of those women, suffering from "too rigid a restraint, too absolute a stagnation." As she tries to overcome her sense of repression and powerlessness, her sole relief is "to open my inward ear to a tale that was never ended—a tale my imagination created, and narrated continuously; quickened with all of incident, life, fire, feeling that I desired and had not in my actual existence" (95–96). The passage is a frank revelation of a discourse of desire, a first step toward Jane's ultimate achievement, which is her narrative itself, in which she finds the power to open her tale to other ears, to progress from imaginary narration to actual

49. Richard Chase, "The Brontës; or, Myth Domesticated," in *Forms of Modern Fiction*, ed. William O'Connor (Minneapolis: Univ. of Minnesota Press, 1948), pp. 102–13.

writing, not only expressing but fulfilling her desire in the process. There is no doubt, moreover, that Rochester is the intended audience for her discourse, since he sees and hears all else through her: "He saw nature—he saw books through me; and never did I weary of gazing for his behalf, and of putting into words the effect of field, tree, town, river, cloud, sunbeam—of landscape before us; of the weather round us—and impressing by sound on his ear what light could no longer stamp on his eye. Never did I weary of reading to him" (397). Since she mentions books in the first line, one wonders why she returns in the last line to reading, unless she intends to draw a subtle distinction between fiction and some other writing—namely, the narrative at hand, which she never tires of reading (or writing). Like other amorous epistolary discourses, indeed, this one appears to be written with a specific addressee in mind: the beloved master who listens, responds, remembers as Jane puts into words the effect he had on the psychic landscape now behind them, for Jane "impresses by sound on his ear" what he had previously refused to see.

These heroines do initially seem to embrace lovers who epitomize patriarchal values, but they have few resources in the law books or the book of life that articulate an alternative model or an alternative logic from which to argue. Each heroine must therefore set about to create such a document herself, as Clarissa does in writing a last will and testament that reverses the attempts of civil and ecclesiastical authorities to negate, to nullify the female. Every love letter is thus a legal challenge. Every discourse of desire is a testament, testimony of a *process*: of confronting oppression, of articulating injustice, of inventing other modes of logic and response, modes based on feeling as a way of knowing. Jane Eyre's narrative is a retrospective record of her illusions, her innocence, her blind idolatry. It resurrects the child within her, her fallen idol, and her idolatrous desire. Her writing records her penance and nostalgia; it is both an evocation and an exorcism of a passion that has been chastened and subdued.

One need not be a chamber to be haunted
One need not be a house;
The brain has corridors surpassing
Material place.
        . . .
Ourself, behind ourself concealed,
Should startle most;
Assassin, hid in our apartment,
Be horror's least.

EMILY DICKINSON

Essential oils are wrung:
The attar from the rose
Is not expressed by suns.
It is the gift of screws.

EMILY DICKINSON

6
The Author of Our Woe:
Virtue Recorded in
The Turn of the Screw

Flora. Mariette Lydis' drawing appeared in Henry James's *The Turn of the Screw* (New York: Plantin Press, 1949). It is reproduced courtesy of Ms. Lillian Marks and the William Andrews Clark Memorial Library, University of California, Los Angeles.

Copies of Desire

In his preface to the New York Edition of *The Turn of the Screw*, Henry James confesses to writing the tale with "cold artistic calcula-tion . . . to catch those not easily caught (the 'fun' of the capture of the merely witless being ever but small), the jaded, the disillusioned, the fastidious."[1] James's trap is not for the unwary reader but for the sophisticated one, fastidious enough to look for snares, false leads, phantasms in the narrative. Yet critical controversy has traditionally revolved around a single aspect of the governess' imagination: are the ghosts real or does she invent them?[2] This is precisely the trap James set, for in puzzling about the reality or unreality of the ghosts, readers overlook the larger role of desire in both the tale and the prologue. James turns the screw by turning attention away from the governess' desire, diverting our attention from her extraordinary imaginative powers, her aesthetic sensibility, and her considerable craft. *Craft,* indeed, reverberates throughout the tale: the crafty governess is skilled in the crafts of reading, writing, and rhetoric and is obsessed with witchcraft. Moreover, she concocts a powerfully crafted version of events that would sound plausible in any court of law.

The language of courts and trials is, of course, one sign of the tale's place in the genre of amorous epistolary discourse, which, as we have seen, the heroine writes with an underlying awareness of re-sistance to her point of view, an aim of accusation, and an eye on self-

1. Henry James, *The Art of the Novel*, introd. Richard P. Blackmur (New York: Scribner's, 1934), p. 172.
2. Critics who believe in the reality of the ghosts include Robert B. Heilman, "*The Turn of the Screw* as Poem," *University of Kansas City Review* 14 (1948), 272–89; Elmer Edgar Stoll, "Symbolism in Coleridge," *PMLA* 63 (1948), 214–22; and Krishna Baldev Vaid, *Technique in the Tales of Henry James* (Cambridge: Harvard Univ. Press, 1964), pp. 90–122. The opposite view is taken by Thomas Mabry Cranfill and Robert Lanier Clark, Jr., *An Anatomy of "The Turn of the Screw"* (Austin: Univ. of Texas Press, 1965); Joseph J. Firebaugh, "Inadequacy in Eden: Knowledge and *The Turn of the Screw*," *Modern Fiction Studies* 3 (1957), 57–63; John Silver, "A Note on the Freudian Reading of *The Turn of the Screw*," *American Literature* 29 (1957), 207–11; and Mark Spilka, "Turning the Freudian Screw: How Not to Do It," *Literature and Psychology* 13 (1963), 105–11.

justification. Unlike Jane Eyre's, this governess' passion is neither chastened nor subdued when she writes her narrative. Jane Eyre's amorous discourse was addressed to Rochester, but when the governess in *The Turn of the Screw* sits down to write, whom does she address? She certainly does not envision Douglas as her reader, for the manuscript is already ten years old when they meet. He does not see it for another twenty years, and by the time Douglas shares its contents, it is forty years old.[3] Whereas Ovid's heroines and Heloise begin by urging the beloved to read their letters, James's governess knows that her intended reader will never see her narrative. Yet she has only one reader in mind when she composes. Her entire literary effort stems from her passion for her employer, the master in Harley Street. He is the absent beloved, the embodiment of her desire.

That desire has not gone unnoticed, but the evaluation of such critics as Edmund Wilson set the tone by reducing the governess to a stereotypical spinster—one who is by definition abnormally frustrated since she lives without a man. (One recalls nearly identical assumptions applied to Sappho by George Devereux and D. L. Page.) Edmund Wilson, moreover, specifically relates the governess' neurosis to a lack of creativity, thus compounding his error; he describes her as the "thwarted Anglo-Saxon spinster; and we remember unmistakable cases of women in James's fiction who deceive themselves and others about the origins of their aims and emotions. . . . James's world is full of these women. They are not always emotionally perverted. Sometimes they are apathetic. . . . Or they are longing, these women, for affection but too inhibited or passive to obtain it for themselves." The problem with Wilson's analysis is, of course, that James's fiction is also full of such men. The governess, furthermore, is neither apathetic nor inhibited nor passive. As Robert Heilman has argued, her "feelings for the master are never repressed: they are wholly in the open and joyously talked about." In contrast to Edmund Wilson and Edna Kenton, whose analysis of the governess' sexual repression is based on stereotypes of female sexuality, Heilman emphasizes the

3. Several critics have suggested that Douglas is really Miles grown up. See, for example, Carvel Collins, "James' *The Turn of the Screw,*" *Explicator* 13:8 (1955), item 49. Louis D. Rubin, Jr., in "One More Turn of the Screw," *Modern Fiction Studies* 9 (1963–64), 314–28, argues that the governess' manuscript is a confession to the man, Douglas, for the love she felt for him at Bly. Stanley Trachtenberg, in "The Return of the Screw," *Modern Fiction Studies* 2 (1965), 180–82, sees the tale as Douglas' confession after suffering for fifty years from some unspecified guilt for the events at Bly.

governess' energetic declaration of desire.[4] He overstates her candor, however, for the act of writing is itself a lie, a disguise. It is not her desire but her confession that she represses. More remains unsaid and inscrutable at the end than ever before.

Just as the writing heroines in previous chapters appear to submit to the tyranny of forms while actually encoding their desire, the governess writes duplicitously too. Her narrative records the contradictory impulses toward confession and release, on the one hand, and toward repression and control, on the other. The imagery of salvation and expiation is related to the governess' first impulse, but it is continually checked by the second impulse, which is marked by a proliferation of images related to the act of writing. Sometimes the two impulses shift in midsentence, as when the governess speaks of her "disguised tension, that might well, had it continued too long, have turned to something like madness."[5] One wonders if the tension did indeed continue too long and turn to madness. For that matter, what makes the tension cease? The governess' answer is framed in the language of salvation: "What saved me, as I now see, was that it turned to another matter altogether." She implies that she might have been saved by confession and expiation, but her sentence, although it seems aimed in this direction at the outset, takes a curious detour before it ends. The narrative thus evades the question of madness by abruptly changing directions to "another matter altogether." What she disguises is not just her own tension but her complicity in the death of a child. Temporal prolepsis, in the phrase "as I now see" serves to authenticate her version of the past and to guarantee the veracity of her memory.[6] The narrative purposely brings into the foreground both the distant past (of her first impressions of Bly) and the immediate present to deflect attention from the gap in between,

---

4. Edmund Wilson, "The Ambiguity of Henry James," *Hound and Horn* 7 (1934), 385–406 (revised for the first edition of *The Triple Thinkers*, and further revised for *The Triple Thinkers*, rev. and enl. ed. [New York: Oxford Univ. Press], pp. 88–132); Robert B. Heilman, "The Freudian Reading of *The Turn of the Screw*," *Modern Language Notes* 62 (1947), 436; Edna Kenton, "Henry James to the Ruminant Reader: *The Turn of the Screw*," *Arts* 6 (Nov. 1924), 245–55.

5. Henry James, *The Turn of the Screw*, ed. Robert Kimbrough (New York: W. W. Norton, 1966), p. 28, hereinafter cited parenthetically in the text by page number. See also Shoshana Felman's analysis of this passage in "Turning the Screw of Interpretation," *Literature and Psychoanalysis: The Question of Reading: Otherwise*, ed. Shoshana Felman (Baltimore: Johns Hopkins Univ. Press, 1977), p. 181.

6. See Gérard Genette, *Narrative Discourse: An Essay in Method*, trans. Jane E. Lewin (Ithaca: Cornell Univ. Press, 1980), pp. 67–69.

for in that narrative gap lies the death of Miles. "As I now see" brings us to the present moment, the moment in which language and meaning are manufactured in writing. What could be construed as the governess' impulse to be saved by confession is thus immediately checked by the opposite impulse to control, to take hold: "It [her disguised tension] didn't last as suspense—it was superseded by horrible proofs. Proofs, I say, yes—from the moment I really took hold" (28). The rhetoric, the insistence, the urgency and pitch of intensity in this sentence all negate the initial expiatory impulse. One wonders at what precise moment the governess believes she "really took hold." Syntactically and structurally, "from the moment I really took hold" belongs with "as I now see": in other words, from the moment the governess begins writing, she is disguising her tension, concealing what she appears to reveal. Like Othello and Hamlet, two other tragically erring murderers, she is obsessed not just with proof but with "horrible proofs"; she assumes an evil where she finds it not.

Her obsession is so compelling that the reader is drawn into the tale, diverted from noticing the proliferation of references to writing, narrating, transcribing, corresponding. But even before the governess meets her employer, she has been engaged in a literary activity with him, for his advertisement "had already placed her in brief correspondence with the advertiser" (4). As in so many amorous epistles, the narrative is oblique; we see only the consequences of events that are never narrated. That initial correspondence between the governess and the master is the first of many epistolary exchanges of which we see only the repercussions. What are those repercussions? First, from that initial correspondence, the governess (falsely) assumes many more letters will follow. Her subsequent disappointment is the more severe for her inflated hopes. Second, by the time she meets her employer, she has already constructed an imaginary idol. He may in fact be "handsome and bold and pleasant, off-hand and gay and kind," but what James describes is not the facts but the governess' imaginative powers. Rather than simply state that the master is gallant, James writes, "he *struck her*, inevitably, as gallant and splendid. . . . She *figured* him as rich . . . *saw* him all in a glow of high fashion, of good looks, of expensive habits, of charming ways with women" (4, my italics). James thus deliberately suggests some disparity between what the master actually is and how he strikes the governess, for the "inevitably" can only be the result of her inexperience and romantic reading. In his revisions for the New York Edition, indeed,

James systematically shifted attention away from details of actions that the governess observed, emphasizing instead the reactions she felt, replacing verbs of thought with verbs of feeling and intuition in order to involve the reader more intimately with her impressions—as opposed to the craft of her narrative.[7] Her experience comes not from life but from books; throughout her narrative she sees herself, her charges, and her ordeal in terms of craft, of fiction, of fairy-tale nightmares and daydreams.

The nursery is transformed into a place of romance; the school-room, of poetry. As Flora gives the governess a tour, she feels as if she is in "a castle of romance inhabited by a rosy sprite, such a place as would . . . take all colour out of story-books and fairy-tales. Wasn't it just a story-book over which I had fallen a-doze and a-dream?" (10). *Day/dream* reveals the underlying logic, the adversarial chain of signification that commences with her first sentence: "I remember the whole beginning as a succession of flights and drops, a little see-saw of the right throbs and the wrong" (6).[8] Although prolepsis disguises its adversarial nature, her narrative revolves around the seesaw logic of antithesis: either she is entrapped in a ghost story or she is dozing in a fairy tale; either the children are demons or they are angels; either the ghosts exist and she is sane, or the children are innocent and she is mad. The first term of the dichotomy is typically the privileged one, used by the governess to condemn her adversaries and to illuminate her virtue, her sanity, her heroism. The dangers of such logic become apparent immediately, for the governess compares her charges to "a pair of little grandees, of princes of the blood, for whom everything, to be right, would have to be fenced about and ordered and arranged, the only form that, *in my fancy*, the afteryears could take for them was that of a romantic, a really royal extension of the garden and the park" (15).

In early editions James wrote "enclosed and protected" instead of "ordered and arranged." His revision reemphasizes the governess' mode of perceiving in terms of artistic composition, of imposing form where there was none before. The connection of *form* to *fancy* is particularly notable, because in the absence of dialogue with the beloved

7. Leon Edel, *The Ghostly Tales of Henry James* (New Brunswick: Rutgers Univ. Press, 1948), p. 434. See also Cranfill and Clark, pp. 18–20.

8. On *daydream* as the first link in an adversarial and antithetical structure, see Roland Barthes, *S/Z: An Essay*, trans. Richard Miller (New York: Hill and Wang, 1974), pp. 17–18.

master, the governess forms the discourse according to her fancy. The passage reveals the depth of her desire to arrest the children's development and even time itself; this desire, indeed, is one of her motives for writing. The passage also explains why she so frequently "fixes" others; she longs for the permanent control of art; she yearns to fix, to frame, to freeze time.[9] The first of many such arrested moments comes when she sees Peter Quint. Everything—sound and movement and all—stops as Quint rises up, "as definite as a picture in a frame," and next appears framed at the window. The governess' narrative is an attempt to fix the meaning of her experience, to dispel all doubts and ambiguities. Most fixed of all is her mind—about the significance of her experience and the greatness of her merit. Injured merit—like that of Milton's Satan, indeed—is a primary motive for her writing. She is convinced that she merits her employer's recognition of her heroism, her desire, her desirability.

What gave her such ideas? This is one of the questions that is never narrated, but the repercussions are clear. The governess writes, like the other heroines, of her seduction and betrayal, and, in so writing, places the tale in the genre of discourses of desire. The master in Harley Street cultivates the fiction of friendship, pretending that she would be doing him an enormous favor by taking the job; rather than represent himself as he really is—an employer striking a bargain, exchanging services for cash—he relies on the intimacy of equals to win her over. Douglas reinforces the genteel view, commenting uncritically, "What took her most of all and gave her the courage she afterwards showed was that he put the whole thing to her as a favour, an obligation he should gratefully incur"; the second narrator fills in the gaps by adding that the governess "succumbed" to "the seduction exercised by the splendid young man" (4, 6). Neither of these narrators condemns the employer's duplicity, perhaps because both are blind to their own class biases; Douglas, remember, remarks with what could be construed as condescension: "She [the governess] was the most agreeable woman I've ever known *in her position;* she'd have been worthy of any whatever" (2, my italics).

The fiction of helping the master takes the governess far. Both in her actions at Bly and later in writing, she always has him in her mind's eye; she imagines the property as her own and that her con-

9. See Kevin Murphy, "The Unfixable Text: Bewilderment of Vision in *The Turn of the Screw," Texas Studies in Literature and Language* 20 (Winter 1978), 538–51.

duct gives "pleasure . . . to the person to whose pressure I have
yielded. . . . I fancied myself . . . a remarkable young woman and took
comfort in the faith that this would more publicly appear" (15). The
implication may be that she was wrong to view herself as remarkable,
but all her other proleptic observations negate this possibility; such
passages are meant to damn not herself but her employer. This sentence, indeed, reveals her motive for writing—as well as revealing her
great expectations—for since further admiration from the master
turns out not to be forthcoming, she writes her own story to make
sure her virtue is recorded. She expects events to unfold as in story-
books—or governess novels—and when they do not, she takes up her
pen. The figure of the absent beloved augments her desire as she
writes. Her wish for him pervades many passages of the narrative:
"One of the thoughts that, as I don't in the least shrink now from
noting, used to be with me in these wanderings was that it would be as
charming as a charming story suddenly to meet some one. Some one
would appear there at the turn of a path and would stand before me
and smile and approve" (15). The first sentence here seems utterly
superfluous unless the governess envisions her beloved master as
reader. Furthermore, while she writes, like so many heroines before
her, she is aware that he will never read it. Here again, the two
narrators in the prologue do not see such absence as a detriment; they
agree in their estimation that it enhances the "beauty of her passion."
Someone does immediately appear in the passage above, whom she
mistakenly identifies as her beloved. The fact that he appears elevated
at a great distance reveals his inaccessibility and the vast differences in
social status that his seduction initially masked. More significantly, his
elevation suggests that the governess has transformed him into an
idol, as her many allusions to her "services," her "offices," her "devotion," and "sacrifices" reveal. Like Jane Eyre, she idolizes her master;
her worship of this man instead of God may explain why, when she
sees Peter Quint's face instead of the master's, the entire scene is
"stricken with death."

In looking back on this first encounter with Quint, the governess
asserts, "I saw him as I see the letters I form on this page" (17). Once
again, this prolepsis serves to underscore the validity of her vision and
her veracity. She immediately proceeds to relate her writing to her
reading, asking herself if Bly holds some "mystery of Udolpho or an
insane, an unmentionable relative kept in unsuspected confinement?"
(17). The governess' allusion is, of course, to Jane Eyre, the narrative

model for her desire.[10] She yearns for Brontë's happy ending. Her naïve assumption is that books should, after all, imitate life, and her deepest desire is to see her own story end with marriage to the master. She unwittingly reveals her great expectations upon arriving at Bly, the grandness of which "suggested that what I was to enjoy might be a matter beyond his promise" (7). The multiple parallels between *Jane Eyre* and *The Turn of the Screw* are close and compelling, for both deal with an inexperienced governess, a mysterious master, and a house of secret horrors. In Brontë's novel, a Master Miles teaches John Reed; in James's, Master Miles is the schoolboy himself. Writing and reading are activities that dominate each novel: just as Miles retires to the "red cushion of a deep window-seat" to read, Jane sits "shrined in double retirement" in a window seat with a "red moreen curtain" in the novel's opening scene. In Brontë's life and in this novel, the governess' position is uneasy and ill defined; she is a threshold figure whose status is ambiguous sexually as well as economically. James doubles the ambiguities of class and sex by juxtaposing the governess with her predecessor, Miss Jessel. Where the governess is a poor parson's daughter who has led a "small, smothered life," Miss Jessel was a genuine lady, whose name, like the Brontë name at the Hegers', is taboo. Jane sees herself full-length in a mirror for the first time when she is locked in the red room; James's governess has the same experience when she arrives at Bly. When Jane arrives at Thornfield, she hears Bertha Mason laugh; the governess hears a child cry. Just as the scene is "stricken with death" when the governess sees Quint at the tower instead of the master she idolizes, Jane's blind idolatry results in death, destruction, and betrayal. Even the fantasy of the master's sudden appearance while the governess wanders the grounds is a repetition, for Jane engages in precisely the same activity for precisely the same reasons. Her boredom, loneliness, and restlessness, she says,

---

10. Leon Edel briefly compares the governess to Becky Sharp and Jane Eyre, pp. 430–31; Oscar Cargill, in *"The Turn of the Screw* and Alice James," *PMLA* 78 (June 1963), 238–49, suggests that James is posing "the dilemma which confronts the reader as well as the governess—he must choose between a supernatural explanation, such as confronts the reader of *The Mysteries of Udolpho* or a natural one such as is given him in *Jane Eyre:* a mad woman." In my view, René Girard's thesis about triangular desire and his explanation of the ways in which reading mediates between the hero and the object of his desire offers the most illuminating approach to the governess' desire, although he does not discuss Henry James directly. See *Deceit, Desire, and the Novel: Self and Other in Literary Structure,* trans. Yvonne Freccero (Baltimore: Johns Hopkins Univ. Press, 1965).

agitated me to pain sometimes. Then my sole relief was to walk along the corridor of the third story, backwards and forwards, safe in the silence and solitude of the spot and allow my mind's eye to dwell on whatever bright visions rose before it—and, certainly, they were many and glowing; to let my heart be heaved by the exultant movement, which, while it swelled it in trouble, expanded it with life; and, best of all, to open my inward ear to a tale that was never ended—a tale my imagination created, and narrated continuously; quickened with all of incident, life, fire, feeling, that I desired and had not in my actual existence. (95–96)

There are multiple ironies here, for although Jane allows her fancies free rein, she does not yet have any idea of the delusions involved in her "bright visions." Bertha Mason's savagely ironic laugh at this instant marks the depths of Jane's delusion, however, for Bertha can testify that desire for Rochester results not in "exultant movement" and expanded life but in restriction and imprisonment. Peter Quint's appearance at the tower serves precisely the same function as Bertha's laugh: it punctures the governess' wish-fulfillment dreams with anxiety.

James's tale is thus both an absorption of and a reply to Brontë's. *The Turn of the Screw* appeared in 1897, but the tale is set fifty years earlier—the very year (1847) that marked the publication of *Jane Eyre*. Curiously, James maintains that he first got the idea for the tale from a story that Edward Benson, the Archbishop of Canterbury, told him. It is perhaps merely coincidental that in 1839, Charlotte Brontë was a governess to the archbishop's cousin, William Sidgwick. Arthur C. Benson, son of the archbishop, writes that as governess Charlotte was, "according to her own account, very unkindly treated, but it is clear that she had no gifts for the management of children, and was also in a very morbid condition the whole time. My cousin Benson Sidgwick . . . certainly on one occasion threw a Bible at Miss Brontë!"[11] In view of the fact that James's governess also suffers from nervousness and morbidity and is also a poor parson's daughter, it seems possible that the writing governess who supplied James for his model in *The Turn of the Screw* was Charlotte Brontë herself!

11. Cited in T. J. Wise and J. A. Symington, eds., *The Brontës: Their Lives, Friendships, and Correspondence*, 4 vols. (Oxford: Shakespeare Head Edition, Basil Blackwell, 1932), 1:177, 182. See also Christine Brooke-Rose, *The Rhetoric of the Unreal: Studies in Narrative and Structure, Especially of the Fantastic* (Cambridge: Cambridge Univ. Press, 1981), p. 138.

Although Benson insists that everyone who knew the Sidgwicks loved them, Charlotte's letters reveal considerable bitterness toward them. Upon her departure, she writes, "I never was so glad to get out of a house in my life." Her own account of her unhappiness with the Sidgwicks is in Clement Shorter's *Charlotte Brontë and Her Circle* (1896). Oscar Cargill suggests that since James wanted the tale published by Clement Shorter, it would be natural for James to familiarize himself with his new editor's tastes by reading his just-published work on Brontë, as well as by rereading Brontë's novels.[12] Although these parallels are merely speculative, Cargill's accuracy is uncanny when he concludes that "in some way, the Shorter relationship was generic to the story," for what is "generic" is amorous epistolary discourse, which resurfaces once again in a dynamic dialogic relationship.

As in previous amorous discourses, James's governess is a reader as well as a writer, but in her preoccupation with Brontë's happy ending, she overlooks such cautionary elements of the novel as Rochester's sexual excesses while traveling through Europe (which have a possible parallel in her own employer's "spoils of travel" and "trophies of the chase"). She also forgets Rochester's imperiousness, his erratic treatment of Jane alternately as employee and confidante, although the uncle in Harley Street does precisely the same thing to her. He cultivates the fiction of her equality, of his great obligation to her, but once she accepts the job, he quickly drops the pretense and reverts to the arrogance of his class. The enormity of the shock the governess experiences at this reversal has been wholly overlooked, although the moment of her disappointment can be fixed quite precisely; it comes with the letter the uncle sends from Miles's schoolmaster. This is the crucial rupture in the text. We know the governess has been expecting the master to show his gratitude by writing to her, because she has been waiting for the mail; she notes with dismay that the postbag comes late. When it does arrive, her expectations first seem to have been fulfilled, but they are shattered directly: "The postbag . . . contained a letter for me which, however, in the hand of my employer, I found to be composed but of a few words enclosing

---

12. James's notebook entry, 12 Jan. 1895, states that he got the story from the archbishop. See *The Notebooks of Henry James*, ed. F. O. Matthiesen and Kenneth B. Murdock (Oxford: Oxford Univ. Press, 1947), pp. 178–79; rpr. Kimbrough, *The Turn of the Screw*, p. 106. See also Cargill, pp. 238–49; Clement K. Shorter, *Charlotte Brontë and Her Circle* (New York: Dodd and Mead, 1896), pp. 79–84.

another, addressed to himself, with a seal still unbroken. 'This, I
recognize, is from the head-master, and the head-master's an awful
bore. Read him please; deal with him; but mind you don't report. Not
a word. I'm off'" (10).[13] The governess is so distraught that she does
not sleep, nor does she even open the second letter (from the head-
master) because the effect of the first is so devastating. It is at this
point that she must begin to see the discrepancy between her desire
and its model in *Jane Eyre*. The whole bitterness of her realization
comes when she sees how little the master cares for the children and,
by extension, for her. Thus when Miles asks later how she plans to
explain his absence from school, her cruel and bitter retort is, "I don't
think your uncle much cares" (57). Similarly, in another statement,
the governess is forced to abjure what she has already revealed as her
deepest desire—to have the master come to her. Whereas she had
previously imagined him appearing before her at a turn in the path,
when Mrs. Grose implores her to write the master, she rejects the idea
as she thinks of "his derision, his amusement, his contempt for the
breakdown of my resignation at being left alone and for the fine
machinery I had set in motion to attract his attention to my slighted
charms" (50). The passage reveals that she does feel slighted; it is a
clear confession of her sense of abandonment and betrayal: she is
dismissed as indifferently and as irrevocably by her master as Miles is
by his schoolmaster. Discourses of desire like the governess', then, can
best be viewed as exercises not in wish-fulfillment but in wish-for-
mulation, for desires are repeatedly articulated only to be thwarted,

13. Cargill's observation that the Shorter relationship was in some way generic to
The Turn of the Screw is again relevant. Compare this passage in *Villette* (which is particularly significant in light of the Brontë-Heger relationship discussed in my last chapter):
"My hour of torment was the post-hour. Unfortunately, I knew it too well, and tried as
vainly as assiduously to cheat myself of that knowledge; dreading the rack of expecta-
tion, and the sick collapse of disappointment which daily preceded and followed upon
that well-recognised ring. . . . The letter—the well-beloved letter—would not come;
and it was all of sweetness in life I had to look for" (chap. 24). Cargill argues (157–60)
that in James's tale the unopened letter sets in motion what Freud calls "conversion
hysteria"; it constitutes the "painful idea" that is repressed. He makes a convincing (if
circumstantial) case for James's familiarity with Freud and discusses the tale's parallels
to Freud's case study of Lucy von R., an English governess who came to him in 1891
complaining that the servants were conspiring against her. Freud concluded that she
wanted to take the place of the dead mother in the household. Lucy's love for her
employer, like that of James's governess, had "sprung out of a single intimate interview
with the master." His behavior, similarly, subsequently became harsh and erratic, shattering all her hopes.

and it is precisely because her desires are thwarted that the governess takes up her pen.[14]

It is thus significant that James's governess has no name, for a name would give her an individual identity and a past. Instead, she is an interchangeable element in the children's education—a mere repetition of former and future governesses. The uncle's note implies tedious past experiences with such employees, for while declaring that the schoolmaster is a bore, between the lines he is warning the governess that he will regard *her* as a bore if she complains, appeals, or seeks help. For the governess, the master is a romantic novelty, a mysterious figure from an old book, but for him she is merely one of a series of schoolmasters, servants, surrogates necessary to the children's maintenance. That is why he imposes an absolute injunction when he hires her: "She should never trouble him—but never, never: neither appeal nor complain nor write about anything; only meet all questions herself, receive all moneys from his solicitor, take the whole thing over and let him alone" (6). One of the many unanswerable questions the text poses is why the uncle makes so absolute a prohibition against contacting him. Did Miss Jessel obey his injunction too? Or did he issue the edict precisely because she proved to be a nuisance, perhaps importuning him not only about the children's needs, but her own? In other words, was "the seduction exercised by the splendid young man" on the governess merely a repetition of his seduction of Miss Jessel?

We learn very little about Miss Jessel. She was respectable, she was a lady, and she "went off," according to Mrs. Grose, who also remarks that she did nothing to prevent Miles and Quint from being "perpetually together." The facts are scarce, but the range of evils that are suggested is immense: Did she have sex with the master at some point? Or with Quint? Was she made pregnant by one of them? (Is that why a child's cry greets the governess' arrival?) Did she "take herself off" to have this child and subsequently die in childbirth? Did she and Quint initiate the children sexually? All we learn from Mrs. Grose is that Quint was "much too free"; he moved freely between the ranks of highest and lowest classes and "he did what he wished."

14. D. W. Harding, "Psychological Processes in the Reading of Fiction," in *Aesthetics in the Modern World*, ed. Harold Osborne (London: Weybright and Talley, 1968), pp. 313–14, cited in Wolfgang Iser, *The Implied Reader: Patterns of Communication in Prose Fiction from Bunyan to Beckett* (Baltimore: Johns Hopkins Univ. Press, 1974), p. 294.

Somehow, in the process, Miss Jessel was, like the ghost of Hamlet's father, "dishonored, unhouseled, unaneled." For Hamlet, either his father is a saint or his mother is a whore; either the ghost is a demon or his uncle is a murderer. The tragedy revolves around the same flawed logic of absolutes and extremes that infects the governess. The children initially are not merely well behaved but "angelic"; when she reverses her opinion, they are not merely bad but lost and damned. Either the ghosts exist and she is sane, or the children are innocent and she is mad. Like Hamlet's, her entire identity hinges on one choice or the other.

Thus, as happens so often in amorous epistolary discourse, the heroine's predecessor reveals something essential about her own identity. Miss Jessel shares Bertha Mason's symbolic function; each tormented woman is the dark, determined, vengeful double that each dutiful, diligent heroine tries to repress. Just as Bertha is Jane's "truest and darkest double: she is the angry aspect of the orphan child, the ferocious self Jane has been trying to repress ever since her days at Gateshead"[15]—the governess' double is Miss Jessel. Mrs. Grose tells her that Jessel was "almost as young and almost as pretty . . . even as you" (12). Later, while describing Jessel's awful eyes, the governess realizes that Mrs. Grose "stared at mine as if they might really have resembled them" (32). The governess' own "dreadful boldness of mind," moreover, comes to resemble Jessel's "deliberation" and her "fury of intention." The replication of psychic traumas is particularly pronounced in the resemblance of Miss Jessel to Bertha. Each had once been a lady and is subsequently dishonored; each is a terrible figure of rage, jealousy, destructive power; each is condemned for excesses that are specifically sexual in nature. Furthermore, each is absolutely mute (discounting Bertha's bestial sounds), yet each has some vital knowledge to impart to the heroine. Each "could a tale unfold" that would harrow her successor's soul. (Clarissa echoed the same sentiment in her torn fragments [5:36:333].) The greatest irony of all is that each scorned woman wanted precisely the same recognition that each heroine yearns for: to be accepted as desiring and desirable.

Jane Eyre, as we saw in the last chapter, comes to feel her close

15. Sandra M. Gilbert and Susan Gubar, *The Madwoman in the Attic: The Woman Writer and the Nineteenth-Century Literary Imagination* (New Haven: Yale Univ. Press, 1979), p. 360.

connection to Bertha Mason. She discovers that the male prerogatives of discourse and reason coerce women, consigning them to silence and madness. Rochester's systematic alteration of the sign systems that make the world intelligible brings her to the brink of madness, and this experience enables her to fully comprehend the enormity of Bertha's oppression. Rochester shut Bertha up, but Jane speaks in her defense and identifies with her plight. The difference between the happy resolution of Jane Eyre's story and the horrible resolution of the governess' has much to do with their relation to their doubles, for where Jane eventually sees an identity, James's governess sees only a difference. She tenaciously maintains the illusion that she can succeed where every other girl has failed and repudiates her double by calling her "my vile predecessor." When she and Jessel come face to face in the schoolroom, she meets Jessel's challenge "that her right to sit at my table was as good as mine to sit at hers" with "a wild protest against it. . . . 'You terrible miserable woman!'" (*Woman* isn't just the opposite of *lady*; it connotes "whore" here as well.) James, however, carefully establishes the similarity of the governess and her predecessor: she feels herself becoming "ugly and queer"; she sinks on the staircase "tormented with difficulties and obstacles" in exactly the same place that Jessel sank; as she collapses, she recalls that moment with "revulsion" when "in the darkness of night and just so bowed with evil things, I had seen the spectre of the most horrible of women" (59). While acting out the compulsion to repeat, she denies it vehemently. By thus denying Miss Jessel, in all her mute suffering and vague terror, the governess denies herself, and it is the self denied that proliferates. Because the governess is incapable of identifying with Miss Jessel, it is Jessel who triumphs at the end by possessing not only Miles but the governess herself. *The Turn of the Screw* thus repeats the fundamental pattern of previous amorous epistolary discourses, for the heroine's predecessor reveals the repetitive structure of desire. The heroine's discourse involves the interpretation of repetition and the trauma of interpretation; if the heroine fails to acknowledge the connection, as James's governess fails, then she is doomed to replication. The governess fails to acknowledge that she and Miss Jessel occupy the same exiled place in relation to the beloved, even though Mrs. Grose spells it out for her. After the governess confesses to being "carried away" by the master, Grose warns her, "Well, Miss, you're not the first—and you won't be the last!" (9).

The governess' most crucial strategy of denial is her writing, the difficulty of which she points out for us again and again. She describes the past as "a time so full that as I recall the way it went it reminds me of all the art I now need to make it a little distinct. What I look back at with amazement is the situation I accepted" (14). The same insistent tone of self-congratulation sounds after Quint's death is described:

> I scarce know how to put my story into words that shall be a credible picture of my state of mind; but I was in these days literally able to find a joy in the extraordinary flight of heroism the occasion demanded of me. I now saw that I had been asked for a service admirable and difficult; and there would be a greatness in letting it be seen—oh in the right quarter!—that I could succeed where many another girl might have failed. It was an immense help to me—I confess I rather applaud myself as I look back!—that I saw my response so strongly and so simply. (28)

The last sentence veils the implication of the previous one, for what the governess plans is to succeed where other girls failed, to snare the master. Since the master fails to notice her "heroism," she spells it out, applauding herself because no one applauds for her. (Inasmuch as her "heroism" results in Miles's death, her self-congratulation is particularly inappropriate.) Her narrative reenacts a fundamental generic trait of amorous discourse: it is a performance that transforms the beloved's absence into an activity involving many roles, much drama. Self-dramatization, as the passage above demonstrates, is the governess' forte. The metaphor of the stage, indeed, pervades her narrative. Because of the maddening ambiguity of her role, she must "rehearse" before meeting the children daily; they "play at innocence"; Peter Quint looks like an actor (although she has never seen one). As summer gives way to fall, Bly comes to resemble a "theatre after the performance—all strewn with crumpled playbills" (52). Before meeting Quint on the staircase, the governess lays down her book "with all the marks of a deliberation that must have seemed magnificent had there been anyone there to admire it" (40). She repeatedly laments her lack of an audience; in its absence, she becomes her own theater, staging a performance, which is her narrative.

James's description of the tale as a trap comes to mind again; a text that sets out to trap a reader must be not a portrayal of the eternal verities but a performance.[16] As a performance, the text brings the status of the reader into play. James, remember, aimed at a specific kind of reader, the kind not easily fooled, the "jaded, the disillusioned, the fastidious."

Wolfgang Iser has explored the paradox involved in the reading process, in which "the reader is forced to reveal aspects of himself in order to experience a reality which is different from his own. The impact this reality makes on him will depend largely on the extent to which he himself actively provides the unwritten part of the text."[17] In James's tale, the reader will actually invent the evils that are never narrated, as James points out in the preface: "Only make the reader's general vision of evil intense enough . . . and his own experience, his own imagination . . . will supply him quite sufficiently with all the particulars. Make him *think* the evil, make him think it for himself" (123). This the governess does to perfection, and the readers of her narrative—both those in the prologue and we readers—repeat the process without end, without resolving it into a univocal, unequivocal meaning. The characteristic strategy of Ovidian doubleness is at play in another sense as well, for while James is making the reader reflect upon his capacity for imagining evil, the governess is using the same script to fortify her fixed self-conception. Composition, indeed, is her most cunning form of self-dramatization, as when she composes herself in yet another proleptic passage: "I find that I really hang back; but I must take my horrid plunge. In going on with the record of what was hideous at Bly I not only challenge the most liberal faith— for which I little care; but (and this is another matter) I renew what I myself suffered, I again push my dreadful way through it to the end" (40). She refers obliquely here to the liberality of the master's faith in making her "supreme authority" at Bly, but she is also the supreme authority as author. As in so many discourses of desire, retrospective narration allows her to relive, to recollect, to reenvision and revise, but what the governess chooses to stress is her own martyrdom; the act of writing, she insists, is far from pleasurable. She is setting the record straight: "It was not, I am as sure to-day as I was sure then, my mere infernal imagination" (50).

16. See Barbara Johnson, *The Critical Difference: Essays in the Contemporary Rhetoric of Reading* (Baltimore: Johns Hopkins Univ. Press, 1980), p. 143–44.
17. Iser, pp. 281–82.

It is in the writing itself that the governess becomes possessed by the demon of repetition. The scene occurs at the end of Chapter 15; the governess has just risen in revulsion from the staircase, remembering that Miss Jessel once sat in the identical pose and place; she flees to the schoolroom, only to discover Miss Jessel seated at her writing desk among "my pens, ink and paper." What strikes the governess most of all, significantly, are the difficulties of composition. Miss Jessel reminds her of a housemaid applying herself "to the considerable effort of a letter to her sweetheart. There was an effort in the way that, while her arms rested on the table, her hands, with evident weariness, supported her head; but at the moment I took this in I had already become aware that, in spite of my entrance, her attitude strangely persisted." Jessel then rises with "grand melancholy"; stares at the governess as if "to say that her right to sit at my table was as good as mine to sit at hers. While these instants lasted indeed I had the extraordinary chill of a feeling that it was I who was the intruder" (59). This crucial scene reiterates many of the distinguishing traits of the genre I am tracing. First, the roles of rival-mistress-servant are blurred; as in *Jane Eyre,* the ambiguous social position of governess is underscored here by the transformation in these few lines of Miss Jessel from housemaid (the governess' initial impression) to grand personage. Second, the rivals engage in a silent struggle over precedence, privilege, and the appropriation of the schoolroom in general and the writing materials in particular. (In his revision of the tale, James changed "*the* schoolroom" to "*my* schoolroom.") The governess first capitulates, sensing that she is the intruder at the site where language, education, meaning are manufactured, but then "as a wild protest against it," she repudiates her rival with the cry: "You terrible miserable woman!" Finally, most telling of all is the governess' assumption that Miss Jessel is writing a love letter, for she has no objective reason to believe this. Her belief is clearly a projection of her own desires, her own letter writing and literary productivity. And indeed, in the next scene but one after seeing Jessel, the governess herself sits "for a long time before a blank sheet of paper" as she attempts to communicate her "endless obsession" to *her* sweetheart: the master in Harley Street. The attempt fails, for we later learn (when Miles opens it) that this letter contains nothing. It never reaches the master; instead Miles steals and burns it.

The Game of Equivocations

As in *Clarissa*, a prodigious amount of writing takes place in this tale, yet most of it is incomprehensible, unread, or meaningless. There is the letter about Miles's conduct at school; the letters Miles may have stolen at school; the letters Mrs. Grose had the bailiff write in the past; the whole elaborate framing device, in which Douglas refuses to paraphrase the tale but instead writes to his servant to send the written manuscript. The children never receive letters from their uncle, but they compose many to him; these, however, are merely "charming literary exercises," the governess explains. "They were too beautiful to be posted; I kept them myself; I have them all to this hour" (54). The emphasis on beauty echoes Douglas' phrase about "the beauty of her passion" and the second narrator's admiring description of Douglas' reading as "rendering to the ear . . . the beauty of his author's hand" (6). As Roland Barthes explains in *S/Z,* the code of beauty obliterates the distinction between origin and result, model and copy, supernatural and subnatural: "The essence of the code (perfection) has in the end the same status as what is outside the code . . . for life, the norm, mankind, are but intermediary migrations in the field of replications. . . . This confusion . . . enables the discourse to engage in a game of equivocations: to speak of the 'supernatural' perfection of the Adonis is also to speak of the 'sub-natural' deficiency of the castrato."[18] Similarly, since the governess comes to believe that the children are copying the behavior of the ghosts and being modeled by the demons, to speak of the supernatural perfection of the children in *The Turn of the Screw* is also to speak of the subnatural deficiency of the ghosts. Copying thus becomes a disturbing image indeed, and references to it are plentiful. Just as Miss Jessel sits among the governess' pens, ink, and paper inscribing her desire, Flora is supplied with a "sheet of white paper, a pencil, and a copy of nice round O's." Language is the inscription of loss, a hole that cannot be filled, like Flora's O's and like the hole Flora tries to fill with a mast. In light of the fact that the governess' own desire is a copy of Jane Eyre's, it is significant that the children's entire education consists of copying, reciting, imitating, and repeating. "We had all three, with repetition, got into such splendid

18. Barthes, *S/Z,* pp. 71–72.

training that we went, each time . . . almost automatically through the very same movements" (53), like the movement of a turning screw that never progresses but merely spirals repetitiously.[19] An education that consists of copying and repetition, James seems to suggest, is given to children to prepare them for a life conceived of as replication, a tragic reenactment of emptiness and loss. These particular children are presented as preternatural mimics by the governess in a passage in which she unaccountably shifts, like a true paranoiac, to speaking of herself in the third person:

> They had never . . . wanted to do so many things for their poor pro-
> tectress . . . in the way of diverting, entertaining, surprising her; read-
> ing her passages, telling her stories, acting her charades, pouncing out
> at her, in disguises, as animals and historical characters, and above all
> astonishing her by the "pieces" they had secretly got by heart and could
> interminably recite. I should never get to the bottom—were I to let
> myself go even now—of the prodigious private commentary, all under
> still more private correction, with which I in these days overscored their
> full hours. (38)

In the last sentence the governess not only shifts back to the first person and the present but emphasizes her firm conviction that the children are being tutored privately by others than herself; it is this that is giving them their false air of perfection. The obvious implica-tion is that tots adept at mimicking Shakespeareans, tigers, Romans, and navigators will be equally adept at imitating the sexual rites and forbidden sports of a Jessel and Quint.

The vision is indisputably very different from the Rousseauistic one of innocence in a state of nature, and ironic variations of the word *nature* reverberate, like the word *craft*, throughout the tale. In *Emile*, however, Rousseau reflects on the relation of writing, copying, nar-cissism, and obedience; his description is an uncanny evocation of Flora's O's:

> I know a young person who learned to write before learning to read. . . .
> Of all the letters, she first wanted only to make O's. She incessantly made
> big and little O's, O's of all sizes, O's inside one another, and always drawn
> backward. Unfortunately, one day when she was busy with this useful
> exercise, she saw herself in a mirror; and finding that this constrained
> attitude was not graceful for her, like another Minerva she threw away

19. Felman, "Turning the Screw of Interpretation," pp. 172–73.

the pen and no longer wanted to make O's. Her brother did not like to write any more than she did, but what irritated him was the discomfort and not the appearance it gave him.

After thus commenting on the essential narcissism of the female sex, Rousseau goes on to proclaim that in young girls

> idleness and disobedience are the two most dangerous defects. . . . They ought to be constrained very early. . . . All their lives they will be enslaved to the most continual and severe of constraints—that of the proprieties. They must first be exercised in constraint, so that it never costs them anything to tame all their caprices in order to submit them to the wills of others. If they always wanted to work, one would sometimes have to force them to do nothing. . . . A decent woman's life is a perpetual combat against herself.[20]

The passage brings to mind the opening chapter of *Jane Eyre,* in which Jane suffers for her disobedience, is persecuted by John Reed, discovers that she is embattled against herself, and is forcefully brought to submit to the will of others. It also reminds us that Flora's education is a repetition of that of previous little girls. Thus as governesses, Miss Jessel and her successor are agents in replicating and enforcing the coercive pattern of their own early education. The word *form,* therefore, has sinister connotations throughout the tale, for the governess clearly sees her function as being "to watch, teach, 'form' little Flora"; she goes so far as to exclaim, "I call the sisterhood to witness!" (19). (The repetitive pattern spills into the prologue: Douglas meets the governess because she is "forming" yet another girl—his own little sister.) Significantly, girls are formed through language, but they are never its masters; instead they discover that males master them and language, while girls must be "exercised in constraint . . . to submit to the wills of others." In Brontë's novel, Jane must keep silent until she can speak pleasantly, for "there is something truly forbidding in a child taking up her elders," and to be disobedient is to become invisible, unnamable ("author of evil . . . Unnamed in heaven"), to be an "unmentionable relative kept in unsuspected confinement." That the governess is a repetition of Miss Jessel, that Flora's education is an exercise in repetition and repression, is brought home when the governess describes the "forbidden

20. Jean-Jacques Rousseau, *Emile; or, On Education,* trans. Allan Bloom (New York: Basic Books, 1979), p. 369.

ground" she skirts while giving lessons when she refers obliquely to Miss Jessel as "the lady who had prepared them for my discipline." (In earlier versions, James wrote, "The lady—never once named—who had prepared them for my discipline.") It is no accident that her successor, the governess who writes the narrative, herself remains unnamed.

Miss Jessel's name is particularly relevant to the amorous discourses we have been tracing, for it is here that the simile of woman as bird, as prey, as captive creature reappears. A *jess* is a short leather strap fastened to a hawk's leg in falconry (a sport as ancient as the card game of *quint*). The jess has been specifically associated with the transportation of letters, as in George Sandys' 1615 example, cited in the *Oxford English Dictionary:* "[They] make tame doves the speedy transporters of their letters; which they wrap about their legs like jesses." Tennyson, similarly, associates the jess with "training, terms of art . . . jesses, leash, and lure" (in *Merlin*, 1874). But the predatory connotations are pronounced by Othello, who is speaking of his attempt to prove Desdemona unfaithful: "If I do prove her haggard, though that her jesses were my dear heart strings, I'd whistle her off, and let her down the wind to prey at Fortune" (III, iii, 261). The governess' obsession with "horrible proofs" thus connects her to Othello as well as to Hamlet, for she says of Miss Jessel: "She rose . . . with an indescribable grand melancholy of indifference and detachment. . . . even as I fixed and, for memory, secured it, the awful image passed away. Dark as midnight in her black dress, her haggard beauty and her unutterable woe, she had looked at me long enough" (59). *Haggard* describes not only a wild, intractable person but one not to be tamed. Othello's desire to prove Desdemona haggard is thus oxymoronic, for a *haggard* by definition cannot be proved, cannot be fixed—as the governess tries to fix Jessel's image or as readers try to fix the tale's meaning.

James's use of *haggard*, like Shakespeare's, is figuratively consistent with the word *jess*, for a *haggard* is a wild female hawk, caught when in her adult plumage, which may be disordered and ragged. The imagery intensifies the irony of Lovelace's analogy of the ways in which first birds, then women are subjected to the "sportive cruelty" of men. His description of Clarissa as an "ensnared Volatile" comes to mind. Jane Eyre, similarly, is compared to a captured bird beating against its cage shortly after she discovers Bertha Mason, who herself is described as a "carrion-seeking bird of prey" (185). A *haggard*, indeed, is also a bewitched hag, a witch; the governess, remember, confesses that she had made Mrs. Grose "a receptacle of lurid things, but there was an odd recognition of my superiority—my accomplishments and my function—in her patience under my pain. She offered her mind to my disclosures as, had I wished to mix a witch's broth and propose it with assurance, she would have held out a large clean saucepan" (46). All the imagery of jesses, haggard hawks, and predators illuminates the slow transformation of the governess into Miss Jessel. The more recent meaning of *haggard* as an adjective involves "want of rest, anxiety, terror, wildness of expression, especially in the eyes" and charts her metamorphosis, for when she realizes she has lost Flora by the lake, she says, "I must have thrown myself, on my face, to the ground and given way to a wildness of grief" (73). Haggard hawks, moreover, are caught by falconers who try to reclaim them and make them prey on other quarry, just as Jessel and the governess first try to reach Flora and, failing that, turn to "other quarry" in the form of Miles. Miles seems to realize that he has become the quarry in the tale's final scene, for he thinks Miss Jessel is in the room, and his "supposition [is] some sequel to what we had done to Flora," the governess declares. The *we* here is intensely ambiguous. Does it refer to Mrs. Grose and the governess or to the governess and (or *as*) Miss Jessel? The latter view is enforced by the ejaculation Miles addresses to the governess when she asks whom he sees, for Miles turns on her with the words, "Peter Quint—you devil!" In my view, Miles never does see Quint, but he does see the devil in front of him—the governess, who is now fully possessed. His movement, she writes, "made *me*, with a single bound and an irrepressible cry, spring straight upon him. For there again, against the glass, as if to blight his confession and stay his answer, was the hideous author of our woe—the white face of damnation. I felt a sick swim at the drop of my victory and all the return of my battle, so that the wildness of my veritable leap only served as a great betrayal" (87–88). In the attempt to "reclaim" Miles, as falconers reclaim haggard hawks, the governess dispossesses him of his heart. ("Though that her jesses were my dear heart strings.") The climax is Miles's "supreme surrender" to the governess, who grasps him with all the passion of one who is herself demonically possessed: "With the stroke of the loss I was so proud of he uttered the cry of a creature hurled over an abyss, and the grasp with which I recovered him might have been that of catching him in his fall. I caught him, yes, I held him—it may be imagined with what a passion" (88).

Perhaps what is finally so provocative about *jess* as an image is precisely the futility of movement, for although the hawk has the impulse to fly free, the jess perpetually thwarts that desire. It is an image of restriction, of movement without progression, as futile as the turning of a screw.[21] Throughout her narrative, the governess depicts language as just as futile, for again and again the rhetorical strategy of prolepsis allows her to congratulate herself for her attempt to describe events and simultaneously to take refuge in the ineffability of her experience. "No no," she writes at one point, "it was useless to attempt to convey to Mrs. Grose, just as it is scarcely less so to attempt to suggest here, how, during our short stiff brush there in the dark, [Miles] fairly shook me with admiration" (47). To lament what language cannot describe, indeed, is one of the duplicitous strategies of amorous epistolary discourse, but in the governess' narrative, the lamentation disguises a murder as well as desire. In previous examples of this genre, I have described how stereotypical representations of gender have been subverted and transgressed repeatedly; James's tale similarly reveals the artifice of the literary construction of gender, for rather than being the helpless victim of unrequited love, the governess demonstrates an aggressive will to power. It is she who turns desire into dread, dread into destruction, destruction into death. Since his reflections on doubles could have been written with Jessel and the governess in mind, it is surprising that René Girard leaves Henry James out of the picture:

> After Dante, almost no one but Dostoevski reveals how truly infernal desire can be, not in the absence of the object and the incapability of reaching it, but in the constant attachment to this double, a slavish imitation growing all the more invincible as escape is attempted. Even where all the positive data seem to preclude it, the relationship of rivalry moves irresistibly toward reciprocity and identity. . . . Both of

21. The image of a *jess*—and of the thwarting of the desire for movement—is also provocative in *The Golden Bowl*, another text in which two women, Maggie and Charlotte, fight for possession of the beloved, Prince Amerigo. Charlotte's final fate is to be bound with a "silken noose," an "immaterial tether," which, like a jess, has a small ring, or varvel, attached to the swivel of the leash. Thus constricted, Charlotte's "straight neck had certainly not slipped it; nor had the other end of the long cord—oh, quite conveniently long!—disengaged its smaller loop from the hooked thumb that, with his fingers closed upon it, her husband kept out of sight. To have recognised, for all its tenuity, the play of this gathered lasso might inevitably be to wonder with what magic it was twisted, to what tension subjected, but could never be to doubt either of its adequacy to its office or of its perfect durability" (Henry James, *The Golden Bowl* [New York: Dell, 1963], pp. 486–87).

the doubles become entangled in the obligatory reciprocity of one and the very same game.[22]

The Body in the Prologue

To what genre does *The Turn of the Screw* belong? The answer is important because it has largely determined the direction of critical controversy. Those critics who see the novel as a ghost story are naturally preoccupied with the issue of the reality or unreality of the ghosts. Leon Edel, for example, places it generically with such other ghost stories as "The Jolly Corner" and "The Altar of the Dead."[23] Jerome Beaty, on the other hand, places the tale in the genre of the governess novel, the characteristics of which include "a poor but respectable orphan . . . who undergoes some sort of humiliation because of her dependent status, who attends the deathbed of a pious child, who has or comes to have a deep religious, providentialist conviction, and who, when she is the heroine, marries a gentleman or clergyman."[24] *Jane Eyre* is Beaty's model, and since I have shown that Brontë's novel is a subtext throughout James's tale, it seems appropriate to consider the extent to which the two texts belong to this genre, rather than to the generic tradition I have been tracing. Obviously, both heroines are governesses, and they do suffer certain humiliations. Yet Jane Eyre certainly does not seem humiliated when she describes Blanche Ingram as being "a mark beneath jealousy; she was too inferior to excite the feeling," and when she writes that, where Rochester is concerned, *"she could not charm him"* (164). This is hardly the tone of humiliation. Nor is the self-congratulatory tone of James's governess, which seems to ward off humiliation at every turn. Indeed, every detail of Beaty's evidence is reversed in James's tale: the governess' "supreme authority" is herself, not God. She does not attend the deathbed of a pious child, but, in James's macabre twist, is herself the agent in the death of a child she considers not pious but demonically possessed. The problem, I think, is that Beaty's definition relies ex-

22. René Girard, *"To Double Business Bound"* (Baltimore: Johns Hopkins Univ. Press, 1978), pp. 40–41.
23. Edel, *The Ghostly Tales of Henry James.*
24. Jerome Beaty, *"Jane Eyre* and Genre," *Genre* 10 (Winter 1977), 619–53.

clusively on plot. A shift in focus to the diegetic aspects of narrative reveals a different set of characteristics, those of amorous epistolary discourse. Jane Eyre's words above, for example, do not reveal Jane's humiliation; they anticipate her eventual triumph. They are, moreover, addressed directly to Rochester; he is her "dear Reader," as I demonstrated in the previous chapter. Thus when Beaty (following Harold Bloom) goes on to reflect that *Jane Eyre* may be Brontë's anxious misreading of Richardson's *Pamela,* he again misses the mark by focusing on plot, for the diegetic aspects of narrative and the generic similarities shared by all amorous discourses link it far more directly to the characteristics we have already charted in *Clarissa.* The problem with classifying James's tale as either a governess novel or a ghost story is that neither classification does justice to the range and resourcefulness of the heroine as writer. To neglect the diegetic aspects of narrative discourse is to fall right into one of the traps James set for the sophisticated reader.

An even larger limitation is that neither the governess novel nor the ghost story can account generically for the tale's prologue, despite some ingenious attempts to show the relation of the two parts.[25] James's dilemma in the tale is the same fundamental dilemma that marks epistolary discourse: how to reconcile the exigencies of story (communication between novelist and reader) with the exigencies of interpersonal discourse (communication between correspondents).[26] The dilemma is complicated by the fact that there are so many levels of correspondence circulating in James's tale: the governess' narrative is a disguised love letter to her employer; Douglas not only interprets but enacts her narrative; Douglas' "reading" is then interpreted by the audience assembled around the fire, one of whom literally rewrites the entire story.

The first point to be made is that "prologue" is a misnomer, falsely implying an inside and outside, a rhetorical hierarchy between two parts of the story—a difference where in fact there is only an identity. The notions of genesis and a bipartite structure are disrupted in the very first sentence, for another tale has just ended which is described

25. To relate the prologue to the governess' narrative, many critics have relied on either thematic similarities or on characterization, arguing that her manuscript was addressed to Douglas or that Douglas is Miles grown up. See note 3 above.

26. Janet Gurkin Altman, *Epistolarity: Approaches to a Form* (Columbus: Ohio State Univ. Press, 1983), p. 210.

as "the last story, however incomplete and like the mere opening of a serial" (3). There is no point of origin in this tale, for even the governess' written statement "took up the tale at a point after it had, in a manner, begun" (4). There are, moreover, prologues within prologues, for the speaker whose voice we first hear is not Douglas, but someone who feels the need to explain: "It appeared that the narrative he had promised to read us really required for a proper intelligence a few words of prologue" (4). This speaker then launches into a prologue entirely different from the one Douglas subsequently provides, for the speaker says: "Let me say here distinctly, to have done with it, that this narrative, from an exact transcript of my own made much later, is what I shall presently give. Poor Douglas, before his death—when it was in sight—committed to me the manuscript that reached him on the third of these days" (4). This narrative, then, is an object of exchange. Just as the tale the governess tells is inseparable from certain economic realities—her employer's unbridgable distance from her in terms of class and status—so too the narrative itself is a contract ruled by several economies: of language, gender, and the human body. Barthes has suggested that the motive of all narrative is "to obtain by exchanging; and it is this exchange that is represented in the narrative itself: narrative is both product and production."[27] From the *Heroides* onward, contract and transgression have been major motifs in discourses of desire. The heroine laments a contract broken, a vow violated; as she writes, she ponders what writing is worth, what it will gain, what wrongs it can redress. But the passage above raises more questions than it answers: why does this speaker make a transcript? Is there a relation, as in *Clarissa*, between death and writing? In a tale where the number *two* seems so obvious everywhere (two children, two turns of the screw, two parts to the story), why does the number *three* seem to proliferate to disrupt the symmetry? If there are two clearly identifiable authorities about this tale— Douglas and the governess—why is the shadow of a third inscribed? What does the act of transcribing imply? Just who writes the words above?

The common answer has been Henry James. The evidence for this view is James's letter to Arthur C. Benson, "a little confession" written in 1898, in which James says he had first heard the gruesome story of

27. Barthes, *S/Z*, p. 89.

dead servants and victimized children from Arthur's father, Edward Benson, the Archbishop of Canterbury. The boundaries of the letter as literature, literature as a letter, have been blurred ever since, for innumerable critics have approached the tale with little reference to the second narrator's fictiveness. The unexamined assumption is that if James got the tale from the archbishop, then Benson is simply transformed in the tale into Douglas, and James is the second narrator. It is certainly interesting to speculate that James got the tale from the archbishop, although some critics dispute his account of its genesis.[28] But the real point is that James's source for the story has absolutely no bearing on the identity of the second narrator in the prologue. The hypothesis that James is the second narrator does violence to the tale because it is one of "writerly texts" in which, in Barthes's words, "the symbolic field is occupied by a single object from which it derives its unity. . . . This object is the human body."[29] In my view, the assumption that the author is the narrator obscures not just the genre the tale belongs to but the human body in the prologue, for sophisticated readers have failed to consider the gender of the narrator to whom Douglas mainly speaks. My primary aim is to point out that critics have simply assumed that the narrator is male; my secondary aim is to speculate briefly on the ways in which the tale and the prologue are transformed if one reads *as if* that second body in the prologue were female. For one thing, the figure in the carpet takes on an entirely different pattern. Suppose, for example, that the governess' unrequited love for her employer leads her to write her narrative, which she gives to Douglas before she dies; Douglas' unrequited love for the governess replicates her love for her employer; the second narrator loves Douglas as he loves the governess; she reenacts the governess' writing by making an exact transcript of her narrative, which Douglas commits to her before his death. This transcript is the source of the narrative we read. It is a "copy" of desire in triplicate, for the governess' desire is copied from *Jane Eyre*, Douglas' is copied from the governess, and the second narrator has made her own copy. But no repetition, as we have seen, is exactly the same. In all amorous discourses, the acts of remembering and transcribing simultaneously reconstruct and deconstruct desire. Why would the second narrator

28. See Robert Lee Wolff, "The Genesis of *The Turn of the Screw*," *American Literature* 13 (1948), 1–8.

29. Barthes, *S/Z*, p. 215.

transcribe at all unless the tale was in some sense her story too? The meaning of the tale thus lies in its infinite reduplication; it is yet another testament to the dialogic dynamism of the genre. Here, again, is Barthes: "The meaning of a text can be nothing but the plurality of its systems, its infinite (circular) 'transcribability': one system transcribes another, but reciprocally as well: with regard to the text, there is no 'primary,' 'natural,' 'national,' 'mother' critical language: from the outset, as it is created, the text is multilingual; there is no entrance language or exit language."[30] The statement illuminates all the false starts in the tale, in the prologue, in the prologue within a prologue. There is, moreover, substantial evidence of the second narrator's romantic interest in Douglas. She has been "fixing" him from the outset, observing the effect Griffin's ghost story has on him. Her "acuteness" is immediately apparent, for Douglas has only to mention that the governess never told anyone her story for this narrator to conclude that she was in love, to which he responds, "You *are* acute." She is acute because of her own empathetic identification—so like that of the governess, who divines that Miss Jessel is writing her sweetheart because she herself wants to do the same. The same close identification of the governess with the second narrator recurs throughout the prologue, as when she says what she would have done in "her successor's place." Literally, she is referring to the governess as Miss Jessel's successor, but she herself is the governess' successor in the sense that her love for Douglas remains as little recognized as his for the governess or the governess' for the master. That her love is not returned is clear from the repeated descriptions of Douglas' obliviousness to her. She feels invisible, indeed, for he looks through her at one point "as if, instead of me, he saw what he spoke of" (2). When she suggests that the story will tell whom the governess loved, Douglas is derisive (just as the governess fears her employer will be if she attracts his attention to her slighted charms): "The story won't tell—not in any literal vulgar way" (3). Finally, when she says she has a title for the tale (could it perhaps be "Unrequited Love"?), Douglas begins to read "without heeding me." Her absorbed interest in him contrasts to his utter self-absorption and inattention. Barthes writes: "The subject painfully identifies himself with some person (or character) who occupies the same position as himself in the amorous structure. . . . I see myself in the other who loves without being loved, I recognize in

30. Ibid., p. 120.

him the very gestures of my own unhappiness."[31] The words, which so well express her own position in James's narrative, might have been written by the second narrator.

The probability that James, like Barthes, was homosexual may seem to contradict the speculations I have been advancing, but that fact actually serves to reinforce rather than to undermine my argument, for it points once again to those characteristic Ovidian strategies of doubleness and dissimulation in discourses of desire. The text, in other words, is no mere transcription of authorial sexual preference; instead James's tale, like Barthes's amorous discourse, consciously subverts the stereotypes of gender—as well as genre—and stages a radically antimimetic performance. There are, of course, many Jamesian tales involving two narrators who are male, but to view this particular narrator as female, one must abandon dichotomous thinking about male/female, prologue/tale proper, inside/outside. (It is the governess' own habit of dichotomizing, after all, that undoes her.) If one allows for the possibility that the second narrator is female, then one is forced to pay as much attention to the margins as to the tale proper; one is forced to reinscribe diegesis rather than mimesis, for the prologue frames the governess' narrative, obliterating the boundaries, making the impressions received from the narrative as significant as the narrative itself. (The entire prologue, indeed, is a study in contrast between those who respond inappropriately and those, like the second narrator, whose imaginations are engaged. It is a study in the diegetic aspects of narrative, for the drama of the telling is quite consciously staged by James as a performance on Douglas' part: Douglas creates suspense by withholding the narrative until the written version arrives; he performs "with immense effect"; he "worked us up" [4].) In short, even if one argues that the gender of the narrator who reports all this is indeterminate, the very fact that this indeterminacy has been overlooked is in itself significant, for it shows how well James succeeded in diverting our attention elsewhere.

If the second narrator is female, Douglas' characterization is transformed as well, for he then resembles John Marcher in "The Beast in the Jungle." Like Marcher, he certainly does not entirely grasp the signifi-

31. Roland Barthes, *A Lover's Discourse: Fragments*, trans. Richard Howard (New York: Hill and Wang, 1978), pp. 129–30.

cance of the events he relates. Like Douglas, Marcher is completely self-absorbed, oblivious to May Bartram, who only signifies as a reflection of himself. He thinks at one point that she has some knowledge of his eventual fate: "She had no source of knowledge he hadn't equally—except of course that she might have finer nerves. That was what women had where they were interested; they made out things, where people were concerned, that the people often couldn't have made out for themselves. Their nerves, their sensibility, their imagination, were conductors and revealers, and the beauty of May Bartram was in particular that she had given herself so to his case."[32] Viewed in this light, Douglas also resembles Lovelace and Rochester; the second narrator's function is to signify as a reflection, as a mirror, to be, in Clarissa's words, "but a *cypher*, to give *him* significance and *myself* pain." May Bartram, moreover, is repeatedly compared to a sphinx who knows the riddle of Marcher's fate; the irony, of course, is that the beast in the jungle is his egotism. Just as May "set him to wondering if she hadn't even a larger conception of singularity for him than he had for himself" (*BJ*, 344), the transcriber in *The Turn of the Screw* is wholly responsible for Douglas' sense of significance. In the first paragraph, it is she who is watching for signs that "he had himself something to produce and that we should only have to wait"; it is she who brings our attention to his obsession, which is as compelling as that of the governess; it is she who urges him "to sit right down and begin" and who is "charmed" by his "scruples" when he cannot begin. That frequent technique of amorous discourse, prolepsis, intensifies and authenticates her memory: "I can see Douglas there before the fire," she writes. Yet in so standing, he is repeatedly described as having his back to her. Because he has been so consistently oblivious to her, she is surprised at his response when she observes that the beauty of the governess' passion was that she only saw her employer twice; Douglas confers upon her his full attention in assenting, "It *was* the beauty of it" (6).

The "beauty" of the governess' passion is that it is "ordered and arranged" into art. For the same reason, the governess kept the children's letters because they were "too beautiful" to be posted: she turned them into artifacts. Throughout the tale, failed communication

32. "The Beast in the Jungle," in *The Portable Henry James*, ed. Morton Dauwen Zabel (New York: Viking Press, 1968), p. 354, hereinafter cited parenthetically in the text as *BJ*, with page number.

is turned into an aesthetic value again and again. Douglas reads the governess' narrative "with a fine clearness that was like a rendering to the ear of the beauty of his author's hand." The death of the author-governess gives birth to Douglas the reader, who not only reads the text but enacts it as a performance: he creates suspense with "quiet art" and builds slowly to a climax; he "prepared his triumph" by evoking "a rage of curiosity . . . produced by the touches with which he had already worked us up" (4). He plays on the listeners' sense of inclusion in the magic circle, for those unworthy to hear the tale depart. Significantly, the transcriber reinforces this sense of exclusivity; it is she who conveys the impression of just how select a group has the aesthetic sensibility to appreciate the tale's significance, for the departure of the others, she says, "only made his little final auditory more compact and select, kept it, round the hearth, subject to a common thrill" (4). Thus they all participate in the code of perfection, which is precisely what disguises the violence of the governess' desire, just as Lovelace's aesthetic sensibility disguises the violence of his quest for novelty regarding Clarissa's perfection. Just as Clarissa is treated as an artifact, locked up like silver plate and returned home in a silver coffin, the code of perfection similarly results in death in *The Turn of the Screw*. Indeed, as in Richardson, in James's tale eros is an ordeal of fascination. It is an ordeal, moreover, marked by the same obsession with legalities and contracts. There is the contract of employment between the governess and the uncle; the implied contract she imagined of an ongoing correspondence; economic and legal contracts related to her role as the uncle's legal substitute—the "supreme authority" who handles all monies, deals with all employees, corresponds not about love to the uncle but about legalities to his solicitor. Like previous amorous epistolary discourses, therefore, this one is yet another contract and transgression, impelled by desire. As Barthes points out: "At the origin of Narrative, desire. . . . Narrative: legal tender . . . *merchandise*, barter [of] which . . . [one asks] *What should the narrative be exchanged for? What is the narrative 'worth'?*"[33] James's tale encodes the unbridled circulation of economies, of desire and its copies, in the prologue as well as in the governess' narrative. Her written record, indeed, is imbued with the power of a fetish; the prologue records the process by which the audience strikes a bargain to have it told, and the very fact that it has

33. Barthes, *S/Z*, pp. 88–90.

never been heard before is "naturally declared by several voices to give the thing the utmost price" (1). Instead of an economy based on giving, loving, or feeling, however, each lover reenacts a transaction based on hoarding, possession, and repression. It is as if words and feelings must be kept under lock and key, lest they be appropriated, as the governess feels that Miss Jessel has appropriated the schoolroom in their recognition scene. (It is a *failed* recognition scene, since the governess repudiates her double.) No wonder the passing on of the manuscript—from the governess to Douglas to the woman who loves him—becomes a deadly transaction, one that can occur only when the writer-lover is at the point of death, of "passing on." (An archaic meaning of the word *jess* is a stage of a journey—a journey one might say without end for Miss Jessel and all tormented souls.) Only in art can one achieve perfection and immortality, yet permanent deathlessness is also permanent lifelessness, as the governess reveals in "dispossessing" Miles at the end.

Naming, of course, is another form of possession, but what is most remarkable in this tale is how much remains unnamed. The governess hesitates for a long time before she can name evil and thereby make it real, yet ultimately, she does name it, asking Flora, "Where, my pet, is Miss Jessel?" and eliciting from Miles before he dies "the supreme surrender of the name" of "the hideous author of our woe" (88). Her allusion to Milton's Satan ("author of evil unknown till thy revolt, Unnamed in Heaven") reveals that even in moments of supreme crisis, the governess resorts to literature. Miles's "supreme surrender" echoes the governess' own "supreme authority"; since she becomes an author herself, to record her virtue, it is no accident that she defines Miles's surrender as a "tribute to her devotion to the master." The master, remember, had thanked her "for the sacrifice" at the outset; at the end Miles is the sacrifice she places before her idol. What remains unnamed in this strange story is love. In introducing it, Douglas "had broken a thickness of ice, the formation of many a winter; and had his reasons for a long silence," just as the governess never names her love for her employer, although Douglas says "I saw it, and she saw I saw it; but neither of us spoke of it" (3). An oppressive silence dates from the master's injunction that the governess "never write about anything" and poisons all communication, in the prologue and narrative alike. Love is unexpressed or unattainable or unrecognized in all the relationships: between the uncle and the children, between the governess and the uncle, between Douglas and the governess, between the second narrator and Douglas. What is said is lost, transitory, indefinite, insubmissible evidence; what is written is fixed, ordered and arranged, formed, as, says the governess, "I form the letters on this page." The contrast between what is written and what is spoken is particularly haunting in light of Miles's great "crime" at school: in his own words, "I said things." These remarks were not repeated to everyone—"Only [to] a few. Those I liked"; the words were subsequently repeated by these boys to others—"to those *they* liked," he explains (86–87). At this point it occurs to the governess that Miles may indeed be innocent, yet she brushes the feeling aside, sternly demands that he spell things out more clearly, and, "blind with victory," terrifies him to death. It seems just possible, then, that Miles's "crime" may have been to speak to his schoolmates of love, but for his schoolmasters, this is too *bad* even to write home about. In any case, since all the governess' conclusions derive from what she imagines are his crimes at school, there is great pathos in looking back on her first impression of him: "What I then and there took him to my heart for was something divine that I have never found to the same degree in any child—his indescribable little air of knowing nothing in the world but love" (13).

   The Turn of the Screw is about the unnamable; the savage *turn* James gives is that what remains unnamed is not evil but good, not hate but love. The same tragic irony is the climax of "The Beast in the Jungle." Like the governess, Marcher wastes his life waiting in dread for the beast to pounce; what finally "brushed him . . . with the disrespect of chance" is that May Bartram "was what he had missed. . . . The escape would have been to love her; then, *then* he would have lived" (*BJ*, 381–82). The governess almost has an epiphany too, but when the "mere brush of the question" of Miles's innocence touches her, she is compelled to dismiss it. Why? Because to accept it would mean the transgression of the antithesis by which she has ordered her teaching, her conduct, her existence: "for if he *were* innocent what then on earth was I?" (87). The tale encodes the collapse of one economy after another: the "much too free" intercourse between Quint and Jessel marks the breakdown of class divisions (a breakdown that is nonetheless exactly what the governess would like to duplicate with her employer). The ambiguity of the ghosts' influence on the children marks another breakdown of the dichotomies of innocence and evil, youth and age, for the governess' relationship with Miles resembles that of "some young couple . . . on their wedding-journey, at the inn, [who] feel shy" (81), and Flora comes to appear to the governess as withered and as haggard as Miss Jessel herself. The economy of gender collapses too, most notably in the prologue, where the transcriber's sex, like her desire, remains oblique.[34] The governess' narrative exhorts us to contemplate evil, just as the little boy in the opening tale that Griffin tells wakes his mother not to dissipate the evil presence but to engage her in it. The tragedy of *The Turn of the Screw* is that characters find the courage to name evil and thereby confirm its reality, but they never find the courage to name love. All of James's fiction, indeed, is full of such cowards, characters with feelings kept under lock and key. Perhaps that is why, in a letter about *The Turn of the Screw*, James refers to the "exposure, indeed the helpless plasticity of childhood that isn't dear or sacred to *some*body! That *was* my little tragedy."[35]

James speaks volumes in these few words, for *plasticity*—a term so rich in artistic connotations—illuminates the gap between aesthetics and compassion that lies at the center of *The Turn of the Screw*. It dramatizes the dangers of treating others as art objects, a crucial theme of James's from *The Portrait of a Lady* to *The Golden Bowl*. The tone, the sympathy, the empathetic identification James reveals in the letter above certainly contradicts the "confession" he makes in the preface to writing the tale with "cold artistic calculation"; that spurious confession, however, is meant to entrap the reader—just as the governess' own spurious confession does. The trap James set is precisely the one into which the sophisticated reader falls by responding aesthetically rather than empathetically to the tale. The aesthetic response, moreover, is the source of the tragedy for the governess in "reading" the children, for Douglas' audience in "reading" her narrative, and for the modern reader of the tale. James juxtaposes those who read the tale aesthetically with those who read it empathetically: Douglas, who "took down . . . nothing but the impression . . . [in] his heart," and the narrator—possibly female—who transcribes it. Mark Spilka, in a recent analysis of Dickens' view of childhood, comments that it is time to "reformulate or perhaps reinvent Sigmund Freud, whose appearance at the end of the last century signalled the return of a doctrine rather like that of Original Sin: the doctrine . . . of the

---

34. Ibid., pp. 215–16.
35. Henry James to Dr. Louis Waldstein, 21 Oct. 1898, in *The Turn of the Screw*, ed. Kimbrough, p. 110.

sexual nature of childhood experience in its unconscious aspects, and of the neurotic nature of family experience in its rivalries and tensions and repressive romances. . . . it seems necessary now to reexamine the unconscious powers of the repressed affections in our domestic freeways."[36] Since in James, diegesis is as telling as mimesis, what his emphasis on narrative discourse demonstrates in this tale are precisely the limitations of sophisticated reading, with all its irony, its aesthetic distance, its connoisseurship. In this tale, James presents all the motifs of sentimental fiction—the trust of innocent children, the vulnerability of a sick child, the pathos of a child's death—as an elegy to the sensibility of an earlier age, with its emphasis on the suffering and the powerlessness endemic to childhood. The wish to elegize those earlier sensibilities is yet another motive for making *Jane Eyre* a subtext in his tale. *The Turn of the Screw* is far removed from Lady Bradshaigh's empathetic identification with Clarissa and from Brontë's "Reader, I married him." Rather than stating it, James *demonstrates* the limitations of modernist irony, which makes "the jaded, the disillusioned, the fastidious" reader so expert in aesthetic distance, so blind to the tragedy the tale presents, and thus so unprepared for the trap James sets. Just as the novel is turning from the nineteenth to the twentieth century, *The Turn of the Screw*, written in 1898, memorializes an earlier age's turn away from sentimentality and the modern turn toward irony. The etymology of the word *sentiment* is instructive, for the Latin verb *sentire* means "to discern mentally and to feel physically"; the modern devaluation of sentimentality may be related to the loss of the connotations of mental discernment, judgment, and intellect that the word carried from *Clarissa* on.[37]

One of Richardson's aims in *Clarissa*, one of the aims of all sentimental fiction, was to train readers to feel and to respond to suffering; it is that ability that our "domestic freeways" now repress, and it may well have been this repression that James was counting on to distract the jaded, sophisticated reader. In one passage of unconscious self-revelation, James's governess reflects that when she looks back on the entire experience at Bly, it seems to her to have been

36. Mark Spilka, "On the Enrichment of Poor Monkeys by Myth and Dream; or, How Dickens Rousseauisticized and Pre-Freudianized Victorian Views of Childhood," in *Sexuality and Victorian Literature*, ed. Don Richard Cox, Tennessee Studies in Literature, vol. 27 (Knoxville: Univ. of Tennessee Press, 1984), p. 177.

37. Jean Hagstrum, *Sex and Sensibility: Ideal and Erotic Love from Milton to Mozart* (Chicago: Univ. of Chicago Press, 1980), pp. 6–7.

"pure suffering" (40). These are precisely the sentiments her narrative, by focusing on herself, deflects from the child-victims. If the governess "takes hold" with one kind of passion, the children's suffering reminds us of the etymological meaning of passion as suffering. These ambiguous, duplicitous meanings of *passion* and its treacherous causes and consequences time and again inform James's sense of the tragic in the tales and novels, from *What Maisie Knew* to "The Altar of the Dead" and *The Wings of the Dove*. The betrayal of trust, the denial of love, the displacement of desire, the repudiation of selves that consequently proliferate—these are the psychic traumas that blight childhood and maturity alike; these are the "inutterable woes" the governess inadvertently reveals when she sits down to record her virtue.

Language (that meager and fragile thread . . . by
which the little surface corners and edges of men's
secret and solitary lives may be joined for an instant
now and then before sinking back into the darkness
where the spirit cried for the first time and was not
heard and will cry for the last time and will not be
heard then either).

GRANDFATHER COMPSON

*There is something in the touch of flesh with flesh which
abrogates, cuts sharp and straight across the devious intricate
channels of decorous ordering, which enemies as well as
lovers know because it makes them both—touch and touch of
that which is the citadel of the central I-Am's private own.*

ROSA COLDFIELD

7
Devious Channels of Decorous Ordering: Rosa Coldfield in *Absalom, Absalom!*

Paula. 1889. This photograph by Alfred Stieglitz is from the Alfred Stieglitz Collection, George Eastman House, Rochester, New York.

Alien Discourse

Before language, desire: the spirit, the darkness in which the spirit cries, the need that makes the spirit cry, and the touch that abrogates—all are represented as being prior to language in *Absalom, Absalom!*[1] The novel explores the solipsism of individual consciousness, the magnitude and meagerness of language, the insatiability of desire. Language is a thread, but a touch has the power to cut (like the knives, sabres, and scythes in the novel) through language—to annul the word through the far greater potency of the flesh. Like James's governess in *The Turn of the Screw*, Rosa Coldfield recognizes the aesthetic attractions of language—its intricacy and decorum—but she also sees its devious, evasive, abstract elements, which the governess exploits but never confesses. Rosa recognizes that all the artificial barriers of caste, color, and code that divide humankind are sustained by language; yet she envisions in the touch of flesh with flesh *"the fall of all the eggshell shibboleth of caste and color too."*[2]

Although Rosa does not state it, the context in which she utters these words—when Clytie stops her on the stairs at Sutpen's Hundred—makes it clear that even though the shibboleths may crumble, the touch of Clytie's flesh on her own does not necessarily result in unity, reconciliation, union. Every major character—black and white, lover and beloved, son and father—shares her yearning for that touch. But that desire is thwarted at every turn. Denial, displacement, and repudiation blight the lives in *Absalom, Absalom!* not only of individuals but of entire generations. Faulkner's novel, like *The Turn of the Screw*, is burdened with multiple voices and multiple hauntings, with

1. On the relation of desire to language, see Jacques Lacan, *The Language of the Self*, trans. Anthony Wilden (Baltimore: Johns Hopkins Univ. Press, 1968), and *Ecrits: A Selection*, trans. Alan Sheridan (New York: W. W. Norton, 1977). In Lacanian terms, desire lies in the gap between the demands made in speech and the needs of the body; since those needs are unarticulated, they can be said to precede language, although one never escapes from the web of language. See pages 256, 261n., 272 below.
2. William Faulkner, *Absalom, Absalom!* (New York: Modern Library, 1966), p. 139, hereinafter cited parenthetically in the text by page number.

baffled ghosts and psychic possession. Sutpen is commonly viewed as the most potent figure in the novel, despite—or because of—his death. What hasn't been noticed, however, is that the operative dichotomy that reveals the underlying structure of adversarial antithesis is *dead/alive*, just as day/dream was in *The Turn of the Screw*.[3] Sutpen is more "alive" than Quentin, who is a pale shade, his "very body was an empty hall echoing. . . . he was not a being, an entity, he was a commonwealth" (12). Sutpen, moreover, has been the focus of exhaustive critical analyses of the relation of history to myth in the novel, but the relation of myth to love has been wholly overlooked.[4]

Of all the narratives in the novel then, which one is a discourse of desire? Who exactly is the lover in the text? It is not Quentin, recreating his incestuous desire for his sister in an imaginative reconstruction of the relationship between Henry and Judith Sutpen. It is not Mr. Compson, lingering lovingly on the sensuousness of Charles Bon's octoroon mistress. It is not even Charles himself, writing love letters to Judith while awaiting his destiny. The female lover, who is herself related to myth, for Faulkner compares her to Cassandra, has remained invisible as the lover in the novel because she, like Cassandra, has been dismissed as mad. Rosa Coldfield is the lover in *Absalom, Absalom!*, endlessly reconstructing her desire and deconstructing its object, lamenting her pain and sustaining her passion by weaving her narrative. Her narrative is not epistolary, yet it is an amorous discourse, a long meditation in the absence of the beloved, spoken out loud. The emphasis on her voice is indeed crucial, for she does not merely tell what happened, she shows the effects. Her narrative, indeed, lies at the extremes of showing and telling, so far removed from mere plot that it could simply be called talking, and it is that talking which gives her voice its overwhelming intensity. Her discourse thus

3. Roland Barthes, *S/Z: An Essay*, trans. Richard Miller (New York: Hill and Wang, 1974), p. 18.

4. On the relation of history to myth, see Melvin Backman, "Sutpen and the South: A Study of *Absalom, Absalom!*," *PMLA* 80 (1965), 596–604; Lennart Bjork, "Ancient Myths and the Moral Framework of Faulkner's *Absalom, Absalom!*," *American Literature* 35 (1963), 196–204; Donald M. Kartiganer, "The Role of Myth in *Absalom, Absalom!*," *Modern Fiction Studies* 9 (1963), 357–69; Michael Millgate, "The Firmament of Man's History: Faulkner's Treatment of the Past," *Mississippi Quarterly* 25 (Spring 1972 supplement), 25–35; Lewis P. Simpson, "Faulkner and the Legend of the Artist," in *Faulkner: Fifty Years after "The Marble Faun,"* ed. George H. Wolfe (Tuscaloosa: Univ. of Alabama Press, 1976).

disrupts the dichotomies of diegesis and mimesis, of present and past, for what Quentin hears is not a mere story but its repercussions, not a memory but its living presence as trace.[5]

Diegesis signifies a journey already made. Like all the heroines of amorous discourse, Rosa is a haunted woman whose very talking evokes the trace of Sutpen. Sutpen, like Quint and Jessel, is "un-houseled, unaneled"; while Rosa speaks, "the ghost mused with shadowy docility as if it were the voice which he haunted where a more fortunate one would have had a house" (8). Not only does Faulkner underscore the dialogic dimensions of Rosa's discourse in this passage by stressing Rosa's voice, but her dialogue is a soliloquy as well, imaged as a struggle for discourse staged in discourse. Language itself is a struggle; Rosa tries to put her experience into words, but it defies all attempts at articulation and comprehension. This is why she is as haunted and as haggard as her predecessors (both Jessel and the governess) in James's tale: her "wan haggard face" watches Quentin as she speaks in a "grim haggard amazed voice." The very fact that she is still amazed after forty-three years of attempting to understand what happened to her simultaneously highlights the necessity of the attempt and its futility. Even her senses are confounded as she talks: "hearing-sense [would] self-confound and the long-dead object of her impotent yet indomitable frustration would appear, as though by outraged recapitulation evoked, quiet inattentive and harmless, out of the biding and dreamy and victorious dust" (7–8).[6] (*Impotent/indomitable* rephrases the fundamental structural dichotomy of *dead/alive*.) Furthermore, not only is the dead Sutpen excusably inattentive, but so is the live Quentin. His entire perception of Rosa is shaped by a similar dichotomization of youth and age, which prevents him from ever really "attending" her. In speculating about her voice, for instance, his words echo the tragic ones of his grandfather. Quentin thinks: "Maybe it (the voice, the talking, the incredulous and unbearable amazement) had even been a cry aloud once . . . long ago when she was a girl—of young and indomitable unregret, of indictment of

---

5. Cf. Gérard Genette, *Narrative Discourse: An Essay in Method*, trans. Jane E. Lewin (Ithaca: Cornell Univ. Press, 1980), pp. 167–68.

6. On diegesis and voice, see Genette, chap. 5. On diegesis as a repetitive journey, see J. Hillis Miller, "Ariachne's Broken Woof," *Georgia Review* 31 (1977), 44–60, and "The Figure in the Carpet," *Poetics Today* 1:3 (1980), 107–18. Homer Barron's corpse in "A Rose for Emily" lies, too, in an "even coating of the patient and biding dust." On the relation of the two texts, see note 22 below.

blind circumstance and savage event" (14). His attempt at empathetic identification fails, because he cannot recognize that Rosa's talking is a discourse of desire, the cry of a spirit who deserves to be heard. He never succeeds in joining the "surface edge" of his life to hers through language. Nor is he capable of imagining that a young girl's spirit may lie immured in "old flesh," as the repetition of the word *old* reveals when he rejects the possibility that she is crying out now too: "Not now: now only the lonely thwarted old female flesh embattled for forty-three years in the old insult, the old unforgiving outraged and betrayed by the final and complete affront which was Sutpen's death" (14). In my view, Rosa's narrative is a last cry from one who remembers not only her youth, her hopes, and her capacity for love but her sexual desire; who is, moreover, capable of imagining a world of possibility beyond the one that has negated her, as Quentin negates her here.

Most critics, however, find Rosa not a passionate but a pathetic creature. Given the sophistication of the analyses of narrative in the novel, it is remarkable how many critics accept Quentin's evaluation of Rosa without recognizing how much more his negation reveals about himself than about her. Critics who discuss Rosa at all choose to emphasize her grotesqueness, her Gothicism, her bitterness. Why her desire and the rhetoric of amorous discourse has been overlooked is a matter for speculation. The oversight is related, I think, to what Barthes calls the philosophical solitude of the lover, which arises because no modern system of thought accounts for love. Instead, "Christian discourse . . . exhorts [the lover] to repress and to sublimate. Psychoanalytical discourse . . . commits him to give up his [beloved] as lost. As for Marxist discourse, it has nothing to say. If it should occur to me to knock at these doors in order to gain recognition *somewhere* . . . for my 'madness' (my 'truth'), these doors close one after the other; and when they are all shut, there rises around me a wall of language which oppresses and repulses me."[7] The female lover faces even greater oppression and repulsion, for as we have seen, she has been reduced to a few well-worn clichés: the mannish intellectual (Heloise); the seduced virgin (the Portuguese nun); the frigid martyr (Clarissa); the gullible plain Jane (Jane Eyre); the frustrated spinster (the governess in James's tale). The female lover is

---

7. Roland Barthes, *A Lover's Discourse: Fragments*, trans. Richard Howard (New York: Hill and Wang, 1978), p. 211.

frequently regarded merely as a madwoman, frigid and furious. No system of discourse seriously considers her suffering, her passion, or the range and resourcefulness of her imaginative powers. Scholarly descriptions of Rosa reveal how quick modern critics have been to dismiss lovers as repressed, disturbed, or mad. Cleanth Brooks describes Rosa's language as a "dithyramb of hate . . . [a] shrill, tense voice . . . [of] Norn-like frenzy."[8] As in *The Turn of the Screw,* the clear implication is that female "tension" is sexual, as Albert Guerard reveals: "Her ornate, often sexualized rhetoric and rhythms of almost insane intensity . . . admirably convey a particular disturbed personality. . . . [Her] ranting [is] controlled by exquisitely timed . . . sentences . . . [in a] hysterical narrative . . . of wild rhetoric."[9] Guerard is representative of all those critics whose "systems"—psychoanalytic or otherwise—have failed to recognize Rosa. He is particularly provocative because he senses that there is a language in *Absalom, Absalom!* that he can neither define nor assimilate. He notes that "all the narrators share Faulkner's ironic love of hyperbole and paradox, of absurd oxymoron and analogy drawn from an alien area of discourse."[10] Here again, as in *The Turn of the Screw,* perhaps the limitations of modernist irony obscure one of the fundamental strains of discourse in Faulkner's masterpiece. My aim, by showing the close connection of Rosa's narrative to the genre of amorous epistolary discourse, is to make it a little less alien.

Of all the narratives in the novel, Rosa's has the most personal immediacy. She—not Quentin—is the character who is most passionately engaged in her discourse, yet she is dismissed as readily as James's governess as a "frustrated spinster," as if the words were redundant. This distorted perception of her is wholly shaped by Mr. Compson, Quentin, and Shreve, none of whom ever really see Rosa as anything but a warped, bitter, outraged, pathetic old woman.[11] She is like the enigmatic letter announcing her death, which Quentin cannot decipher.

Here again, the dichotomy *dead/alive* is central, for it is one thing

8. Cleanth Brooks, "The Poetry of Miss Rosa Canfield [*sic*]," *Shenandoah* 21 (Spring 1970), 199–206.

9. Albert Guerard, *The Triumph of the Novel: Dickens, Dostoevsky, Faulkner* (New York: Oxford Univ. Press, 1976), pp. 323, 329.

10. Ibid., p. 321.

11. See J. Gary Williams, "Quentin Finally Sees Miss Rosa," *Criticism* 21 (Fall 1979), 331–46. Williams maintains, "Quentin really has not heard, in any profound sense, anything Rosa has said in Chapter 5" (335).

to indulge in imaginative reconstructions of the long-dead Sutpen, Bon, and Judith, but Rosa is not remote. She has personal, immediate relations with the characters who negate her. The Sutpens may be ghosts, but she is not, although both Compsons try to make her one. When Quentin asks his father why he must obey Rosa's summons, he replies, "Years ago we in the South made our women into ladies. Then the War came and made the ladies into ghosts. So what else can we do, being gentlemen, but listen to them being ghosts?" (12). They try to distance themselves from her by thus reducing her complexity—to gain the kind of aesthetic distance that is ordered and arranged into art. But how, one wonders, can they hope to understand the long-dead Sutpens if they cannot even comprehend the woman who is their contemporary, as Shreve implies when he confronts Quentin at the end with the challenge: "You dont even know about the old dame, the Aunt Rosa. . . . You dont even know about her." Rosa resists reduction, however, as Shreve senses when he perceives that "she refused at the last to be a ghost" (362).

Her narrative, then, is no mere diatribe by a mad woman. She refuses to conform to the town's view of "an old lady that died young of outrage." Rosa remarks that touch makes enemies as well as lovers, and she herself is both: the object of her love is Charles Bon; the object of both her desire *and* her enmity is Thomas Sutpen. Her narrative thus reflects the characteristic Ovidian doubleness and dissimulation. Her motives for summoning Quentin are as duplicitous as the duality of her focus on Sutpen and Bon. She wants to set the record straight, but she also has some purpose that she withholds. As in previous discourses, Rosa is torn by a thousand conflicting emotions; she oscillates from love to hate, forgiveness to revenge, pathos to despair. She sounds like the preacher without a pulpit, the judge without power to punish, the prophet without a following, reminding us that the discourse of pathos is always a surrogate for an earlier genre—that of amorous epistolary discourse. Her very name records the doubleness in her rhetoric, her desire, her character; she combines the passion of courtly love (*Le Roman de la rose*) with cold fascination and fury. Although she invests Charles Bon with all the qualities of courtly romance, Sutpen is the focus of her fury. Bon is the absence to which Rosa gives shape, as she herself explains:

> There must have been some seed he left, to cause a child's vacant fairy-tale to come alive. . . . even before I saw the photograph I could have recognized, nay, described, the very face. But I never saw it. I do not even know of my own knowledge that Ellen ever saw it, that Judith ever loved it, that Henry slew it: so

who will dispute me when I say, Why did I not invent, create it?—And I know this: if I were God I would invent out of this seething turmoil we call progress something . . . which would adorn the barren mirror altars of every plain girl who breathes with such as this . . . this pictured face. It would not even need a skull behind it; almost anonymous, it would only need vague inference of some walking flesh and blood desired by someone else even if only in some shadow-realm of make-believe. (146–47)

The passage is a remarkable revelation of desire: Bon is the idol who adorns Rosa's mirror altar; he is the sacrifice on the altar of Sutpen's design. Rosa worships someone she never saw, yet she is one of three surviving witnesses to his having lived at all. (The others are Clytie and Henry.) What she worships is an image, framed and frozen in a photograph, as removed from the actual being as language is. That photograph, moreover, is an altar that transforms Rosa from plain girl into devotee. Thus, in contrast to such lover-tyrants as Lovelace and Rochester, Rosa is not narcissistic. She worships not her own "barren" reflection but a photo, which gives her an image—what Barthes would call an "Image-repertoire." Like a face in a mirror, furthermore, language is a mirror not of presence but of the image of presence.[12] The repeated emphasis on vacancy, vagueness, and make-believe reveals that Bon is not only absent in retrospect, that for Rosa he was always absent. She is, actually, acutely aware of the fictiveness of her desire and of her own highly self-conscious literary powers, for what she worships is not Bon but the idea of Bon and his very absence: his footprint obliterated by the rake, the fading sound of his breathing, *"his foot, his passing shape, his face, his speaking voice, his name: Charles Bon, Charles Good, Charles Husband-soon-to-be"* (148). The Keatsian and Shakespearean images with which she endlessly recreates her passion illuminate her attachment to the idol she has built for herself, the receptacle of all her hopes and illusions. If, as we saw in the previous chapter, the ambiguous beauty of the governess' passion is that she only saw her employer twice, the "beauty" of Rosa's is that she never sees Charles Bon at all. Thus when John Irwin argues that Rosa can never become Bon's lover because Judith never becomes Bon's wife, his approach to Rosa's remarkable imaginative powers is far too literal.[13] My point is just the opposite: Rosa sees herself as a

12. Sharon Cameron, *Lyric Time: Dickinson and the Limits of Genre* (Baltimore: Johns Hopkins Univ. Press, 1979), pp. 198.
13. John T. Irwin, *Doubling and Incest/Repetition and Revenge* (Baltimore: Johns Hopkins Univ. Press, 1975), pp. 74–75.

more perfect lover precisely because her emotions are centered on the idol she invents. Just as unheard melodies are sweeter in Keats's "Ode on a Grecian Urn," Rosa's desire is perfect because it is conceived, nurtured, and sustained solely in the imagination. The same code of perfection that makes the governess' desire ambiguous in *The Turn of the Screw* is endorsed by Rosa in relation to Charles Bon.

Unlike James's governess, however, Rosa does not insist on coercing her narrative into one fixed meaning for all time. One sign that she lacks her predecessor's fixity of intention is that she does not even bother to write down her narrative, although she is a skilled and prolific writer of thousands of odes and eulogies. As in James's tale, the question of what the narrative is worth arises; here, as there, it is an object of exchange, of barter. Rosa speculates that Quentin may one day write down her story to buy a gown or a chair for his wife, since the only kind of production left for southerners after the war is literary production about their loss, their despair, their failure (9–10). Quentin's skepticism, however, does not accurately reflect Rosa's real attitude about her story, although the same paradoxical explanation is repeated again and again: "It cant matter . . . and yet it must matter" (127).

Indeed, just as the governess mythologizes the children in *The Turn of the Screw,* Rosa retrospectively mythologizes Sutpen, transforming him from a damn fool into a demon. In both James's text and Faulkner's, the mythologizing tendency belongs in the "province of the antithesis" between angel and demon.[14] We saw in the last chapter how in mythologizing the children, the governess' organizing dichotomy was good/evil; Rosa falls into precisely the same pattern, retrospectively regarding Charles Bon as "Charles Good" and Thomas Sutpen as the devil incarnate. But the distinction between Rosa the *focus* and Rosa the *voice* is crucial here, for at the time the events that she narrates occurred, her views of Sutpen went through three distinct stages: she is raised to regard him as an ogre; when he comes home from the war her attitude softens; and it is not until he repudiates her that she reverts—with some justice—to her initial opinion of his bedevilment.

Thus if Bon is at first the receptacle of Rosa's illusions, Sutpen is the one who shatters them. She never invests Sutpen with the kind of perfection that she attributed to Bon; neither is her hatred uniformly

14. Barthes, *S/Z*, p. 17.

consistent throughout her narrative. Most critics overlook the fact that Sutpen becomes the focus of Rosa's desire because she saw in him the possibility of salvaging something of *"the old lost enchantment of the heart."* He is, in short, as much the epitome of lack as Bon is, astounding as it seems. Sutpen is the very figure of absence, despite the fact that Rosa cannot even say how often she sees Sutpen "for the reason that," according to Mr. Compson, "waking or sleeping, the aunt had taught her to see nothing else" (62).

Like all the other characters in the novel, Sutpen never does "see" Rosa herself. Her experience with him, indeed, consists of repeated nullification. Even after he "proposes," Rosa realizes that *"My presence was to him only the absence of black morass and snarled vine"* (166). Yet once their marriage is planned, she allows herself to hope anew, to believe that he *"was not oblivious of me but only unconscious and receptive"* (167). Unfortunately, as in *Jane Eyre* and *The Turn of the Screw*, a critical moment of rupture comes because the beloved is a destroyer of love. Sutpen suggests that he and Rosa breed first and marry later, if she bears a son who survives. As in the earlier texts, the scene is stricken with death precisely because the heroine realizes that the beloved is incapable of recognizing her humanity:

> [I] *did believe there was that magic in unkin blood which we call by the pallid name of love that would be, might be sun for him. . . . And then one after-noon . . . the death of hope and love, the death of pride and principle, and then the death of everything save the old outraged and aghast unbelieving . . . oh I told you he had not thought of it until that moment, that prolonged moment which contained the distance between the house and wherever it was he had been standing when he thought of it: and this too coincident: it was the very day on which he knew definitely and at last exactly how much of his hundred square miles he would be able to save and keep and call his own on the day when he would have to die. . . . he stood with the reins over his arm (and no hand on my head now) and spoke the bald outrageous words exactly as if he were consulting with Jones or with some other man about a bitch dog or a cow or mare.* (168)

Significantly, Rosa specifically draws attention to the absence of Sutpen's touch here; this is no more "coincident" than that the death of love coincides with the decimation of Sutpen's Hundred and with Sutpen's own death day. No coincidence, it is the *consequence*, fore-shadowed by the allusion to the mare, for it is Sutpen's comparison of Milly to a mare which leads Wash to murder him, Milly, and the newborn. Sutpen is thus a symbol not just of a megalomaniacal male principle, but of the other, inaccessible and unknowable; it is partly because he is unknowable that all the characters in the novel are obsessed with him. For Rosa, too, he is the magical other who holds the keys to the edifice but denies her access.

Rosa the *focus* compares both Bon and Sutpen to fairy-tale figures: Bon "makes a vacant fairy-tale come alive," whereas the child Rosa saw Sutpen as "an ogre, a djinn, a Bluebeard." (The latter, one remembers, hangs his wives in the turret chamber.) Brontë's Rochester, significantly, is also compared to Bluebeard because of his cruel treatment of Bertha Mason. Not only do Bluebeard, Rochester, and Sutpen all stand convicted of inhospitable treatment of their wives, but in Sutpen the enigmatic character of a Rochester is combined with scores of depraved—albeit mysterious—activities, including wrestling with Negroes in the barn. The cumulative mystery of his depravities brings to mind the range of unspecified evils that Henry James leaves to the reader's imagination in *The Turn of the Screw*. Thus, if the heroines who write discourses of desire are Rosa's predecessors, Sutpen's are the lover-tyrants. Rosa, indeed, recognizes her place in the repetitive structure of seduction, betrayal, and abandonment. Like Ovid's heroines, Heloise, Mariane, Clarissa, Jane Eyre, and James's governess, Rosa, too, discovers that she is neither the first to be seduced nor the last to be betrayed. Where she draws on Keats, Shakespeare, and romance in her re-creation of Bon, for Sutpen her sources are the Old Testament, Milton, and the Brothers Grimm. In one poetic passage, full of Miltonic cadences, she notes the replication of her rivals while describing Wash Jones as

> that brute progenitor of brutes whose granddaughter was to supplant me, if not in my sister's house at least in my sister's bed to which (so they will tell you) I aspired—that brute who (brute instrument of that justice which presides over human events which, incept in the individual, runs smooth, less claw than velvet: but which, by man or woman flouted, drives on like fiery steel and overrides both weakly just and unjust strong, both vanquisher and innocent victimized, ruthless for appointed right and truth) brute who was . . . to preside upon the various shapes and avatars of Thomas Sutpen's devil's fate. (134)

In the elevation and intensity of her rhetoric, Rosa is unquestionably theatrical here, and such self-conscious theatricality is a distinguishing feature of amorous discourse; the heroine creates roles, plots, dramas, and fictions to occupy herself in the beloved's absence. Rosa, moreover, is acutely aware of her theatricality where both Bon and Sutpen are concerned. Her motive for her frequent forays into

Judith's room to look at Bon's picture is *"not to dream . . . but to renew, rehearse, the part as the faulty though eager amateur might steal wingward in some interim of the visible scene to hear the prompter's momentary voice"* (147). This passage illuminates the difference between her desire for Bon and for Sutpen: with Bon she nurtured the illusion of perfection, but her desire was completely imaginative; with Sutpen she was willing to forgo perfection, to accept the vagaries of fortune and the change that the war wrought in him and, instead of remaining a spectator, to take the risk of becoming a principal player in the drama.

Instead, Rosa is devastated to discover that Sutpen's view of her is purely utilitarian. He must have a male heir, and to insure that he gets one, he proposes to beget the heir before signing the contract of marriage. Outrageous as the proposition is, Rosa reacts so vehemently because it reenforces the fundamental trauma of nullification that marks every stage of her existence. Her entire childhood is described in terms of lack. She has only her aunt for mother and father; her sister, she is taught, "vanished, not only out of the family and the house but out of life too" (60); her childhood is marked by the absence of play and is passed in "that aged and ancient and timeless *absence of youth* which consisted of a Cassandralike listening beyond closed doors, of lurking in dim halls" (60, my italics). Sutpen's obliteration of her thus has far more cumulative force than it might otherwise have. Since nullification has been the pattern of her life, she dedicates herself to hating him to break the pattern, combating nullification by mythologizing Sutpen and herself. Ignored by her father, excluded from her cousins' company, ridiculed by her sister when she offers to help Judith, she describes herself as a *"small plain frightened creature whom neither man nor woman had ever looked at twice"* (141). Rosa's narrative, like so many amorous discourses, thus arises from extreme silence and solitude, as she explains: *"Instead of accomplishing the processional and measured milestones of the childhood's time I lurked, unapprehended as though, shod with the very damp and velvet silence of the womb, I displaced no air, gave off no betraying sound, from one closed forbidden door to the next"* (145). That closed forbidden door is a multifaceted metaphor for the deprivation Rosa suffers—of light, of touch, of love, of the entire range of experiences in human development. Indeed, an astonishing number of forbidden doors, gates, and corridors appear in the novel: Goodhue Coldfield nails the attic door shut; Henry stops Bon at the gate; Clytie stops Rosa on the stair; Sutpen

forbids Wash entrance; there is a door in Quentin's consciousness
through which he cannot pass. All these images contribute to the
sense of the novel as a labyrinth and to the narrative line as a thread.
Many of the images replicate Sutpen's humiliation at the door of
Pettibone's mansion, which in turn is a reenactment of the psychic
shock Pip in *Great Expectations* suffers at the door of Satis House.
(Satis: desire increases in direct proportion to humiliation and rejection, as in Rosa's narrative.) The connection of humiliation to narration and naming can be seen by comparing the reactions of young Pip
and young Thomas Sutpen. Just as Thomas "couldn't get it straight
yet. . . . he was seeking among what little he had to call experience for
something to measure it by, and he couldn't find anything" (233), Pip
describes himself as being "so humiliated, hurt, spurned, offended,
angry, sorry—I cannot hit upon the right name for the smart—God
knows what its name was. . . . As I cried I kicked the wall . . . so bitter
were my feelings, and so sharp was *the smart without a name*, that
needed counteraction."[15] Rosa Coldfield's own efforts to find the
words to express her pain are similarly related to humiliation and to
the frustration of her desire. From abandonment, then, comes the
birth of language; loss is the structure. Loss, indeed, is what structures
the lives of all the characters in the novel: Sutpen's loss of innocence
at Pettibone's door, Eulalia's loss of Sutpen, Charles Bon's search for
the lost father, Judith's unmarried widowhood. And looming over all
these losses is the loss of the Civil War. Language is a means of
exorcism or of enchantment, a ceaseless lament against the underlying structure of loss, lack, absence.

Like previous writing heroines, Rosa is attempting to reorder experience and make it comprehensible, to reconstruct her desire while
exorcising its object, Sutpen. Her narrative is an effort to comprehend
and, simultaneously, an acknowledgment of the futility of that effort.
One source of her frustration, indeed, is that no telling can express the
meaning of her tale; it has to be traced and retraced, as Theseus

15. Charles Dickens, *Great Expectations* (Baltimore: Penguin Books, 1965), p. 92 (bk.
1, chap. 8), my italics. One thinks as well of Clarissa locked in her room, and of the
closed, forbidden doors in Brontë's novel: Jane Eyre is locked behind a massive door to
the red room, and Bertha Mason is locked behind another door in the attic. Like the
governesses in both *Jane Eyre* and *The Turn of the Screw*, Rosa is a threshold figure,
poised between past and present, between the world before and after the Civil War,
between the world of Sutpen and that of Quentin Compson. She is, however, not so
much poised as cramped: she summons Quentin in a letter "out of another world
almost," written on an "archaic" sheet of notepaper in a "cramped script" (10).

retraces Ariadne's thread in the labyrinth. This, too, is one of the distinguishing characteristics of amorous discourse: "to deplore that words should betray an 'ineffable' emotion which nevertheless demands to be avowed."[16] Amorous discourses are always critiques of language, for the alphabet of the body has to be replaced with what is considered an inadequate system of signs: words. Rosa reveals her awareness both of the inadequacy of language and of her compulsion to repeat when she tells Quentin: *"I will tell you what he did and let you be the judge. (Or try to tell you, because there are some things for which three words are three too many, and three thousand words that many words too less, and this is one of them. It can be told; I could take that many sentences, repeat the bold blank naked and outrageous words just as he spoke them, and . . . leave you only that Why? Why? and Why? that I have asked and listened to for almost fifty years)"* (166–67). Rosa's amorous discourse is thus a self-address as well as an address to the other. As a critique of language, it is a lament at the enormity of the pain and the paucity of the words to describe it. As one critic, writing of Emily Dickinson, puts it, "Pain is the space where words would be, the hole torn out of language."[17] One thinks not only of Rosa's reference to the blank, naked words but of Clarissa's earlier lamentation that, if she had received a kind word from her family before she died, she would have "filled in the blanks" that pain made when she was very weak and very ill. Hatred is a way of filling in the blanks in Sutpen's enigmatic character, but hatred is not Rosa's only response to Sutpen. Quentin is wrong when he reflects: *"Maybe you have to know anybody awful well to love them but when you have hated somebody for forty-three years you will know them awful well so maybe it's better then, maybe it's fine then because after forty-three years they cant any longer surprise you or make you either very contented or very mad"* (14). Quentin exaggerates by formulating solutions to the unsolvable mystery of personality in terms of either/or dichotomies. The fact is that Rosa expresses as much love, pity, and regret for Sutpen as she does hatred, as the opening strophe and antistrophe make clear: Sutpen *"died. Without regret, Miss Rosa Coldfield says—(Save by her) Yes, save by her"* (9). Save

---

16. Denis de Rougemont discusses the ineffable in *Love in the Western World*, trans. Montgomery Belgion (London: Faber and Faber, 1940), p. 159–60. While tracing the "origins" of the ineffable as a motif, de Rougemont overlooks the considerable cunning, duplicity, and evasiveness that may be at play in any lover's exhortation of the ineffable, as is certainly the case in *The Sorrows of Young Werther* and in *The Turn of the Screw*.

17. Cameron, p. 158.

signifies not only "except" but "salvation." In Shakespeare's Sonnet 12, there is no way to triumph over time, "Save breed, to brave him when he takes thee hence." In *Absalom, Absalom!* the idea that breeding is the braving of time is particularly ironic, since it is Sutpen's view of women as mere breeders which leads Wash, like the Grim Reaper and Father Time, to behead him with the scythe.

Sutpen's proposition to Rosa is most devastating, finally, because he makes no effort to reciprocate. What is outrageous, ultimately, is the utter disparity between how Rosa thought Sutpen saw her—as a source of sunlight and hope—and his actual attitude toward women as brood mares.

His mare's name, incidentally, is Penelope; in the short story, "Wash," the mare is Griselda—ironic allusions to the patient figure of the woman who waits. Now Rosa is not the only one who waits in the novel. All the women whose men go to war are waiting. Judith, moreover, is poignantly contrasted to other women, for she waits not only "not knowing for what, but . . . not even knowing for why" (126) after Henry repudiates his birthright and departs with Charles. But it is Rosa—intractable and unforgetting—who remains to interpret events in the end. It is Rosa who summons Quentin. It is Rosa who conjures up the past and is the catalyst for the entire plot. She embodies the classical figure of absence—its textuality. She is the writing heroine whose predecessors are Penelope, Phaedra, Medea, Ariadne. Indeed, that familiar contrast from Ovid onward between the men at war for their country and the women warring with their passion is reinforced here by Rosa's single-minded obsession with her passion, by her imaginative powers, and by the private theater of her emotions. Rosa's iterative narrative is a vocation. What makes it so memorable is the passionate intensity of her internal battle as she weaves fictions while waiting for the end of war and Sutpen's return, and embroiders them in the long aftermath of solitude and despair.

Her narrative is a defiant effort to break the pattern of nullification that has plagued her entire existence. But no matter what she says, she knows that she will always be called a *"warped bitter orphaned country stick,"* who *"caught a man but couldn't keep him"* (168). No matter how she embroiders and elaborates, she remains trapped in the flesh, in the social system she inherits, in the perceptions of those around her. Barthes's amorous discourse contains a similar lament: "All the solutions I imagine are internal to the amorous system. . . . I order myself to be still in love and to be no longer in love. This kind of identity of the problem and its solution precisely defines the *trap*: I am trapped because it lies outside my reach to change systems: I am 'done for' twice over: inside my own system and because I cannot substitute another system for it. This double noose apparently defines a certain type of madness."[18] Significantly, it is the body that is both trap and release. The needs of the body are made into demands articulated in speech; desire signifies the gap between body and speech, need and demand.[19] For Rosa, the flesh itself is the reminder of what once might have been, of all the potential for fulfillment that is thwarted. Like Clarissa's, her discourse of desire takes the form of an elegy, a testament to all the processes of nature that are stillborn. This stillbirth is what Rosa laments when she describes the trap and the systems that imprison her: *"There are some things which happen to us which the intelligence and the senses refuse just as the stomach sometimes refuses what the palate has accepted but which digestion cannot compass— occurrences which stop us dead as though by some impalpable intervention, like a sheet of glass through which we watch all subsequent events transpire as though in a soundless vacuum, and fade, vanish; are gone, leaving us immo- bile, impotent, helpless; fixed, until we can die. That was I"* (151–52). Like those of other heroines, Rosa's meditations rely on imagery drawn from the realm of the senses and the body's functions. The lines above are a remarkably acute epiphany about the limits of human comprehension, a vivid contrast between the stasis of Rosa's develop- ment and the endlessness of grief, between the intractability of lan- guage and the flux of despair. Amorous discourses have no exits; the only way out, as Clarissa demonstrates, is death. In Faulkner's novel, Sutpen escapes his obsession with his grand design by dying; Rosa remains trapped in hers. She rages because she cannot disentangle herself from the threads of memory, frustration, and desire, whereas Sutpen has "kicked himself loose of the earth," like Conrad's Kurtz. This is ultimately what Rosa can never forgive: for Sutpen the rest is silence; for Rosa there is no rest, only recollection, reflection, repetition.

There is thus great poignancy in Mr. Compson's letter to Quentin describing Rosa's death, for he hopes that Rosa gains a bourne where there are actual people to be recipients of her outrage *and* her com- miseration, her hatred *and* her pity (377). These words signal once

18. Barthes, *A Lover's Discourse*, p. 143.
19. The formulation is Jacques Lacan's, in "The Insistence of the Letter in the Unconscious," *Yale French Studies* 36/37 (1966), 112–47.

again the doubleness of all lovers' discourses and reveal that reciprocity is the key. Traditionally, as we have seen, the abandoned lover
prefers anything, even active hatred, to indifference. Hatred, after
all, at least involves engagement. I think this sense of *engagement* is
what Faulkner means when Shreve describes Rosa as "irrevocably
husbanded . . . with the abstract carcass of outrage and revenge" (180,
my italics). What moves lovers to rage is the utter lack of involvement
or recognition, and this aloofness has far-reaching ramifications in
Absalom, Absalom! not only in Sutpen's relations with women but in his
refusal to recognize Charles Bon as well. Reciprocity is the vital ingre-
dient missing in Sutpen's recipe for morality, in his grand design, and
in all his relations.

Another Lost Father, Another Search

Sutpen denies to each character what each most desires: the touch
of flesh with flesh—the only means by which the shibboleths of caste
and color are ever even momentarily breached. Like Rosa, Charles
Bon yearns for Sutpen's touch beyond all else; he is willing to forsake
Henry, Judith, the octoroon, and his son to satisfy this desire:

> There would be that flash, that instant of indisputable recognition be-
> tween them and he would know for sure and forever—thinking maybe
> *That's all I want. He need not even acknowledge me; I will let him understand
> just as quickly that he need not do that, that I do not expect that. . . .* Because he
> knew exactly what he wanted; it was just the saying of it—the physical
> touch even though in secret, hidden—the living touch of that flesh
> warmed before he was born by the same blood which it had bequeathed
> him to warm his own flesh with, to be bequeathed by him in turn to run
> hot and loud in veins and limbs after that first flesh and then his own
> were dead. (319)

The passage reiterates the desire that "the little surface corners and
edges of men's secret and solitary lives may be joined for an instant . . . before sinking back into the darkness" (251). What is devastating here is that, even if Sutpen had ever known how little Bon
wanted, it is doubtful that he would have given it. One of the many
tragedies for Sutpen's descendants is that they ask so little but receive
still less. Denied his father's touch, Charles Bon chooses to destroy
himself. Since the father who could have touched him "declined to do

it, nothing mattered to him now, revenge or love or all, since he knew
now that revenge could not compensate him nor love assuage" (343).
Compare these lines from Swinburne's *Anactoria*:

> Alas, that neither moon nor snow nor dew
> Nor all cold things can purge me wholly through,
> Assuage me nor allay me nor appease,
> Till supreme sleep shall bring me bloodless ease.

As Geoffrey Carter points out, *bloodless* here is a pun in which *blood*
has, besides its obvious sense, the Shakespearean-Jacobean connotation of "hot blood" (passion) that cannot be allayed or cooled. This
observation multiplies Faulkner's allusiveness, since Charles Bon
meditates on the warm blood Sutpen bequeathed him. As is well
known, Faulkner was a great admirer of Swinburne and imitated him
in his own poetry. Faulkner's Swinburnian allusions reinforce the
dialogic intertextuality in lovers' discourses, moreover, for it is Sappho who addresses these lines to Anactoria in a lament of unrequited
love. Carter goes on to observe that "the violence and suddenness of
Sappho's shifts in mood remind us of Pope's 'Eloisa to Abelard,' for
Swinburne too is dealing with the ultimate anguish and despair of a
lover."[20]

As happened when the governess rejected Miss Jessel, the self
denied merely proliferates in *Absalom, Absalom!* The pattern of self-
destruction set off by Sutpen's repudiation is reenacted generation
after generation. Bon's suicidal passivity; Charles Etienne de St. Vel-
ery Bon's masochistic quest for physical contact through beatings he
provokes; Jim Bond's bellows—all are motivated by the same psychic
trauma of denial of any and all human bonds that should unite this
family—indeed, the human family. We need because we are in the
body; we demand in speech. While the Sutpen mansion burns, Bond
is a mere *thing* howling: "Somewhere something lurked which bel-
lowed, something human since the bellowing was in human speech,
even though the reason for it would not have seemed to be" (375).
The reason "would not have seemed to be" because to trace the direct
relation of Bond's desire back to Sutpen seems to be beyond the
capacity of reason. The heart has questions that the mind can't an-

20. Geoffrey Carter, "Sexuality and the Victorian Artist: Dickens and Swinburne,"
in *Sexuality and Victorian Literature*, ed. Don Richard Cox, Tennessee Studies in Literature, vol. 27 (Knoxville: Univ. of Tennessee Press, 1984), p. 153.

swer; the spirit cries unheard at the beginning and at the end; desire precedes language.

The relation is nonetheless directly traceable to Sutpen's own thwarted desire to speak and to be heard. Central to *Absalom, Absalom!* as to *The Turn of the Screw,* is silence, "the long silence of notpeople, in notlanguage" in which the ordeal of consciousness unfolds. As in *The Turn of the Screw,* the source of the entire tragedy lies in the unsaid—specifically in an undelivered message, for Sutpen's grand design stems from his humiliation at Pettibone's door. He undertakes the mission to deliver the message in "good faith" and finds himself brutally confronted with the distinctions of caste and code, forcibly made to understand that as "white trash," he can be silenced, sent around back by the Negro butler. As Thoreau observed, no one can combat injustice as effectively as someone who has experienced a little of it in his own person. (One thinks of Rochester's redemption, which is achieved when he comes to comprehend powerlessness by experiencing it. He discovers what it feels like to be silenced, as he silenced Bertha Mason.) But Sutpen proceeds to dedicate his life not to combating such injustice but to perpetuating it. Here, the consequence of being "shut up" is Sutpen's entire design. Sutpen, however, utterly dissociates himself from the powerless little boy who stood in front of the mansion. Instead, he resolves to become powerful enough to be one of the oppressors rather than the oppressed. At his hands, Eulalia and Charles Bon suffer the same inexplicable and unspoken rejection he experienced. He repudiates their desire for "the physical touch . . . the living touch." The hot, loud blood, like the spirit crying unheard, is doomed to be denied, cooled, silenced, sepulchered. Words—tranquil and taunting, illuminating and inscrutable, impotent and ineradicable—are the only legacy passed on.

The yearning for the touch of love is what led Faulkner to reflect (speaking of Emily Grierson) that if a natural instinct is repressed, it comes up somewhere else in a tragic form.[21] The form it takes in *Absalom, Absalom!,* as in "A Rose for Emily" and *The Turn of the Screw,* is murder. Furthermore, Faulkner gives his ghost story two turns by doubling the figure of female fury; two women are betrayed by the same man. Sutpen brutally betrays first Eulalia, the mother of his son,

---

21. *Faulkner in the University: Class Conferences at the University of Virginia, 1957–1958,* ed. Frederick L. Gwynn and Joseph L. Blotner (New York: Vintage, 1965), p. 185.

then Rosa, the barren spinster doomed to be the chronicler of the age, the critic of language and society. As we have seen, one of the ways in which amorous discourse is dialogic is in its positing of another logic that defies society's view. Rosa therefore counterpoints her own discourse with the refrain from another discourse: the collective voice of the town. She punctuates the story she is telling by revealing her awareness of the story the town tells about her: "*Oh yes, I know*" (of their gossip); "*they will have told you doubtless already how*" (this or that happened); "*doubtless you already know*" (what the gossips have said) (134, 168). The town's voice has reduced Rosa to a bit of doggerel: "*Rosie Coldfield, lose him, weep him; caught a man but couldn't keep him*" (168). Indeed, part of the intensity and tension of Rosa's narrative is the result of the disparity between what she felt and what the gossips report. Their reports, actually, attain the status of truth by sheer volume and ceaseless repetition. The same thing happens to Emily Grierson; the irony of Faulkner's "A Rose for Emily" lies in the disparity between the townspeople's voyeurism, their smug certainty, and the grisly remains of Homer with which Emily surprises them in the end. In view of the ways in which amorous discourse is a reply to and an absorption of other texts, one might say that just as Jane Eyre speaks for Bertha Mason, Rosa Coldfield speaks for Emily Grierson. Just as Rosa's narrative becomes interwoven with others within the novel, the novel itself is interwoven with subsequent tales; Rosa subsequently speaks the silence of the mute woman in "A Rose for Emily"; indeed the very title—particularly the word *rose*—points to the relation between the two women and their desire. Faulkner's characteristic counterpointing of themes and characters in a continuing chronicle also characterizes the dialogic dynamism of amorous discourse from the *Heroides* onward.[22]

22. Faulkner wrote "A Rose for Emily" in 1929, the same year that *The Sound and the Fury* appeared; *Absalom, Absalom!* was published in 1936. The Faulknerian embroidering of one tale in another also illustrates that no repetition is exactly the same and no telling is univocal, unequivocal, or determinate. Some scholars insist that *The Sound and the Fury* should be viewed autonomously from *Absalom, Absalom!* (Guerard, p. 311, for example). Although Faulkner is not always reliable, his view is at least worth noting: "Quentin Compson, of the Sound & Fury, tells it, or ties it together; he is the protagonist so that it is not complete apocrypha. I use him because it is just before he is to commit suicide because of his sister, and I use his bitterness which he has projected on the South in the form of hatred of it and its people to get more out of the story itself than a historical novel would be." *Selected Letters of William Faulkner*, ed. Joseph Blotner (New York: Random House, 1977), p. 79. John T. Irwin, *Doubling and Incest/Repetition and Revenge*, and Cleanth Brooks, "The Narrative Structure of *Absalom, Absalom*," *Georgia Review* 29:2 (Summer 1975), 366–94, are among the critics who stress the interrelation of the two novels.

Of all the narrators in the novel, it is Rosa who is most aware of the desire for the human touch and of its implications, for she comments on it repeatedly. When Sutpen returns from the war, she tells us that he touches Judith, speaking *"four sentences of simple direct words behind beneath above which I felt that same rapport of communal blood which I sensed that day while Clytie held me from the stairs"* (159). In this scene, she is once again the outsider, excluded from the magic circle of the beloved and from the rapport for which she yearns. Later, she seems briefly included in that circle when Sutpen declares their engagement. What she remembers most of all is his touch. As she tries to comprehend her birth, her childhood, her dawning womanhood, her imagery centers on the body: the womb, gestation, the embryo, and desire. Her spirit cried out when she was young, and it cries out in her narrative, but no one hears either the first or the last time. No one ever asks her what she remembers, what memory means to her, what its relation is to the body. But she answers all these questions when she observes how the body goes on remembering long after mind and words evaporate: *"That is the substance of remembering—sense, sight, smell: the muscles with which we see and hear and feel—not mind, not thought: there is no such thing as memory: the brain recalls just what the muscles grope for: no more, no less. . . . Ay, grief goes, fades; we know that— but ask the tear ducts if they have forgotten how to weep"* (143).[23]

Rosa thus restates the fundamental value system of amorous discourse, valorizing the heart as sign, the senses as signifiers, the body as alphabet. She has a great deal to offer Quentin, if he could but hear her, for throughout her narrative she relates body to mind, feeling to thought, words to senses, intuition to intellect. Quentin, however, sees only discontinuities. Quentin's obsession with the Henry-Bon-Judith relationship, for example, mirrors his obsession with Caddy's virginity. Virginity epitomizes all absolutes: either his sister is a virgin or she is a whore. Upon that minute membrane, he constructs all his elaborate abstractions about honor, and—like Abelard, the Portuguese nun's family, and the Harlowes—Quentin conceives of honor as the exclusive property of the male. Rosa, in contrast, describes virginity not as an absolute but as a continuum, a process. She com-

---

23. Over twenty years later, Faulkner mentioned the same contrast between facts and truth, between memory as a mere log or catalogue and memory as a muscle, an instinct, something prior to language, when he described his own memory as being "phenomenal . . . in the sense that the muscle remembers. . . . it's not anything that's really catalogued into the mind, it's catalogued into whatever muscles of the human spirit produce the book," *Faulkner in the University*, p. 203.

pares herself to the lover *"who spies to watch, taste, touch that maiden revery of solitude which is the first thinning of that veil we call virginity"* (147–48). Of her own sexuality, moreover, she speaks frankly in terms that are not a condemnation but a celebration: she affirms her own potential for love and the urge of her own desire by comparing herself to a *"warped chrysalis of what blind perfect seed: for who shall say what gnarled forgotten root might not bloom yet with some globed concentrate more globed and concentrate and heady-perfect because the neglected root was planted warped and lay not dead but merely slept forgot?"* (144). In the imagery of Keatsian ripeness and ecstasy (heady-perfect), Rosa affirms the potential her sexuality had to be fuller, more vital, more "concentrate," precisely *because* her desires had been so long deferred. Indeed, she continually contrasts the masculine obsession with such abstractions as honor, courage, and glory to the *"indomitable woman-blood* [which] *ignores the man's world in which the blood kinsman shows the courage or cowardice, the folly or lust or fear, for which his fellows praise or crucify him"* (153). Therefore, Mr. Compson errs when he describes women as deluded, determined to live in an air of unreality, to ignore the *"shades and shapes of facts"* (211); women simply affirm values that he and Quentin find alien. Rosa, like all heroines of amorous discourses, demonstrates that the discourse itself is an affirmation, made in the full awareness that it goes against the facts and figures; for as Faulkner was fond of saying, truth is whatever touches the heart. Again and again he contrasts the meagerness of facts with the heart's powers of invention, the paucity of literalism with the richness of infinitely transcribable desire.

Theseus, Dionysus, and Ariadne's Thread

The same issues of authority, authorship, ownership, and identity that are so central in amorous discourse also dominate Faulkner's novel. Legitimacy, paternity, and lineage are indeed Sutpen's overriding obsessions, and Faulkner uses the thread as a metaphor for the narrative line, reenforcing the motif of doubling and repetition. The relation of Rosa to Ariadne is particularly provocative, for the doubling of Ariadne's relation to Theseus and Dionysus is compressed in the novel into one male figure: Sutpen. Sutpen's traits are frequently specifically associated with threads on a spool, signifying the conflicts in his own character. One thread contains Theseus' characteristics:

shrewdness, courage, will, rationality. The other contains Dionysian elements: impulsiveness, unpredictability, instinct.

Sutpen is Thesean when he tries to discover where he made his "mistake"; he explains to Grandfather Compson how eminently rational and judicious he was when he abandoned his first wife and son:

> 'I was faced with condoning a fact which had been foisted upon me without my knowledge during the process of building toward my design, which meant the absolute and irrevocable negation of the design; or in holding to my original plan for the design in pursuit of which I had incurred this negation. I chose, and I made to the fullest what atonement lay in my power for whatever injury I might have done in choosing, paying even more for the privilege of choosing as I chose than I might have been expected to, or even (by law) required.' (273)

Like Rochester, Sutpen abandons a Creole wife from the West Indies whose heritage is tainted by some unspecified hereditary evil; a crucial aspect of the novel is the fact that the allegation of Eulalia Bon's Negro blood is never proven. This demonstrates once again that those who can define are the masters, for those who make the laws and enforce them do so by a selective manipulation of the facts that they pride themselves on collecting objectively. Sutpen's justification of his actions resembles Rochester's rationalization of bigamy. The writing heroines in amorous discourses invariably address their letters to lovers who themselves have much in common. Sutpen is a lover-tyrant who combines the traits of Ovid's warriors and who exhibits Abelard's tyranny, Lovelace's violence, and Rochester's specious logic. Mr. Compson ironically calls it *"the old logic, the old morality which had never yet failed to fail him"* (279–80). It fails him because there are so many Dionysian forces that cannot be reduced and constrained by intellect and rationality, by a "code of logic and morality, his formula and recipe of fact and deduction" (275). The Dionysian facets of Sutpen's character, moreover, create internal and external pressures. His insulting proposition to Rosa, for instance, is an unpremeditated act—sheer impulse, Rosa insists: *"He had never once thought about what he asked me to do until the moment he asked it because I know that he would not have waited two months or even two days to ask it"* (166). His drunken bouts in the scuppernong arbor with Wash further connect him to the god of wine, who was also known as the sufferer who grieves for his own pain. Since Dionysus is also the vine pruned so severely that it seems incapable of producing again, it is significant that during the battle in the West Indies, one wound "came pretty near leaving [Sutpen] that virgin for the rest of his life" (254). Potency and fertility, of course, are the roots of Sutpen's obsession: "*he was now past sixty and . . . possibly he could get but one more son, had at best but one more son in his loins, as the old cannon might know when it has just one more shot in its corporeality*" (279).

While evoking the images of loom, thread, and spool, Faulkner makes it clear that Sutpen weaves nothing from these threads of Theseus and Dionysus in his character. Instead, the images represent the thwarting of desire and the coming of death: "*The thread of shrewdness and courage and will ran onto the same spool which the thread of his remaining days ran onto and that spool almost near enough for him to reach out his hand and touch it*" (279). Unlike Rosa, Sutpen creates nothing. Instead, like Dionysus, like Lovelace, like Rochester, he is the "ambiguous seducer-rescuer in a family romance involving defeat or death for the father figures, and a complex role for the female figures as murderous mothers, as self-slaying victims, and as transfigured mates for the god."[24] In Faulkner's family romance, one thinks of Eulalia Bon as the murderous mother; Clytie as the self-slayer; and Milly Jones as the mate for Sutpen. Defeated or dead father figures also abound: Goodhue Coldfield, Charles Bon, Wash Jones, and Sutpen himself. Therefore, the multiplication of images of the phallus at the end (Sutpen's horse, his whip, the rusty scythe, the butcher knife) merely inscribes its loss.[25]

Like Persephone, Dionysus dies with the coming of cold, reduced to a gnarled stump. The connection of Sutpen to the god of the vine gives us an added insight into Rosa's preoccupation with wisteria, snarled vines, and roots. Indeed, if Sutpen resembles Dionysus dying of cold, Rosa believes that she "*might be sun for him*" (168), that she can bring him to life again. She describes him as being "*like the swamp-freed pilgrim feeling earth and tasting sun and light again and aware of neither but only of darkness' and morass' lack*" (167–68).

Rosa's responses to Sutpen are thus remarkably varied and complex and Shreve's and Quentin's repeated emphasis on her hatred must not be allowed to overshadow her hope, her pity, her compassion for Sutpen. Clarissa tells Lovelace that if he could be sorry for himself, she could be sorry too; Rosa manages to make a similar

24. Although J. Hillis Miller never mentions Faulkner, I am indebted to his essay "Ariadne's Thread: Repetition and the Narrative Line," *Critical Inquiry* 3 (Autumn 1976), 57–77.
25. Ibid., p. 76.

imaginative leap from her own suffering to empathetic identification with Sutpen's. She vanquishes her childhood vision of him as an ogre, for when he comes home from the war, she sees him not as *"the ogre; villain true enough, but* [as] *a mortal fallible one less to invoke fear than pity . . . victim . . .* [of] *solitary despair"* (167). Now Rosa knows something about both solitude and despair, but she is less solipsistic and monomaniacal than Sutpen, and she makes a supreme effort to hear and to respond to the last cry of another spirit.

Sutpen, too, is conscious of spirit, but of an entirely different order: he is obsessed with the waste and loss of potency, with "th'expense of spirit in a waste of shame." Like previous lover-tyrants, he views woman metonymically. He merely wants a womb in which to deposit his seed, as one deposits money in the bank. Sutpen equates sexuality with depletion, as he reveals when he notes that he could have reminded Eulalia of "these wasted years, these years which would now leave me behind with my schedule not only the amount of elapsed time which their number represented, but that compensatory amount of time represented by their number which I should now have to spend to advance myself once more to the point I had reached and lost" (264). This fundamental fear leads him to calculate and compute everything: he wars with his flesh, carefully devising strategies for the dispersal of his seed, and tactics for conserving it, remaining a virgin until he marries in order to preserve his potency. Like Lovelace, he is not motivated by love or even lust; instead sex is merely a vehicle for his power, his ambition, his design. Significantly, not one male narrator ever notices or challenges Sutpen's assumptions about the depletion of potency. None of the men ever examines the implications of using economic metaphors of getting, spending, paying, for male sexuality. They overlook the angle of vision that female sexuality may offer; objectively, after all, the female has far more to fear than the male, since the loss of her reproductive powers occurs some twenty years sooner than Sutpen's "last shot." (He is past sixty when he impregnates Milly.) Thus the obsession with impotence is not rooted in biology but is yet another of those imprisoning abstractions that paralyze so many of the male characters in Faulkner's fiction.

If the male vision of sexuality is of depletion, the female's is of plenitude. Sexuality is as bountiful as the sun in the comparison Rosa makes repeatedly. It is infinite, inexhaustible, measureless—utterly beyond all boundaries, all male categories of worth and value. Yet male characters see female sexuality as a labyrinth, treacherous and mysterious. As Grandfather Compson asks Sutpen, "Didn't the dread and fear of females which you must have drawn in with the primary mammalian milk teach you better?" (265). If to Rosa, sexuality is a cup overflowing, to the male it is always in danger of being drained. In my view, the male narrators never challenge Sutpen's view because they share it; it is so deeply rooted that they don't even recognize it, and this primary dis-ease with sexuality is a vicious circle, for it makes them sterile and impotent. Where Lovelace's existence is a "cursed still-life," Sutpen is, like Sam Fathers, "himself his own battleground, the scene of his own vanquishment, and the mausoleum of his defeat."[26] Quentin's body, similarly, resembles "a barracks filled with . . . ghosts still recovering . . . from the fever which had cured the disease, waking from the fever without even knowing that it had been the fever itself which they had fought against and not the sickness, looking with stubborn recalcitrance backward beyond the fever and into the disease with actual regret, weak from the fever yet free of the disease and not even aware that the freedom was that of impotence" (12). This fever is the Civil War, which cures them of the disease which is slavery. Slavery made them powerful; so they regret being cured, since the cure leaves them impotent. Apparently, male potency derives from and depends on the oppression of others, sexually and racially. This understanding sheds new light on the obsession with the phallus in the novel, which is a stark contrast to the metaphors from nature (wisteria, the sun, honeysuckle, the earth) that Rosa uses to describe love and sex.

The Ledger

I have argued that *dialogism* in discourses of desire signifies not just dialogue, but an entirely different *logic,* one opposed to Aristotelianism and, as the conflict between Ovid and Virgil demonstrates, to all officially endorsed structures and institutions (law, economics, politics) that have their roots in formal logic. Heloise, for example, stands in stark opposition to the master logician Abelard; Clarissa and Jane Eyre both defy the "eminently rational" logic of Lovelace and Rochester. As we have seen, everything conspires to render the heroine's alternative logic invisible, as when the Portuguese nun gets "lost in translation" because of the publisher, Claude Barbin. Among so

26. Faulkner, *Go Down, Moses* (New York: Modern Library, 1955), p. 168.

many male narrators in *Absalom, Absalom!*, Rosa Coldfield gets lost in translation too. In order to appreciate the scope of her affirmation and her rebellion, I must, therefore, digress briefly to delineate the dominant logic that she defies. Because all the male narrators endorse the same logic, which she opposes, and because so many of our judgments of Rosa are filtered through their perceptions, it is doubly important to reveal the specious argument upon which their judgments are based. Theirs is the logic of the phallus, and among the many multiple figures of the phallus in the novel, I shall examine just one: the ledger. Inscribed in the ledger is an entire economy of sexuality that marks the radical difference between Rosa and the males in the novel. The ledger's columns and computations of spending and getting, its list of Negroes bought, bred, and sold—all reveal how fundamental the equation of sex and money is in the false economy of Sutpen's design and, alas, in the entire South. The ledger, moreover, dominates the imagination of every male character in the novel: Goodhue Coldfield, Grandfather Compson, and Wash Jones, as well as the main narrators, all view existence in terms of what is spent and what is saved, in terms of debts owed, bills paid, credits accumulated. Every male who tells even a fraction of the story not only repeats but validates the sterile economy that Sutpen's sexuality encodes. For instance, it is not Rosa but Mr. Compson who insists that Rosa was "born at the price of her mother's life." It is Mr. Compson who (probably quite accurately) describes Goodhue Coldfield as he spent "three days in a mental balancing of his terrestrial accounts, found the result and proved it. . . . Doubtless the only pleasure which he had ever had was not in the meager spartan hoard which he had accumulated . . . —not in the money but in its representation of a balance in whatever spiritual counting-house he believed would some day pay his sight drafts on self-denial and fortitude" (84). In contrast to Rosa, who affirms the possibility that sexual fulfillment might be "more perfect" because it has been so long deferred, who thinks not in terms of numbers or computations, Mr. Compson goes so far as to calculate copulations when he describes the Sutpens as being "integer for integer, larger, more heroic . . . [than we who are] author and victim too of a thousand . . . copulations and divorcements" (89). Shreve and Quentin are equally infected with this niggardly debit-credit mentality. Their imaginations, too, are ruled by the ledger. Shreve imagines that Charles Bon woke up one spring morning and "lay right still in bed and took stock, added the figures and drew the balance" (330). It is

Shreve, moreover, who refers to God as a "Creditor" whom Sutpen hopes to fool "by illusion and obfuscation by concealing behind the illusion that time had not elapsed and change occurred the fact that he was now almost sixty years old, until he could get himself a new batch of children to bulwark him" (179–80). Quentin protests that Shreve "sounds just like father," but he too sounds like his father. The very nature of male sexuality, in fact, makes all the male narrators sound alike because they share the fundamental assumptions that Sutpen enacts. Quentin automatically validates Sutpen's sexual economy here, for he proceeds to describe him as

> the old wornout cannon which realizes that it can deliver just one more fierce shot and crumble to dust in its own furious blast and recoil . . . the old demon, the ancient varicose and despairing Faustus fling his final main now with the Creditor's hand already on his shoulder, running his little country store now for his bread and meat, haggling tediously over nickels and dimes with rapacious and poverty-stricken whites and negroes, who at one time could have galloped for ten miles in any direction without crossing his own boundary, using out of his meager stock the cheap ribbons and beads . . . with which even an old man can seduce a fifteen-year-old country girl. (181–83)

While Sutpen haggles and hoards, Milly's "increasing belly" grows in mocking juxtaposition to Sutpen's shrunken stature.

The same patriarchal economy that makes sex a commodity devalues the female; this devaluation too remains unchallenged by all the male narrators in the text. Indeed, when Shreve realizes that Milly's infant is not a boy but a girl, his only response is not a protest, but simply, "Oh." Women are chattel whom men price according to a complex system of computation involving the exact fractions of blood, as with Charles Bon's octoroon mistress. Charles justifies this system by first accusing God, then white women of perpetrating it to protect their own chastity; in reality it is yet another indictment of the economics of male sexuality. Woman is viewed metonymically; the octoroon's vagina and the white virgin's hymen are assigned market values correlated to their function: the octoroon serves the white man's lust as the white virgin serves his honor. (Dr. Johnson's declaration that chastity is of the utmost importance because all property depends upon it comes to mind.) Mr. Compson imagines Charles explaining that the octoroon was made by white men,

> created and produced [by] them; we even made the laws which declare that one eighth of a specified kind of blood shall outweigh seven eights

of another kind. . . . we do save that one, who but for us would have
been sold to any brute who had the price, not sold to him for the night
like a white prostitute, but body and soul for life to him who could have
used her with more impunity than he would dare to use an animal,
heifer or mare, and then discarded or sold or even murdered when
worn out or when her keep and her price no longer balanced. (115–16)

Thus Sutpen's "domain" signifies more than his compulsion to dominate all, more than his compulsion to name (and thus to define) not
only all his children ("the entire fecundity of dragon's teeth") but all
abstractions, all the "eggshell shibboleth of caste and color." He dominates not just by *defining* such abstractions as Beauty, Woman, Virginity, Honor, and Negro but by assigning a dollar value to those
abstractions in the marketplace. When he returns from the war, for
instance, Rosa reflects retrospectively that marrying her would have
"gained him at the lowest possible price the sole woman available to
wive him" (166). Women are synonymous with virgin land, the sole
function of which is to turn fertile crops into cash. Thus, whether
Rosa is "cold" is debatable, but—in the logic of male sexual economy—she is definitely a *field*; as she discovers in the aftermath of
abandonment. Eulalia Bon's lawyer epitomizes the *reductio ad absurdum* of a masculine economy that turns human emotions and sexuality
into financial transactions. He is imagined as having a secret drawer
or a secret safe with a secret paper in it, which computes Sutpen's
success and plots his ruin: *"Today Sutpen finished robbing a drunken
Indian of a hundred miles of virgin land, val. $25,000. . . . 7:52 p.m. today
married. . . . Say 1 year. . . . Son. Intrinsic val. possible though not probable
forced sale of house & land. . . . Emotional val. plus 100% times nil. plus val.
crop. . . . Daughter . . . 1859. . . . Query: bigamy threat, Yes or No. Possible
No. Incest threat: Credible Yes. . . . Certain"* (301, 310). The lawyer is
merely an exaggeration of Sutpen himself, whose obsession with time
is as pronounced as it is with money; like sex, time indeed *is* money. A
close analysis of the novel's rhetoric would reveal how consistently the
use of legal language reveals a debased moral code.[27] Faulkner's
theme, however, is not simply that lawyers are corrupt or that legality
is diametrically opposed to morality. His characterization of the lawyer reminds us once again of the close connection of amorous discourse to the language of courtrooms and trials. The lawyer is the

27. See Marvin Singleton, "Personae at Law and in Equity," *Papers on Language and
Literature* 3 (Fall 1967), 354–70.

extreme embodiment of all those—from Goodhue Coldfield to Sutpen and Mr. Compson—who exploit and control, who view life in terms of facts and computations and whose debit-credit mentality makes them obsessed with possession, domination, and settling accounts.

"Bond," as the Negro Luster points out, is "a lawyer word. Whut dey puts you under when de Law ketches you" (215). This law is always a negation, and an unbearable bondage to negativity enslaves all the characters infected with this niggardly economy. Not only is the South's economic system corrupt, not only is Sutpen's morality myopic, but the male equation of sex with money makes the very idea of meaningful bonds savagely ironic. Just as the lawyer is the extreme example of male acquisition, of male "getting," in economic terms, Jim Bond is the epitome in sexual terms. He is the *reductio ad absurdum* of the logic of the phallus, of the law that measures fractions of blood, computes the number of copulations, and counts ejaculations. The phallic ledger looms largest on the last page of the novel, which is devoted to Shreve's final nihilistic vision:

> "So it took Charles Bon and his mother to get rid of old Tom, and Charles Bon and the octoroon to get rid of Judith, and Charles Bon and Clytie to get rid of Henry; and Charles Bon's mother and Charles Bon's grandmother got rid of Charles Bon. So it takes two niggers to get rid of one Sutpen, dont it? . . . Which is all right, it's fine; it clears the whole ledger, you can tear all the pages out and burn them, except for one thing. . . . You've got one nigger left. One nigger Sutpen left. Of course . . . you never will be able to use him. But you've got him there still." (377–78)

Yet even on the last page of the novel, an alternative to Shreve's dark vision opens out, spills over. As with Rosa's analogy of sexuality to sunlight, one might posit an entirely different economy based on giving and loving rather than on hoarding here, for one might argue that instead of lack, there is always something left, something from which human existence can replenish itself, as in a few thousand years we may replenish the human race from the loins of African kings. Faulkner sees time and existence as cyclical, like the sun, not linear, like the ledger. He does not endorse either Shreve's vision or Quentin's, although he gives the last word to Quentin. As in Henry James's tale, what is named and thus given a reality is hatred rather than love. The tragedy (for even if Sutpen is not tragic, his descendants are) is that rather than *do* and *love,* Quentin's final words are *dont* and *hate.* Rather than being able to affirm anything, his final words are a denial and a lie, for he does hate the South, as men hate what they don't understand.

Quentin hates women for the same reason. He confesses that he still hears Jim Bond howling at night, but he hates being haunted and he hates being a ghost. In my view, he hates Rosa too, because all he can see in her is his own eventual fate—to be yet another living ghost. He thus demonstrates that in Rosa he sees not a face but a mirror, a projection of his own deepest doubts and fears. He never does decipher her, although he stares steadily at the letter announcing her death: "It was becoming quite distinct; he would be able to decipher the words soon, in a moment; even almost now, now, now" (377). Her spirit was not heard when it cried for the last time, and *now* never comes.

As in *The Turn of the Screw,* Faulkner's novel is filled with written agreements, contracts, papers, ledgers, and letters that seem to be without origin or end. When the novel opens, Rosa has already sent a written summons to Quentin "out of another world almost—the queer archaic sheet of ancient good notepaper written over with the neat faded cramped script" (10). Sutpen's rise depends on a written agreement involving a bill of lading which gives Goodhue Coldfield cash and Sutpen a wife, as well as a wedding license, a "patent" of respectability. There are, moreover, all sorts of certificates that fail to certify, binding agreements that fail to bind. Sutpen receives a citation for bravery from Lee, but as Wash discovers, it certifies neither his honor nor his humanity. A letter, furthermore, is the focal point of desire in myriad ways: Quentin and Shreve speculate that Charles is hoping for a letter from Sutpen saying *"I am your father. Burn this,"* but the letter never comes. The letters in *Absalom, Absalom!* repeat the pattern so characteristic of amorous epistolary discourse: they have no date, no salutation, no signature, yet the more inscrutable they are, the more they seem to signify. What is astonishing about the passage below is the degree to which Mr. Compson's response to the letter partakes of literature; his many allusions to formulas, proportions, and miscalculations are all revealing. He is describing a love letter that Charles Bon wrote to Judith:

> It's just incredible. It just does not explain. Or perhaps that's it: they dont explain and we are not supposed to know. We have a few old

272   Discourses of Desire

mouth-to-mouth tales; we exhume from old trunks and boxes and
drawers letters without salutation or signature, in which men and wom-
en who once lived and breathed are now merely initials or nicknames
out of some now incomprehensible affection which sound to us like
Sanskrit or Chocktaw; we see dimly people, the people in whose living
blood and seed we ourselves lay dormant and waiting, in this shadowy
attenuation of time possessing now heroic proportions, performing
their acts of simple passion and simple violence, impervious to time and
inexplicable. . . . They are there, yet something is missing; they are like
a chemical formula exhumed along with the letters from that forgotten
chest, carefully, the paper old and faded and falling to pieces, the
writing faded, almost indecipherable, yet meaningful, familiar in shape
and sense, the name and presence of volatile and sentient forces; you
bring them together in the proportions called for, but nothing happens; you re-read, tedious and intent, poring, making sure that you
have forgotten nothing, made no miscalculation; you bring them together again and again nothing happens: just the words, the symbols,
the shapes themselves, shadowy inscrutable and serene, against that
turgid background of a horrible and bloody mischancing of human
affairs. (100–101)

As Lacan has said, "A cryptogram takes on its full dimension only when
it is in a lost language."[28] The statement is a psychoanalytic version of
Keats's "unheard melodies are sweeter," for Lacan is referring to the
agency of the Imaginary in the unconscious. Rather than freeing one
from language, the Imaginary exists in dynamic interrelation with the
realms of the Symbolic and the Real. My interest in the passage involves
Faulkner's representation of lack and loss, and the ways those representations structure the narratives. As we saw with Clarissa's crypt,
letters in Faulkner's text overflow their bounds, yet remain cryptic. Mr.
Compson's reflections shed light on the paradoxes involved in viewing
the letter as literature and literature as a letter, for Faulkner might well
be describing the fate of the reader of the novel. Within the novel, the
death of the authors of the letters, of course, gives birth to reader-
narrators like Mr. Compson, readers who invest the correspondents
with the heroic proportions of the past. Rosa Coldfield is both in and
out of this world, "a crucified child," imprisoned in a house that "like
her . . . had been created to fit into and complement a world in all ways
a little smaller than the one in which it found itself" (8, 10). Rosa is
isolated from "general space," from the world at large, by time and
space; she lives "partitioned" in a "dim hot airless" office, in the

28. Lacan, "Insistence of the Letter in the Unconscious," p. 129.

"coffin-smelling gloom . . . as if there were prisoned in it like in a tomb all the suspiration of slow heat-laden time" (7, 8, 10). Rosa's room resembles the cloisters of Heloise and the Portuguese nun, as well as Clarissa's crypt. Rosa's eloquent speech issues from this funereal environment; as with all amorous discourses, it is a self-address—internal as well as external. Derrida explores the ambiguities of interiority and exteriority when he describes a crypt as a kind of forum, "like a closed rostrum or speaker's box, a *safe*: sealed, and thus internal to itself, a secret interior within the public square. . . . The inner forum is (a) safe, an outcast. . . . That is the condition, and the strategem, of the cryptic enclave's ability to isolate, to protect, to shelter from any penetration, from anything which can filter in from outside along with air, light, or sounds, along with the eye or the ear, the gesture or the spoken word."[29] Like Clarissa's writing of her last will and testament, Rosa's "office" is to encrypt desire and inscribe the memory of what might have been. Clarissa is indeed her closest analogue among the writing heroines in this book, for the discourse of desire once again takes the form of an elegy. Yet it is paradoxically also an affirmation.

The Loom

Rosa consciously affirms the existence of something beyond the literal, legalistic language of ledger-books, beyond language itself, indeed. She speaks of her desire as being made of myriad elements that language cannot begin to describe. Desire *"has no words to speak with other than 'This was called light,' that 'smell,' that 'touch,' that other something which has bequeathed not even name for sound of bee or bird or flower's scent or light or sun or love"* (145). What Rosa, like all the heroines of amorous discourses, posits is another logic, one that defies all the calculations and abstractions of all the eggshell shibboleths. She demonstrates once again that amorous discourse is an affirmation, for she maintains that *"there is that might-have-been which is the single rock we cling to above the maelstrom of unbearable reality"* (149–50). Even more remarkable than her affirmation here is her definition of that "might-have-been," for despite the brutality of Sutpen's rejection, despite all the waste and grief and sorrow, she defines it as love and faith. This

29. Jacques Derrida, "Fors," trans. Barbara Johnson, *Georgia Review* 31 (Spring 1977), 64–116.

affirmation is the way to surmount all the imprisoning abstractions that reduce the human spirit to economic matters, that negate truth with mere facts, for Rosa possesses the *"true wisdom which can comprehend that there is a might-have-been which is more true than truth"* (143), which consists of *"love and faith at least above the murdering and the folly, to salvage at least from the humbled indicted dust something anyway of the old lost enchantment of the heart"* (150).

The qualifiers—"at least," "something anyway"—point to the difficulty of finding something, anything, to affirm in the aftermath of devastation. The Civil War reveals the catastrophic results of assigning dollar values to human beings as if they were livestock, of equating sex with money, of reducing human emotions to economic integers. Rosa realizes the folly of trying to balance accounts—emotionally, morally, spiritually—for one can never settle accounts because nothing is ever "settled"; *was is*. Rosa, like Clarissa before her, affirms that *"there is no all, no finish"*; even as the soul leaves the body, the soul contains *"that spark, that dream which, as the globy and complete instant of its freedom mirrors and repeats (repeats? creates . . .) all of space and time and massy earth, relicts the seething and anonymous miasmal mass which in all the years of time has taught itself no boon of death but only how to re-create, renew"* (143).[30] Not only is nothing ever finished, but whatever is left over will be used to renew, to recreate, as Rosa recreates her passion in her narrative. She is the chronicler of the time, the one who records births, deaths, and disasters not only in the family Bible but in the imaginations of a younger generation. Like Ariadne, she is the one who waits, who gives shape to absence and weaves its fictions. Faulkner finally makes Rosa's relation to Ariadne explicit when he juxtaposes Rosa's sewing with the slow unraveling of the South during the war. She steals the cloth from her father's store and spends her days and nights

> sewing tediously and without skill on the garments which she was making for her niece's trousseau and which she had to keep hidden . . . whipping lace out of raveled and hoarded string and thread and sewing it onto garments while news came of Lincoln's election and the fall of Sumpter [*sic*], and she scarce listening, hearing and losing the knell and

---

30. Compare the affirmation in *Go Down, Moses,* another novel that contrasts the logic of ledgers and legalities with the myriad ways in which accounts can never be settled nor anything in life ever finished: "You always wear out life long before you have exhausted the possibilities of living. . . . all that could not have been invented and created just to be thrown away. . . . And the earth dont want to just keep things, hoard them; it wants to use them again" (186).

doom of her native land between two tedious and clumsy stitches on a garment which she would never wear and never remove for a man whom she was not even to see alive. (78)

What Rosa demonstrates here is the opposite of the debit-credit mentality of niggardly economy; she toils to give a gift of love to the woman who will marry the man she loves. Significantly, Judith repeats the same act of generosity for her rival. She not only raises her lover's bastard son but dies while tending his yellow fever. It is the female who weaves and spins, and this creative impulse is closely allied with identity, as Judith reflects: "You are born at the same time with a lot of other people, all mixed up with them, like trying to, having to, move your arms and legs with strings only the same strings are hitched to all the other arms and legs and the others all trying and they dont know why either except that the strings are all in one another's way like five or six people all trying to make a rug on the same loom only each one wants to weave his own pattern into the rug" (127). This vision of interdependence is what Sutpen never manages to achieve or even to comprehend. Therefore, he creates nothing, despite the fact that his design, his very life, and all the lives his touches draw on the imagery of loom, thread, and spool. In contrast, Judith, Clytie, and Rosa form a triumvirate: they are like the three fates who "*spun thread and wove the cloth*" (155). Sex becomes "*some forgotten atrophy like the rudimentary gills we call the tonsils*," and they cease to be circumscribed by such abstractions as Woman or Negro, for they endure "*amicably, not as two white women and a negress, not as three negroes or three white, not even as three women, but merely as three creatures. . . . as though we were one being, interchangeable and indiscriminate*" (155). In my view, the radical proportions of Rosa's vision have been entirely overlooked. The three women can do anything a man can do—chop wood, plow fields, mend fences; the fact that they are indiscriminate highlights the hollowness of the dominant means by which the white man "discriminates" between himself and Negro, between himself and woman. The logic of male sexual economy requires that woman and Negro be reduced to the level of abstraction so the white male can define himself in terms of what he is not; the self/other dichotomy imprisons all others in the vague category of "other-than-himself." The miracle, in my view, is that despite her imprisonment in the rigid structures of male logic and patriarchal discourse, Rosa Coldfield manages to defy those structures and to make an affirmation by embroidering her vision of what might-have-been.[31]

The loom is thus an alternative to the ledger: a collaborative creative endeavor among women, "above the murdering and the folly," "the fine dead sounds" of glory, honor, warfare. One thinks again of the contrast between Socrates' condemnation of Eros as a sophist, and Sappho's celebration of Eros as a weaver of tales, for the loom leads directly back to Sappho, weaving her lyric-webs, and Ariadne, affirming the primacy of the heart's desires. Yet those desires are continually in danger of being effaced by others. In "The Figure in the Carpet," for instance, J. Hillis Miller is fascinated by Ariadne, but he compares his essay to Theseus' impossible attempts at mastery: "the dance of the too rational Theseus . . . marked out ever-changing, winding figures . . . compulsively retracing the labyrinth in an always frustrated desire to master it. . . . The present essay is one more execution of the dance of Theseus."[32] Miller acknowledges the limitations of language, but one wonders why Ariadne—her role, her fate, her desires—seems to have disappeared. As in the case of the *Portuguese Letters*, when critics set about discussing the difficulty of writing or translating, what gets lost in translation is frequently the woman. Barbin, the interpreter who appears to efface himself, instead ends up erasing the nun. Here, similarly, Ariadne's desire gets lost amid the obsession with mastery (and masters) and the labyrinth of narrative. Thus, in charting Theseus' quest, Miller replicates his crime. By focusing on Sutpen's quest, on his obsession with mastery, critics have consistently done the same thing to Rosa Coldfield. When Quentin confronts Henry at the end, he sees Clytie as "the one who owns the terror" (369). But the drama of the telling belongs to Rosa; she is the one who articulates not only the doom, the curse, and the fatality of Sutpen's downfall, but the sorrow and the pity of it as well.

31. I should note that even when Rosa is not being interpreted by Mr. Compson, Quentin, or Shreve, there are moments when her own voice is clearly Calvinistic. Nevertheless, those passages can be attributed to Rosa as *voice*—looking back after Sutpen injures her—rather than to Rosa as *focus*. As stated earlier, her aunt's Calvinism imbues the child Rosa with the sense of Sutpen's evil; when he returns from the war she views him as mortal, fallible, and despairing; and when he repudiates her, she reverts to her initial opinion of his inherent evil. What I have focused on in this chapter is her second, softer attitude towards Sutpen, since the male narrators so distort this phase by labeling her merely as the Scorned Woman.

32. Miller, "The Figure in the Carpet," p. 107, n. 1. See also Miller, "Ariadne's Thread," pp. 71–74.

Her narrative establishes a pattern that is but one of many woven on the loom, one with a complex texture of hatred *and* love, fury *and* faith. She dedicates herself to what Barthes, in his amorous discourse, calls the Loquela: "The flux of language through which the subject tirelessly rehashes the effects of a wound or the consequences of an action: an emphatic form of the lover's discourse. . . . I spin, unwind and weave the lover's case, and begin all over again (these are the meanings of the verb μηρύομαι (*meruomai*): to spin, to unwind, to weave)."[33] Thus in the absence of the touch of flesh with flesh, Rosa gives shape to lack and elaborates the fictions of loss that structure all the lives around her. She makes her presence felt by transforming passion into art, weaving and reweaving through "devious intricate channels of decorous ordering."

33. Barthes, *A Lover's Discourse*, p. 160.

The allegorical question "She? Who?" will thus remain unanswered. The text, nonetheless, will play out the question to its logical end, so as to show in what way it *precludes* any answer, in what way the question is set as a trap. The very *lack of the answer* will then write itself as a *different* question, through which the original question will find itself dislocated, radically shifted and transformed.

SHOSHANA FELMAN,
Women and Madness: The Critical Phallacy

8

Poetics, Passion, and Politics in *The Three Marias: New Portuguese Letters*

The Portuguese Nun. This engraving by R. J. Beedham of a
painting by Joanne Gill appeared in *The Letters of a Portuguese
Nun,* trans. E. Allen Ashwin (Talybont Dyffryn, North Wales:
Francis Walterson, 1929). It is reproduced courtesy of the
William Andrews Clark Memorial Library, University of Cal-
ifornia, Los Angeles.

Laws and Outlaws

> This text . . . seems to be made . . . to make light of all
> the tranquil categories of genre-theory and history in
> order to upset their taxonomic certainties, the
> distribution of their classes and the presumed stability
> of their classical nomenclatures. . . . I am convinced
> that fundamental rights are bound up in all of this:
> the law itself is at stake.
>
> JACQUES DERRIDA, "La Loi du genre/
> The Law of Genre"

The Three Marias: New Portuguese Letters is the collaborative work of three Portuguese women, Maria Isabel Barreño, Maria Teresa Horta, and Maria Velho da Costa. When it was written in 1971, Horta was literary editor of a Lisbon newspaper; Barreño and Velho da Costa were writers and researchers at the Ministry of Economics. The text consists of letters, poems, and fragments inspired by the original *Letters of a Portuguese Nun.* The impact of the modern text can perhaps best be measured by the severity of the backlash against it. Published in the spring of 1972, it was immediately hailed as a masterpiece, but by May it had been banned, and within a month a censorship committee ruled that the authors and everyone else involved in the book's publication would be prosecuted for "abusing the freedom of the press and out-raging the public morals and decency." The government was apparently counting on them to assume the roles of powerless victims. Monique Wittig suggests that the Portuguese censors were furious at the text's immediate success and that this anger accounts for the unusual severity of their treatment.[1] The trial began in October 1972 and, in order to ruin the women financially, it was prolonged well into the spring of 1974. The authors were imprisoned, feminist protests were mobilized internationally, embassies were besieged with protests, and a statement was prepared for the United Nations Human Rights Commission.

1. Monique Wittig and Evelyne Le Garrec, trans., Introduction, *Nouvelles Lettres portugaises* (Paris: Editions Seuil, 1973), p. 8.

The Portuguese government was clearly unprepared for the feminist mobilization; it apparently expected to imprison the women (one of whom is tubercular) for six months to two years without a public outcry, much less one of such massive international proportions. On 18 April 1974, one day before the three women were to be sentenced, the court inexplicably adjourned; a week later the Caetano-Salazar dictatorship was overthrown by a junior officers' coup. Even after the coup, however, the three women still had to stand trial. This is why they consistently maintain that revolutions come and go, but women remain oppressed; this is why they maintain that they owe their freedom not to the coup but to the concerted effort of the feminist movement throughout the world. Three days after they were acquitted, the Movimento de liberacão das mulheres was founded, with prominent participation by Barreño and Horta.[2]

Why did the text arouse such a vehement response? What were the three Marias' crimes? Clearly, some transgression of the law was at stake, but what? First, a transgression of gender: the three women write "like men"; they are sexually explicit, frank about their bodies, their desires, their fantasies, their sexuality. They analyze the patriarchal structures and the repression that creates violence between lovers, within families, throughout society, continuously interweaving the personal plight of individuals with the political consequences of repression. They give women who have been silenced through the ages a name, a voice, a heritage, creating a female history and genealogy in the letters of mothers, daughters, sisters, aunts, nieces. They break the law of genre as well as of gender by interweaving "historical" letters that are fictional, interpolating tales of Gothic horror, essays, poems, puzzles, and legal documents. The text is an incitement to insurrection, based on the conviction that "when woman rebels against man, nothing remains unchanged" (158).

It is simultaneously a radical reenvisioning of writing and revolt, defiance and desire, *and* it is an amorous epistolary discourse. I have

2. See Wittig and Le Garrec, pp. 7–11; and Robin Morgan, "International Feminism: A Call for Support of the Three Marias," in *Going Too Far* (New York: Random House, 1975), pp. 220–27; Helen R. Lane, Translator's Preface to Maria Isabel Barreño, Maria Teresa Horta, Maria Velho da Costa, *The Three Marias: New Portuguese Letters* (New York: Bantam, 1976), pp. ix–xv (the edition hereinafter cited by page number parenthetically in the text); Dan Hofstadter, review of *The Three Marias: New Portuguese Letters*, *New Leader*, 23 June 1975, p. 18. An earlier volume of poems by Maria Teresa Horta had also been banned as "erotic." See H. M. Macedo, *Times Literary Supplement*, 12 Dec. 1975, p. 1484.

chosen to conclude with *New Portuguese Letters* because, although some would argue that its achievement does not match that of the other texts in my study, it does reiterate all the essential characteristics that I have been tracing. These traits, indeed, reappear in unexpected combinations. The three Marias' lament of exile evokes the *Heroides*; the seclusion of the cloister returns us to Heloise and Mariane; the tyranny of families and social codes recalls Clarissa and Rosa Coldfield. *New Portuguese Letters* thus demonstrates that the more a genre evolves and the more complex it becomes, the better it remembers its past. The three Marias revisit and revise the original nun's letters, casting them in a new light that illuminates their subsequent literary history, and history in general. That reaccentuation is dialogic: it is simultaneously a multilingual (French and Portuguese) discourse and an assertion of another logic and another modality based on dialogue. *The Three Marias* combines the erotic and educational strains of epistolarity; it is both a love letter and a legal challenge. It is also a theoretical experiment, a narrative performance that purposely subverts the traditional divisions between reading and writing, fiction and reality, politics and poetics. By focusing on politics and history, the three Marias make explicit what was implicit in the nun's original letters— the parallels between the colonization of Portugal and of woman, between the country as colony and woman as conquest.

Genre theory maintains that no new contribution to a genre is merely a product of a preexisting system; "to signify in history," says Todorov, "is to proceed from difference not merely from repetition. Hence the work of art . . . always involves a transforming element, an innovation of the system."[3] As with my previous texts, this one must be viewed in terms of its innovative experiments. By including an anticanonical text, I mean to call into question the process by which the critical reception of a text influences its canonical status; I shall return to this question in the last section of this chapter. As an experiment, moreover, *New Portuguese Letters* points to new directions in which the genre of the amorous epistle might move. One of the three Marias' many innovations involves multiple addressees; although we have seen multiple correspondents in previous discourses such as

3. On dialogism, see M. M. Bakhtin, *The Dialogic Imagination: Four Essays*, ed. Michael Holquist, trans. Holquist and Caryl Emerson (Austin: Univ. of Texas Press, 1981), pp. 415–21. On generic systems, see Tzvetan Todorov, *The Poetics of Prose*, trans. Richard Howard (Ithaca: Cornell Univ. Press, 1977), p. 186.

Clarissa, here for the first time three authors collaborate, writing directly to one another. They make visible in the text itself the kind of dialogue and critical exchange that went on behind the scenes in Lady Bradshaigh's collaboration with Richardson. They also write letters directly to the original Portuguese nun, thus blurring the boundaries between the letter as literature and literature as a letter once again. Among all the texts in my study, indeed, this is the first that presents the other as a woman. She is addressed with all the passion that was reserved for the absent male in previous discourses.

The exercise of passion is the Marias' subject from their opening declaration: "...Granted, then, that all of literature is a long letter to an invisible other, a present, a possible, or a future passion that we rid ourselves of, feed, or seek. We have also agreed that what is of interest is not so much the object of our passion, which is a mere pretext, but passion itself" (1). By beginning with an ellipsis, they reveal that something prior has already taken place; they have made agreements before writing, and they begin by laying out their theoretical premises. The scholars who wrote about the Portuguese nun, we may recall, were obsessed with issues of authority and authorship, with discovering her identity, proving or disproving the authenticity of her letters, with giving the text a father. The three Marias share no such obsession; instead they offer an empathetic vision of the nun's sensibility, her sexuality, her society. What interests them is her passion and its exercise, her *mouvements,* her fate and feelings before and after her abandonment. They are interested, in other words, in imagining precisely those aspects of the nun's experience which J. Hillis Miller overlooks in Ariadne. Just as Rosa Coldfield affirms that there is a *"wisdom . . . a might-have-been which is more true than truth,"* the three Marias aim to reconstruct the nun's predicament and her passion, to make a "mosaic. . . . Letter by letter . . . via the volatile written word. . . . And never has love been such a fiction, and hence absolutely true" (18).

The three Marias' approach to the Portuguese nun revolves around the purposeful transgression of the boundaries of fiction and reality. By maintaining that it is immaterial whether the experience and emotion described in the nun's letters is fictive or real, the three modern women are liberated from the controversies of traditional scholarship about authorship of the original *Portuguese Letters.* They never claim that a real nun wrote authentic letters; they simply write their own letters to her, letters that are themselves an enigmatic mixture of fiction and reality. (Indeed, one Maria ridicules the efforts of one enterprising male critic who, conjecturing about her life from her art, concludes that she must be sexually frustrated since her poetry is so erotic. Classical scholars, remember, drew similarly erroneous conclusions about Sappho.) As if to repay Barbin for completely effacing the nun in his *avis* to the reader when he published the original *Portuguese Letters*, the three Marias never mention him or Guilleragues. They see their writing as a process of restoration and recuperation: what they reinscribe is the woman in the text. *New Portuguese Letters* is thus a work of criticism as well as of fiction, one that intentionally subverts the conventions of scholarly discourse that so frequently nullify the female. The Marias' theoretical motives for writing are to transform the reader into writer-critic. The fluid roles of writer and reader create a forum for investigations of nature and culture, past and present, desire and the law, the body and language. The writing is a process of searching for the law of their own desires.[4]

They inscribe those desires in part by speaking *to* the nun rather than about her and by transforming her from victim into victor, famous in all the courts of Europe for her celebrated letters. The significance of this departure is enormous, for the popularity of the *Portuguese Letters* through the centuries was based on the conviction— one might almost say the celebration—of the nun's victimization. All of Europe wept for her, but the orgy of tears was aroused by her desolation, her disorder, her disillusionment to the point of delirium and self-destruction. The three Marias evoke this literary history while revising it: the nun, after all, does not destroy herself; instead, she writes. The same distinction, remember, distinguishes Virgil's representation of Dido as victim from Ovid's emphasis on her writing. The three Marias dramatize the nun's dedication to her desire and celebrate her final epiphany: "It was not so much you as my own passion to which I was attached." Where her letters end, theirs begin:

4. Julia Kristeva says the same thing about Roland Barthes in *Desire in Language: A Semiotic Approach to Literature and Art*, ed. Leon S. Roudiez, trans. Thomas Gora, Alice Jardine, and Leon S. Roudiez (New York: Columbia Univ. Press, 1980), chap. 4. The theoretical aim and method underlying the three Marias' mode of response to the Portuguese nun can be compared to Roland Barthes's response to Werther in *A Lover's Discourse: Fragments*, trans. Richard Howard (New York: Hill and Wang, 1978). In the course of this chapter, I sometimes compare the ideas of the three Marias to those of Barthes simply because readers are more likely to be familiar with his texts than with theirs, but the Marias' text is not merely an "application" of Barthesian theories.

In my heart of hearts I do not believe in love as a totally genuine feeling apart from my imperative need to invent it (in which case it is real but you are not), I nonetheless refuse to deny it, since it truly does exist in and of itself. . . .
    It is not false, then, if I write you:
    'I know that . . . I am also losing myself because I am completely powerless to make you love me.'
    And so I suffer, apparently because I love you, but in reality because I am losing the motive that will sustain my passion, which most likely I am more fond of than I am of you. (2–3)

Like so many previous amorous epistolary discourses, the *New Portuguese Letters* are filled with such contradictions and paradoxes. In some fragments, the three Marias address "Sister Mariana of the five letters" directly; in fragments like the one above, however, they write from the place of the nun—a very different procedure from mere projection. It is, in fact, another facet of their theoretical project, for what critics have dismissed as mere naïve projection is actually *production*, based on the ideas that reading is a kind of writing and that the textual reader yields to language as an erotic practice. The three Marias thus enact a poetics of reading that could be called an erotics of reading. Indeed, that is what Roland Barthes does call it later, in another context: the erotic practice of language takes place "whenever the 'literary' Text (the Book) transmigrates into our life, whenever another writing (the Other's writing) succeeds in writing fragments of our own daily lives."[5] The three Marias' project is to write to the imaginary other, Mariane, interweaving their own writing and desire with hers, just as their shared names—Maria, Mariana, Mariane—connect them like the threads on a loom.

    Yet the nun's past and even her personality are unsolvable enigmas for the three modern women; they invent possible answers to questions that no reader, no scholar, no critic has ever been able to answer. Why, for instance, was Mariane incarcerated in the convent in the first place? The three Marias (all convent-educated themselves), agree that "a daughter put in a convent is not loved in her house"; why was she not loved? In imagining her family and her relationship with her mother, they compare their own families and conclude that, like Mariane, they are orphans, exiled, unassimilable in the social

5. Roland Barthes, *Sade, Fourier, Loyola*, trans. Richard Miller (New York: Hill and Wang, 1976), pp. 7–8.

system around them. One Maria laments that a woman can give birth but remain stillborn herself; another grieves that a woman's entire life is "all like the act of giving birth; a solitary, painful, furtive act, hidden from the eyes of everyone in the name of modesty" (155). The legacy passed down from mothers to daughters is self-loathing and suicide, a blood curse that is the result of a mother's disappointment at having brought forth a child like herself: "From our earliest days as suckling babes in diapers we have had no mother; no one ever told us we were wanted and needed for our unique presence. And for this reason too our interchanges with each other—and all friendship between women—has a uterine air about it, the air of a slow, bloody, cruel, incomplete exchange, of an original situation being repeated all over again" (90). They are engaged in repeating a trauma and interpreting a repetition, the same process that marks all discourses of desire. One of their motives for writing is to alter this pattern, to invent the mothers and sisters they have been denied and to create a new model of exchange with women by exchanging letters. Each Maria thus serves as analyst as well as reader-critic for the other two, and all three are seeking to define the "original situation being repeated all over again." The search leads them from critiques of their childhoods to criticism of one another: "We found ourselves touched by . . . the common childhood that we *made it our task* to discover . . . going on from accusing our mothers to accusing each other to our faces, and discovering that we could tolerate this—and that is how we made each of ourselves the mother and the daughter of each of the others, and sisters determined to talk about precisely why we were orphans and suffering and destitute. A new family" (106). Theirs is a theoretical procedure, drawn from psychoanalytic models of transference and countertransference. In the language of psychoanalysis, one would say that the three Marias practice the Imaginary in full awareness that they are doing so. They purposely shift roles from analyst to analysand repeatedly, so that no single woman becomes the "authority" on the other two. Their own image for the process is an *open parabola*—a plane curve that is the locus of a moving point, equidistant from a fixed point, or focus, and a fixed straight line—the image suggests the dynamic relationship between three shifting entities, three bodies that want to remain open to experimentation, to suggestion, to analysis, to each other. Their experiment in reinventing mothers and sisters is far from sentimental, for they see how much damage has been done by the mystiques of marriage, pregnancy, and motherhood.

Each Maria, moreover, is a critic as well as a reader of the theories of the other two. They disagree about the uses and value of the women's movement; about the causes, consequences, and remedies for patriarchy; about the solutions to women's misery in the modern world. Their motives, their methods, their writing styles all differ as well: one is lyrical, emotional, erotic; another is incisive and analytic; the third is detached and ironic.

They call their process of writing, their final product, and their relationship a trialectic in order to disrupt all dichotomies, all binary oppositions that, as we have seen before, are so often exploited to define and circumscribe woman, desire, discourse. Their aim is to block the reconciliation of opposites, to resist synthesis, unity, and closure. In addition to shifting the roles of analyst and analysand, they subvert the hierarchies of authorship and mastery by not signing their letters. To write without authority is also to write without the authorization of scholars and critics; it is to write "unprotectedly." They also write without the exclusive endorsement of any one language system (Marxism, feminism, or psychoanalysis). Instead, their collaborative effort allegorizes the process of reading by which woman as critic is transformed into critic as woman writer: she leaves parents, family, and authorities behind and speaks in her own voice, but "unprotectedly," "without authority," literally without signature.[6] To describe the result in the language of transference: "The primary effect of writing is registered in the writer—one writes *for oneself* as a kind of ethical exercise."[7] With that model in mind, the three Marias return to the Portuguese nun, enabling us to see her for the first time, illuminating the significance of her final radical declaration: "I write more for myself than for you."

6. In deference to their political motives for not signing their letters, I have purposely chosen to focus on the text as a "trialectic," rather than discussing each Maria's individual contribution and identifying her separately from the collective.

7. Gregory L. Ulmer, "The Discourse of the Imaginary," *Diacritics* 10:1 (March 1980), 61–75. See also Jacques Lacan, *The Language of the Self: The Function of Language in Psychoanalysis*, trans. Anthony Wilden (Baltimore: Johns Hopkins Univ. Press, 1968). Jane Gallop's *The Daughter's Seduction: Feminism and Psychoanalysis* (Ithaca: Cornell Univ. Press, 1982) examines the relation of Freudian and Lacanian psychoanalysis to the theories of (among others), Hélène Cixous, Catherine Clément, Julia Kristeva, and Luce Irigaray. Since I refer to these women below, I must note at the outset that these French theorists by no means all share the same theoretical methods and beliefs. An analysis of their differences, however, lies outside the scope of this book, which is limited to a general demonstration of the relevance of recent French, feminist, and psychoanalytic theories to *The Three Marias* within the context of amorous epistolary discourse.

The result of the dual focus on their own oscillating impressions and on the Portuguese nun are letters that are simultaneously topical and timeless. The Marias subvert authorial mastery by simply arranging their letters chronologically, leaving them unsigned but dated at the bottom from 1 March to 25 October 1971. One of the functions of amorous narrative, we recall from the *Heroides*, is the invention of one time scheme in terms of another; the dates at the bottom of the three Marias' letters are frequently juxtaposed with opening dates ranging from 1669 to 1800 to 1940 to the present, marking significant political moments in history and personal moments in women's lives. One result of such temporal juxtaposition is that the letters are timely and polemical. One Maria notes that sexual liberation in Portugal merely means that pornography and media images of violence against women are now rampant. But the same letters are historical, for that pornography, that glorification of crimes of passion, reached its apogee during the reigns of Louis XIV and of the Philips in Spain (114–15). The invention of one time scheme in terms of another makes the *New Portuguese Letters* not just topical and historical but timeless. For woman, the personal is the political. That point is conveyed, paradoxically, by demonstrating how little her condition has changed through history, for even if man rebels against the colonizer, his personal arrangements, his rights as master of women and children are never challenged, never disturbed. In one letter, a niece of the nun's, "Dona Maria Ana, born around 1800," asks: "What woman is not a nun, sacrificed, self-sacrificing, without a life of her own, sequestered from the world? What change has there been in the life of women through the centuries? In Aunt Mariana's time women did embroidery or spun or wove or cooked, obeyed their husband's will, became pregnant, had abortions, or . . . sometimes died in childbed. . . . a king of France has been sent to the guillotine . . . the United States of America has gained its independence. . . . [but] what has changed in the life of women?" (154). Thus each letter is the site of eternal recurrence, a reiteration of Ariadne's asking not just what she is doomed to suffer but what all women are doomed to suffer. Each "new" Portuguese letter is simultaneously a testament to the personal and the political, to type and to history, to the timeless and the polemical. The same effect is achieved by giving many of the correspondents, like the niece, the name Maria Ana, or a variation of that name, or by marking the "coincidence" of the three Marias' shared bond with that name. Reading backward and forward through history, the three modern women discover not their differences from their great-great-grand-mothers but their similarities. The reliance on resemblance, on like recognizing like, is one of the distinguishing features of the discourse of the Imaginary.[8] What they record is a polyphony of female voices that had been silenced, sepulchered, and forgotten. Just as Clarissa concludes her discourse by proclaiming, "I am Nobody's," the three Marias invent an entire female genealogy that celebrates woman as disorder, as scandal, as marginal; it is

> a lineage opposed to the forgetting and the diluting, the rapid absorp-tion of a scandal within the peace of the family circle and the reigning social order.
>
> If men create families and lineages in order to ensure that their names and property are passed along to their descendants, is it not logical for women to use their nameless, propertyless line of descent to perpetuate scandal, to pass along what is unacceptable?
>
> Like religious orders in essence. (153)

The three Marias also "perpetuate scandal" by demonstrating that discourse is what they fight to obtain and that the fight is waged in discourse; their analysis of language revolves around the issues of male domination, male narcissism, and the dichotomies of patriarchal logic. Just as Clarissa protested against being a cipher to give Lovelace significance, the three Marias condemn men for dividing themselves "into men and masters. But all men are masters of women. In the houses of masters, of men and of cavaliers, we give them their mean-ing, for they define themselves by their opposites" (66).

The three Marias expose the contradictions, the injustice, the re-pression inherent in the civil and ecclesiastical definitions of woman by including fragments from such documents as the Portuguese penal code, which gives husbands the right to murder adulterous wives for insulting their honor "with the full sanction of the law, with the agree-ment, the approbation of an entire society that complacently con-dones this crime." A wife, however, only has legal recourse if her husband's concubine lives under the same roof, and even then, she may not act in the name of her honor, but only in the name of "established morality" (276). (Ironically, these were the very grounds upon which the three Marias were prosecuted—they outraged "estab-lished morals.") The three Marias are the latest of the long line of

---

8. Ulmer, p. 68.

heroines of amorous discourse from the *Heroides* forward who dedicate themselves to the inscription not just of desire but of honor. It was in the name of honor, one recalls, that Heloise proclaimed her preference for being Abelard's whore over being Augustus' wife, that Clarissa wrote her will, that Jane Eyre refused Rochester's seduction, and that Mariane dedicated herself to her passion. The three Marias defiantly assert their right to action in defense of "our name or our wrath or our jealousy or our honor, the defense of which is a right granted only to the man" (276–77). That assertion marks the culmination of one dominant strain of amorous epistolary discourse which we have traced from Ovid: its relation to courts, trials, evidence, and legalities. Like Clarissa, the three Marias expose the codes responsible for the reduction of woman to "a legal fiction"; instead, they give her an individual name and a legal identity, reinscribing her in the law books and the book of life. No longer will they stand as objects of status and exchange among men, and never again will honor merely be a matter of male property rights. The reclamation of honor is thus a subversive assertion of self-possession and self-worth. Besides the penal code, the three women expose numerous other codes that have repressed women through the ages, defiantly challenging the systematic depiction of woman as evil, as disorder, and analyzing how such negative images of women have been perpetuated out of fear, loathing, and ignorance. The vastness of the compendium, which ranges from a *Dictionary of Sorcery* to the Bible, illustrates once again the extent to which woman is a cipher in patriarchal culture, the quintessential blank page, waiting to be filled by man's negative image of her as "a castrated man . . . Eve . . . the virgin-mother, a witch, the devoted, self-sacrificing mother, the vampire . . . man's plot of earth . . . Adam's rib, man making himself the mother of the woman to reorganize her very creation out of chaos" (87, 89). The three Marias repudiate these roles; each is "a woman ridding herself of the image of the woman created by men" (35). One Maria helps the other to stop being "trapped by the myth of the male" (112); another repudiates "any man who creates a false image of me" (74).

One strategy for surmounting the definitions imposed from the outside is to write from the place of the other. Just as Ovid experimented with "writing like a woman," the three Marias experiment with "brazenly stripping ourselves of our habits . . . and riding life bareback, as though we were males" (17). They thus enact what the original Portuguese nun imagined when she took everything the chevalier did for herself.[9] It is an act of appropriation and exposure, a deliberate mimicking of the attitudes, obsessions, oppressions of the colonizer. Speaking from the place of chevaliers, husbands, and lovers through the ages, the three Marias stage the ordeal of abandonment as colonization, for the letters they invent come from men fighting in colonial wars in Europe, Angola, or Africa, addressing the women they leave behind. In one fragment, the chevalier recollects his conquest of Mariane, his victory over "the battlefield of [her] body" (105). In another, he advises her "to accept the world that has been forced upon you and mold yourself to it, inasmuch as there is no possible escape for you" (57). In others, husbands absent for twelve years write letters home, blithely describing new mistresses, new families they have engendered, while their Portuguese wives remain faithful, dressed in widow's weeds.

Just as Rosa Coldfield's narrative exposed all the shibboleths of such abstractions as virginity, one of the primary objectives of the three Marias is the "deflowering of myths." Like the loss of virginity, it is a bloody process, a necessary penetration of stereotypical clichés. In some fragments, the copybook exercises of little girls are included to show, as in *The Turn of the Screw*, how early the "necessary" job of indoctrination begins. The Marias' strategy is to defuse the cumulative power of these myths by making travesties of them, exposing them as the fictions that they have been all along: the devouring mothers, frustrated spinsters, crimes of passion, sex-as-death, woman as goddess and demon. It is a "quiet, stealthy work of undermining" (23), carried out by miming the dominant images the culture disseminates.

Despite substantive differences between Mexico and Portugal, Oc-

9. Curiously, a collection of tales by Joyce Carol Oates that appeared about the same time as the Marias' text is another example of writing from the place of the other. *The Poisoned Kiss and Other Stories from the Portuguese* begins with the assertion: "The tales in this collection are translated from an imaginary work, *Azulejos*, by an imaginary author, Fernandes de Briao. To the best of my knowledge he has no existence and has never existed, though without his very real guidance I would not have had access to the mystical "Portugal" of the stories—nor would I have been compelled to recognize the authority of a world-view quite antithetical to my own." Oates signs the collection, "Fernandes/Joyce Carol Oates." Her strategy thus reverses the procedure of Claude Barbin in *Lettres portugaises;* where he effaces the nun to authenticate his "translation," Oates invents a male author to give her text authenticity and to dramatize that antithetical perspectives are the result not just of national boundaries but of literary inventions of gender. See Fernandes/Joyce Carol Oates, *The Poisoned Kiss and Other Stories from the Portuguese* (Greenwich, Conn.: Fawcett, 1971), p. 10.

tavio Paz's analysis of the Mexican man's view of woman validates the view that the Marias condemn in Portuguese men: woman, Paz writes, is "an instrument, sometimes of masculine desires, sometimes of the ends assigned to her by morality, society and the law . . . as a 're-pository' for certain values. . . . In a world made in man's image, woman is only a reflection of masculine will and desire. . . . Wom-anhood, unlike manhood, is never an end in itself. . . . [Woman] has no will of her own. Her body is asleep and only comes really alive when someone awakens her. She is an answer rather than a question, a vibrant and easily worked material that is shaped by the imagination and sensuality of the male."[10] Woman is thus the conquest even of those who are themselves colonized, whether in Mexico or in Por-tugal. Men in love seek not a face but a mirror; it is that narcissism, that mystification and manipulation that the Marias set about to dismantle.

One of their methods is to speak of the silence that enshrouds women. Writes one Maria, "Let no one tell me that silence gives consent, because whoever is silent dissents" (291). All three writers describe the experience of colonization as being stripped of language, of positive self-images, and systematically deprived of a viable cultural community in which to create those images. Even the smallest com-munal effort of women is perceived as a potent threat, as the reactions of men to the trio's project reveals: one tells them it "might be the death of us"; another says, "What monsters you three are!"; a third accuses them of lesbianism. They receive vicious letters and death threats in the mail. Yet they persevere, coming through the process of writing to understand how literally "the law itself is at stake" in pre-venting transgressions of roles, prohibiting the subversion of cultural myths, and fostering division and competition among women. They note that, although even "a black extremist is now respectable . . . a feminist is slandered; she is someone raising the frightening specter of what has never been put into words, a trouble-maker, a ridiculous creature" (90–91). For the three Marias, the revolt lies in the telling, putting into words "what terrifies us . . . just as we must combat all the frightening, monstrous, confusing charges that others will levy against us" (90). The government's reaction after the book was pub-lished demonstrates just how potent any group of women, however

10. Octavio Paz, *The Labyrinth of Solitude: Life and Thought in Mexico*, trans. Lysander Kemp (New York: Grove Press, 1961), p. 37.

small, is perceived to be, for Monique Wittig suggests that one woman writer would not have been treated so harshly, but that three women united to denounce the condition of women constitutes a veritable organization, a "menace to the established order."[11]

They dedicate themselves not just to imagining a different future but to making it a reality by raising a new generation to respond differently to women. They speak frankly of their rage as they watch their sons become "little tyrants" when they discover how society diminishes the importance of mothers, sisters, and all women. As mothers, they vow to break the chains of tradition by treating their sons as "people and not phalluses of our males" (70). They vow never to live through their sons; sons "will never be our way of asserting ourselves or our only work in the world: we shall refuse to allow them to be the bridges of our longings or our dissension" (83).

Masks and Veils, Miming and Mimesis

Instead, the bridge is writing. As in previous amorous epistolary discourses, the effect the Marias are striving for is *aleatory*; they want the text to be a fluid interplay that, rather than fortifying a fixed social and sexual identity, dissolves it. The text also dissolves the hierarchies of active writer and passive reader, which is why the verb *exercício* recurs in a variety of contexts. The reflexive form connotes drilling, training; *exercício* also means to influence, to wield power, to exercise, as in gymnastics. The text is thus an active exertion, an acrobatic exercise, a performance that involves many postures of passion. *Exercício* thus parallels Barthes's *figures*: "The word is to be understood, not in its rhetorical sense, but rather in its gymnastic or choreographic acceptation . . . the body's gesture caught in action and not contemplated in repose: the body of athletes, orators, statues . . . the lover at grips with his figures . . . struggles in a kind of lunatic sport . . . 'phrases,' like an orator . . . is caught, stuffed into a role, like a statue. The figure is the lover at work."[12] The three Marias similarly perform dazzling feats while "exercising." Like the original Portuguese nun, they discover ingenious ways to arouse desire by writing letters and to arouse letters by rehearsing the literature of

11. Wittig and Le Garrec, p. 8.
12. Barthes, *A Lover's Discourse*, pp. 3–4.

desire. They mime the roles women have been stuffed into, discarding one mask after another and imagining new roles with dizzying speed. Their postures pose a challenge to the values of unity, consistency, and clarity. What they posit as an alternative is simultaneously a renewal and an elusive revision of the Ovidian rhetorical ideal of the decentered self—capricious and changeable, equivocal and equivocating, full of masks and poses, playfully subverting the hierarchies of high seriousness and mimesis. Their theories of the relation of the body to knowledge, to self, to style lead directly back to the Ovidian strategies of doubleness, duplicity, and dissimulation.

Octavio Paz helps us see the political implications, for in analyzing the Mexican's reaction to successive invasions, he describes dissimulation and mimicry as strategies of rebellion against colonization by noting that

> dissimulation . . . is almost habitual with us. It does not increase our passivity; on the contrary, it demands an active inventiveness and must reshape itself from one moment to another. We tell lies for the mere pleasure of it, like all imaginative peoples, but we also tell lies to hide ourselves and to protect ourselves from intruders. . . . The dissembler pretends to be someone he is not. His role requires constant improvisation, a steady forward progress across shifting sands. Every moment he must remake, re-create, modify the personage he is playing. . . . In its most radical forms dissimulation becomes mimicry. . . . Mimicry is a change of appearance rather than of nature.[13]

In earlier amorous discourses, the kinds of strategies the Marias use were consciously rhetorical; here they are political and theoretical as well, based on an attempt to overcome the "repression of the feminine" in language by acting it out, performing a "playful rehearsal," in the words of Luce Irigaray. By mimicking the roles the culture assigns them, they expose the underlying absurdity of the roles. That their identification with the Portuguese nun involves more than mere projection can perhaps best be demonstrated by seeing how they exploit mimesis to expose its limitations. As Luce Irigaray explains:

> To play with mimesis, is, therefore, for a woman, to attempt to recover the place of her exploitation by discourse, without letting herself be simply reduced to it. It is to resubmit herself . . . to "ideas," notably about her, elaborated on/by masculine logic, but in order to make "visible," by an effect of playful repetition, what should have remained

13. Paz, pp. 40, 43–44.

hidden: the recovery of a possible operation of the feminine in language. It is also to "unveil" [*dévoiler*] the fact that, if women mime so well, they do not simply reabsorb themselves in this function. They also remain elsewhere.[14]

Implicit in every discourse of desire in this book is the same impulse to make the hidden visible, to recover something that has been repressed. Clarissa's purpose in substituting feminine pronouns in the Book of Job certainly involves the recovery of the feminine in language. Indeed, from Heloise to Rosa Coldfield, each heroine initially seems to submit to the tyranny of masculine logic, yet she recovers her own place in the process of writing and redefines herself. Each, moreover, in some sense remains elsewhere: Heloise refuses to be circumscribed by Abelard's tyranny; Clarissa's crypt overflows its bounds; Rosa affirms that nothing is ever settled, that there is no all, no finish.

The three Marias do not, however, merely celebrate "the feminine mystique"; nor do they endorse the "essentialist" theories of some of their French feminist contemporaries about woman's nature. Instead, they parody the stereotypes of woman, ironically miming masculine logic, unveiling all the habits by which culture cloisters them. They deflower the myths that have kept women virginal, childish, frozen in time, forgotten in history. Like woman, love itself has been relegated to the margins, blighted by myths of inevitable separation, unfulfillment, and death. One Maria laments, "Abelard is castrated, and Tristan is forever separated from Isolde, and all the myths of love describe this relation as something forbidden and unfulfilled, and all love stories are stories of suicides" (86).

Like previous amorous discourses, this one offers the alternative of another logic, one that is an affirmation of surrender without destruction and domination, of loving as a way of knowing. Having unveiled the causes, the consequences, and the pervasiveness of their colonization, each Maria discovers that until she finds a means of self-possession she will never surmount the self-loathing that the culture engenders. Before they can love others, they must learn self-love; this

14. Luce Irigaray, *Ce sex qui n'en est pas un* (Paris: Minuit, 1977), p. 25, cited and trans. in Mary Jacobus, "The Question of Language: Men of Maxims and *The Mill on the Floss*," *Critical Inquiry* 8 (Winter 1981), 207–22. Just as the three Marias are familiar with Lacanian psychoanalysis and the theories of French women, French feminists demonstrated their enthusiasm for *The Three Marias* with a reading for their legal defense fund in Paris on 25 Oct. 1973. The three Marias had sent *New Portuguese Letters* to Christiane Rochefort in March 1973 because they admired her work.

is what the trialectic enables them to attempt. In forging a new family, they recombine in novel ways the fundamental characteristics of amorous discourse, for their emotions toward one another run the gamut from love to hate, passion to compassion. One wants to leave the group because love is too demanding; another is wounded by the hostility of the third; in short, the same motifs of rivalry, jealousy, fear, possessiveness that mark other discourses mark their letters, too. Yet the act of writing becomes a fluid, volatile process of continual metamorphosis—of ideas, forms, modes, styles, passions.

The trialectic method allows for continual exploration and immediate response, for the exploration in writing of woman's role, in Hélène Cixous' words, as the

> outcast [who] has never ceased to hear the resonance of fore-language. She lets the other language speak—the language of 1,000 tongues which knows neither enclosure nor death. To life she refuses nothing. Her language does not contain, it carries; it does not hold back, it makes possible. When id is ambiguously uttered—the wonder of being several—she doesn't defend herself against these unknown women whom she's surprised at becoming, but derives pleasure from this gift of alterability. I am spacious, singing flesh, on which is grafted no one knows which I, more or less human, but alive because of transformation.[15]

The three Marias put all these elements into practice, exploring the women that they are becoming through the process of writing, celebrating the human gift of metamorphosis that has been such a marked characteristic of amorous discourse since Ovid. Recalling the sensuousness of Sappho's lyrics, the flesh itself seems to sing, and the idea of grafting rather than fathering once again subverts the notion of a primary source engendered in a father-text. The last line is particularly telling, for transformation is not mere play but a necessary strategy of survival; alterability is what keeps one alive. The three Marias draw on the same recurrent images that mark previous amorous discourses: links in a chain, threads spun, webs woven; the multiple images of interdependence, indeed, recall Judith Sutpen's loom: "All this linked in a chain, each of us intermingling and trying on

---

15. Hélène Cixous, "The Laugh of the Medusa," trans. Keith Cohen and Paula Cohen, *Signs* 1:4 (Summer 1976), 875–93, rpr. in *New French Feminisms*, ed. Elaine Marks and Isabelle de Courtivron (New York: Schocken Books, 1981), p. 260.

forms of the others. . . . Passion threatening to become the same thing
in another form (that is the nature of passion): that is how the pact
was sealed. . . . The time of discipline began. Each of us the pupil of
whichever one of us could best teach what each of us needed to learn"
(106–7). They thus combine the educational strain of the epistolary
genre with the erotic strain, for each Maria becomes mentor and
pupil in a constantly shifting relation that suspends all hierarchies and
metamorphoses continuously, like passion itself. They "play with
mimesis" through laughter too; one laughs while sending her lover a
sex manual; the second composes a Beckettian dialogue in capital
letters, the third composes games, puzzles, anagrams. The trace of
Ovidian stylistics remains intact, for the three Marias delight in doubleness and dissimulation, in parodic laughter, and in sexual and
textual transgressions. They indeed race back and forth (*dis-cursus*: to
run to and fro) from sexual pleasures to textual ones, recalling how in
their "comradeship . . . we did not weave on anyone else's loom, certainly not on that of any male, since we are fond of men (very fond, in
fact), but never in secret, and only if they are not expert horse-
men . . . and in the end we laughed. Oh, sisters, how we laughed!"
(332). This laughter demonstrates that discourses of desire are not
mere exercises in sorrow, a ceaseless counting of beads on the rosary
of grief and loss. Instead, desire is celebrated with gusto, irreverence,
and joy. Laughter is also a theoretical and political strategy; it de-
mystifies the male, demolishing the distance of time and space that his
myths and epics have engendered. The three Marias explicitly make
the epic pretensions of national glory, Portuguese machismo, a heroic
past of omnipotent patriarchs the butt of their laughter. In contrast to
the reverential distance of epic, the women subject these pretensions—and men—to a minute scrutiny. In some fragments, this is a
loving scrutiny, as when one Maria sketches the body of a naked man
sleeping. At other times, however, particularly when man views his
body as a weapon, a source of power and intimidation, the three
Marias defuse the threat. The process of demystification reveals that
most men are ordinary; many, mediocre. (The original Portuguese
nun, remember, concludes her letters by revealing all the chevalier's
méchantes qualités; in one of The Three Marias' fragments, the women
imagine a man confronting his own mediocrity.) The laughter is
sometimes cheerful, sometimes annihilating; the aim is a comical operation of dismemberment of the phallus as signifier ("a pocket sig-

nifier," says Hélène Cixous in an essay appropriately entitled, "The Laugh of the Medusa").[16] The three Marias laugh at male posturing—their bull fights, their automobile races, their wrestling matches: "O my Portugal of males concealing their impotence, copulators, stallions at stud, such bad lovers, in such a tearing hurry in bed, their attention entirely devoted to demonstrating their virility" (84). Laughter is thus an integral part of their poetics and their politics. They have grafted onto the original *Portuguese Letters* their own pressing preoccupations, confronting political and ideological conflicts in a polyphonic female chorus. This polyphony demonstrates once more that the enterprise is far more complex than mere projection of their desires onto the Portuguese nun; the text is a multifaceted production of ambitious proportions. They mimic, they "play with mimesis" by assimilating numerous genres and styles in their letters, parodying "higher" genres that take these *ficciones* seriously. All these characteristics—the love of miming, the refusal to glorify, the irreverence towards national heroes, the exposure of epic as fraud, the valorization of the present over the past, the personal over the public, the individual over the state—lead directly back to Ovid. Julia Kristeva has placed these traits in a tradition older than Ovid; following Bakhtin, she relates them to Menippean satire, which she describes as

> a festival of cruelty, but also a political act. It transmits no fixed message except that itself should be "the eternal joy of becoming," and it exhausts itself in the act and in the present. . . . the dialogism of Menippean and carnivalesque discourses, translating a logic of relations and analogy rather than of substance and inference, stands against Aristotelian logic. From within the very interior of formal logic, even while skirting it, Menippean dialogism contradicts it and points it towards other forms of thought. Menippean discourse develops in times of opposition against Aristotelianism, and writers of polyphonic novels seem to disapprove of the very structures of offical thought founded on formal logic.[17]

In amorous epistolary discourse, one finds the same disapproval in Ovid's resistance to Virgil, in Heloise's resistance to Abelard, in Rosa Coldfield's "alien" discourse. Kristeva's description further illuminates the theoretical foundations of the three Marias' experiment. The intertextual dynamics between the original letters and the *New Portuguese Letters* depends on a logic of relations and analogy. The

16. Cixous, "The Laugh of the Medusa," p. 261.
17. Kristeva, *Desire in Language*, pp. 84–85.

strategy allegorizes reading into partial illuminations, fragmentary insights, open-ended discoveries about writing and desire, about honor and "established morals," about the colonizing and cloistering of woman. The dynamics of the three women themselves similarly rely on a logic of relations and analogy. They explore commonalities without glossing over substantive differences, without resorting to some generalized, "politically correct" attitude about feminism or femininity. Indeed, they subscribe to no predetermined theory of the feminine any more than of the masculine; they would, I think, reject theories of the French feminists who valorize woman's feminine "essence," for they would see such essentialist arguments as another repression, another mystique that mythicizes woman, confining her to the very roles that they have set out to expose through parody. Their masks and poses create critiques of genre, gender, and class, for they even go so far as to critique their own privileged class status, drawing attention to the vast differences in women on various parts of the globe and to the enormity of the suffering of most women all over the world. That global perspective also mitigates against any formulation of a "universal feminine." What is effaced when one argues that women are universally alike are all the distinguishing differences that make their suffering profound. For example, while celebrating the "universal" experience of motherhood, one can too easily ignore the substantive differences in prenatal care and infant mortality rates that distinguish the so-called "feminine condition" of middle-class American and European women from that of poor women in Ethiopia. Says one Maria: "I consider it an urgent task to dismantle the mystique of pregnancy . . . Let our dialectic of women-born-and-raised-in-the-urban-middle-class-of-this-society-whose-values-we-are-all-too-familiar-with-and-hence-sympathize-with-all-exploited-classes-and-groups-with-the-heart-felt-feeling-of-belonging-to-the-exploited-group-'women' come out in print then" (316).

What is erased, in short, by erasing differences among women is history, injustice, and politics. This Maria explicitly exposes the class biases that underlie the essentialist theories of the feminine. She sees how easy it is to use language to co-opt any political action, and she protests against the ways in which even the project in which she is engaged can be defused by reducing each writer to the category of middle-class woman. She addresses the traps that make language a refuge from political realities and action when she protests that aesthetic style can be a refuge, yet she simultaneously criticizes her own tendency to be pedantic. In this manner, the trialectic method prevents any one of the three Marias from taking over the project; all points of view, all "isms" and "ologies" are continually being decentered, whether they involve the feminine or feminism.

Disjointed Letters, Long Farewells

Every act of protest is also an affirmation—of an alternative, of another logic, of an *elsewhere*. The three Marias reveal in their final letters more than anywhere else just how committed they are to open-endedness as an artistic and ideological orientation, for they reject resolution and closure. Despite the tensions that the collaborative experiment produced, despite many disappointments and frustrations with writing, they write one farewell letter after another. One Maria commences her "first final letter . . . probably very long and disjointed" by confessing: "This is good-bye, my dear ones, I've been trying to tell you so for two letters now, writing you without having any news from you, yet a further proof of the spitefulness and arrogance involved in the act of writing" (320). In farewell after farewell, they illuminate the "mourning that is language."[18] It unites their solitary lives momentarily but does not alleviate either their loneliness or their longing. Therefore, every single discourse of desire resists closure. The heroine continues to try to record "the *might-have-been* that is more true than truth"; she always envisions another letter that will express another facet of her desire. Just as the Portuguese nun anticipates writing another letter to follow her fifth (and final) one, the three Marias describe in their final letters all the others they had in mind. One meaning of this volubility is certainly the "eternal joy of becoming."

One of the Marias envisions the *topos* of utopia when she imagines writing a love letter to the man of the future,

> the man who will eventually come to be. . . . It is necessary to cure the man; to tell him both that his body is not sterile and that it is not only his phallus that is creative; to tell him that it is not always necessary to erect things in order to create, and that creating first and then building and

18. See Sharon Cameron, *Lyric Time: Dickinson and the Limits of Genre* (Baltimore: Johns Hopkins Univ. Press, 1979), chap. 4.

raising can cease to be a woman's privilege alone. He must be told many things, but *there is no way to say them yet that I know of.* (313, my italics)[19]

And this indeed is the crucial discovery of every single discourse of desire: there is no way to articulate desire, for it is prior to language. The yearning to articulate it, in speech or in writing, is the desire to express the inexpressible. ("It seems to me," says the Portuguese nun, "that I am doing the greatest possible wrong to the feelings of my heart in trying to make them clear in writing to you. How happy I should be if you could guess them by the violence of your own!" [353].) All language is self-reflexive; it always contains the seeds of its own critique; it is the site of struggle. What makes the language of amorous discourse distinctive, however, is that in every discourse of desire a lament like the Portuguese nun's is inscribed; every single heroine is engaged in the act of writing, but paradoxically, what she writes, in one guise or another, is, "Words fail me." Because desire lies between the needs to which the body responds and the demands that speech articulates, it is always a gap in language that cannot be filled, and consequently, every discourse of desire is a critique of language: it cannot encapsulate, enclose, sum up desire—much less satisfy it. Nostalgia and revenge, expiation and exorcism must be obsessively reiterated in amorous discourse because they reveal the heroine's longing and frustration not just toward the absent lover but toward language. In the absence of the beloved's touch of recognition, "revenge cannot compensate nor love assuage." This paradox illuminates the profound ambivalence toward language in every discourse of desire, an ambivalence, moreover, that is as decentered ideologically as it is emotionally. Since dialogism implies a radical decentering of the belief systems language institutionalizes, the result is a decentering that is simultaneously political and psychic. Dialogism gives amorous discourses their characteristic duplicity, dubiousness, and despair about the efficacy of language. Ovid, in looking back at Sappho, is simultaneously looking away from Virgil, from Rome, from Latin, just as the three Marias, in looking back at Mariane, are looking away from Portugal, from Portuguese, addressing their mothers with

---

19. The idea of curing man of destructiveness and sterility and teaching him that all power does not reside in the phallus, recalls the image of the Civil War in *Absalom, Absalom!* as the fever that cured the sickness of slavery, upon which man's sense of potency depended. See page 266 above.

the vengeful words, "All of my imaginings have been cast in a language that is not my mother tongue and far from maternal (and thus I reject you, I free myself from you)" (53).

But while the heroine mourns its limitations, she acknowledges that language is the only medium she has. Writing, moreover, may not succeed in expressing, much less fulfilling, desire, but it does augment desire: "My passion increases with every moment," writes the Portuguese nun—meaning, of course, every moment of writing. What is more, other texts can be sources of consolation by reinforcing, repeating, signifying desire. Other texts, in fact, arouse desire: the *Portuguese Letters* are a fictional discourse inspired both by the *Heroides* and by the authentic letters of Heloise; *The Turn of the Screw* renews and revises Jane Eyre's desire for the master; the three Marias transcribe the desire of the Portuguese nun. Desire circulates, and therefore there is no exit from language. Nor is there any entrance, origin, original text of desire, for as we have seen, behind Heloise stands Ovid, behind Ovid stands Sappho, and Sapphic lyrics are testaments of infinite transcribability. No better example, indeed, can be found of the process by which later readers must supplement, embroider, embellish; they must, in other words, fill in the blanks in the worn papyrus. Perhaps it is precisely because the worn papyrus is so enigmatic, so fragmentary that it arouses such passionate speculation. (One thinks again of cryptograms that only take on their full dimensions when they are in a lost language, and of the obsessive embroidering on exhumed letters that resemble Chocktaw or Sanskrit in *Absalom, Absalom!*) Sapphic lyrics are the opposite of a totality, a symbolic unity that conveys univocal meaning through the ages; they survive instead as fragmentary testaments to the impulse to narrate, to supplement, to fill in the blanks.

Paradoxically, amorous discourse may arouse the writer and seduce subsequent readers, but the lover to whom it is addressed is never persuaded to return. Despite its futility, it is nonetheless an affirmation. The three Marias explore this paradox by alternately asking "What can words do?" and "What can love do?" It is precisely the *correspondence* between the two, between a mode of loving and a mode of writing, that they address in their long, disjointed, and disruptive farewell letters:

> None of us ever ventured beyond the edge of many things, and above all simply hovered at the edge of this wild and solitary thing that love-writing is, which is not a thing that depends merely on circumstances, a

thing that can be done only if and when the relations between men, the relations between men and women, the social-ethical-economic circumstances that determine them change, but a thing involving art, a thing involving a way of responding by asking questions—love in short, a permanent proof by the absurd that it is possible to say *yes*. (320–21)

The letter enacts its own affirmation, for it is itself a response to the preoccupations of one of the other two Marias with the social and political implications of the relations between men and women. Each woman responds to the other two by asking questions, anticipating responses, and altering her own responses accordingly. The text is a methodological field that exposes its tensions and contradictions and invites deconstruction in the process of reconstructing the original nun's desire. One thinks again of the *Heroides*, for by unweaving by night what she weaves by day, the heroine disrupts resolutions, defers both pleasure and death, and keeps the circuit of desire open. Just as Mariane encourages her lover at the end of one letter to continue to make her suffer, the three Marias disrupt closure in their concluding letters by disowning all that went before. One "disruptively break[s] away; to hell with the whole thing; I'm fed up" (317); yet that is not her final word. Another mourns the death of writer friends, and of "talent and capabilities [that] will die before your eyes, as this book is dying. Different and separated. Unless we have loved and hated more passionately than is indicated by what we have written and done, much more, each one awaiting the other two, isn't that true, sisters? Isn't that true, brother writers and readers?" (323). The question reminds us once again of the fluid boundaries between the readers within the text and readers of the text, for the three Marias invite, incite, arouse the reader to embroider on their text, as readers embroidered Heloise's letters, as Lady Bradshaigh collaborated on *Clarissa*, as they themselves revise the *Portuguese Letters* and reenvision Mariane. With each other and with the nun, their method involves a way of reading and responding by asking questions.

To evoke a response, after all, is one aim of all amorous epistolary discourse. One asks the beloved questions in the implicit hope and faith that the beloved will answer, not just once but again and again. But whether answers are forthcoming or not, to respond by asking questions is a strategy that makes all discourses of desire allegories of reading, for the questions preclude closure, finality, resolution. So Heloise addresses question after question about food, wine, the bodies of nuns to Abelard, and the Portuguese nun, knowing that she takes pleasure in doing so, asks if she is obliged to describe all her diverse desires. One may view the allusion to the things the three Marias never ventured beyond as a confession of failure, but it is also a celebration of the things that remain unsettled, unassimilated; love is permanent proof of sorts, but only of the absurd, of the possible. It is thus an affirmation of all that is paradoxically indelible and most transitory: the trace of the body's touch, memory, desire. Desire, discourse, and woman herself are relegated to the margins, subjected to extreme solitude, exiled; the three Marias see their experiment as an exercise that resembles

> rivers [that] must drain if the sea is to be cleansed for us women who are polluted by the flow of time and words, driven out of so many places, or left behind by men. . . .
>   Let us hope that our hands will not be crippled or our bodies shattered . . . that those who love us for what we are and do will not divide themselves by dividing us. This is what is meant by poverty and chastity. (44–45)

The production of writing, then, is what makes the three Marias come to comprehend the meaning of a nun's vocation; its essential solitude, sacrifice, sacredness. Something that is affirmed but not seen, believed by thousands, but forsaken in modern times—what is theirs but a confession of faith, like Heloise's faith in Abelard? That faith may not be completely communicable in language, but language is all one has. To describe the indescribable, to describe passion (passion-as-suffering as well as passionate love), despite its relegation to the margins of the conceptual universe—isn't it this impulse that unites saints, mystics, nuns?[20]

From Heloise to Mariane, from the passion-as-suffering of Clarissa to the devious, intricate weaving of Rosa Coldfield, amorous discourses are affirmations of faith in a might-have-been, an elsewhere, a possible, a yes. Discourses of desire are thus always a *tissu de greffes*, a fabric of grafts, in which something is always added on, borrowed from something else, embroidered.[21] From Sappho's Eros as weaver of tales to Belfour's embroidering on the text of *Clarissa*, amorous heroines take pleasure, as the three Marias say, in interweaving desire

20. Barthes, *A Lover's Discourse*, pp. 231–34.
21. Jacques Derrida, *Dissemination*, trans. and introd. Barbara Johnson (Chicago: Univ. of Chicago Press, 1981), pp. 355–58.

in writing. Punning on *abandon, habit,* and *distaff,* they celebrate their "voracious hungers . . . at last . . . unveiled. . . . we are stitching ourselves other garments for our happiness and abandon. For abandon is another supposed habit, or a right traditionally granted us, a distaff for spinning the threads of our pleasure . . . letter by letter" (18).

The duplicitous meaning of *abandoned* as "left behind" or (sexually) "let loose," as wanting or wanton, is one of the many multilingual puns—like habit, distaff, pleasure—that make language such a fertile source of pleasure for the three Marias. Their shared sense of exile, their defiance of both the authorities and the authorized languages that have abandoned them commit the three women to the dream of a common language that they are in the process of inventing. Significantly, they call the original Portuguese nun a philosopher; it was indeed as a philosophy that her letters were discussed in the literary salons of seventeenth-century Paris. The formula of *Questions of Love* was a favorite method for analyzing the passions in the salons frequented by La Rochefoucauld, Racine, Guilleragues, Mme de Sévigné, Mme de Lafayette, and Bussy-Rabutin. (It was Bussy-Rabutin, remember, whose *tissu de greffes* made his translated paraphrase of Heloise's letters resemble the *Lettres portugaises* so closely.)[22] One might go so far as to say that the *Questions of Love* provided the theory, *Lettres portugaises* the practice. The first text, for example, asks if it is better to love or to avoid embracing love at all costs, to which the Portuguese nun responds by asking: "What would I do if my heart were not filled with so much hate and so much love? Could I possibly survive all my incessant obsessions that occupy me so completely merely to live a tranquil and tedious life again? That abyss, that emptiness, that insensibility can never come again to me."[23] The three Marias respond once again by asking the same questions: "Will love ever find any other way save this: love that uses or is used? Love that devours or is devoured; that pretends to be devoured only to devour in its turn?" (34). "Can there possibly be any reason for a woman to still believe in love? . . . How to invent a love that will recognize all the abysses" (41). By asking such questions, the three Marias evoke a language and a philosophy that has long been lost in modern times; they thus draw attention to the erasure and the trace of such a language and they ponder its uses in politics and history. "Will," they ask,

22. See Frédéric Deloffre and J. Rougeot, "Analyse d'un chef-d'oeuvre," in *Lettres portugaises, Valentins, et autres oeuvres de Guilleragues* (Paris: Garnier, 1962), pp. 14–20.
23. *Lettres portugaises,* p. 54, my translation.

"the threads running from me to you, from us to the others, be woven together in silence, in meek gestures, in delicate vibrations beneath the surface, or in action?" (315).

Again and again the three Marias ask one another, "What can words do?" What is literature worth? What is the relation of language to action, to politics, to economics? From the *Heroides* forward, we have seen how amorous discourse is simultaneously a lament and a legal challenge; in this light Derrida's speculations about the relation of genre and gender to the law take on new meaning. Throughout amorous discourse, moreover—from the bargains struck in the *Heroides* to the narrative transactions in the prologue of *The Turn of the Screw*—every narrative involves not only the circulation of desire but some kind of contract or exchange. Barthes echoes Derrida's analogy when he presents his own version of what is at stake in narrative. Narrative, Barthes writes, is "subject to contract, economic stakes, . . . which . . . can turn into haggling . . . but [these stakes are] represented, *en abyme*, in the narrative. . . . This is the question raised, perhaps by every narrative. . . . *What is the narrative 'worth'?* . . . by a dizzying device, narrative becomes the representation of the contract upon which it is based: . . . narrating is the (economic) theory of narration."[24] We saw earlier how Faulkner's text involves multiple representations of lack; *New Portuguese Letters* involves multiple representations of contracts. There are many other things to notice here. Just as the three Marias try to negotiate a settlement by inventing a love that recognizes the abysses, Barthes sees negotiation framed *en abyme* in every narrative. Barthes's observation is particularly provocative when one considers the impulse that makes the heroine put pen to paper. She simultaneously confronts the beloved for breaking their vows and uses the letter to negotiate a new contract (Heloise's procedure with Abelard is a good example). The letter itself is highly seductive; the heroine explicitly states time and again that it should be exchanged for her body, as when Mariane laments that her letter will be held in her lover's hands and adds, "How I wish I were in its place" (341). Amorous discourses are thus "representations of the contract upon which they are based," and complaints about the transgression of that contract. They are sites that take the place of courts of law, as

24. Barthes, *S/Z: An Essay*, trans. Richard Miller (New York: Hill and Wang, 1974), pp. 88–89.

when Clarissa, having been prosecuted *in absentia* by her family, serves as witness for her own prosecution and "executes" her will.

The Critical Reception

The three Marias ask each other whether the words that join them to one another and to others will be woven in meek silence and gestures, in "delicate vibrations beneath the surface, or in action." Julia Kristeva asks the same question when she contrasts women who "valorize phallic dominance" and "identify with power" to women who shun power, flee from everything phallic, and valorize the "silent underwater body, thus abdicating any entry into history."[25] In my view, the three Marias manage to avoid celebrating phallic dominance without shunning power or abdicating history. Their laughter deprives the phallus of its power as signifier, but they simultaneously take pains to bring the silent, underwater woman to the surface. They painstakingly elucidate women's perpetual colonization historically, from Louis XIV to Angola.

I turn now briefly to consider the critical reception of this experimental text, because it sheds light on certain kinds of unconscious critical assumptions—assumptions about mimesis, about calculation and spontaneity, about language, about the relation of politics to art, about the formation of a canon. What the responses to *New Portuguese Letters* demonstrated was the lack in 1971 of a vocabulary that could encompass the anticanonical, theoretical, and transgressive strategies of this particular text. There was, moreover, no tradition like the one I am tracing that could provide a context for critical consideration; the sole example of an attempt—and the most intelligent review— places *The Three Marias* in a long tradition of Portuguese feminism, showing its similarities to the cycles of stories in which an older woman has a dialogue with a younger woman about love.[26] (The dialogism here is once again worth noting.) In some regards, critics continued to make the same mistakes that classical scholars of Sappho made in later antiquity: they assumed that one can deduce the life from the art. As a

25. Julia Kristeva, "Oscillation du 'pouvoir' au 'refus,'" an interview by Xavière Gauthier, *Tel Quel* 58 (Summer 1974), rpr. as "Oscillation between Power and Denial," trans. Marilyn A. August, in *New French Feminisms*, pp. 165–67.
26. See H. M. Macedo, *Times Literary Supplement,* 12 Dec. 1975, p. 1484.

result, they were not a little puzzled by (among other things) the sexuality of the three Marias. One critic described them as "proud prisoners of sex."[27] Another criticized their "adolescent, groping, overheated displays of narcissism, fantasies that are often dull."[28] What such reviews overlook is that within the text itself, such criticisms recur: one Maria critiques the writing of another, asking, "Which of us did not gorge herself on your obsessive, narcissistic description . . . [of your] furious desire for your own self" (313). Yet this very criticism is immediately displaced by the recognition that the Maria who was the most obsessed with sex was also the "one who exposed herself the most." The writers' aims, in other words, were to let stand all the vacillating impulses without endorsing one perspective—political, sexual, emotional, aesthetic—over another. But the critical reception had just the opposite effect; disparate elements were isolated, then criticized, as if they were the central message, and the conscious attempt of the authors to decenter the text was ignored. Reviewers attacked form and content alike. One criticized its "formless approach to the genuine problems that face the world's women now."[29] In other words, it was not enough of a political tract to suit some critics, but others found it excessively polemical.

In my view, the three Marias oscillate between power and denial.[30] Their strategy is to combine incitements to political action with the gestures and codes of love. *New Portuguese Letters*, however, far from being perceived either as an avant-garde experiment or as a condensation of history and myth or as a theoretical text whose very fragmentation is a political posture, was instead attacked by those who misunderstood the ways in which the project combined poetics and politics. In fact, all the vituperative criticisms that we have traced since Sappho have been directed at this single text. The three women are accused of lesbianism, man-hating, narcissism, sexual hysteria, wantonness, frigidity, unnaturalness. The opposite charge is leveled by other critics; the writing is too spontaneous, too natural, too formless, "born out of experience, not introspection,"[31] consisting of "amorphous . . . epistolary oddments."[32] Even the *ad feminam* attacks that

27. Jane Kramer, review, *New York Times Book Review*, 2 Feb. 1975, pp. 1–2.
28. Doris Grumbach, review, *New Republic*, 15 Feb. 1975, pp. 32–33.
29. Ibid., p. 33.
30. The term is Julia Kristeva's; see "Oscillation between Power and Denial," rpr. *New French Feminisms*, p. 165.
31. Christopher Hitchens, review, *New Statesman*, 7 Nov. 1975, p. 580.
32. Hofstadter, review, p. 19.

we traced from Sappho's to Charlotte Brontë's critics recur here, for rather than accept the motives for not signing the letters, one reviewer accuses the three Marias of purposeful provocation, of forcing the reader to focus on each woman's identity, to "read for clues, as if the book were one of those thinly disguised pulp novels about Jacqueline Onassis or Frank Sinatra."[33] Even the subsequent lack of unanimity between the three authors in recent times is cited as evidence of the text's failure.[34]

The Three Marias thus demonstrates one of the central ideas that I have been tracing in amorous epistolary discourses from Ovid onward: there is no language-system that has historically encompassed antimimetic stances toward art, politics, sexuality, and love. As if to demonstrate the force of the oppression and repulsion of love in modern systems of discourse, one recurrent strain of criticism—like eternity in a grain of sand, perhaps more revealing than all the others—finds that the book is antiquated, outmoded, sentimental. The Marias' view of love, says one reviewer, is out of date: "they are positively Stendhalian . . . or at least . . . early 19th century."[35] Another calls it "a strangely outmoded way of looking at love, or better, of looking at women's role in love. There are no sexual politics here, only rhapsodies and lavish displays of passion, erotic passages that are easy targets for parody. . . . it precedes feminist developments of the last ten years."[36] In my view, the text comes not too late but too early. No one thought to place *New Portuguese Letters* in the context of either structural, linguistic, or poststructural theories, despite the allusions of the authors themselves.[37] Such a context, as I have shown, elucidates their aleatory "music in letters"; their acrobatic exercises, their polyphonic innovations.

Julia Kristeva's comments on the strategies of the avant-garde help to illuminate the three Marias' project (albeit retrospectively, since her speculations appeared several years after *New Portuguese Letters*). The avant-garde, she notes,

33. Kramer, review, p. 1.
34. Antonio de Figueiredo, review, *Listener*, 2 Oct. 1975, pp. 451–52.
35. Kramer, review, p. 1.
36. Grumbach, review, p. 32.
37. The three Marias allude specifically to Freud, Lévi-Strauss, the Imaginary, deciphering signs and texts, to linguistics, psychoanalysis, anthropology, Marxism, semiology, and to a range of feminist theorists, from Shulamith Firestone to Simone de Beauvoir. For their familiarity with French feminism and psychoanalysis, see note 14 above.

has been introducing ruptures, blank spaces, and holes into language.
It is what Mallarmé called "the music in letters" . . . multiplied condensation of myths, philosophy, history, and verbal experience. . . . All of
these modifications in the linguistic fabric are the sign of a force that
has not been grasped by the linguistic or ideological system. . . .
   However, in a culture where the speaking subjects are conceived of
as masters of their speech, they have what is called a "phallic" position.
The fragmentation of language in a text calls into question the very
posture of this mastery. The writing . . . confronts this phallic position
either to traverse it or to deny it.[38]

Traversal and transgression are precisely what the three Marias
achieve. Rather than being "easy targets for parody," they parody
themselves and each other. Rather than avoid politics and history,
they explore the relations between writing and revolution, between
their feminist poetics and global politics. *Novas Cartas portuguesas* signifies more than mere identification with the original *Portuguese Letters*. It is a point of departure, for *cartas* is not just a letter but a map
and a charter. Like the Magna Carta, *Novas Cartas* is a charter of
human rights, a weaving of women's voices that enables one to read
back and forth in history. The final letter, indeed, inscribes the relation between writing and revolution, for after describing the "madness and vertigo" of love-making that defies time, this Maria ends as
she began, with an avowal that woman must be free or she will die.
Yet, as we have seen from the *Heroides* onward, the very act of imagining, threatening, lamenting, describing death is a deferral, a detour
that lets the narrative—and desire—linger a little longer.
   One question remains: can one reevaluate love without being
hopelessly sentimental? Can one discuss desire without being hopelessly self-indulgent, given the atrocities in history that mark the modern age? Are love and history, in other words, irreconcilable, as
Roland Barthes suggests when he describes a "historical reversal: it is
no longer the sexual which is indecent, it is the *sentimental*—censured
in the name of what is in fact only *another morality.* . . . The lover's
sentiment is old-fashioned, but this antiquation cannot even be recuperated as a spectacle: love falls outside of *interesting* time; no historical, polemical meaning can be given to it; it is in this that it is
obscene."[39] Barthes's title for this fragment, "Love's Obscenity,"
opens yet another "way of responding by asking questions," for the

38. Kristeva, "Oscillation between Power and Denial," p. 165.
39. Barthes, *A Lover's Discourse*, pp. 177–78.

question inevitably arises: was it the sex that led *The Three Marias* to be banned as obscene, or did its obscenity lie closer to the grounds on which its reviewers attacked it as sentimental, outmoded, antiquated, as "uninteresting, unhistorical, unpolemical"? The three Marias demonstrate that "the lover's sentiment" *can* "be recuperated as spectacle," for they "recuperate" the Portuguese nun. They dramatize the exercise of passion as spectacle in love letters that crisscross from the plains of Portugal to the salons of Paris, celebrating that grand passion in fiction and in history. They further demonstrate the dialogic dynamism of amorous epistolary discourse by interweaving so many other reinventions of the *Portuguese Letters* with their own. The subsequent literary history of Mariane's letters, indeed, is part of the spectacle they stage, for by writers from Aphra Behn to Elizabeth Barrett Browning, from Rousseau to Rilke, the nun's letters have been rewritten, reinvented, reaccentuated in all ages and in many countries.[40] By creating correspondences first with one another, then with other women and men, the three Marias reenvision love, restoring it to time and history, exploring the dynamic dialogism of discourse, the myriad mediations of desire.

40. The most recent reaccentuation prior to *New Portuguese Letters* was Madeleine L'Engle's *The Love Letters* (New York: Ballantine Books, 1966), which counterpoints the story of a modern American woman with a reinvention of the Portuguese nun.

But [all] he who utters this discourse . . . knows is that what passes through his mind at a certain moment is marked, like the printout of a code (in other times, this would have been the code of courtly love, or the Carte du Tendre).

ROLAND BARTHES, *A Lover's Discourse: Fragments*

Epilogue

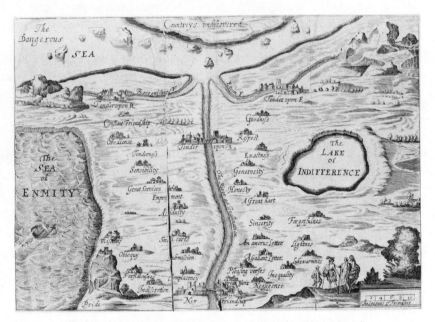

The Map of Tenderness. An engraving published in Madeleine de
Scudery's *Clélie* (Paris: Augustin Courbé, 1678) is reproduced
courtesy of the William Andrews Clark Memorial Library,
University of California, Los Angeles.

My aim in plotting these treacherous traces and forking paths has thus been to chart a typology of discourse that places certain formal characteristics in high relief, maps shared thematic preoccupations, and situates theoretical landmarks. In analyzing modes of circulation and repression, valorization and appropriation, we can begin to see that the subversion of classical categories is a profoundly political act—one that leads from Ovid's exile to the three Marias' prosecution. From the *Heroides* to *New Portuguese Letters,* the texts in this book all demonstrate the justice of Derrida's observation that some law is at stake when one makes light of all the tranquil categories of genre and gender. Certain critical assumptions—about mimesis, about canons, about genre, about masculine and feminine—have permitted the discourses, the heroines, and the authors in my study to be perceived only in certain prescribed ways: Sappho's art reflects her lesbianism; Ovid lacks Virgil's "high seriousness"; feminine writing is unnatural and hysterical, masculine is vigorous and rational. What Ovid teaches us by mimicking these received ideas is that the literary construction of gender is always artificial, that one can never unveil the *essence* of masculinity or femininity. Instead, all one exposes are other *representations.*

Rather than fearing that challenges to the assumptions of mimesis will once again obliterate the female authors or characters, I believe that antimimesis is a particularly fertile field of investigation for feminist criticism because mimesis has been employed as an ideological weapon to demonstrate the "unnaturalness" of women as lovers, as writers, and in myriad other roles, from Sappho to Brontë to the three Marias. What should lead logically from the examination of images of woman in literature—as witch, as monster, as sphinx, as devourer—is the examination of the production and dissemination of those images. Whose ideology is served by sustaining mimesis as an ideal? By confronting the strategies and ideologies at work in representation itself, feminist perspectives on both literature and politics stand to gain. "The post-age"—by which I mean postmodernism and postrepresentation—is upon us.[1] I am also alluding to the ways in which literature is implicated in the letter, and the letter in literature—the postal agelessness of intertwined motives and motifs in discourses of desire. Whether we trace the remarkable similarities between Charlotte Brontë's authentic love letters to Monsieur Heger and the fictional letters of the nun to the chevalier, the same codes of love are reiterated ceaselessly, because they are all inevitably drawn from literature itself. Despite the transformations of amorous epistolary discourse from the *Heroides* to Richardson's *Clarissa,* the generic characteristics of this discourse remain intact. Even when the genre seems to undergo a crucial deformation in the first-person narratives of Jane Eyre, James's governess, and Rosa Coldfield, the trace of the Ovidian genre remains visible, for it is simultaneously assimilated and reaccentuated in these texts. From the critical crossroads that these three first-person narratives represent, amorous epistolary discourse reemerges in a form closest to its Ovidian model in the dialogic collaboration of the three Marias. In all these texts, time, memory, and fiction inevitably augment desire, prolonging both passion and the production of writing, providing new models at every turn. I have tried to avoid presenting definitive new interpretations of each of these texts, but new perspectives inevitably arise when one shifts the critical ground from mimesis to diegesis, from generic traditions to generic transgressions, from literary exegesis to the performative aspects of narrative. At this juncture I am particularly aware of the many roads not taken—of the absence of Emily Dickinson and Elizabeth Barrett Browning, for example—but I have omitted them in order to focus solely on the assimilation of amorous epistolary discourse into the *novel.*

Finally, certain fissures recur throughout the particular typology I have mapped in amorous epistolary discourse. Letter/literature, natural/artificial, presence/absence, sexual/sentimental—these are some of the boundaries that are transgressed and transformed. The censors considered *New Portuguese Letters* sexually obscene, but American reviewers found it "sentimental, outmoded, antiquated." Throughout

1. See Gregory L. Ulmer's review-essay of Jacques Derrida's *La Carte postale,* "The Post-Age," *Diacritics* 11 (Fall 1981), 39–56. On the implications of the age of postrepresentation for feminist criticism, see Alice Jardine, "Pre-Texts for the Transatlantic Feminist," *Yale French Studies* 62 (1981), 220–36, and *Gynesis: Configurations of Woman and Modernity* (Ithaca: Cornell Univ. Press, 1985).

this book, I have tried to expose the devaluation of the sentimental as another form of repression, with ramifications as serious at the end of the twentieth century as sexual repression was at the end of the nineteenth. Barthes asks, "(How do History and Type combine? Is it not up to the type to formulate—to form—what is out of time, ahistorical? In the lover's very tears, our society represses its own timelessness, thereby turning the weeping lover into a lost object whose repression is necessary to its 'health.' In Rohmer's film *The Marquise of O.*, the lovers weep and the audience giggles.)"[2] In the genre of amorous discourse, the writing heroine is the Type, who formulates what society represses, which is far more, in fact, than a few tears. Tear-stains on the paper, as we have seen from Ovid onward, are visible signs of the body's pain, "permanent proofs" of the disproportion between the signified and the means of signifying, transmissions of the body to the text. Thus in the *Portuguese Letters*, what gets lost in translation in Barbin's "authoritative" preface is the body of a woman, the nun, whom the three Marias reinscribe. In *The Turn of the Screw*, a sentimental response is what the "sophisticated, fastidious reader" overlooks. It is no coincidence that the same "sophisticated" reader simultaneously overlooks the transcriber's body in the prologue, for the very fact that it does not occur to the reader to consider either the gender of that transcriber or the realm of emotion is part of the problem I am discussing. James's tale at the turn of one century elegizes the turn away from eighteenth-century sentiment and toward twentieth-century irony; from the sexual repression that Freud unlocked, it is perhaps time to turn the same intense scrutiny on our affectional as on our sexual lives.[3] The result might point the way to a new direction in writing and criticism. Significantly, in reviewing Barthes's *Lover's Discourse* Geoffrey Hartman asks, "Is criticism finding its own style at last? Or recovering a formal possibility that is, in truth, very old? To make criticism creative, to reconcile learning with the language of love, inspired one of the first essays of the vernacular muse in the Renaissance, appropriately entitled by Dante, 'La Vita

2. Roland Barthes, *A Lover's Discourse: Fragments*, trans. Richard Howard (New York: Hill and Wang, 1978), p. 181.
3. Cf. Mark Spilka, "On the Enrichment of Poor Monkeys by Myth and Dream; or, How Dickens Rousseauisticized and Pre-Freudianized Victorian Views of Childhood," in *Sexuality and Victorian Literature*, ed. Don Richard Cox, Tennessee Studies in Literature, vol. 27 (Knoxville: Univ. of Tennessee Press, 1984), p. 177.

Nuova.' "[4] My aim has been to show that the impulse to reconcile the language of love with that of criticism is actually far older than Dante, for the erotic poetics of discourses of desire show the ineradicable trace of Ovid. In addition to Barthes, two other theorists, moreover, have demonstrated that recent experiments in such a reconcilation are already well underway. Viktor Shklovsky is well known as the father of Russian formalism, but he also wrote an epistolary novel entitled *Zoo, or Letters Not about Love* (his second subtitle: *The Third Heloise*). Jacques Derrida, similarly, is famous as the founder of deconstruction, but in *La Carte postale*, he, like Barthes, experiments in "writing unprotectedly" in a series of meditative amorous postcards.[5] The fact that three major theorists have taken the same turn by reaccentuating the Ovidian genre of amorous epistolary discourse may point the way to further reconsiderations of the masks, illusions, adornments of the "harlot" rhetoric, and of theories of loving as a way of knowing, with the body as sign, as figure, as alphabet, as style. (The figures of Erté, who designed letters of the alphabet in the shape of women comes to mind; Barthes wrote the introduction to a recent edition of this stylish text.)[6] The *exercises* of the three Marias are, as we have seen, closely related to the *figures* Barthes celebrates in his *Lover's Discourse*.

What these examples point to is both another turn and a return. I began my study by describing the futility of the search for the lost father, for Ovid did not engender the genre of amorous epistolary discourse parthenogenically. Behind him, mimed by him, was the erotic and emotional intensity of Sappho. Just as the formal features of Ovidian stylistics lead back to the fragments of Sappho's lyrics, Barthesian poetics have a prior source too. It is surprising to discover that there is a theoretical text on amorous discourse that anticipates the elegant formulations of Roland Barthes, one that, like his, is the "site of an affirmation," dedicated to the poetics of reading and the production of writing. Barthes, after all, is justly renowned for such strategies. Yet there is a prior text that employs all these strategies,

4. Geoffrey H. Hartman, "Signs and Symbols" (review of *Image/Music/Text* and *A Lover's Discourse*), *New York Times Book Review*, 4 Feb. 1979, pp. 12, 34–35.
   5. Viktor Shklovsky, *Zoo, or Letters Not about Love*, ed. and trans. Richard Sheldon (Ithaca: Cornell Univ. Press, 1971); Jacques Derrida, *La Carte postale: De Socrate à Freud et au-delà* (Paris: Flammarion, 1980).
   6. Gregory L. Ulmer, "The Discourse of the Imaginary," *Diacritics* 10 (March 1980), 61–75.

that anticipates his interest in the performative aspects of narrative and the staging of the Imaginary: *The Three Marias.*

The final gesture of transforming and transgressing the "tranquil categories" of genre and gender comes here, for the three Marias' *New Portuguese Letters* was already six years old when Barthes's *Lover's Discourse* appeared. Not only do the three Marias reenvision the original nun, but they show the relation of poetics to politics precisely by reflecting on the historical, polemical meaning of her passion and her fate. They illuminate the relation of history to type, for rather than relegating love to the margins of the conceptual universe, their letters are situated in history and in time. The dating of letters from Angola to America, Portugal to Paris, from 1671 to 1971 dramatizes the eternal recurrence of passion and war, conquest and colonization, pleasure and betrayal, solitude and despair—all the themes so obsessively reiterated in the *Heroides.* As with Ovid's heroines, the three Marias chart the relation of the personal to the political, of myth to utopia in their *novas cartas* through a multilingual, polyphonic dialogue. From the *Heroides* to *The Letters of a Portuguese Nun* to *New Portuguese Letters,* every discourse in the genre I have been tracing creates correspondences among the heroines within the text and with other texts, thus keeping the circuit of desire open and demonstrating that the act of writing is the revolution—one that explores the treacherous traces and forking paths of sex and politics, nostalgia and revenge, myth and utopia, discourse and desire.

Index

Library of Congress Cataloging-in-Publication Data

Kauffman, Linda S., 1949–
  Discourses of desire.

  Includes index.
  1. Love in literature. 2. Love-letters—History
and criticism. 3. Letters in literature. 4. Epistolary
fiction—History and criticism. 5. Women and literature.
I. Title.
PN56.L6K38 1986   809'.93354   85-48196
ISBN 0-8014-1853-4 (alk. paper)